CONCURRENCY
IN DEPENDABLE COMPUTING

T0138023

Concurrency
in Dependable Computing

Edited by

Paul Ezhilchelvan

University of Newcastle-upon-Tyne

and

Alexander Romanovsky

University of Newcastle-upon-Tyne

KLUWER ACADEMIC PUBLISHERS
BOSTON / DORDRECHT / LONDON

A C.I.P. Catalogue record for this book is available from the Library of Congress.

ISBN 978-1-4419-5278-3

Published by Kluwer Academic Publishers,
P.O. Box 17, 3300 AA Dordrecht, The Netherlands.

Sold and distributed in North, Central and South America
by Kluwer Academic Publishers,
101 Philip Drive, Norwell, MA 02061, U.S.A.

In all other countries, sold and distributed
by Kluwer Academic Publishers,
P.O. Box 322, 3300 AH Dordrecht, The Netherlands.

Printed on acid-free paper

Printed in the Netherlands.

Contents

Part II Application Specific Modelling for Dependable Design and Analysis

Part III Event Ordering and its Application

Part IV   Transactions and Consistent Checkpointing

Part V   Concurrency in Real-Time Applications

Foreword

One frequently-encountered quotation regarding the dependability of computers, and in particular software, is that by Tony Hoare, who famously said: "The price of dependability is utter simplicity – and this is a price that major software manufacturers find too high to afford!" Both parts of this aphorism are true, but – regrettably – so is Einstein's remark that: "Everything should be made as simple as possible, but not simpler". One can gain much simplicity by making assumptions as to the nature of the faults that will not occur (whether in system specification, design or operation). But this will be a spurious simplicity if the assumptions are false.

Concurrency and faults, both in computing systems and in their environments, constitute two major sources of complexity, both individually and especially in combination, which unfortunately cannot be simply wished away, at least in the so-called real world. Thus one of the main challenges of system dependability research is that of finding means of coping with this unavoidable complexity, and so retaining as much simplicity as can be properly justified.

This challenge applies both in the case of operational computing systems, and of the systems that are used for their design and evaluation. As always, one of the best ways of coping with complexity is to devise and use effective "divide and conquer" techniques, i.e. methods of system structuring.

In the former case, i.e. for operational computing systems, various types of transaction scheme are often used for such structuring. They do this both by providing means of confining parts of computations that can be designed, and executed, independently – and by factoring out some of the subtle coordination and confinement algorithms that are required into standard "middleware" that can be re-used by a variety of applications.

Such transaction schemes vary according to the (it is hoped justified) assumptions that are made by the designers employing them regarding (i) the extent and forms of concurrency involved, (ii) the faults that can occur, and (iii) the types of demands that are placed on a system

P. Ezhilchelvan and A. Romanovsky (eds.), Concurrency in Dependable Computing, ix–x.
© 2002 *Kluwer Academic Publishers. Printed in the Netherlands.*

by its environment. For example, in some circumstances it may well be regarded as satisfactory to assume that there will be no concurrent faults of any type, and that the environment has an ability to back-up after an error has been detected or reported to it. At the other end of the spectrum, so to speak, there may be a need to deploy very subtle means of concurrency control, to allow for the occurrence of further faults during error recovery, and to admit that the environment is by no means always able simply to back-up in order to recover from faulty data it has received from the computing system.

In the latter case, regarding systems used for computing system design and evaluation, the notations, logic schemes, and any associated tools all in effect divide up the design and evaluation task and hence reduce its complexity. For example, by embodying some of the overall design and evaluation task in a tool, or indeed in a high-level notation, the task is in effect divided between the creator of the tool or notation and its user – the results of whose efforts can therefore presumably be trusted with rather more confidence than might otherwise be the case. Moreover, well-designed notations prompt the discovery of simple yet elegant solutions to design problems, and the re-use of tried and trusted validation arguments.

My own researches over recent years have concentrated on the structuring of fault-tolerant concurrent systems. However, in my early career I was very much involved in language design and compiler implementation. I am thus delighted that Newcastle should have been the venue for the workshop on "Concurrency in Dependable Computing" that provided an initial impetus for the present book, since both the workshop and the book are so neatly focused on the twin problems of faults and concurrency, and on both the problems of structuring operational systems, and of systematically designing and evaluating them. As a result, the breadth and depth of the coverage that is provided by these papers of recent research in these two related forms of system structuring are particularly striking, and the organizers and the authors are both to be congratulated.

Brian Randell

Department of Computing Science
University of Newcastle upon Tyne

Preface

The aim of this book is to expose readers to recent research results in certain important areas of computer science. Concurrency and dependability are the two chosen themes. There are applications (e.g., airline reservation systems, bank teller systems) in which many users are allowed to interact with the system at the same time. Similarly, any system meant for practical use must provide some guarantee on dependability. Such a guarantee may be in the form of the system's ability to tolerate faults of certain types, its ability to withstand security attacks of certain kinds, an assurance that the system will not fail in a catastrophic manner, and so forth. Concurrency control and dependability provision are thus two important issues firmly rooted in building practical systems.

The contributions contained in this book advance the reader's knowledge in two ways. First, they describe how concurrency theory and formalisms can be applied in the design, development and verification of dependable systems generally and also in some application-specific contexts. Secondly, they present new concurrency management schemes in the pursuit of dependability, specifically fault-tolerance and timeliness guarantees. The book is a balanced blend of conceptual principles and their applications. It has fifteen chapters divided into five parts.

Part I expands on the role of modelling and formalisms in the design, development and verification of dependable systems.
Part II extends the focus of part I for systems built for specific applications. The aspects of dependability concerns addressed are security, safety, and reliability.
Part III presents distributed protocols for reliable multicast and event ordering, and also an application of such protocols in achieving coordinated, forward error recovery.
Part IV considers concurrency control in the context of backward error recovery.
Part V considers the problem of concurrency control in distributed, real-time systems with design-level guarantees on the timely provision of services.

P. Ezhilchelvan and A. Romanovsky (eds.), Concurrency in Dependable Computing, xi–xvii.
© 2002 Kluwer Academic Publishers. Printed in the Netherlands.

An Outline of the Contents

Part I consists of four chapters. The first chapter addresses an important problem encountered in the step-wise refinement of a specification into a corresponding implementation. An implementation component, often expressed at a lower level of abstraction than its specification component, can have a different interface from that of the specification. Yet, despite this difference, an implementation must be verified against its specification. The authors describe an approach which is illustrated by outlining the development of a fault-tolerant system based on Co-ordinated Atomic actions.

The authors of chapter 2 view a dependable system design to be essentially an enforcement, even in the presence of rare faults, of a model of system behaviour expressed in a formal specification. The enforcement approaches proposed by them take into account two important practical aspects which ought not to be ignored. Firstly, the added complexity due to dependability enforcement should not be allowed to become a source of undependability. Secondly, enforcement of a global model of a system should be made feasible and pragmatic by decomposing the model. The applicability of the proposed approaches is illustrated by two case studies.

Building complex fault tolerant applications in which several participants need to coordinate their activity is a challenging task. Multiparty interaction is a structuring mechanism that helps meet this challenge. Chapter 3 incorporates dependability into this mechanism and formally describes the dependable multiparty interaction (DMI) scheme using Temporal Logic of Actions. In particular, it shows how DMI deals with exceptions raised concurrently during an interaction.

The task of building a reliable system is considerably simplified when that system is built out of 'idealised' fault-tolerant components which incorporate error detection and correction redundancies. Chapter 4 applies this notion in modelling a dependable system for verification. It illustrates the importance of, and also the feasibility of, componentised modelling that incorporates the means to observe specific system behaviour of interest. It also demonstrates that the support for behaviour observation can be constructed in a modular fashion, and that verification formulae and aspects of fault-tolerance can be easily evaluated based on the observations made.

Part II is made up of three chapters. Chapter 5 is concerned with the design of a digger and dumper truck by digging (literally!) into concurrency through the use of Petri nets. The work described here is complete from design to a Lego implementation, and then to evaluation. It also focuses on security issues lest any unauthorised diggers make use of the system.

Chapter 6 considers concurrency control and safety in an industrial setting. The competing processes here are guided vehicles in an automated manufacturing system, which contend for traffic zones to make progress toward their destinations. The presence of more than one vehicle in any given zone is construed as a collision, which must be avoided without causing deadlock. Developing a safe and deadlock-free control algorithm is made difficult, as vehicle movements, unlike recoverable computations of transactions, cannot be undone. Beginning with a survey of earlier works, the author argues that the coloured Petri Net approach offers a very powerful tool for modelling vehicle behaviour and develops a controller algorithm.

Chapter 7 considers the task of modelling Enterprise Information Systems (EIS). Such systems are typically characterised by long-running and autonomous business processes coordinated to meet a specific set of user requirements. Performance and reliability are the two most sought-after qualities. The authors take a view that known techniques, e.g., Markov Chains, Petri Nets, etc., for system modelling and analysis, are not popular with the EIS architects; these techniques cannot however be done away with if the analysis performed is to be realistic. The chapter presents a practical way to bridge this gap. It describes an environment which enables specifications of EIS architectures to be described and provides a tool support for automated generation of models for subsequent quality analysis.

Part III has three chapters on protocols for reliable multicast and event ordering, and one chapter on the application of group communication for forward error recovery. Lamport in one of his classical papers has highlighted the need for, and the difficulties in obtaining, a total order on events. Since then, ordering algorithms have been developed under various fault models and message delay assumptions. Chapter 8 specifies a distributed fault-tolerant sequencer by means of which independent processes can obtain a sequence number to globally order the events they generate. It also provides an implementation of the sequencer in a timed asynchronous system.

In chapter 9, a QoS (quality of service) analysis of two ordering broadcast protocols for a wireless network has been performed. Particular consideration has been paid to the effects of the fading phenomenon caused by the interference of message copies arriving at a receiver through different paths. Analyses use experimental data obtained in realistic environments and illustrate, among other things, the need for fault-tolerant protocols to ensure that successive transmissions from a given source are sufficiently spaced apart in time.

Fundamental to obtaining a total order on events is that the events are observed by all participants concerned. In a failure-prone environment, an event may remain unobserved by some correct participants due, say, to message loss and buffer shortage. The protocol presented in chapter 10 guarantees that either all or none of the correct participants observes all relevant events and employs a mechanism which deduces, using semantic information, events that are not relevant in a given context. It promises increased efficiency with no compromise on correctness.

Chapter 11 presents a model for generating globally co-ordinated response to exceptions that cannot be effectively handled locally. The power and richness of the proposed architecture are due mainly to the combined use of paradigms for exception handling and those for group communication. The former are used for the acquisition of appropriate knowledge to handle an exception raised and the latter for transforming such knowledge into an agreed knowledge common to all concerned participants.

Part IV has three chapters, two of which focus on enriching transactions and the third one on consistent checkpointing. Chapter 12 presents an alternative to the traditional way of handling concurrency in transaction systems. In the traditional approach, concurrency is handled by avoiding information flow between active transactions. Consequently, each transaction autonomously decides its fate of either aborting or committing. Reminiscent of fault avoidance versus fault tolerance approaches, the model presented in this chapter permits flow of information between transactions and deals with the consequence by treating an aborted transaction as a potential source of error propagation. The chapter formalises the behaviour of such an interference-tolerant system and derives a criterion for committing transactions in a safe and lively manner.

Chapter 13 investigates integrating transactions with group communication. On one hand, groups of processes can deal with persistent data in a consistent way with the help of transactions. On the other hand, transactional applications can take advantage of group communication to build distributed co-operative servers as well as replicated ones. An additional advantage of an integrated approach is that it can be used as a base for building transactional applications taking advantage of computer clusters.

Chapter 14 presents a non-intrusive, co-ordinated checkpointing protocol for distributed systems with the least overhead during failure-free executions. The protocol also has optimal communication and storage overheads, requiring only O(n) messages to take a global consistent checkpoint.

Part V has one chapter which is concerned with concurrency in systems which are to be designed with guarantees to provide timely services. The author presents a novel object structure in which the traditional, message-triggered method calls of an object are distinguished from the real-time specific, time-triggered ones. The proposed scheme is shown to ease the burden of building a distributed, real-time system with design-level timeliness guarantees in such a way that the design appears not as an esoteric specialisation but as a requirements-driven extension of a non-real-time design. The rules for concurrency management that facilitate the provision of timeliness guarantees are presented together with some interesting open research problems.

Acknowledgements

We are thankful to the organisers of the International Conference on Application of Concurrency to System Design (ICACSD) and the 22nd International Conference on Application and Theory of Petri

Nets in Newcastle upon Tyne, 2001. They encouraged and supported us in organising an one-day workshop on Concurrency in Dependable Computing, as a side event. Preliminary versions of seven chapters of this book were presented in the workshop. The encouragement we received from the workshop participants led us to embark on the task of publishing this book. We are also thankful to the reviewers for their careful scrutiny of the submitted chapters and for the many constructive suggestions they made. Finally, and most importantly, we are very much indebted to the contributors of all the chapters for their brilliant research work which led to this book.

Paul Ezhilchelvan

Alexander Romanovsky

The List of Reviewers

Anish Arora
Roberto Baldoni
Didier Buchs
Andrea Coccoli
Felicita Di Giandomenico
Paul Devadoss Ezhilchelvan
Maria Pia Fanti
Jean-Michel Helary
Teresa Higuera
Ricardo Jimenez-Peris
Jörg Kienzle
Christos Kloukinas
Maciej Koutny
Lalit Kumar
Achur Mostefaoui
Michael Mock
Y. Narahari
Marta Patiño-Martinez
Michel Raynal
Alexander Romanovsky
Detlef Schwier
Simeon Veloudis
Alex Yakovlev
Avelino Zorzo

I

ROLE OF MODELLING AND FORMALISMS FOR DEPENDABLE SYSTEM DESIGN

Chapter 1

COMPOSITIONAL DEVELOPMENT IN THE EVENT OF INTERFACE DIFFERENCE

Jonathan Burton, Maciej Koutny

Dept. of Comp. Science, University of Newcastle, Newcastle upon Tyne NE1 7RU, U.K.

{j.i.burton, maciej.koutny}@ncl.ac.uk

Giuseppe Pappalardo

Dip. di Matematica e Informatica, Università di Catania, I-95125 Catania, Italy

pappalardo@dmi.unict.it

Marta Pietkiewicz-Koutny

Dept. of Comp. Science, University of Newcastle, Newcastle upon Tyne NE1 7RU, U.K.

marta.koutny@ncl.ac.uk

Abstract

We present here an implementation relation which allows compositional development of a network of communicating processes, in the event that corresponding specification and implementation components have different interfaces. This relation is compositional, in the sense that a target composed of several connected systems may be implemented by connecting their respective implementations. In addition, an implementation, when plugged into an appropriate environment, is to all intents and purposes a conventional implementation of the target. We illustrate our approach by outlining the development of a fault-tolerant system based on coordinated atomic actions (CA actions).

Keywords: Theory of parallel and distributed computation, behaviour abstraction, communicating sequential processes, compositionality, CA actions.

P. Ezhilchelvan and A. Romanovsky (eds.), Concurrency in Dependable Computing, 3–22.

Introduction

Consider the situation that we have a specification network, P_{net}, composed of n processes P_i, where all interprocess communication is hidden. Consider an implementation network, Q_{net}, also composed of n processes, again with all interprocess communication hidden. Assume that there is a one-to-one relationship between component processes in P_{net} and those in Q_{net}. Intuitively, P_i is intended to specify Q_i in some sense. Finally, assume that the interface of Q_{net}, in terms of externally observable actions, is the same as that of P_{net}.

In process algebras, such as those used in [10, 14], the notion that a process Q_{net} *implements* a process P_{net} is based on the idea that Q_{net} is more deterministic than (or equivalent to) P_{net} in terms of the chosen semantics. (In the following, we shall also refer to such specifications as *target* or *base* systems.)

The process of refining the target into the implementation also allows the designer to change the control structure of the latter. In such a case, Q_{net} has implemented P_{net} by describing its *internal* structure in a more concrete and detailed manner. However, we are able to hide the details of that internal structure, and then verify that this new internal structure still gives correct behaviour at the interface of Q_{net}, which is still that of P_{net}. Indeed, the standard notions of refinement, such as those of [10, 14], are interested only in *observable* actions, i.e., in the behaviour available at the *interface* of processes. However, the interfaces of the specification and implementation processes must be the same to facilitate comparison.

What if we wish to approach this verification question compositionally? What if we want to verify that Q_{net} implements P_{net} simply by verifying that Q_i implements P_i, for each $1 \leq i \leq n$. In general, this is only possible if Q_i and P_i have the same communication interface. Thus, Q_i may implement P_i by describing its computation in a more concrete manner, but it may not do so by refining its interface, at least if we wish to carry out compositional verification.

Yet in deriving an implementation from a specification we will often wish to implement abstract, high-level *interface* actions at a lower level of detail and in a more concrete manner. For example, the channel connecting P_i to another component process P_j may be unreliable and so it may need to be replaced by a data channel and an acknowledgement channel. Or P_i itself may be liable to fail and so its behaviour may need to be replicated, with each new component having its own communication channels to avoid a single channel becoming a bottleneck (such a scenario was one of the major historical motivations behind the present work [3, 4, 7, 8]). Or it may simply be the case that a high-level action of P_i has been rendered in a more concrete, and so more implementable, form. As a result, the interface of an implementation process may end up being expressed at a lower (and so different) level of abstraction to that of the corresponding specification process. In the process algebraic context, where our interest lies only in *observable* behaviour, this means that verification of correctness must be able to deal with the case that the implementation and specification processes have different interfaces.

The relation between processes detailed in the remainder of this paper allows us to carry out such compositional verification in the event that Q_i and P_i have different interfaces.

An important notion in the development of this relation is that of *extraction pattern*. Extraction patterns interpret the behaviour of a system at the level of communication traces, by relating behaviour on a set of channels in the implementation to behaviour on a channel in the specification. In addition, they impose some correctness requirements upon the behaviour of an implementation; for example, the traces of the implementation should be correct with respect to the interface encoded by the extraction pattern. The set of extraction patterns defined for all channels in an implementation system appears as a formal parameter in a generic *implementation relation*.

The motivating framework given above for the implementation relation presented here leads to the identification of two natural constraints which must be placed upon any such implementation relation.

The first, *realisability*, ensures that the abstraction built into the implementation relation may be put to good use. In practice, this means that plugging an implementation into an appropriate environment (see, e.g., [7]) should yield a conventional implementation of the specification. A related requirement arises when the implementation relation is parameterized with a special set of extraction patterns, known as *identity* extraction patterns, which essentially formalise the fact that implementation and specification processes are represented at the *same* level of abstraction; in this case, the implementation relation should reduce to a satisfactory notion of behaviour refinement.

Compositionality, the other constraint on the implementation relation, requires it to distribute over system composition. Thus, a specification composed of a number of connected systems may be implemented by connecting their respective implementations. It is remarkable that although in general Q_i and P_i do not have the same interface, we know that, when all of the components Q_i have been composed, the result — namely Q_{net} — will have the same interface as the corresponding specification process — namely P_{net}. Compositionality is important in avoiding the state explosion problem when we approach automatic verification, algorithms for which have been developed in [3].

The paper is organised as follows. In the next section, we introduce some basic notions used throughout the paper. In section 2, we present extraction patterns — a central notion to characterising the interface of an implementation. Section 3 deals with the implementation relation, while section 4 applies our approach to the compositional development of a concurrent system based on coordinated atomic actions.

All proofs of the results presented here have been already published, or will appear in a forthcoming technical report. Comparison with other work, in particular [1, 2, 5, 9, 13, 15], can be found in [4, 8].

1.   Preliminaries

Processes are represented in this paper using the failures-divergences model of Communicating Sequential Processes (CSP) [6, 14] — a formal model for the description of concurrent computing systems. A CSP *process* can be regarded as a black box which may engage in interaction with its environment. Atomic instances of this interaction are called *actions* and must be elements of the *alphabet* of the process. A *trace* of the process is a finite sequence of actions that a process can be observed to engage in. In this paper, structured actions of the form $b{:}v$ will be used, where v is a *message* and b is a communication *channel*. For every channel b, μb is the *message set* of b, i.e., the set of all v such that $b{:}v$ is a valid action, and $\alpha b \stackrel{\mathrm{df}}{=} \{b{:}v \mid v \in \mu b\}$ is the *alphabet* of b. For a set of channels B, $\alpha B \stackrel{\mathrm{df}}{=} \bigcup_{b \in B} \alpha b$.

Throughout the paper we use notations similar to those of [6]. A trace $t[b'/b]$ is obtained from trace t by replacing each action $b{:}v$ by $b'{:}v$, and $t{\restriction}B$ is obtained by deleting from t all the actions that do not occur on the channels in B. For example, if $t = \langle b{:}2, c{:}3, b{:}2, c{:}6, d{:}7 \rangle$, then $t[e/b] = \langle e{:}2, c{:}3, e{:}2, c{:}6, d{:}7 \rangle$ and $t{\restriction}\{b, d\} = \langle b{:}2, b{:}2, d{:}7 \rangle$. A mapping from a set of traces to a set of traces $f : T \to T'$ is *monotonic* if $t, u \in T$ and $t \leq u$ implies $f(t) \leq f(u)$, where $\leq$ is the prefix relation on traces. For a set T of traces, $Pref(T)$ is the set of all prefixes of the traces in T. Finally, $\circ$ is the concatenation operation for traces.

We use the standard failures-divergences model of CSP [6, 14] in which a process P is a triple $(\alpha P, \phi P, \delta P)$ where αP (the *alphabet*) is a non-empty finite set of actions, ϕP (the *failures*) is a subset of $\alpha P^* \times \mathbb{P}(\alpha P)$, and δP (the *divergences*) is a subset of αP^*. Moreover, $\tau P \stackrel{\mathrm{df}}{=} \{t \mid \exists R \subseteq \alpha P : (t, R) \in \phi P\}$ denotes the *traces* of P. If $(t, R) \in \phi P$ then P is said to *refuse* R after t. We will associate with P a set of channels, χP, and stipulate that the alphabet of P is that of χP.

For our purposes neither the syntax nor the semantics of the whole CSP is needed. Essential are only the parallel composition of processes, $P\|Q$, hiding of the communication over a set of channels, $P\backslash B$, and renaming of channels, $P[b'/b]$. In the examples, we also use deterministic choice, $P[]Q$, non-deterministic choice, $P \sqcap Q$, and prefixing, $a \to P$ (see [6, 14] for the definitions and intuitions concerning all these operations).

Processes $P_1, \ldots, P_n$ form a *network* if no channel is shared by more than two P_i's. We define $P_1 \otimes \cdots \otimes P_n$ to be the process obtained by taking the parallel composition of the processes and then hiding all interprocess communication, i.e., the process $(P_1 \| \cdots \| P_n) \backslash B$, where B is the set of channels shared by two different processes in the network. Network composition is commutative and associative. As a result, a network can be obtained by first composing some of the processes into a subnetwork, and then composing the result with the remaining processes. Moreover, the order in which processes are composed does not matter.

We can partition the channels of a process P into the input channels, *in P*, and output channels, *out P*. It is assumed that no two processes in a network have a common input channel or a common output channel. In the diagrams, an outgoing arrow indicates an output channel, and an incoming arrow indicates an input channel (being an input or output channel of a process is, in general, a purely syntactic notion).

A channel c of a process P is *value independent* if, for all $(t, R) \in \phi P$, $\alpha c \cap R \neq \emptyset$ implies $(t, R \cup \alpha c) \in \phi P$. We then define an *input-output process* (*IO* process) to be a non-diverging process P such that all its input channels are value independent. Intuitively, in an *IO* process the data component of a message arriving on an input channel c is irrelevant as far as its receiving is concerned; if one such message can be refused then so can any other message. In practice, this is not a restrictive property and, in particular, the standard programming constructs like $c?x$ for receiving messages give rise to value independent input channels. The requirement that an *IO* process P should be non-diverging, i.e., $\delta P = \emptyset$, is standard in a CSP based framework, as divergences basically signify totally unacceptable behaviour. The class of base *IO* processes is compositional, i.e., a network of *IO* processes is an *IO* process (provided that the composition does not generate a divergence).

2.   Extraction patterns

We first explain the basic mechanism behind our modelling of behaviour abstraction, viz. the extraction pattern, using a simple example. Consider a pair of base processes, DBL and BUF, shown in figure 1. DBL receives a signal (0 or 1) on its input channel at the very beginning of its execution, forwards this signal followed by its converse on its output channel and terminates. BUF is a buffer of capacity one, forever forwarding signals received on its input channel. In terms of CSP, we can represent them as $\text{DBL} \overset{\text{df}}{=} []_{i \in \{0,1\}} c{:}i \to d{:}i \to d{:}(1-i) \to \text{STOP}$ and $\text{BUF} \overset{\text{df}}{=} []_{i \in \{0,1\}} d{:}i \to e{:}i \to \text{BUF}$, and one can see that $\text{DBL} \otimes \text{BUF}$ is semantically equal to $\text{DBL}[e/d]$, i.e., the composition of the two processes behaves like DBL with its output channel renamed to e.

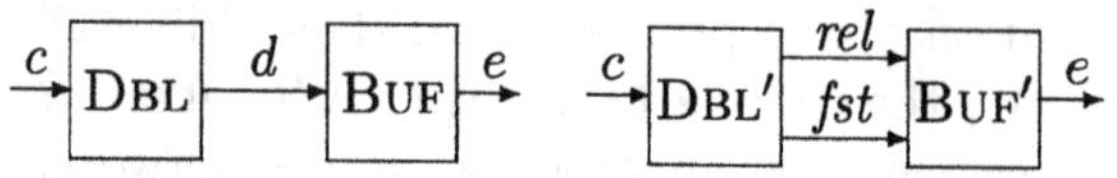

Figure 1 Two base processes and their implementations.

Suppose now that the signal transmission between the two processes has been implemented using two channels, *rel* and *fst*, as shown in figure 1. The transmissions on d are now duplicated and the two copies sent along *rel* (reliable but slow) and *fst* (fast but unreliable). That is, DBL′ sends a duplicated signal, while BUF′ accepts the first received copy of the signal and passes it on ignoring the other one: $\text{DBL}' \overset{\text{df}}{=} []_{i \in \{0,1\}} c{:}i \to (rel{:}i \to rel{:}(1-i) \to \text{STOP} \| fst{:}i \to fst{:}(1-i) \to \text{STOP})$ and $\text{BUF}' \overset{\text{df}}{=} \text{BUF}^{\langle \rangle}$, where

$$\text{BUF}^{\langle \rangle} \overset{\text{df}}{=} []_{i \in \{0,1\}} rel{:}i \to e{:}i \to \text{BUF}^{\langle fst{:}i \rangle} \ []$$
$$[]_{i \in \{0,1\}} fst{:}i \to e{:}i \to \text{BUF}^{\langle rel{:}i \rangle}$$
$$\text{BUF}^{\langle fst{:}k \rangle \circ z} \overset{\text{df}}{=} []_{i \in \{0,1\}} rel{:}i \to e{:}i \to \text{BUF}^{\langle fst{:}k \rangle \circ z \circ \langle fst{:}i \rangle} [] \ fst{:}k \to \text{BUF}^{z}$$
$$\text{BUF}^{\langle rel{:}k \rangle \circ z} \overset{\text{df}}{=} []_{i \in \{0,1\}} fst{:}i \to e{:}i \to \text{BUF}^{\langle rel{:}k \rangle \circ z \circ \langle rel{:}i \rangle} [] \ rel{:}k \to \text{BUF}^{z} \ .$$

In the above, the traces appearing in the superscripts indicate which messages should be ignored, as their copies have already been received.

Such a scheme clearly works as we have $\text{DBL} \otimes \text{BUF} = \text{DBL}' \otimes \text{BUF}'$. Suppose next that the transmission of signals is imperfect and two types of faulty behaviour can occur: $\text{DBL}_1 \overset{\text{df}}{=} \text{DBL}' \sqcap \text{STOP}$ and $\text{DBL}_2 \overset{\text{df}}{=} \text{DBL}' \sqcap []_{i \in \{0,1\}} c{:}i \to rel{:}i \to rel{:}(1-i) \to \text{STOP}$. In other words, DBL_1 can break down completely, refusing to output any signals, while DBL_2 can fail in such a way that although channel *fst* is completely blocked, *rel* can still transmit the signals (DBL_2 could be used to model the following situation: in order to improve performance, a 'slow' channel d is replaced by two channels, a potentially *fast* yet unreliable channel *fst*, and a slower but *reliable* backup channel *rel*). Since $\text{DBL} \otimes \text{BUF} = \text{DBL}_2 \otimes \text{BUF}'$ and $\text{DBL} \otimes \text{BUF} \neq \text{DBL}_1 \otimes \text{BUF}'$, it follows that DBL_2 is much 'better' an implementation of the DBL process than DBL_1. We will now analyse the differences between the behavioural properties of the two processes and, at the same time, introduce informally some basic concepts used subsequently.

We start by observing that the output of DBL_2 can be thought of as adhering to the following two rules: (R1) the transmissions over *rel* and *fst* are consistent w.r.t. message content (the set of all traces over *rel* and *fst* satisfying such a property will be denoted by *Dom*); and (R2) transmission over *rel* is reliable; there is no such guarantee for *fst*. The output produced by DBL_1 satisfies R1, but fails to satisfy R2, unlike DBL_2 which satisfies R1-2. To express this difference formally, we need to render these two conditions in some form of precise notation.

To capture the relationship between traces of DBL and DBL_2, we will employ an (extraction) mapping *extr*, which for a trace over *rel* and *fst* returns the corresponding trace over *d*. For example, keeping in mind that duplicates of signals should be ignored by the receiving process, some extraction mappings will be: $\langle \rangle \mapsto \langle \rangle$, $\langle rel{:}0 \rangle \mapsto \langle d{:}0 \rangle$, $\langle fst{:}0 \rangle \mapsto \langle d{:}0 \rangle$, $\langle fst{:}1, rel{:}1 \rangle \mapsto \langle d{:}1 \rangle$ and $\langle fst{:}1, rel{:}1, fst{:}0 \rangle \mapsto \langle d{:}1, d{:}0 \rangle$. Notice that the extraction mapping need only be defined for traces satisfying R1, i.e., those in *Dom*. We further observe that, in view of R2, some of the traces in *Dom* may be regarded as *incomplete*. For example, $\langle fst{:}1, rel{:}1, fst{:}0 \rangle$ is such a trace since channel *rel* is reliable and so the duplicate of $fst{:}0$ (i.e., $rel{:}0$) is bound to be eventually offered for transmission. The set of all other traces in *Dom* — i.e., those which in principle may be *complete* — will be denoted by *dom* (in general, $Dom = Pref(dom)$, meaning that each interpretable trace has, at least in theory, a chance of being completed). For our example, *dom* will contain all traces in *Dom* where the transmission on *fst* has not overtaken that on *rel*. (As another example, suppose that the whole sequence of actions $a_1, \ldots, a_k$ is extracted to a single action a, i.e., $\langle a_1, \ldots, a_i \rangle \mapsto \langle \rangle$, for $i < k$, and $\langle a_1, \ldots, a_k \rangle \mapsto \langle a \rangle$; then we do not consider such a transmission complete unless the whole sequence $a_1, \ldots, a_k$ has been transmitted.)

Although it will play a central role, the extraction mapping alone is not sufficient to identify the 'correct' implementation of DBL in the presence of faults since $\tau DBL = extr(\tau DBL_1) = extr(\tau DBL_2)$, while DBL_1 is incorrect. What one also needs is an ability to relate the refusals of potential implementations DBL_1 and DBL_2 with the possible refusals of the base process DBL. This, however, is much harder than relating traces. For suppose that we attempted to 'extract' the refusals of DBL_2 using the mapping *extr*. Then, we would have had $(\langle c{:}0 \rangle, \{fst{:}0\}) \in \phi DBL_2$, while $extr(\langle c{:}0 \rangle, \{fst{:}0\}) = (\langle c{:}0 \rangle, \{d{:}0\}) \notin \phi DBL$. This indicates that the crude extraction of refusals is not going to work. What we need is a more sophisticated device, which in our case comes in the form of another mapping, *ref*, constraining the possible refusals a process can exhibit on channels in the implementation, after a given trace $t \in Dom$.

For example, we should not allow the refusal of *rel*:0, after an incomplete communication $t = \langle fst{:}0 \rangle$.

The refusal bounds given by *ref* may be thought of as ensuring a kind of liveness or progress condition on sets of channels upon which composition will occur when implementation components are composed to build the full implementation system Q_{net}. Since these channels are to be composed upon and so hidden, the progress enforced manifests itself in the final system as the occurrence of a τ (invisible) transition, which leads to the instability of the states in which those τ transitions are enabled. This then means that these states will not contribute a failure of Q_{net}. Conversely, if we may not enforce progress after a *complete* behaviour, then it is possible that the relevant state reached *will* contribute to a failure, (t, R), of Q_{net}. Since, in the failures model of CSP, if Q_{net} 'implements' P_{net}, $\phi Q_{net} \subseteq \phi P_{net}$, then we must ensure that the relevant failure, (t, R), also occurs in P_{net}. We do this by ensuring that progress will not be possible on the corresponding channel in the specification component. Here, lack of progress on internal channels leads to stability and the fact that the relevant state *will* give rise to a failure of P_{net}.

Therefore, a sender implementation process, like DBL2, can admit a refusal disallowed by $ref(t)$ if the target process, DBL, admits after the extracted trace $extr(t)$ the refusal of all communication on the corresponding channel and, moreover, the trace t itself is complete, i.e., $t \in dom$.

Finally, it should be stressed that $ref(t)$ gives a refusal bound on the sender side (more precisely, the process which implements the sender target process). But this is enough since, if we want to rule out a deadlock in communication between the sender and receiver (on a localised set of channels), it is now possible to stipulate on the receiver side that no refusal is such that, when combined with any refusal allowed by $ref(t)$ on the sender side, it can yield the whole alphabet of the channels used for transmission.

Formal definition of extraction pattern.   The notion of extraction pattern (introduced and used in [7, 8], and slightly simplified here) relates behaviour on a set of channels in an implementation process to that on a channel in the target process. It has two main functions: that of interpretation of behaviour, necessitated by interface difference, and the encoding of some correctness requirements.

Definition 1 *An extraction pattern is a tuple* $ep \overset{\text{df}}{=} (B, b, dom, extr, ref)$, *where:* $B \neq \emptyset$ *is a set of* source *channels, and* b *is a* target *channel;* $dom \neq \emptyset$ *is a set of traces over the sources;* $extr$ *is a monotonic mapping* *defined for traces* $t \in Dom \stackrel{df}{=} Pref(dom)$ *such that* $extr(t)$ *is a trace over the target and* $extr(\langle \rangle) = \langle \rangle$; *and ref is a mapping defined for traces* $t \in Dom$ *such that* $ref(t)$ *is a non-empty family of proper subsets of* αB *(it is assumed that* $R \in ref(t)$ *and* $R' \subset R$ *always implies* $R' \in ref(t)$).

As already mentioned, the mapping *extr* interprets a trace over the source channels B (in the implementation process) in terms of a trace over a channel b (in the target process), and defines functionally correct (i.e., in terms of traces) behaviour over those source channels by way of its domain. The mapping *ref* is used to define correct behaviour in terms of failures as it gives bounds on refusals after execution of a particular trace sequence over the source channels. *dom* contains those traces in *Dom* for which the communication over B may be regarded as complete; the constraint on refusals given by *ref* is only allowed to be violated for such traces. The intuition behind this requirement is that we cannot regard as correct a situation where deadlock occurs in the implementation process when behaviour is incomplete, for regarding this as correct behaviour would imply that the specification process could in some sense deadlock while in the middle of executing a single (atomic) action. The extraction mapping *extr* is monotonic as receiving more information cannot decrease the current knowledge about the transmission. $\alpha B \notin ref(t)$ will be useful to forbid the sender to refuse all possible transmissions after an unfinished communication t.

The extraction pattern discussed informally for the example in figure 1 can be formalised as ep_0, where $B \stackrel{df}{=} \{rel, fst\}$ and $b \stackrel{df}{=} d$. To define the remaining components, for a trace t over B and a channel $x \in B$, we denote by t_x the trace obtained by first projecting t onto x and then renaming the channel x to d, i.e., $t_x \stackrel{df}{=} (t \restriction x)[d/x]$. Then *dom* is the set of all traces t over B such that $t_{fst} \leq t_{rel}$, and so *Dom* is the set of all traces t over B such that $t_{fst} \leq t_{rel}$ or $t_{rel} \leq t_{fst}$. Moreover, for every trace t in *Dom*, $extr(t)$ is the longest of the traces t_{fst} and t_{rel}, and $ref(t)$ is the set of all sets $R \subseteq \alpha B$ such that $rel:0 \notin R$ or $rel:1 \notin R$.

Intuitively, the extraction mapping always returns a trace derived from the longer of the two communications over *fst* and *rel* (this is acceptable since these communications are consistent, see the definition of *Dom*). Complete traces are those where *rel* has not fallen back behind *fst* in transmitting the signals. The $ref(t)$ component states that if behaviour is not complete on *rel* and *fst*, then at least one action must be possible on *rel*.

To relate incoming communication of DBL and DBL2, we will need another kind of extraction pattern. An *identity* extraction pattern for a channel c, id_c, is one for which $B \stackrel{df}{=} \{c\}$, $b \stackrel{df}{=} c$, $dom = Dom$ is the set of all traces over channel c, $extr(t) \stackrel{\text{df}}{=} t$ and $ref(t)$ is the set of all proper subsets of αc. The idea here is that the extraction mapping is simply the identity mapping, i.e., the specification and implementation processes have the same input interface. Any such communication can therefore be a terminated one, i.e., it can be regarded as complete.

We lift two of the notions introduced above to any set of extraction patterns $Ep = \{ep_1, \ldots, ep_n\}$, where $ep_i = (B_i, b_i, dom_i, extr_i, ref_i)$. Dom_{Ep} is the set of all traces t over channels $B_1 \cup \ldots \cup B_n$ such that $t{\restriction}B_i \in Dom_i$, for every $i \leq n$. Moreover, $extr_{Ep}(\langle\rangle) \stackrel{\text{df}}{=} \langle\rangle$ and, for every $t \circ \langle a \rangle \in Dom_{Ep}$ with $a \in \alpha B_i$, $extr_{Ep}(t \circ \langle a \rangle) \stackrel{\text{df}}{=} extr_{Ep}(t) \circ u$, where (possibly empty) u is such that $extr_i(t{\restriction}B_i \circ \langle a \rangle) = extr_i(t{\restriction}B_i) \circ u$.

In what follows, different extraction patterns will have disjoint sources and distinct targets.

3.   The implementation relation

Suppose that we intend to implement a base process P using another process Q with a possibly different communication interface. The correctness of the implementation will be expressed in terms of two sets of extraction patterns, *In* and *Out*. The former (with sources *in Q* and targets *in P*) will be used to relate the communication on the input channels of P and Q, the latter will serve a similar purpose for the output channels.

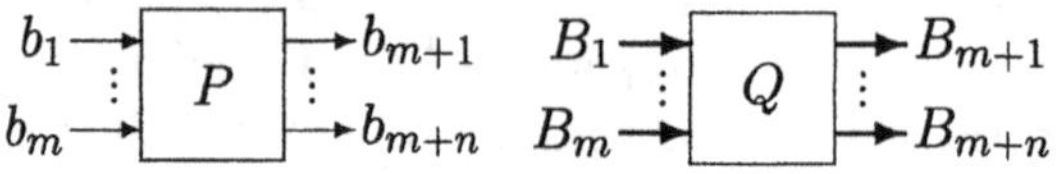

Figure 2 Base process P and its implementation Q.

Let P be a base *IO* process as in figure 2 and, for every $i \leq m + n$, let $ep_i \stackrel{\text{df}}{=} (B_i, b_i, dom_i, extr_i, ref_i)$ be an extraction pattern. We will denote by *In* the set of the first m extraction patterns ep_i, and by *Out* the remaining n extraction patterns. We then take any non-diverging process Q with the input channels $B_1 \cup \ldots \cup B_m$ and output channels $B_{m+1} \cup \ldots \cup B_{m+n}$, as shown in figure 2, where thick arrows represent *sets* of channels. We will further say that channels B_i are *blocked* at a failure $(t, R) \in \phi Q$ if either $i \leq m$ and $\alpha B_i - R \in ref_i(t{\restriction}B_i)$, or $i > m$ and $\alpha B_i \cap R \notin ref_i(t{\restriction}B_i)$. (Note that in both cases this signifies that the refusal bound imposed by ref_i has been breached.) We denote this by $i \in Blocked(t, R)$.

Definition 2 *Under the above assumptions, Q is an* implementation *of P w.r.t. sets of extraction patterns In and Out, denoted $Q \preceq_{Out}^{In} P$, if the following hold, where $All \stackrel{\text{df}}{=} In \cup Out$.*

1 $\tau Q \subseteq Dom_{All}$ and $extr_{All}(\tau Q) \subseteq \tau P$.

2 If $t \leq t' \leq \ldots$ are unboundedly growing traces of Q, then the traces $extr_{All}(t) \leq extr_{All}(t') \leq \ldots$ also grow unboundedly.

3 If $(t, R) \in \phi Q$ and $i \in Blocked(t, R)$, then $t{\restriction}B_i \in dom_i$.

4 If $(t, R) \in \phi Q$ is such that $t{\restriction}B_i \in dom_i$ for all $i \leq m + n$, then

$$\left(\; extr_{All}(t) \;, \quad \bigcup_{i \in Blocked(t,R)} \alpha b_i \; \right) \in \phi P \; .$$

In the above definition, (1) states that all traces of Q can be interpreted as traces of P. According to (2), it is not possible to execute Q indefinitely without extracting any actions of P. According to (3), if refusals grow in excess of their bounds on a source channel set B_i, communication on B_i may be interpreted as locally completed. Finally, (4) states a condition for refusal extraction, whereby if a trace is locally completed on all channels, then any local blocking on a source channel set B_i in Q is transformed into the refusal of the whole αb_i in P.

A direct comparison of an implementation process Q with the corresponding base process P is only possible if there is no difference in the communication interfaces. This corresponds to the situation that, in the definition of $\preceq_{Out}^{In}$, both In and Out are sets of *identity* extraction patterns. In such a case, we simply denote $Q \preceq P$ and then we can directly compare the semantics of the two processes in question.

Theorem 3 *If $Q \preceq P$ and $(t, R) \in \phi Q$ then*

$$\left(t, \; (\alpha in\,P \cap R) \cup \bigcup_{b \in out\,Q,\, \alpha b \subseteq R} \alpha b \right) \in \phi P \; .$$

That is, $Q \preceq P$ implies that Q is a process whose functionality in terms of traces conforms to that of the specification process P (to see this, it suffices to take $R = \emptyset$). Moreover, all the *essential* refusals of Q are also present in P. That is, all the refusals on input channels are preserved *entirely*, while for output channels any refusal to output anything on a given channel b is also present in P. The latter should indeed be considered as a very satisfactory state of affairs: Q will never fail to provide an output consistent with the specification, unless the specification process explicitly allows no output at all to be produced. We therefore consider that the above result embodies a fully adequate notion of *realisability* in any practical framework consistent with our setup. It is also worth mentioning that $\preceq$ is a preorder (i.e., it is a reflexive and transitive relation), and is preserved by the hiding of communication channels, i.e., if $Q \preceq P$ and B is a set of channels of P such that $P \backslash B$ is divergence-free, then $Q \backslash B \preceq P \backslash B$.

In the light of theorem 3, relation $\preceq$ provides us with a direct measure of the closeness of the approximation of the base process P by an implementation process Q. It therefore deserves further discussion, in particular with regard to its relationship with the standard *refinement* ordering of CSP, denoted by $\sqsupseteq$. In our framework, $Q \sqsupseteq P$ (i.e., Q 'CSP implements or *refines*' P) basically amounts to stating that $\phi Q \subseteq \phi P$.

To start with, it is not difficult to check that $Q \sqsupseteq P$ implies $Q \preceq P$. Moreover, $\preceq$ collapses to $\sqsupseteq$ for the rather wide class of *output-determined IO* processes. A process P is said to be output-determined if, for any traces $t \circ \langle c{:}v \rangle$ and $t \circ \langle c{:}v' \rangle$ of P such that c is an output channel, it is the case that $v = v'$ (i.e., the result produced by P on a given output channel c is determined at any given point of its execution).

Theorem 4 *If P is output-determined, then $Q \preceq P$ implies $Q \sqsupseteq P$.*

We will now investigate what can be established by considering the way P and Q interact with a possible environment. Let P be a (specification) base *IO* process, which is not assumed to be output-determined, and Q be its implementation w.r.t. suitable identity extraction pattern, i.e., let $Q \preceq P$. Therefore Q can be used in place of P in an environment T accepting all their outputs, as shown in figure 3. Our aim now is to relate the behaviour of Q and P in the environment provided by the process T.

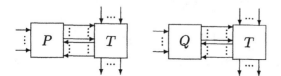

Figure 3 Relating base and implementation processes in the context of an environment.

We assume that, besides P, also T is an *IO* process, their composition is non-diverging, and *out* $P \subseteq in\,T$. We then obtain

Theorem 5 *If $Q \preceq P$ then $Q \otimes T \sqsupseteq P \otimes T$.*

Thus $Q \otimes T$ is at least as *deterministic* a process as $P \otimes T$ in the sense of CSP (see [6, 14]). This makes Q at least as good as P (and possibly much better) as a process to be used in practice. Hence we conclude that $Q \preceq P$ captures an adequate notion of realisability in the context of an environment T.

We finally present a fundamental result, that the implementation relation is compositional.

Theorem 6 *Let K and L be two base IO processes whose composition is non-diverging, as in figure 4, and let Ep_c, Ep_d, Ep_e, Ep_f, Ep_g and Ep_h be sets of extraction patterns whose targets are respectively the channel sets C, D, E, F, G and H. Then*

$$M \preceq_{Ep_d \cup Ep_e}^{Ep_c \cup Ep_h} K \ \wedge \ N \preceq_{Ep_g \cup Ep_h}^{Ep_d \cup Ep_f} L \implies M \otimes N \preceq_{Ep_e \cup Ep_g}^{Ep_c \cup Ep_f} K \otimes L \, .$$

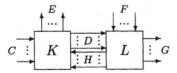

Figure 4 Base processes used in the formulation of the compositionality theorem.

Hence the implementation relation is preserved through network composition, and the only restriction is that the network of the base processes should be designed in a divergence-free way. However, the latter is a standard requirement in the CSP approach (recall again that divergences are regarded as totally unacceptable).

Returning to the example in figure 1, it can be shown that $\text{DBL}_2 \preceq_{ep_0}^{id_c} \text{DBL}$ and $\text{BUF}' \preceq_{id_e}^{epo} \text{BUF}$. Hence, it follows from theorem 6 and $\text{DBL} \otimes \text{BUF} = \text{DBL}[e/d]$ that $\text{DBL}_2 \otimes \text{BUF}' \preceq \text{DBL}[e/d]$. Thus, by theorem 4, $\text{DBL}_2 \otimes \text{BUF}' \sqsupseteq \text{DBL}[e/d]$, as process $\text{DBL}[e/d]$ is easily seen to be output-determined. But we can go one step further since $\text{DBL}[e/d]$ is a *deterministic* process in the sense of CSP (see [6, 14]). This means, in particular, that $Q \sqsupseteq \text{DBL}[e/d]$ implies $Q = \text{DBL}[e/d]$, for any process Q. Thus, we can finally conclude that $\text{DBL}_2 \otimes \text{BUF}' = \text{DBL}[e/d]$ and that we obtained such a result by purely compositional argument, using the results presented in this section together with a well-known property of deterministic CSP processes.

4.   Compositionality and CA actions

The above approach to verification, based on abstraction of interface difference and compositionality, will now be applied to an analysis of Coordinated Atomic (CA) actions [11, 12]. This concept represents an approach to structuring complex activities in a distributed environment, aimed at supporting fault tolerance in object-oriented systems.

The following are some of the essential characteristics of the model: (CA1) a CA action has roles which are activated by some external participants (processes or threads); (CA2) a CA action starts when all the roles have been activated and finishes when each role has completed its execution; (CA3) the execution of a CA action updates the system state (represented by a set of external objects) atomically; (CA4) roles can access local objects as well as participate in nested CA actions; and (CA5)

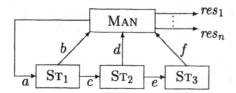

Figure 5 Initial architecture of the system based on a manager process, and three processes responsible for the three stages of processing

CA actions provide a basic framework for exception handling that can support a variety of fault tolerance mechanisms.

We will interpret CA3 as stating that the desired behaviour of external objects constitutes a specification of the system design based on CA actions, and so the CA actions design should respect the main objective which is that the external objects must complete successfully all the stages through which they are passing while being manipulated by the CA actions.

Modelling the production cell. In the rest of this section we will discuss an example inspired by the 'production cell' case study in [12]. The initial architecture of the design is shown in figure 5, where MAN is a *manager* process initially holding n external objects, represented throughout as $\xi^1, \ldots, \xi^n$, which are supposed to pass through the required stages of processing (three stages, in our case). The external objects are passed as messages and every object must be received by processes ST_1, ST_2 and ST_3, representing the three stages. To keep track of progress, the three processes report to the manager after each stage has been successfully completed. The manager MAN, in turn, sends out, over the channels res_i, messages that inform the external environment how the system as a whole is progressing. The initial system specification is given as $SYS \stackrel{df}{=} MAN \otimes ST_1 \otimes ST_2 \otimes ST_3$, where $MAN \stackrel{df}{=} MAN^0$, $ST_1 \stackrel{df}{=} []_{i \leq n} \, a{:}\xi^i \rightarrow b{:}i \rightarrow c{:}\xi^i \rightarrow ST_1$, $ST_2 \stackrel{df}{=} []_{i \leq n} \, c{:}\xi^i \rightarrow d{:}i \rightarrow e{:}\xi^i \rightarrow ST_2$, $ST_3 \stackrel{df}{=} []_{i \leq n} \, e{:}\xi^i \rightarrow f{:}i \rightarrow ST_3$ and:

$$
MAN^k \stackrel{df}{=} \begin{cases} \left(\begin{array}{l} a{:}\xi^{k+1} \rightarrow MAN^{k+1}[] \\ []_{i \leq n, \, ch \in \{b,d,f\}} \; ch{:}i \rightarrow res_i{:}ch \rightarrow MAN^k \end{array} \right) & \text{if } k < n \\ []_{i \leq n, \, ch \in \{b,d,f\}} \; ch{:}i \rightarrow res_i{:}ch \rightarrow MAN^k & \text{if } k = n \end{cases}
$$

Note that the meaning of, e.g., message $res_i{:}f$ is to inform the external environment that ξ^i has successfully passed through the third stage of processing. It is not difficult to see that each of the processes used to define SYS is a base IO process, and so is SYS.

As far as the overall correctness is concerned, we are interested in establishing that every object ξ^i has successfully passed through each

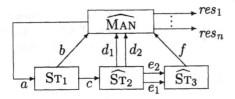

stage, and has done so in the prescribed order. Such a property may be verified by showing that, when restricted to a single output channel res_i, the system behaves as the process $\text{SPEC}_i \stackrel{\text{df}}{=} res_i{:}b \rightarrow res_i{:}d \rightarrow res_i{:}f \rightarrow \text{STOP}$. Indeed, one can show (e.g., using the tool FDR [14]), that for every $i \leq n$, $\text{SYS}@res_i = \text{SPEC}_i$ (for any process P with the same channels as SYS, $P@res_i \stackrel{\text{df}}{=} P \backslash \{res_1, \ldots, res_{i-1}, res_{i+1}, \ldots, res_n\}$).

Introducing exception handling.   As stated by CA5, CA actions provide a basic framework for exception handling. At the level where the roles of CA actions are described, exceptions could be modelled as actions which are followed by exception handling processes. At the current, higher level of abstraction, we will model the effects of exceptions rather than the exceptions themselves. In particular, we can imagine the situation when an exception raised within some CA action, representing an implementation of one of the three stages, is handled by invoking another, alternative CA action. Suppose this can occur during the second stage. To capture this, we replace ST_2 by another process, $\widehat{\text{ST}_2}$, which allows two alternative ways of processing a recently received object ξ^i: it is passed to the next stage using exactly one of the channels, e_1 or e_2, which has replaced e, and the manager is informed about the successful completion using the corresponding new channel, d_1 or d_2, which has replaced d. The process $\widehat{\text{ST}_2}$ uses a non-deterministic choice operator to choose between the two ways of processing an object, and so that process rather than the environment is responsible for resolving this choice: this models the possibility of a fault occurring. The new system is given by $\widehat{\text{SYS}} \stackrel{\text{df}}{=} \widehat{\text{MAN}} \otimes \text{ST}_1 \otimes \widehat{\text{ST}_2} \otimes \widehat{\text{ST}_3}$, where (see also figure 6):

$$\widehat{\text{MAN}} \stackrel{\text{df}}{=} M^0$$
$$\widehat{\text{ST}_2} \stackrel{\text{df}}{=} []_{i \leq n}\, c{:}\xi^i \rightarrow (d_1{:}i \rightarrow e_1{:}\xi^i \rightarrow \widehat{\text{ST}_2} \sqcap d_2{:}i \rightarrow e_2{:}\xi^i \rightarrow \widehat{\text{ST}_2})$$
$$\widehat{\text{ST}_3} \stackrel{\text{df}}{=} []_{i \leq n,\, ch \in \{e_1, e_2\}}\, ch{:}\xi^i \rightarrow f{:}i \rightarrow \widehat{\text{ST}_3}\, .$$

Moreover, $M^n \stackrel{\text{df}}{=} Z^n[]W^n$ and $M^k \stackrel{\text{df}}{=} (a{:}\xi^{k+1} \rightarrow M^{k+1})[]Z^k[]W^k$, for every $k < n$, where: $Z^l \stackrel{\text{df}}{=} []_{i \leq n,\, ch \in \{b,f\}}\, ch{:}i \rightarrow res_i{:}ch \rightarrow M^l$ and $W^l \stackrel{\text{df}}{=} []_{i \leq n,\, ch \in \{d_1,d_2\}}\, ch{:}i \rightarrow res_i{:}d \rightarrow M^l$, for every $l \leq n$.

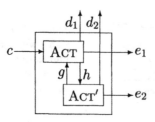

Figure 7 An architecture for a distributed implementation of the second stage of processing

To verify the correctness of $\widehat{\text{SYS}}$ compositionally, we can use the model presented earlier on in this paper. To establish that $\widehat{\text{MAN}}$, $\widehat{\text{ST}}_2$ and $\widehat{\text{ST}}_3$ are respectively implementations of MAN, ST_2 and ST_3, we will use two extraction patterns, both instances of a generic *merge* extraction pattern, mrg_x, for $x \in \{d, e\}$. The sources of mrg_x are two channels, x_1 and x_2, and the target is a channel x such that $\mu x_1 = \mu x_2 = \mu x$. The valid traces are all traces over $\alpha x_1 \cup \alpha x_2$ and $Dom = dom$. The extraction mapping is a trace homomorphism such that $extr(x_i{:}v) \stackrel{\text{df}}{=} \langle x{:}v \rangle$, for $i = 1, 2$. The *ref* mapping is such that, for every trace $t \in Dom$, $ref(t)$ comprises all proper subsets of $\alpha x_1 \cup \alpha x_2$. One can then show (e.g., using the techniques proposed in [3]) that

$$\widehat{\text{MAN}} \preceq^{mrg_d, id_b, id_f}_{id_a, id_{res_1}, \ldots, id_{res_n}} \text{MAN} \ , \quad \widehat{\text{ST}}_2 \preceq^{id_c}_{mrg_d, mrg_e} \text{ST}_2 \quad \text{and} \quad \widehat{\text{ST}}_3 \preceq^{mrg_e}_{id_f} \text{ST}_3 \ .$$

Hence, by theorem 6, we obtain that $\widehat{\text{SYS}} \preceq \text{SYS}$ and so $\widehat{\text{SYS}}@res_i = \text{SPEC}_i$, for every $i \le n$, as the implementation relation is preserved by hiding of channels, $\text{SYS}@res_i = \text{SPEC}_i$, and each process SPEC_i is output-determined (see theorem 4) and deterministic (in the CSP sense).

Refining a stage.   A possible implementation of $\widehat{\text{ST}}_2$ is to employ two processes, ACT and ACT$'$, which represent two intended CA actions: a primary CA action responsible for processing objects at the second stage, and another CA action invoked when the first one cannot be completed successfully (see figure 7). The implementation of $\widehat{\text{ST}}_2$ is $\widetilde{\text{ST}}_2 \stackrel{\text{df}}{=} \text{ACT} \otimes \text{ACT}'$, where:

$$
\begin{aligned}
\text{ACT} \ &\stackrel{\text{df}}{=} \ []_{i \le n} \ c{:}\xi^i \rightarrow (d_1{:}i \rightarrow e_1{:}\xi^i \rightarrow \text{ACT} \ \sqcap \ h{:}\xi^i \rightarrow g{:}go \rightarrow \text{ACT}) \\
\text{ACT}' \ &\stackrel{\text{df}}{=} \ []_{i \le n} \ h{:}\xi^i \rightarrow d_2{:}i \rightarrow e_2{:}\xi^i \rightarrow g{:}go \rightarrow \text{ACT}'
\end{aligned}
$$

Since $\widehat{\text{ST}}_2 = \widetilde{\text{ST}}_2$ (which can be checked using, e.g., the FDR tool [14]), we can now refine the architecture of the design, replacing $\widehat{\text{ST}}_2$ with $\widetilde{\text{ST}}_2$, and obtaining a new system composed of five processes: $\widetilde{\text{SYS}} \stackrel{\text{df}}{=} \widehat{\text{MAN}} \otimes \text{ST}_1 \otimes \text{ACT} \otimes \text{ACT}' \otimes \widehat{\text{ST}}_3$. As $\widetilde{\text{SYS}} = \widehat{\text{SYS}}$, we do not lose the correctness established for $\widehat{\text{SYS}}$, i.e., $\widetilde{\text{SYS}}@res_i = \text{SPEC}_i$, for every $i \le n$.

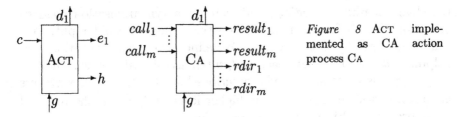

Figure 8 ACT implemented as CA action process CA

Since all the components in $\widetilde{\text{SYS}}$ are *IO* processes, we can again apply the framework developed in this paper, and indeed continue the cycle of development until a sufficiently detailed level of modelling has been reached, at each stage applying a compositional argument as outlined above. We stop this discussion here, but instead look at the way in which ACT could be implemented by a process CA, shown in figure 8, modelling more closely the intended features of CA actions.

Modelling CA actions. CA has $call \stackrel{\text{df}}{=} \{call_1, \ldots, call_m\}$ channels which are intended to carry messages with some input data (parameters) requesting an access to CA, each such message corresponding to starting a role (see requirement CA1). CA waits for a set of m messages, each such message arriving along a different channel $call_i$, before accepting them for further processing (see CA2). In general, it is not the case that any message set will be accepted as a valid call, so it is assumed that there is a non-empty set of *valid inputs* (e.g., two out of three results are successful in majority voting, see [7]), *Valid*, and a *consistent input* is any set of messages which is contained in some valid input. Each $V \in Valid$ is a set of m messages, $\{call_1{:}v'_1, \ldots, call_m{:}v'_m\}$. It is also assumed that for such a V there is a non-empty set $result(V)$ which comprises all possible outcomes of the processing of messages in V. Each element U of $result(V)$ is a set of m messages $\{result_1{:}v_1, \ldots, result_m{:}v_m\}$. It is assumed at this level of abstraction that an execution of any CA action produces a single result for each of the participating threads. Note also that an aborted execution of the CA action can be modelled by $\{result_1{:}abort, \ldots, result_m{:}abort\} \in result(V)$. Below, for any consistent input V, $\rho(V) \stackrel{\text{df}}{=} \{i \leq m \mid \alpha call_i \cap V = \emptyset\}$ identifies those channels $call_i$ on which a suitable input is still expected and, for every $i \in \rho(V)$, the set of all $v \in \mu call_i$ such that $V \cup \{call_i{:}v\}$ is still a consistent input is denoted by $\pi_i(V)$.

After assembling a valid input, CA proceeds in one of two ways. First of all, it can report on channel d_1 that the action has been completed successfully, and then non-deterministically produce one of the possible outcomes in $result(V)$. Alternatively, it can invoke the CA action process CA$'$ implementing ACT$'$, by redirecting the data received on $call$ using the channels $rdir_1, \ldots, rdir_m$, and wait for a synchronisation message $g{:}go$ from CA' before starting to construct another valid input. We can model this by $\mathrm{CA} \overset{\mathrm{df}}{=} \mathrm{CA}_\emptyset$. To define CA_V, some notations are helpful: $redir(V)$ is V with each $call_i{:}v$ replaced by $rdir_i{:}v$, $\psi : Valid \to \{\xi^1, \ldots, \xi^n\}$ is a mapping which describes how an input to CA process is interpreted as an object at the higher level, $\iota(\xi^i) \overset{\mathrm{df}}{=} i$ is the index of every processed object. We may now define:

$$\mathrm{CA}_V \overset{\mathrm{df}}{=} \begin{cases} []_{i\in\rho(V),\, v\in\pi_i(V)}\ call_i{:}v \to \mathrm{CA}_{V\cup\{call_i{:}v\}}\,[] & \\[4pt] []_{i\in\rho(V),\, v\in\mu call_i - \pi_i(V)}\ call_i{:}v \to \mathrm{CA}_V & \text{if } |V| < m \\[4pt] \sqcap_{U\in result(V)}\ (d_1{:}\iota(\psi(V)) \to \widehat{\mathrm{CA}}_U) \sqcap \widetilde{\mathrm{CA}}_{redir(V)} & \text{if } |V| = m \end{cases}$$

where $\widehat{\mathrm{CA}}_\emptyset \overset{\mathrm{df}}{=} g{:}go \to \mathrm{CA}_\emptyset$, $\widetilde{\mathrm{CA}}_\emptyset \overset{\mathrm{df}}{=} \mathrm{CA}_\emptyset$ and, for every $U \neq \emptyset$,

$$\widehat{\mathrm{CA}}_U \overset{\mathrm{df}}{=} []_{a\in U}\ a \to \widehat{\mathrm{CA}}_{U-\{a\}} \text{ and } \widetilde{\mathrm{CA}}_U \overset{\mathrm{df}}{=} []_{a\in U}\ a \to \widetilde{\mathrm{CA}}_{U-\{a\}}\ .$$

Verifying the CA action design.   To show that CA indeed implements ACT, we need to find suitable extraction patterns. Below we show how to devise one capable of relating communication on channels $call$ to that on channel c; for the other channels one may proceed similarly.

We define by induction Dom and $extr$, together with an auxiliary mapping $\zeta : Dom \to \mathbb{P}(\alpha call)$, which for any trace in Dom yields the last unfinished consistent input built along this trace. To begin with, we have $\langle\rangle \in Dom$, $extr(\langle\rangle) \overset{\mathrm{df}}{=} \langle\rangle$ and $\zeta(\langle\rangle) \overset{\mathrm{df}}{=} \emptyset$. Suppose now that $t \in Dom$ and $v \in \mu call_i$. Then $u = t \circ \langle call_i{:}v\rangle \in Dom$ if $i \in \rho(\zeta(t))$. Let $V \overset{\mathrm{df}}{=} \zeta(t) \cup \{call_i{:}v\}$ if $v \in \pi_i(\zeta(t))$, and $V \overset{\mathrm{df}}{=} \zeta(t)$ otherwise. If $|V| = m$ then $extr(u) \overset{\mathrm{df}}{=} extr(t) \circ \langle c{:}\psi(V)\rangle$ and $\zeta(u) \overset{\mathrm{df}}{=} \emptyset$; otherwise $extr(u) \overset{\mathrm{df}}{=} extr(t)$ and $\zeta(u) \overset{\mathrm{df}}{=} V$. Finally, dom is the set of all $t \in Dom$ such that $\zeta(t) = \emptyset$, and for every $t \in Dom$, $ref(t)$ comprises all subsets, R, of $\alpha call$ such that $\alpha call_i \not\subseteq R$, for at least one $i \in \rho(\zeta(t))$.

Having designed the extraction patterns establishing that CA is an implementation of ACT, one might refine our design both by 'looking inside' CA, capturing its internal architectural details (we can handle this using, for instance, FDR and the standard CSP theory) and/or further refining the interface of the process, for example, by specifying in detail communication protocols used to receive inputs on the channels $call$ (we can handle this using the approach proposed in this work, as CA is an IO process, and applying the algorithms presented in [3]).

5.   Conclusions

Compositional development, as outlined in the case study of the previous section, is a cyclic process, which starts with an initial system design given in the form of a process network $\text{SYS}_0 \stackrel{\text{df}}{=} P_1 \otimes \cdots \otimes P_r$ $(r \geq 1)$. For such a high-level description, one can relatively easily verify the relevant correctness requirements, e.g., using FDR or a similar tool. Suppose now that, after a number of iterations, the current system description comes in the form of a network $\text{SYS}_i \stackrel{\text{df}}{=} Q_1 \otimes \cdots \otimes Q_s$ satisfying $\text{SYS}_i \preceq \text{SYS}_0$. According to the argument put forward in the previous section, SYS_i constitutes a suitable implementation of the initial (correct) design. There are now two directions for further development:

- Find a process of SYS_i, e.g., Q_s, and implement it as a sub-network $Q'_1 \otimes \cdots \otimes Q'_q \sqsupseteq Q_s$. By compositionality, the resulting network, $\text{SYS}_{i+1} \stackrel{\text{df}}{=} Q_1 \otimes \cdots \otimes Q_{s-1} \otimes Q'_1 \otimes \cdots \otimes Q'_q$ satisfies $\text{SYS}_{i+1} \preceq \text{SYS}_i$ as $Q \sqsupseteq P$ always implies $Q \preceq P$, and so $\text{SYS}_{i+1} \preceq \text{SYS}_0$.

- Find IO processes of SYS_i, e.g., Q_{s-1} and Q_s, whose intercommunication interface can be refined, and replace them by their respective implementations, Q'_{s-1} and Q'_s, designed according to suitably chosen extraction pattern(s). The resulting network, $\text{SYS}_{i+1} \stackrel{\text{df}}{=} Q_1 \otimes \cdots \otimes Q_{s-2} \otimes Q'_{s-1} \otimes Q'_s$ satisfies $\text{SYS}_{i+1} \preceq \text{SYS}_i$, and so $\text{SYS}_{i+1} \preceq \text{SYS}_0$.

In further stages, if the second kind of development is to be applied, both Q'_{s-1} and Q'_s must be IO processes and, in the previous section, this was always the case. However, if more complex refinement steps are carried out, the situation may require a degree of care. A typical example would be to implement a communication on a channel ch, from Q_{s-1} to Q_s, using two communication channels, *data* and *ack* passing messages of a feedback-controlled protocol. In such a situation, it is usually not the case that *ack* is a value-independent channel of Q'_s and, strictly speaking, such a process is no longer an IO process with *ack* treated as its input channel. Fortunately, channels like *ack* will generally be value-independent in Q'_{s-1}, and a simple way out of the problem is to syntactically make *ack* an output channel of Q'_s and an input channel of Q'_{s-1}, before proceeding with further development of the network.

Of course, the first kind of iteration step can also present us with the problem of maintaining the property of value-independence for the channels internal to the sub-network $Q'_1 \otimes \cdots \otimes Q'_q$. This, however, is usually easy to address by looking up the code of the processes.

Acknowledgments

We would like to thank the anonymous referee for a number of corrections and helpful suggestions for improvement. This research was supported by an EPSRC studentship and the EU-funded DSoS project.

References

[1] M. Abadi and L. Lamport, "The Existence of Refinement Mappings," *Theoretical Computer Science* vol. 82, 1991, pp. 253-284.

[2] E. Brinksma, B. Jonsson, and F. Orava, "Refining Interfaces of Communicating Systems," *Proc. Coll. on Combining Paradigms for Software Development*, Springer, LNCS 494, 1991.

[3] J. Burton, M. Koutny and G. Pappalardo, "Verifying Implementation Relations in the Event of Interface Difference," *Proc. FME 2001*, LNCS 2021, 2001, 364-383.

[4] J. Burton, M. Koutny and G. Pappalardo, "Implementing Communicating Processes in the Event of Interface Difference," *Proc. ACSD 2001*, IEEE Computer Society, 2001, 87-96.

[5] R. Gerth, R. Kuiper and J. Segers, "Interface Refinement in Reactive Systems," *Proc. CONCUR '92*, Springer, LNCS 630, 1992, 77-93.

[6] C. A. R. Hoare, *Communicating Sequential Processes*, Prentice Hall, 1985.

[7] M. Koutny, L. Mancini and G. Pappalardo, "Two Implementation Relations and the Correctness of Communicated Replicated Processing," *Formal Aspects of Computing* vol. 9, 1997, pp. 119-148.

[8] M. Koutny and G. Pappalardo, "Behaviour Abstraction for Communicating Sequential Processes," to be published in *Fundamenta Informaticae*, 2002.

[9] L. Lamport, "The Implementation of Reliable Distributed Multiprocess Systems," *Computer Networks* vol. 2, 1978, pp. 95-114.

[10] R. Milner, *Communication and Concurrency*, Prentice Hall, 1989.

[11] B. Randell, A. Romanovsky, R. J. Stroud, J. Xu and A. F. Zorzo, *Coordinated Atomic Actions: From Concept to Implementation*, tech. report CSTR-595, University of Newcastle, 1997.

[12] B. Randell, A. Romanovsky, R. J. Stroud, J. Xu, A. F. Zorzo, D. Schwier and F. von Henke, *Coordinated Atomic Actions: Formal Model, Case Study and System Implementation*, tech. memo, University of Newcastle, 1997.

[13] A. Rensink and R. Gorrieri, "Vertical Implementation," to be published in *Information and Computation*, 2002.

[14] A. W. Roscoe, *The Theory and Practice of Concurrency*, Prentice-Hall, 1998.

[15] H. Schepers and J. Hooman, "Trace-based Compositional Reasoning About Fault-tolerant Systems," *Proc. PARLE'93*, Springer, LNCS 694, 1993.

Chapter 2

MODEL-BASED DESIGN OF DEPENDABILITY*

Anish Arora

Rajesh Jagannathan

Computer and Information Science
The Ohio State University
Columbus, Ohio USA
{anish,jagannat}@cis.ohio-state.edu

Yi-Min Wang

Microsoft Research
Redmond, Washington USA
ymwang@microsoft.com

Abstract   Distributed systems are notoriously subject to complex faults, of which
some are unanticipated. Towards dealing with the problem of unanticipated faults, we describe in this paper a model-based approach to
the design of dependability. By exploiting models, i.e. abstract descriptions of systems, our approach offers a potentially low-cost alternative
to handling rare faults in a case-by-case manner, while allowing common faults to be handled individually. We illustrate the model-based
approach with two case-studies: one concerning a home-network lookup
service and the other an X10 powerline network.

Keywords: model, formal methods, dependability, unanticipated faults, concurrency, distribution, networking

---

*This work was partially sponsored by DARPA contract OSU-RF #F33615-01-C-1901, NSF
grant NSF-CCR-9972368, an Ameritech Faculty Fellowship and a grant from Microsoft Research.

P. Ezhilchelvan and A. Romanovsky (eds.), Concurrency in Dependable Computing, 23–40.
© 2002 *Kluwer Academic Publishers. Printed in the Netherlands.*

1.   Introduction

Distributed systems are notoriously subject to complex faults. A number of these faults are unanticipated, and one might argue that this number will only increase as distributed systems are increasingly built by dynamic composition of components from diverse sources (using technologies such as COM, CORBA, and JavaBeans). In spite of this trend, it is expected that the systems function acceptably in a variety of user and fault environments.

It is therefore our position that the design of dependability for complex faults should also contend with unanticipated faults. Towards this end, we describe in this paper a model-based approach for dependability design in distributed systems.

1.1   Overview of the Model-Based Approach

Notwithstanding the uncertainties associated with distributed systems composition and their user/fault environments, their designer is typically in a position to specify the desired system behavior. The focal point of our approach is therefore a model of the desired behavior of the system, expressed in terms of a formal specification.

The effect of the faults on the system are only implicitly captured by considering potential violations of the model. By taking into account all possible model violations, the model-based approach contends with complex faults, both anticipated and unanticipated. It reduces the problem of dependability design to "enforcing" the system model at all times. Enforcement may occur at several levels: sometimes, it may be possible to ensure that the system behavior is never violated; at other times, the behavior may be recovered to (re)satisfy the system model; and occasionally the best that may be possible is to provide notification that the behavior has violated the model. (Details of how enforcement is achieved will be discussed in Section 2.)

It should be stressed that model-based design is compatible with several extant approaches that are fault-centric. The compatibility lies in two senses: First, model-based design does not preclude fault-centric design of dependability to handle common-case faults, which are often simple and best handled explicitly. When it comes to rare-case faults, which tend to be more complex, interdependent, and difficult to diagnose, model-based design offers the possibility of dealing with them in an implicit manner. (The combined use of fault-centric design to handle simple, common-case faults and model-based design to handle complex, rare-case faults will be illustrated via a case study in Section 3.) And second, model-based design does exploit knowledge of faults when designing the "enforcers" of the system model. (This will be illustrated in the case studies in Sections 3 and 4.)

Model-based design separates system dependability from system functionality. It allows the two to be modified independently. It also allows the dependability design to be reused for other systems which are expected to satisfy the same system model. Since it builds on more knowledge of the system than is assumed by approaches that essentially treat the system as a black-box, it offers the promise of lower-cost design of dependability. In particular, in the absence of faults, it allows the overhead of the dependability to be kept low, since essentially only the conformance to the model has to be checked. Moreover, in case the model evolves or is enriched, the dependability design may be modified accordingly.

1.2   Rationale underlying Model-Based Approach

Early techniques for system dependability assumed –with good reason– simple fault models, such as limited numbers of stuck-at faults, timing delays, or fail-stop nodes. During the last two decades, many of these techniques (e.g., rollback-recovery, consensus, and voting) have been systematically extended to deal with rich classes of faults, such as any number of concurrent node failures and repairs, or Byzantine processes or arbitrary transient faults. Graceful degradation techniques have also addressed complex faults [10]. In one such technique, faults are decomposed in multiple fault-classes, and the system is designed to tolerate each fault-class in an appropriate manner. In recent work on component-based design of multitolerance [2], tolerances are added one at a time, with each step ensuring that the newly added tolerance component does not interfere with the previously added ones.

As may be expected, while techniques that deal with complex faults often yield elegant designs, there are cases where the added complexity has yielded significant tradeoffs. ISIS is an example of a group communication services platform that dealt with complex faults but was itself so complex that maintainability suffered [6]. In other work, scenarios are reported where the virtual synchrony approach experienced scalability problems [7]. In the case of the Microsoft Cluster Service [11], it is reported that the high overhead of that dependability design prevented it from scaling past 2 to 4 nodes.

A different sort of scalability problem is noted for designs which assume full knowledge of implementation details: stabilization [8] with respect to the rich class of transient faults is a case in point. While there are cases where stabilization yields simpler designs than exception handling on a per-fault basis, it sometimes yields intricate designs because it makes extensive use of the details of system implementation. Also, the designs are rarely reusable for other systems because of their intimate dependence on the particulars of the implementation of the system.

Experience suggests that to keep the design task tractable, the number and composition of the fault-classes should be kept well under control. Handling faults individually and efficiently is reasonable for common-case faults but not necessarily for rare-case faults (this is why we endorse fault-centric design for common-case faults). The added complexity in the latter case is a potential source of undependability. One alternative therefore is to group multiple rare faults together and deal with them collectively. Another alternative is to show that the rare faults are all members of a rich fault class, such as Byzantine faults or transient faults, and now tolerance may be designed more expeditiously with respect to that rich fault class. But in the light of the maintainability, scalability, and reusability problems discussed above, and with a view to dealing with unanticipated faults as well, the alternative that we endorse is to deal with the complex faults in an implicit manner, by enforcing a model of the system.

1.3   Outline of the Chapter

In Section 2 we describe the model-based design in more detail. We illustrate our approach with two case-studies: a dependable lookup service in Section 3 and monitoring of the X10 powerline networking protocol in Section 4. Finally, in Section 5, we make concluding remarks and discuss some directions for future work.

2.   Model-based Dependability

2.1   Model

A *model* specifies the behavior that is desired of the system. This behavior may be expressed using any suitable modeling language, e.g., finite state automata, petri nets, temporal logic specifications, action systems, etc. Per se, a model of the system is independent of the faults that can affect the system. It is therefore assumed that the system satisfies the model when the system is executed in the absence of faults. By the same token, violations of the system model imply occurrence of some fault(s). The goal of the model-based approach, then, is to design dependability components that can be added to the system to "enforce" the model at all times, even in the presence of faults.

Example: Consider a highly available HTTP service. The service is identified by a unique domain name and is hosted by a cluster of workstations. It is assumed that in response to a request for name resolution with respect to this domain name, a DNS service supplies one of several internet addresses assigned to the cluster.

A model of the highly available service may be given with respect to the IP addresses: it is always the case that every IP address supplied by the DNS is assigned to some active node in the cluster. As long as the system satisfies this model the service remains available. Notice that the model is not specified in terms of the possible faults that may occur, e.g., NIC failure, workstation failure, unassigned IP address, duplicate IP address assignment, etc.

2.2 Model Predicates

The task of enforcement of a model is relatively straightforward for monolithic sequential systems. For instance, if the model is specified via an automaton, the model may be enforced by detecting/ensuring at each step that the system only performs valid transitions. But in distributed, concurrent, or otherwise composite systems, enforcement at the level of a global model of the system may be impractical and/or infeasible. For ease of implementation, therefore, we may decompose the model into several components (or processes or localities); component models may include assumptions about the environment under which they provide correct operation. The essential requirement of the decomposition is that every violation of the system model must imply the violation of at least one of the components models, and vice versa. It follows then that enforcement of the system model is achieved by separate enforcement of each component model.

Enforcing a (component) model is, without loss of generality, achieved by enforcing a corresponding "model predicate". While model predicates may, in general, involve temporal modalities, our presentation will focus only on state predicates of the model. This subclass of model predicates suffices in practice; moreover, by allowing the model state to be augmented with "history" or "prophecy" variables, the generality of this subclass is justifiable theoretically. Formally, then, we define a *model predicate* to be a boolean expression on the state of the model. The state of the model comprises all variables existing in the model. Note that these variables exist only in the design space and are not necessarily implemented by the system. Borrowing notation from temporal logic, if P denotes a boolean expression and $\Box$ denotes the *always* operator, then the model predicate $\Box P$ encodes the fact that the system always satisfies P.

Example (contd.): Continuing with our example of the HTTP server, we decompose the model into two parts and establish the corresponding model predicates: (i) each IP address is assigned to at least one active node in the cluster; and (ii) no IP address is assigned to two nodes simultaneously (which is a requirement of the underlying IP protocol). Letting i, j range over the set of nodes and the model variables $up.i$ and $assigned.ip.i$ respectively denote that node i is active and that the IP address ip is assigned to node i, we express the above predicates as

Assigned : $\Box(\exists i : up.i \wedge assigned.ip.i)$
Unique   : $\Box\neg(\exists i, j : i \neq j : assigned.ip.i \wedge assigned.ip.j)$

Thus, there are two model predicates for each *ip* address. Notice that the second predicate (*Unique*) can be further decomposed, on the basis of locality, into smaller predicates each of which refer to only two nodes. Whenever the model is violated, one of these predicates is also violated and, vice versa, whenever one of these predicates is violated the model is also violated.

2.3   Enforcement of Model Predicates

As discussed above, enforcement of all model predicates (corresponding to the component models) implies enforcement of the system model. But what precisely is meant by "enforcement"? Depending upon the level of dependability that is desired by the user of the system and the particular model predicate that is on hand, enforcement may mean any one of the following: (i) the predicate is never violated in the presence of faults; (ii) even if the predicate is violated, the system is restored such that the predicate is (re)satisfied; or (iii) violation of the predicate is notified in case the system functionality is unrecoverable; the notifications can be automatically logged for later analysis or propagated to the user for immediate action.

Enforcement of the individual predicates is achieved by dependability components which we term *predicate enforcers*. Achieving the level of enforcement in (i) above usually implies placing strict restrictions on the system functionality. Such predicate enforcers allow the system to make progress only if the next state can be guaranteed to still satisfy the predicate. In the case of (ii) and (iii) above, a generic strategy for the predicate enforcers is to monitor the corresponding predicate. If faults cause the predicate to be violated, the predicate enforcers execute appropriate corrective actions to resatisfy the predicate.

The corrective actions executed in the predicate handlers are not tied to any particular fault source or fault location, but only to the effects of the faults on the system and, in turn, the predicates. This empowers predicate enforcers to recover from the occurrence of unanticipated faults as well, unlike as in some fault-centric approaches where the handlers are tightly coupled with the source and location of the fault. In cases where the predicate enforcers are unsuccessful in restoring the system via the corrective actions, a notification is raised.

Example (contd.): Let us consider the enforcement of the predicate *Unique* extracted from our server model. The following predicate is for the IP address *ip* and the two nodes *u* and *v* ($u \neq v$):

$$\Box \neg (assigned.ip.u \wedge assigned.ip.v)$$

The level of enforcement we wish to provide for this predicate is as in (ii) discussed above. Now, if due to some fault, say in the DHCP (dynamic host configuration protocol) server, *ip* is assigned to the two nodes *u* and *v* at the same time and hence the predicate is violated, the enforcer for the predicate should take the corrective action to deassign the *ip* address from one of the nodes. Thus the predicate will be eventually resatisfied. Note that this enforcement involves a distributed computation. Interestingly, ensuring strict consistency in the collection of distributed state is not necessary in this example: in case the *ip* address is inadvertently deassigned from all nodes, the predicate enforcer for *Assigned* will ensure that eventually the *ip* is address assigned to one of the nodes.

2.4   Compatibility with Fault-Centric Design

In its pure form, model-based design does not model faults explicitly. However, we do not preclude the use of fault models in conjunction with the approach. The knowledge of fault models can be used to come up with efficient implementations for the predicate enforcers. In particular, a subset of the anticipated faults may be identified that are expected to occur more commonly than the others; a *common-case* fault model can therefore be defined explicitly. Using this fault model, it may be possible to ensure that some model predicates are never violated or more efficiently restored, even though this may not be possible in general for faults not in this fault model. This may be achieved by enforcing an additional predicate, that is stronger than the model demands. An illustration via our running example follows.

Example (contd.): The violation of the predicate *Assigned* from the server example implies that a particular *ip* has not been assigned to any alive node in the cluster. This may occur for example if the node to which the IP address was originally assigned fails, an occurrence which we treat as the *common-case* fault, as opposed to say simultaneous failure of two or more nodes, which we treat as a *rare-case* fault. A proposed enforcement of this predicate involves the failover of this address to some active node in the cluster. (We assume all the nodes are multi-homed, i.e., they are able to host more than one IP on the same NIC). It is possible to ensure that predicate *Assigned* is never violated for the common-case fault. In the implementation of the predicate enforcer, we use the common-case fault model to enforce the stronger predicate that at least two nodes are alive at all times:

$$\square(\exists i, j : i \neq j : up.i \wedge up.j)$$

As long as this stronger predicate holds, even when a common-case single node failure occurs, there is at least one node alive in the system. This along with the failover of the IP addresses ensures that predicate $\square(\exists i : up.i \wedge assigned.ip.i)$ is enforced without violation.

2.5   Comments on the Model-Based Design

In model-based design, the model enables separation of the system functionality from the system dependability. This separation has several advantages: (i) not only is the approach useful for adding dependability to systems during their design process but also a posteriori; (ii) in the absence of faults, the overhead of dependability is limited to that of monitoring that the system continues to satisfy the model; and (iii) the dependability components can be reused for systems that need to exhibit the same model of desired behavior.

The decomposition of the model into model predicates makes the design modular and incremental. If the system evolves or the dependability requirements change over time the dependability does not have to always be re-implemented from scratch. We can selectively add new predicates or modify existing ones, and tailor the set of predicates to the new model. A couple of issues that arise in the implementation are, dependability of the predicate enforcers and possible interference among them. Discussion on these is deferred till after the case studies have been presented.

Structure of case-study presentations. In both of the case-studies which follow, we begin with an informal description of the system, then give a model of desired behavior, and proceed to extract from the model the predicates to be enforced. Next, we discuss the common-case faults and a representative set of the rare-case faults, and finally present the design of the various predicate enforcers.

3. Case Study: Dependable Lookup Service

Aladdin [13] is a system for dependable, extensible control of heterogeneous devices via an in-home PC cluster and heterogeneous network. Aladdin control scenarios include: (i) automatic device discovery and location mapping (e.g., plug a lamp into an outlet in the kitchen, turn it on, and the system will know that a new lamp is now available in the kitchen). (ii) natural language-based home automation (e.g., enter "turn on the lights on the garage side of the kitchen"). (iii) email-based remote home automation (e.g., send a secure email to close your garage door). And (iv) cell phone-based remote notification [12] (e.g., get a cell phone call when your basement is flooded).

Given the above scenarios, one of the keys for the extensibility of Aladdin is the *Lookup service*. This service responds to two types of queries: (i) an attribute based query which returns a list of unique names that match the attributes, and (ii) a name based query which returns the address of an object given the unique name. The lookup service maintains information regarding addressing, location, and status of the various types of objects in the home network, including sensors, devices, and controllers.

Objects typically join and leave the network spontaneously. To automate the discovery process, objects periodically "refresh" their status and location in the lookup service, at a frequency of their choice. This frequency is chosen based on a number of factors, e.g., how often their status changes and how much network bandwidth is available. Depending upon the frequency chosen, refreshes are classified as being either *low-frequency* or *high-frequency*.

3.1 Model and Predicates

The requirements of the lookup service can be stated informally as: "each query to the lookup service returns a unique up-to-date response". For dependability, we replicate the service on an in-home PC cluster. Refresh messages and queries are assumed to be broadcast to all the replicas. The requirements of the lookup service may now be ensured by keeping the lookup server replicas in virtual synchrony.

Alternatively, we could achieve lower-cost dependability by exploiting a model. We postulate the following model of the lookup service: Always there exists a unique server that responds to queries, and this server—which we refer to as the leader—has up-to-date status of the objects.

If i ranges over the replicas, the boolean model variable *alive.i* denotes that node i is running a functioning replica; *leader.i* denotes that replica i believes it is the leader; and *uptodate.i* denotes that replica i has the most recent information. The table below lists the model predicates, extracted from the model.

Lookup service predicates

Activity	: $\Box((\exists i : alive.i) \wedge (\forall i : leader.i \Rightarrow alive.i))$
Uniqueness	: $\Box((\exists i : leader.i) \wedge \neg(\exists i, j : leader.i \wedge leader.j))$
Recency	: $\Box(\forall i : leader.i \Rightarrow uptodate.i)$

3.2   Enforcement

The dependability implementation, then, consists of enforcement of each of the three model predicates. Our implementation essentially (re)satisfies each predicate upon its violation. The enforcer for *Activity* runs a protocol that diagnoses and repairs failed replicas. The enforcer for *Uniqueness* implements a "weak leader election" protocol; in this protocol, only a unique replica knows it is the leader (the term 'weak' is used in the sense that the other nodes need not know the identity of the leader). Only the leader responds to queries.

Recency is automatically enforced in part by the periodic refreshes that are received from the various objects. The refreshes serve to repopulate the lookup database at the replicas once they have been repaired. While this is adequate for high-frequency refreshes, for the case of low-frequency refreshes the replica might respond to queries with out-of-date information for a long interval. Therefore, as part of the diagnosis and repair protocol, the information corresponding to the low frequency refreshes is streamed to the newly repaired servers to ensure *Recency* for low-frequency objects.

We identified the following faults as being common-case: the crash of a single replica and the loss of a single refresh message. To handle the crash of a single replica efficiently, the enforcer for *Activity* ensures that there are always two or more alive replicas with up-to-date information. In case the leader fails, the leader election protocol allows one of the remaining replicas with up-to-date information to automatically assume the role of leader. To handle the single refresh loss efficiently, we add an acknowledgment mechanism in which the leader is required to acknowledge the low-frequency refreshes. Low-frequency objects are expected to re-transmit their refreshes until an acknowledgment is received. In case of high-frequency refreshes, high data-quality is achieved per se and so we do not require the use of acknowledgments.

We conclude our lookup server case study with an example of an unanticipated fault that was handled by the predicate enforcers. During a deployment period of 14 days without any restart, on a cluster of four machines —Jasmine, MagicCarpet, Abu, and Genie— an unidentified 'glitch' caused unanticipated network partitioning on a number of occasions. We briefly describe one such occurrence (which in fact recurred several times): Magiccarpet became isolated from the rest of the nodes; Jasmine lost contact with Genie; and, Abu lost contact with both Jasmine and Genie. As a result of the partitioning, more than one node assumed leader status. In all cases, predicate enforcement restored the system to having a unique leader and subsequently the model was resatisfied.

4. Case Study: X10 Powerline Dependability

The X10 powerline network is one of several networks supported in Aladdin [13]. A typical X10 network consists of multiple controllers (CM11A interfaces) and multiple modules (LM465, PAM22 etc.), which communicate using the X10 protocol, over the common powerline communication medium. An X10 controller issues an address command, consisting of a house code and unit code (e.g., *A 1*), which places the module corresponding to that address in an "addressed" state, and then issues a function command, with the same house code and a function code (e.g., *A On*). The addressed module then responds to the function code specified as part of the function command.

The X10 protocol is a very simple communication protocol where the messages transmitted do not contain the identity of the transmitter (controller) or the receiver (module). The communication medium being a broadcast medium, it is not possible to distinguish the sequence of commands transmitted by any single controller. Moreover, the X10 modules attached to the powerline usually tend to be 'dumb' devices and hence it is not feasible to monitor each device (i.e. controller or module) to detect if any fault has occurred. Therefore, we elected to model the entire powerline network.

4.1 Model

By considering the X10 messages as an input alphabet, we can model the network as an automaton that generates the sequence of transmissions of the powerline. A feature of the X10 protocol is that commands with one house code say h do not affect the addressing or functioning of modules with a different house code. Therefore, the model automaton can be decomposed into independent automata, one for each house code. The simplified automaton in Figure 1 models the legal sequences of X10 commands corresponding to house code *h*. For details regarding how the automaton was developed we refer the interested reader to [4]. The transitions in Figure 1 represent the valid system transitions and are labeled with the X10 commands observed/generated on the powerline. (All other transitions are invalid). The labels on the transitions are as follows: *AUOff(h)* — the AllUnitsOff function command; *ACmd(h,i)* — valid address command corresponding to an existing module (house code *h* and unit code *i*); and, *Brd(h), Mul(h), Uni(h)* refer to broadcast, multicast and unicast function commands respectively.

X10 powerline model

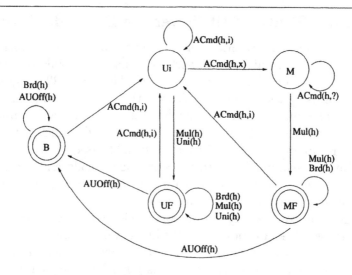

Figure 1. Model automaton for house code *h* ($x \neq i$, ? any unit code).

The legal sequences of X10 commands are governed both by the addressing logic and the function classification. The automata state *B* represents the system configuration where no modules have been addressed and so only the broadcast commands can be issued. In states *Ui, UF* we can execute unicast function StatusReq that polls the state of the household appliance attached to the module. Since the response does not explicitly mention the address of the responding module we require only one module to be addressed so that response can be matched to the request. In the states *M* and *MF* where more than one module has been addressed only multicast commands are executed. The multicast commands, such as On and Dim, do not require a response, so they can be issued in these states also. The addressing logic governs the way the modules transition on the X10 commands.

4.2 Predicates

From the automaton model of the valid sequences, we extract the predicates that encode the valid transitions. If the model variable *state.h* abstracts the current state of the system and the model variable *cmd.h* abstracts the next command on the powerline, then for example the valid transitions from the state M can be encoded as the predicate ($state.h =$ M)$\wedge$($cmd.h =$ ACmd(h) $\vee cmd.h =$ Mul(h)). Alternatively, we can use the invalid transitions which are the complement of the valid transitions, to encode the same information. The advantage of this alternative is that we use the knowledge of the common-case faults to group the invalid transitions. A subset of the model predicates that are to be enforced are listed below. The first three predicates are self-explanatory.

X10 powerline predicates

Broadcast(h) :
  $\Box\neg((state.h =$ B) $\wedge$ ($cmd.h =$ Mul(h) $\vee cmd.h =$ Uni(h)))
Unicast(h)   :
  $\Box\neg((state.h =$ M $\vee state.h =$ MF) $\wedge$ ($cmd.h =$ Uni(h)))
Allunitsoff(h) :
  $\Box\neg((state.h =$ Ui $\vee state.h =$ M) $\wedge$ ($cmd.h =$ AUOff(h)))
Timeout(h)   :
  $\Box\neg((state.h =$ Ui $\vee state.h =$ M) $\wedge$ ($cmd.h =$ TO(h)))
ValidAddr(h) :
  $\Box\neg(cmd.h = InvACmd(h))$

Timeout(h): The states B, UF, MF are final states reached after a complete command sequence. The states Ui and M, on the other hand, are states reached after a command sequence has been only partially issued. Therefore, in these states, we expect progress to be made in terms of the rest of the command sequence transmitted on the powerline. Any lack of progress is detected by using timeouts; the timer is started in the predicate enforcer, when states Ui and M are entered and the command $TO(h)$ captures the event that the timer has expired without any command having been issued. (This is an event seen only in the predicate enforcer and not on the powerline.)

ValidAddr(h): The legitimate controllers on the powerline have knowledge about the valid X10 addresses that are actually assigned to modules. This information is updated in the lookup service on the addition of new modules. Given that *InvACmd(h)* denotes an invalid address not currently assigned to any X10 module, the predicate *ValidAddr(h)* specifies that only valid addresses are to be transmitted on the powerline.

4.3   Enforcement

The enforcement of X10 model predicates is complicated by the presence of "hidden" state. Unlike the lookup server example, where replicas can be polled to determine their status, the status of X10 modules (addressed or otherwise) cannot be determined directly. (The *StatusReq* command can be used to poll the status of the household appliance attached to the module, but not that of the module itself). The system state is therefore hidden and must be deduced indirectly, from the sequence of commands observed on the powerline. We are therefore led to formulate the state deduction task in terms of the observability of the model, a concept which is well studied in discrete-event dynamic systems. We refer the reader to [4] for details.

The powerline medium is inherently unreliable and suffers from disruption due to power spikes and noise from household appliances. Its common-case faults are: the loss of a single message and the crash of a single CM11A interface. To detect and handle these faults, we propose that every PC be equipped with two CM11A interfaces: one serves as the controller through which the commands are issued, and the other to monitor the commands being transmitted. The software controller in the PC handles the loss of a single message by retransmitting it, and restores a crashed interface by resetting it.

All other faults are treated as rare-case and handled implicitly as predicate violations. Our current implementation of the enforcement generates a notification whenever a model predicate is violated. We present a few representative rare-case faults: (i) the crash of the software controller, that occurs in the middle of a command sequence, leaves the system in states Ui or M. This crash is detected when the timeout occurs in the predicate enforcer (TO(h)), causing the violation of the predicate *Timeout(h)*; (ii) if two controllers issue command sequences with the same house code, the resulting interleaved sequence could result in mismatched function commands. The predicates violated are Broadcast(h), Allunitsoff(h) and Unicast(h); and (iii) a security intruder without adequate information about the modules attached to the powerline could end up issuing an invalid address command, leading to violation of the predicate `ValidAddr(h)`.

We conclude our case study of X10 with a complex, unanticipated fault that we observed and which illustrates the value of the model-based approach. A transceiver module, which is supposed to convert radio frequency (RF) signals that it receives from wireless remotes into X10 commands, once erroneously started to convert random RF noise (resulting from RF interference) into an invalid sequence of X10 commands.

5. Concluding Remarks

In this chapter we presented two case studies—a lookup service and an X10 powerline monitor—to illustrate the model-based approach. The lookup service study elicited the unanticipated fault of complex network partitioning. The X10 study dealt with the unanticipated arbitrary behaviors that resulted from RF interference. By dealing with all model violations, the approach handled these and other unanticipated faults implicitly. We expect the approach to be useful in new application domains such as sensor networks and internet services where the environment is rather unknown and hence unanticipated faults are common.

As noted before, the approach does not preclude the use of explicit fault models. We chose to restrict ourselves to just two fault-classes – common-case and rare-case– but in general the designer is free to choose the number of classes as need be. In both case studies, for the common-case faults, the effect of the faults on the model behaviors was explicitly used in calculating the model predicates to be enforced. Rare-case faults were handled only implicitly and uniformly.

An analogy to intrusion detection is worth noting. Intrusion detection approaches are broadly classified as pattern-based and anomaly-based. Pattern-based approaches detect specific intrusions, which are analogous to our explicit handling of common-case faults. On the other hand, anomaly-based approaches start with a model of the ideal system and classify all deviations from the model as intrusions, which is analogous to our implicit handling of rare-case faults in terms of model violations.

By separating system dependability from system functionality and by decomposing a system model into predicates, the approach achieves modular (and incremental) design of dependability. Modular designs have been endorsed in other work: component-based design of multitolerance [2] achieved modular design using detector and corrector components. More recently, [5] illustrated the merits of separating dependability modules, such as node failure detectors and arbitrary behavior violation detectors, from functionality modules, such as consensus builders, in achieving distributed consensus, even in the presence of some number of byzantine faults. Other examples of model-based modular designs may be found in [1, 3].

Modular designs of dependability lend themselves to object-oriented implementations. The predicate enforcer modules used in this paper involved monitoring of model predicates in order to detect their violations, which was sometimes event-driven —as in the case of X10 command transmissions— and sometimes time-driven— as in the case of periodic updates in the lookup service. Therefore, the object model used in an object-oriented implementation must support both types of monitoring. This may be achieved in terms of extant object models such as time-driven message-driven objects (TMO) [9].

Implementation of predicate enforcers also raises the issues of (i) interference with other modules and (ii) "who watches the watchers". The first issue involves interference not only with the underlying system but also with the other predicate enforcers. This issue may be dealt with using existing concurrency control mechanisms. An alternative approach would be to use the semantic information encoded in the predicates to co-ordinate among the predicate enforcers at the semantic level; for a detailed discussion of this alternative we refer the reader to [2].

The issue of the dependability of predicate enforcers arises since enforcers may be subject to the same faults that affect the system. In practice, this issue may not be as severe as the dependability of the functional components of the system, since enforcers are relatively simpler than functionality components. Also, enforcers are more under the control of the designer than are functionality components, and may be instantiated from carefully verified dependability frameworks. In principle, this issue may be dealt with by ensuring predicate enforcer dependability by reusing the model-based design approach. This was the approach taken in the case studies. The enforcers were designed to be themselves self-stabilizing and hence were in a position to deal with a number of rare-case faults, and they were also designed to tolerate the common-case faults efficiently.

Future Work. We envision the need for various services to support predicate enforcer modules. One of these is a core monitoring service. This service monitors all predicate enforcers and restores them if they somehow fail. By requiring only this minimal level of functionality, the core can be designed to be highly dependable and also reused in various implementations. Yet another service would provide scalable and adaptive communication. This service would affect the overhead of monitoring of the predicate enforcers by the core, as well as that of the additional monitoring of the model predicates by the enforcers. Finally, another direction for future research is the automatic synthesis of model predicates and the corresponding predicate enforcers, which would simplify the design and implementation of dependability.

References

[1] A. Arora, M. Demirbas, and S. S. Kulkarni. Graybox stabilization. In *International Conference on Dependable Systems and Networks (DSN 2001)*, pages 389–398, June 2001.

[2] A. Arora and S. S. Kulkarni. Component based design of multitolerance. *IEEE Transactions on Software Engineering*, 24(1):63–78, 1998.

[3] A. Arora, S. S. Kulkarni, and M. Demirbas. Resettable vector clocks. *Proceedings of the 19th ACM Symposium on Principles of Distributed Computing (PODC)*, pages 269–278, August 2000.

[4] A. Arora, Y.-M. Wang, and R. Jagannathan. Model based fault detection in X10 powerline monitoring. Technical report, http://www.cis.ohio-state.edu/~anish/group/papers.html, 2000.

[5] R. Baldoni, J.-M. Helary, M. Raynal, and L. Tanguy. Consensus in byzantine asynchronous systems. Technical Report RR-3655, National Institute for Research in Computer Science and Automatic Control (INRIA), 1999.

[6] K. P. Birman. A review of experiences with reliable multicast. Technical Report TR99-1726, Department of Computer Science, Cornell University, 1998.

[7] K. P. Birman. The Horus and Ensemble projects: accomplishments and limitations. Technical Report TR99-1774, Department of Computer Science, Cornell University, 1999.

[8] E. W. Dijkstra. Self-stabilizing systems in spite of distributed control. *Communications of the ACM*, 17(11), 1974.

[9] K. Kim and C. Subburaman. Dynamic configuration management in reliable distributed real-time information systems. *IEEE Transactions on Knowledge and Data Engineering*, 11(1):239–254, 1999.

[10] D. Siewiorek and R. S. Swarz. *Reliable Computer Systems: Design and Evaluation*. Digital Press, 1992.

[11] W. Vogels, D. Dumitriu, A. Agrawal, T. Chia, and K. Guo. Scalability of the microsoft cluster service. In *Proceedings of the Second Usenix Windows NT Symposium, Seattle, WA*, August 1998.

[12] Y.-M. Wang, P. V. Bahl, and W. Russell. The SIMBA user alert service architecture for dependable alert delivery. In *International Conference on Dependable Systems and Networks (DSN 2001)*, Jul 2001.

[13] Y.-M. Wang, W. Russell, A. Arora, J. Xu, and R. Jagannathan. Towards dependable home networking: An experience report. In *International Conference on Dependable Systems and Networks (DSN 2000)*. IEEE, July 2000.

Chapter 3

TLA SPECIFICATION OF A MECHANISM FOR CONCURRENT EXCEPTION HANDLING

Avelino Francisco Zorzo

Faculdade de Informática - PUCRS - 90619-900 - Porto Alegre - RS - Brazil

zorzo@inf.pucrs.br

Brian Randell

University of Newcastle upon Tyne - NE1 RU - Newcastle upon Tyne - UK

brian.randell@ncl.ac.uk

Alexander Romanovsky

University of Newcastle upon Tyne - NE1 RU - Newcastle upon Tyne - UK

alexander.romanovsky@ncl.ac.uk

Abstract   Recently the concept of *dependable multiparty interaction* (DMI) has been introduced. In a multiparty interaction, several parties (objects or processes) somehow "come together" to produce an intermediate and temporary combined state, use this state to execute some activity, and then leave this interaction and continue their normal execution. The concept of multiparty interactions has been investigated by several researchers, but to the best of our knowledge none have considered how failures in one or more participants of the multiparty interaction could be dealt with. In this paper, we show how this mechanism deals with concurrent exceptions raised during an interaction. This is shown through a formal description of the DMI concept. We use Temporal Logic of Actions (TLA) in order to formally describe the DMI features.

Keywords: Distributed and Parallel Systems, Multiparty Interactions, Concurrent Exception Handling

P. Ezhilchelvan and A. Romanovsky (eds.), Concurrency in Dependable Computing, 41–59.

1.   Introduction

It is very common for software developers to write programs under the optimistic assumption that nothing will go wrong when the program is executed. Unfortunately, there are many factors that can make this assumption invalid. For example, an arithmetic expression that may cause a division by zero; an array that is indexed with a value that exceeds the declared bounds; the square root of a negative number; a request for memory allocation during run-time that may exceed the amount of memory available; opening a file that does not exist; and many more.

When any of such event happens the system will often fail in an unexpected way. This is not acceptable in current programming standards. To improve reliability, it is important that such circumstances are detected and treated appropriately. Conventional control structures, such as the if-then-else command, are inadequate. For example, to check that an index of an array is always valid, a programmer could explicitly test the value of the index each time before using it, which is cumbersome and could often be forgotten or intentionally omitted. A better way would be to rely on the underlying system to trap the situation where array indexes are outside the array bounds. To cope with this kind of situation, several programming languages provide features for handling such circumstances, i.e. exception handling.

Exception handling in sequential programs is a well-known subject with several languages providing mechanisms for handling exceptions. Exception handling in parallel programs is much more complex than in sequential programs. Exceptional termination in a process can have a strong impact on other processes. For example, consider a set of processes that communicate with each other via a rendezvous mechanism. A process may terminate abruptly due to the presence of an exception. Processes that need to communicate with the process that was terminated, may be suspended for ever because the terminated process will not be ready for communication anymore.

The problem of dealing with concurrent exceptions has been addressed in different systems [1] and models [2] [3]. For example, the VAXELN programming environment from Digital [1] provides means for a process to raise exceptions in other processes. The raising of an exception in a different process is done in an unstructured manner. A process can enable or disable this kind of exceptions. Raising an exception in a process that has disabled this kind of exception has no effect. The approach of allowing an exception in a process to be raised in a different process outside a structured framework can have a devastating effect on program modularity. This is especially the case when the raising of exceptions in other processes cannot be restricted.

In [2], a model for dealing with concurrent exceptions explores the use of an exception tree. Exceptions that can be signalled by a component of a parallel block C are organized in a tree structure. The root of this tree contains the *universal exception*, i.e. the exception that represents the whole exceptional domain of C. When more than one exception is raised concurrently, a handler for an exception that is ancestor to all exceptions raised is executed. In the worst case scenario, a handler for the *universal exception* is executed. In [3], a different model that relies on the definition of resolution functions within classes is presented. In this model, a resolution function takes a sequence of exceptions as input parameter and returns an exception.

Despite the aforementioned efforts, mechanisms for dealing with concurrent exceptions in programming languages are still in their early stages. For example, in the Ada 95 [4] rendezvous mechanism, if an exception is raised during a rendezvous and not handled in the **accept** statement, that exception is propagated to both tasks and must be handled in two places. However, Ada 95 does not provide any mechanism to handle concurrent exceptions.

A mechanism that handles concurrent exception has been presented in [5]. This mechanism is called *dependable multiparty interaction* (DMI) and is able to cope with several concurrent exceptions being raised during an activity executed jointly by a set of participants (processes/threads).

The main goal of this paper is to present how Temporal Logic of Actions (TLA) [6] can be applied to describe dependable programming/specification constructs, such as the DMI concept. TLA is a formalism suitable for describing state transition systems and their properties using a uniform notation. Hence being suitable to describe fault tolerance mechanisms. For example, the one described in this paper.

This paper is organized as follow. Section 2 introduces the concept of dependable multiparty interaction. Section 3 presents the formalism used to describe the DMI properties. Section 4 shows the formal description of the DMI properties. Section 5 discusses the related work. Section 6 draws some conclusions.

2.   Dependable Multiparty Interactions

Existing multiparty interaction mechanisms [7] [8] do not provide features for dealing with possible failures that may happen during the execution of the interaction. Typically, the underlying system that is executing those multiparty interactions will simply stop the system in response to a failure. In DisCo [9], for instance, if an assertion inside an action is false, then the run-time system is assumed to stop the whole application. This is unacceptable in many situations, e.g. a flying aircraft or a pacemaker (see [10] for more examples).

In this section, multiparty interactions are augmented with an exception handling facility to form a new construct: the *dependable multiparty interaction* (DMI). The DMI mechanism is based on a structuring mechanism called Coordinated Atomic Action (CA action) [11], which brings together the concept of conversation [12] and transaction [13]. Specifically, a DMI provides facilities for:

- HANDLING CONCURRENT EXCEPTIONS: when an exception occurs in one of the bodies of a participant, and is not dealt with by that participant, the exception must be propagated to all participants of the interaction [2]. A DMI must also provide a way of dealing with exceptions that can be raised by one or more participants. Finally, if several different exceptions are raised concurrently, the DMI mechanism has to decide which exception will be raised in all participants.

  With respect to how the participants of a DMI will be involved in the exception resolution and exception handling, there are two possible schemes: synchronous or asynchronous. In synchronous schemes, each participant has to either come to the action end or to raise an exception; it is only afterwards that it is ready to participate in any kind of exception handling; this means that the participant's execution cannot be pre-empted if another participant raises an exception. In asynchronous schemes, participants do not wait until they finish their execution or raise an exception to participate in the exception handling; once an exception is raised in any participant of the DMI, all other participants are interrupted and handle the raised exceptions together. Although implementing synchronous schemes is easier than asynchronous, because all participants are ready to execute the exception handling, the synchronous scheme can bring the undesirable risk of deadlock. Therefore the asynchronous scheme is adopted;

- ASSURING CONSISTENCY UPON EXIT: participants can only leave the interaction when all of them have finished their roles and the external objects are in a consistent state. This property guarantees that if something goes wrong in the activity executed by one of the participants, then all participants have an opportunity to recover from possible errors.

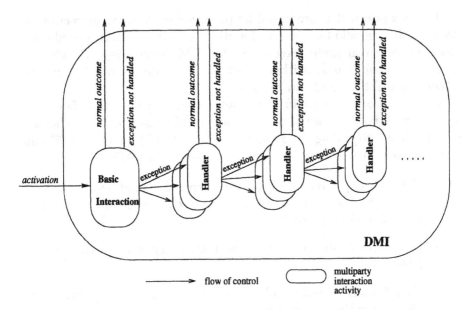

Figure 1. Dependable Multiparty Interaction

The key idea for handling exceptions is to build DMIs out of not necessarily reliable multiparty interactions by chaining them together, where each multiparty interaction in the chain is the exception handler for the previous multiparty interaction in the chain. Figure 1 shows how a basic multiparty interaction and exception handling multiparty interactions are chained together to form a composite multiparty interaction, in fact what we term a DMI, by handling possible exceptions that are raised during the execution of the DMI. As shown in the figure, the basic multiparty interaction can terminate normally, raise exceptions that are handled by exception handling multiparty interactions, or raise exceptions that are not handled in the DMI. If the basic multiparty interaction terminates normally, the control flow is passed to the callers of the DMI. If an exception is raised, then there are two possible execution paths to be followed: *i*) if there is an exception handling multiparty interaction to handle this exception, then it is activated by all roles in the DMI; *ii*) if there is no exception handling multiparty interaction to handle the raised exception, then this exception is signalled to the invokers of the DMI. The whole set of basic multiparty interaction and their associated exception handling multiparty interactions form a single entity: they are isolated from the outside so that internal activities (e.g., the raising of an exception) are not visible to the enclosing environment.

The exceptions that are raised by the basic multiparty interaction or by a handler, should be the same for all roles in the DMI. If several roles raise different concurrent exceptions, the DMI mechanism activates an exception resolution algorithm based on [2] to decide which common exception will be raised and handled.

In view of our interest in dependability, and in particular fault tolerance, we adopt the use of pre and post-conditions, which are checked at run-time. Regarding the remaining alternatives presented in [7] and [14], we have made the following design choices for DMIs:

- although the particular processes involved should be able to vary from one invocation of a DMI to the next, their number in a given DMI should be fixed;

- the processes should synchronise their entry to and exit from the DMI;

- the DMI mechanism should ensure that as viewed from outside the DMI, its system state should change atomically, though inside the DMI intermediate internal states will be visible;

- the way the underlying system executes a DMI can be synchronous or asynchronous.

The choice for allowing a varying set of processes to enrole into a DMI is related to the expressive power of the language construct we intend to provide. In [7] a taxonomy of languages that provide multiparty interactions as a basic construct is presented. In the presented taxonomy, the basic construct that presents the higher degree of expressiveness is a team. A DMI is a team, hence choice (i) was made. Synchronisation upon entry and exit (choice (ii)) is crucial if we want to have some kind of guard to be tested before the DMI commences, or an assertion to be tested before the DMI terminates. For example, if participants in a DMI are allowed to terminate without synchronising upon exit, then the process of involving that participant in the handling of an exception raised by another participant of the DMI will be much more difficult. Paper [15] discusses several issues related to termination of processes that should not interfere with each other, e.g. issues related to error recovery before a process has terminated, or error recovery after a process has terminated the execution of an activity. Choice (iii) is related to the visibility of shared data inside the DMI and outside of the DMI. The related "frozen initial state" property discussed in [14] is used in relation to the participants that are outside the DMI, i.e. they see the change of shared data as being instantaneous when the DMI terminates. Our proposal differs from [14] in relation to the visibility of shared data inside the DMI. In our proposal, participants can exchange data inside the DMI, while in [14] participants of a multiparty interaction view shared data as "frozen" when the multiparty interaction commences.

3.   Formal Semantics

A well-defined syntactic and semantic description of a language is essential for helping good design and programming of a system. The *syntax* of a language describes the correct form in which programs can be written while the *semantics* expresses the meaning that is attached to the various syntactic constructs. While *syntax diagrams* and *Backus-Naur Form - BNF* have become standard tools for describing the syntax of a language, no such tools have become widely accepted and standard for describing the semantics of a language. Different formal approaches to semantics definition exist, e.g. *operational semantics, axiomatic semantics,* or *denotational semantics.* Several authors report how to use these approaches for describing the semantics of programming languages [16] [17].

Concurrent systems are usually described in terms of their behaviour - what they do in the course of an execution [18]. The Temporal Logic formal model [19] was introduced to describe such behaviour of concurrent systems. A variation of Temporal Logic that makes it practical to write a specification as a single formula was presented in [6]. This variation is called Temporal Logic of Actions - TLA. TLA provides the mathematical basis for describing properties of concurrent systems.

3.1   Temporal Logic of Actions

The Temporal Logic of Actions - TLA [6] is a formalism suitable for describing state transition systems and properties of such systems using the same notation.

TLA is a linear-time logic in which expressions are evaluated for non-terminating sequences of states. Each sequence of states is called a behaviour. A state is an assignment of values to variables. Variables that are used to model properties are state functions, which have unique values in each state. A state function is a non-boolean expression built from variables, constants, and constant operators. Semantically, a state function assigns a value to each state. An individual state change is called a step. A step that allows variables to stay unchanged is called a stuttering step.

An action is a boolean expression containing primed and unprimed variables. For any pair of states, primed variables refer to the second

---

```
process example is
  integer x := 0;
  body
    loop x := x + 1; end;
  end body
end process
```

Figure 2.   Simple Program in DIP

state whereas unprimed ones refer to the first state. An action is said to be enabled in a state s if and only if there exists some state t such that the pair of states $< s, t >$ satisfies that action.

Rather than presenting the full description of TLA, a simple program [6] in Dependable Interacting Processes (DIP) [20] is presented with its corresponding TLA formula. The process, in Figure 2, initialises a variable x with 0 and then keeps incrementing x by 1 forever.

The TLA formula for the above DIP process is defined as follows:

$$\prod \ \stackrel{\Delta}{=} \ \wedge \ (x \ = \ 0)$$
$$\wedge \ \Box[x' \ = \ x + 1]_x$$
$$\wedge \ \mathrm{WF}_x(x' \ = \ x + 1)$$

A TLA formula is true or false on a behaviour. Formula $\prod$, presented above, is true on a behaviour in which the ith state assigns the value $i - 1$ to x, for $i = 1, 2, \ldots$. In the above TLA formula, the conjunct (x = 0) specifies that initially, x is equal to 0; the conjunct $\Box[x' = x + 1]_x$ specifies that the value of x in the next state (x') is always ($\Box$) equal to its value in the current state (x) plus 1. The subscript x specifies that stuttering steps are allowed, i.e. steps where the value of x is left unchanged. The $\mathrm{WF}_x(x' = x + 1)$ conjunct rules out behaviours in which x is incremented only a finite number of times. It asserts that, if the action (x' = x + 1) $\wedge$ (x' $\neq$ x) ever becomes enabled and remains enabled forever, then infinitely many (x' = x + 1) $\wedge$ (x' $\neq$ x) steps occur. WF stands for Weak Fairness.

In the next section the specification of the dependable multiparty interaction mechanism is presented in TLA.

4.   DMI in TLA

In this section we will present the semantics of dependable multiparty interactions. However, before we start formally describing the semantics of DMI in TLA, consider the following:

- a DMI is represented by a set of roles that are executed by players;

- a player has to activate a role in DMI in order to execute the commands inside a role;

- a DMI only starts when all roles of the DMI have been activated, and the guard (boolean expression) at the beginning of the DMI is true;

- the DMI only finishes when all players have finished executing their roles, and the assertion at the end of the DMI (boolean expression) is true (if no exceptions were raised);

- roles can only access data that is sent to them when they are activated, or data that is sent to them by other roles belonging to the same DMI;

- exceptions may be raised during the execution of a DMI, in which case all roles that have not raised an exception are interrupted; an exception resolution algorithm is executed when all roles either have raised an exception or have been interrupted.

- if there is a handler to deal with the exception that was decided upon by the exception resolution algorithm, then this handler is activated by all roles;

- if there is no handler to deal with the exception that was decided upon by the exception resolution algorithm, then the exception is raised in the callers of all roles;

- handlers have the same number of roles as the DMI to which they are connected.

In order to formally specify the semantics of a DMI in TLA, we will use the following sets, predicates and state variables:

- Exceptions: the set of exceptions handled by the DMI;

- Commands: a set of commands;

- Objects: a set of objects;

- **Players**: a set of players that can participate in a DMI;

- **Roles**: contains the roles of a DMI. Each element of this set is a record with a field to represent the **state** of the role, a field to represent the **result** of the role after the commands of this role have been executed, a field to store those **commands**, and a field containing the set of **objects** manipulated by the role;

- **Handlers**: the set of handlers for the DMI;

- **GuardExpression(e)**: a predicate representing the execution of the precondition of the DMI. The parameter **e** contains the set of all tuples <p,er,o>, where **p** represents a player that is enroled to the role **er**, and **o** is the set of objects sent to the role by the player;

- **AssertionExpression(e)**: the same as **GuardExpression(e)** but for the post-condition of the DMI;

- **ExecuteCommands(e)**: execute the commands for the corresponding role;

- **Resolve(enroled)**: execute the exception resolution algorithm for all roles in the DMI. After this algorithm has been executed all roles will produce the same exceptional **result**;

- four state variables: *i*) **guard**, which indicates whether the DMI can be started or not; *ii*) **assert**, which indicates whether the DMI was finished successfully or not; *iii*) **enroled**, which stores the roles that have already been enroled to in a particular execution of the DMI; and, *iv*) **elements**, which stores the tuples <p,er,o> that are used when executing the roles commands.

The type invariant specifies that the **guard** and **assert** are BOOLEAN variables, the state of a role can only have one of the values from the set {"wait","ended","started"}, and the result of a role can either have a value from the set {"ok", "interrupted"} or from the set of possible exceptions in **Exceptions**. The type invariant is defined as:

$$
\begin{aligned}
\text{TypeInvariant} \;\triangleq\; & \wedge \; \text{guard, assert} \in \text{BOOLEAN} \\
& \wedge \; \forall r \in \text{Roles}: \\
& \quad \text{r.state} \in \{\text{"wait","ended","started"}\} \\
& \wedge \; \forall r \in \text{Roles}: \\
& \quad \text{r.result} \in \{\text{"ok","interrupted"}\}\cup\text{Exceptions} \\
& \wedge \; \text{enroled} \subseteq \text{Roles} \\
& \wedge \; \text{elements} \subseteq \text{Players X Roles X Objects}
\end{aligned}
$$

The initial condition for the DMI is that all roles are in a waiting state, both `guard` and `assert` have the value `FALSE`, and the `enroled` and `elements` sets are empty. The `Init` predicate is defined in TLA as:

```
Init ≜ ∧ ∀r ∈ Roles: r.state = "wait"
       ∧ guard = FALSE
       ∧ assert = FALSE
       ∧ enroled = {}
       ∧ elements = {}
```

For a player `p` to enrole in a role `er` with a set of objects `o`, it has to execute the action `Enrole(p,er,o)`. This step is only enabled if role `er` belongs to the set of `Roles` in the DMI and no other player has enroled to such a role. This is expressed by the first two conjuncts of the following TLA formula. If this step is enabled, then the role `er` is added to the `enroled` set and the tuple `<p, r, o>` is added to the `elements` set. The `Enrole(p,er,o)` action is defined in TLA as:

```
Enrole(p,er,o) ≜ ∧ er ∈ Roles
                 ∧ er ∉ enroled
                 ∧ enroled' = enroled ∪ {er}
                 ∧ elements' = elements ∪ {<p,er,o>}
                 ∧ UNCHANGED (guard, assert)
```

The DMI only begins if all roles have a player enroled to and the precondition is true. The testing of the guard with all players enroled is defined by the following two TLA conjunctions:

```
Guard ≜ ∧ ∀r ∈ Roles: r ∈ enroled
        ∧ guard' = GuardExpression(elements)
        ∧ UNCHANGED (enroled, elements, assert)

Begin ≜ ∧ guard = TRUE
        ∧ ∀r ∈ Roles: r.state' = "started"
        ∧ UNCHANGED (enroled, elements, assert, guard)
```

The execution of all roles is defined in the action `ExecuteRoles`. This step is only enabled if all roles have `state = "started"`. If enabled, then the result of the execution of the set of commands of a role is stored in the field `result`. The `ExecuteRoles` is defined in TLA as:

```
ExecuteRoles ≜ ∧ ∀r ∈ Roles: r.state = "started"
               ∧ ∀<p,r,o> ∈ elements:
                 r.result' = ExecuteCommands(<p,r,o>)
               ∧ UNCHANGED (enroled, assert, guard)
```

When all roles have executed their commands without raising an exception, i.e. their state is equal to `"ok"`, the post-condition expression can be tested. The `assert` variable changes its value based on the execution of the `AssertionExpression(elements)` action. The post-condition of a DMI is defined as:

```
Assertion  ≜  ∧ ∀r ∈ Roles: r.result = "ok"
              ∧ assert' = AssertionExpression(elements)
              ∧ UNCHANGED ⟨enroled, elements, guard⟩
```

If no exceptions were raised, then the normal termination of a DMI is defined in the `NormalEnd` action. The condition that enables this step is `assert = TRUE`, i.e. the post-condition was passed. This step changes the state of all roles to `"wait"`, meaning that the roles are ready to be executed again. The sets `enroled` and `elements` are emptied. The TLA definition of `NormalEnd` is:

```
NormalEnd  ≜  ∧ assert = TRUE
              ∧ ∀r ∈ Roles: r.state' = "wait"
              ∧ enroled' = ⟨ ⟩
              ∧ elements' = ⟨ ⟩
              ∧ assert' = FALSE
              ∧ guard' = FALSE
```

Figure 3 shows the complete first part of the formal semantics of a DMI. In the figure all conjunctions are related to the normal execution of a DMI. In Figure 4, we define the formal semantics for the steps that are taken in case of one or more exceptions being raised. An exception can be raised during the execution of the set of commands of a role in the `ExecuteCommands` action.

The activation of a handler depends on the state of the roles. A handler is only activated when all roles have the same value for their `result`, and there exists a handler for the exception resolved by the resolution algorithm. The activation of a handler is defined as:

```
ActivateHandler  ≜  ∧ ∀r₁,r₂ ∈ Roles: (r₁.result = r₂.result)
                    ∧ ∃h ∈ Handlers: (∃r ∈ Roles: r.result ∈ h.Exc)
                    ∧ UNCHANGED ⟨enroled, elements, assert, guard⟩
```

The resolution algorithm on the other hand, is activated once all roles have raised an exception, i.e. their `result` belongs to the set `Exceptions`, or have been interrupted. The state of all roles has to be different from `"ok"`. This action is defined as:

```
ExceptionResolution  ≜  ∧ ∀r ∈ Roles: r.result ≠ "ok"
                        ∧ Resolve(enroled)
                        ∧ UNCHANGED ⟨enroled, elements, assert, guard⟩
```

─────────────────── MODULE DMI ───────────────────

EXTENDS Naturals, Sequences
VARIABLES enroled, elements, guard, assert

──

Init $\triangleq$ $\land$ $\forall r \in$ Roles : r.state = "wait"
    $\land$ guard = FALSE
    $\land$ assert = FALSE
    $\land$ enroled = {}
    $\land$ elements = {}

TypeInvariant $\triangleq$ $\land$ guard, assert $\in$ BOOLEAN
      $\land$ $\forall r \in$ Roles : r.state $\in$ {"wait","ended","started"}
      $\land$ $\forall r \in$ Roles : r.result $\in$ {"ok","interrupted"} $\cup$ Exceptions

Enrole(p,er,o) $\triangleq$ $\land$ $\exists r_1 \in$ Roles : r_1 = er
      $\land$ $\forall r_2 \in$ enroled : $r_2 \neq$ er
      $\land$ enroled$'$ = enroled $\cup$ {er}
      $\land$ elements$'$ = elements $\cup$ {<p,er,o>}
      $\land$ UNCHANGED ⟨guard, assert⟩

Guard $\triangleq$ $\land$ $\forall r \in$ Roles : r $\in$ enroled
    $\land$ guard$'$ = GuardExpression(elements)
    $\land$ UNCHANGED ⟨enroled, elements, assert⟩

Begin $\triangleq$ $\land$ guard = TRUE
    $\land$ $\forall r \in$ Roles : r.state$'$ = "started"
    $\land$ UNCHANGED ⟨enroled, elements, assert, guard⟩

ExecuteRoles $\triangleq$ $\land$ $\forall r \in$ Roles : r.state = "started"
      $\land$ $\forall$<p,r,o> $\in$ elements : r.result$'$ = ExecuteCommands(<p,r,o>)
      $\land$ UNCHANGED ⟨enroled, assert, guard⟩

Assertion $\triangleq$ $\land$ $\forall r \in$ Roles : r.result = "ok"
     $\land$ assert$'$ = AssertionExpression(elements)
     $\land$ UNCHANGED ⟨enroled, elements, guard⟩

NormalEnd $\triangleq$ $\land$ assert = TRUE
     $\land$ $\forall r \in$ Roles : r.state = "ended"
     $\land$ $\forall r \in$ Roles : r.state$'$ = "wait"
     $\land$ enroled$'$ = ⟨ ⟩
     $\land$ elements$'$ = ⟨ ⟩
     $\land$ assert$'$ = FALSE
     $\land$ guard$'$ = FALSE

──

Figure 3. TLA Specification of a DMI (part 1)

$$
\begin{aligned}
\text{InterruptRoles} \;\triangleq\; & \wedge\; \exists r_1 \in \text{Roles} : r_1.\text{result} \in \text{Exceptions} \\
& \wedge\; \forall r_2 \in \text{Roles} : \text{IF } r_2.\text{result} \notin \text{Exceptions} \\
& \qquad\qquad\qquad\quad \text{THEN } r_2.\text{result}' = \text{"interrupted"} \\
& \qquad\qquad\qquad\quad \text{ELSE } r_2.\text{result}' = r_2.\text{result} \\
& \wedge\; \text{UNCHANGED } \langle\text{enroled, assert, guard}\rangle
\end{aligned}
$$

$$
\begin{aligned}
\text{ExceptionResolution} \;\triangleq\; & \wedge\; \forall r \in \text{Roles} : r.\text{result} \neq \text{"ok"} \\
& \wedge\; \text{Resolve(enroled)} \\
& \wedge\; \text{UNCHANGED } \langle\text{enroled, elements, assert, guard}\rangle
\end{aligned}
$$

$$
\begin{aligned}
\text{ActivateHandler} \;\triangleq\; & \wedge\; \forall r_1, r_2 \in \text{Roles} : (r_1.\text{result} = r_2.\text{result}) \\
& \wedge\; \exists h \in \text{Handlers} : (\exists r \in \text{Roles} : r.\text{result} \in h.\text{Exc}) \\
& \wedge\; \text{UNCHANGED } \langle\text{enroled, elements, assert, guard}\rangle
\end{aligned}
$$

$$
\begin{aligned}
\text{ExceptionalEnd} \;\triangleq\; & \wedge\; \forall r_1, r_2 \in \text{Roles} : r_1.\text{result} = r_2.\text{result} \\
& \wedge\; \neg\exists h \in \text{Handlers} : (\exists r \in \text{Roles} : r.\text{result} \in h.\text{Exc}) \\
& \wedge\; \forall r \in \text{Roles} : r.\text{state} = \text{"ended"} \\
& \wedge\; \forall r \in \text{Roles} : r.\text{state}' = \text{"wait"} \\
& \wedge\; \text{enroled}' = \langle\;\rangle \\
& \wedge\; \text{elements}' = \langle\;\rangle \\
& \wedge\; \text{assert}' = \text{FALSE} \\
& \wedge\; \text{guard}' = \text{FALSE}
\end{aligned}
$$

$$
\begin{aligned}
\text{Next} \;\triangleq\; & \vee\; \exists p \in \text{Players} : (\exists er \in \text{Roles} : (\exists o \in \text{Objects} : \text{Enrole}(p,er,o))) \\
& \vee\; \text{Guard} \vee \text{Begin} \vee \text{ExecuteRoles} \vee \text{Assertion} \vee \text{NormalEnd} \vee \\
& \vee\; \text{ExceptionalEnd} \vee \text{InterruptRoles} \vee \text{ActivateHandler}
\end{aligned}
$$

$$
\text{Spec} \;\triangleq\; \text{Init} \wedge \square[\text{Next}]_{\langle\text{enroled, elements, assert, guard}\rangle}
$$

THEOREM Spec $\Rightarrow$ $\square$ TypeInvariant

Figure 4. TLA Specification of a DMI (part 2)

When a role terminates by raising an exception, then all other roles have to be interrupted, causing the exception resolution algorithm to be enabled. The step that represents the interruption of roles is Interrupt-Roles. This step is enabled when at least one of the roles has raised an exception. The raising of an exception is represented in the value that the role's result assumes. If the value belongs to the set of Exceptions, then the InterruptRoles action is enabled. The step will then set the state of all roles, which did not raise an exception, to "interrupted". Even if a role has terminated it will be interrupted when another role raises an exception. The InterruptRoles actions is defined in TLA as:

$$
\begin{aligned}
\texttt{InterruptRoles} \ \triangleq\ & \wedge\ \exists \texttt{r}_1 \in \texttt{Roles: } \texttt{r}_1.\texttt{result} \in \texttt{Exceptions} \\
& \wedge\ \forall \texttt{r}_2 \in \texttt{Roles: IF } \texttt{r}_2.\texttt{result} \notin \texttt{Exceptions} \\
& \qquad\qquad\qquad\quad \texttt{THEN } \texttt{r}_2.\texttt{result}' = \texttt{"interrupted"} \\
& \qquad\qquad\qquad\quad \texttt{ELSE } \texttt{r}_2.\texttt{result}' = \texttt{r}_2.\texttt{result} \\
& \wedge\ \texttt{UNCHANGED } \langle \texttt{enroled, assert, guard} \rangle
\end{aligned}
$$

If exceptions were raised and there is no exception handler for the exception that resulted from the exception resolution algorithm, then the exceptional termination of a DMI is defined in the ExceptionalEnd action. This step is enabled when all roles have the same result and there is no exception handler for that result. This step changes the state of all roles to "wait", meaning that the roles are ready to be executed again. The sets enroled and elements are emptied. The TLA definition of ExceptionalEnd is:

$$
\begin{aligned}
\texttt{ExceptionalEnd} \ \triangleq\ & \wedge\ \forall \texttt{r}_1, \texttt{r}_2 \in \texttt{Roles: } \texttt{r}_1.\texttt{result} = \texttt{r}_2.\texttt{result} \\
& \wedge\ \neg \exists \texttt{h} \in \texttt{Handlers: } (\exists \texttt{r} \in \texttt{Roles: } \texttt{r}.\texttt{result} \in \texttt{h.Exc}) \\
& \wedge\ \forall \texttt{r} \in \texttt{Roles: } \texttt{r}.\texttt{state} = \texttt{"ended"} \\
& \wedge\ \forall \texttt{r} \in \texttt{Roles: } \texttt{r}.\texttt{state}' = \texttt{"wait"} \\
& \wedge\ \texttt{enroled}' = \langle\ \rangle \\
& \wedge\ \texttt{elements}' = \langle\ \rangle \\
& \wedge\ \texttt{assert}' = \texttt{FALSE} \\
& \wedge\ \texttt{guard}' = \texttt{FALSE}
\end{aligned}
$$

5.   Related work

The semantics described in Section 4 deals with the basic rules of a DMI, i.e. pre and post-synchronisation, roles activation, exception handling, and roles interruption.

We did not attempt to describe formally the semantics of the execution of the role's commands. The way external objects guarantee ACID properties is also not described (a formal description of the ACID properties can be found in [21]). In [22], for example, formal description of properties for a mechanism similar to the DMI (Coordinated Atomic actions [11] - CA actions differ from DMIs in the way exceptions are handled during the interaction) is given in Temporal Logic. In [23], a formal approach is used to model and verify a safety-critical system (namely the fault-tolerant production cell) designed using CA actions. In order to model-checking, the state transition system corresponding to a CA action based design is expressed in SMV (Symbolic Model Checking) [24] and system properties expressed in CTL [25].

The COALA framework [26] is proposed to allow system developers to model systems using the CA action concept. Within this work a formalisation of the CA action concept is developed that uses CO-OPN/2:

an object-oriented language based on Petri nets and partial order-sorted algebraic specifications.

The ERT model (ERT stands for extraction, refusals and traces) is used for formalising the CA action concept [27]. Refusals and traces are terms coming from CSP; term extraction refers to a specific technique used to relate systems specified at different levels of abstractions.

A mathematical framework based on Timed CSP for representing the use of CA actions in real-time safety-critical systems is proposed in [28]. It allows the interactions between concurrently functioning equipment items to be modelled and their behaviour to be reasoned about in an abstract way. The framework models dynamic system structuring using CA actions by explicitly modeling synchronisation between items and the controlling system. Although the framework is not developed for dealing with erroneously behaving action participants, it allows for better understanding of the CA action concept and can be used in developing general models incorporating mechanisms supporting system safety.

6.   Conclusion

The strategy of dealing with concurrent exceptions by enclosing them in a language mechanism presented in this paper, has been successfuly applied to several case studies [29] [30] [31]. This paper has showed how TLA can be used to formally describe the semantics of a mechanism that implements this strategy. The formal model described in this paper is now being applied to a case study, which will be model-checked using TLA tools.

We believe that based on the description of the formal semantics presented in this paper, the process of implementing languages like Dependable Interacting Processes [5] [20], which include DMIs as a basic language construct will be greatly facilitated.

Acknowledgments

We would like to thank our colleagues from the Department of Computing Science at the University of Newcastle, Robert Stroud and Ian Welch, and from the University of Durham, Jie Xu, for several discussions that helped in formulating the dependable multiparty interaction concept. This work is supported by FAPERGS and CNPq/Brazil (grant number 520503/00-7). Alexander Romanovsky is supported by European IST DSoS project (IST-1999-11585). We also thank the reviewers for their contribution in making this a better paper.

References

[1] Digital Equipament Corporation, Massachusetts, USA. *VAXELN Pascal language reference manual: Programming*, 1986.

[2] R. H. Campbell and B. Randell. Error recovery in asynchronous systems. *IEEE Transactions on Software Engineering*, 12(8):811–826, 1986.

[3] V. Issarny. An exception handling mechanism for parallel object-oriented programming: Toward reusable, robust distributed software. *Journal of Object Oriented Programming*, 6(6):29–39, 1993.

[4] International Standard for Organization. *Ada 95 Reference Manual - ISO/8652-1995*. ISO, 1995.

[5] A. F. Zorzo. *Multiparty Interactions in Dependable Distributed Systems*. PhD thesis, University of Newcastle upon Tyne, Newcastle upon Tyne, UK, 1999.

[6] L. Lamport. The temporal logic of actions. *ACM Transactions on Programming Languages and Systems*, 16(3):872–923, 1994.

[7] Y.-J. Joung and S. A. Smolka. A comprehensive study of the complexity of multiparty interaction. *Journal of ACM*, 43(1):75–115, 1996.

[8] I. Forman and F. Nissen. *Interacting Processes - A multiparty approach to coordinated distributed programming*. ACM Publishers, 1996.

[9] H.-M. Jårvinen and R. Kurki-Suonio. Disco specification language: Marriage of actions and objects. In *11th International Conference on Distributed Computing Systems*, pages 142–151. IEEE CS Press, 1991.

[10] N. G. Levenson. *Safeware: System, safety and computers*. Addison Wesley, Reading, MA, USA, 1995.

[11] J. Xu, B. Randell, A. Romanovsky, C. Rubira, R. J. Stroud, and Z. Wu. Fault tolerance in concurrent object-oriented software through coordinated error recovery. In *25th International Symposium on Fault-Tolerant Computing*, pages 450–457. IEEE Computer Society Press, 1995.

[12] B. Randell. Systems structure for software fault tolerance. *IEEE Transactions on Software Engineering*, 1(2):220–232, 1975.

[13] J. Gray and A. Reuter. *Transaction processing: concepts and techniques*. Morgan Kaufmann Publishers, San Mateo, CA, USA, 2nd edition, 1993.

[14] M. Evangelist, N. Francez, and S. Katz. Multiparty interactions for interprocess communication and synchronization. *IEEE Transactions on Software Engineering*, 15(11):1417–1426, 1989.

[15] C. T. Davies. Data processing spheres of control. *IBM Systems Journal*, 17(2):179–198, 1978.

[16] R. D. Tennent. *Semantics of Programming Languages*. Prentice Hall, Englewood Cliffs, NJ, USA, 1991.

[17] M. Hennessy. *The Semantics of Programming Languages: An elementary introduction using Structural Operational Semantics*. John Wiley & Sons, Chichester, UK, 1990.

[18] L. Lamport. Specifying concurrent systems with TLA$^+$. In M Broy and R. Steinbruggen, editors, *Calculational System Design*. IOS Press, Amsterdam, 1999.

[19] A. Pnueli. The temporal logic of programs. In *18th Annual Symposium on the Foundations of Computer Science*, pages 46–57. IEEE CS Press, 1977.

[20] A. F. Zorzo. A language construct for DMIs. In *II Workshop of Tests and Fault Tolerance*, Curitiba, PR, Brazil, 2000.

[21] N. Lynch, M. Merrit, W. Weihl, and A. Fekete. *Atomic Transactions*. Morgan Kaufmann, 1994.

[22] D. Schwier, F. von Henke, J. Xu, R. J. Stroud, A. Romanovsky, and B. Randell. Formalization of the CA action concept based on temporal logic. In *DeVa - Design for Validation*, 2nd year, pages 3–15. ESPRIT Long Term Project 20072, 1997.

[23] J. Xu, B. Randell, A. Romanovsky, R. J. Stroud, E. Canver A. F. Zorzo, and F. von Henke. Rigorous development of a safety-critical system based on coordinated atomic actions. In *29th International Symposium on Fault-Tolerant Computing*, pages 68–75. IEEE CS Press, 1999.

[24] K. L. McMillan. *Symbolic Model Checking*. Kluwer Academic Press, 1993.

[25] E. A. Emerson. Temporal and modal logic. In J. van Leeuwen, editor, *Handbook of Theoretical Computer Science*, chapter 16, pages 995–1072. Elsevier Science Publishers, 1990.

[26] J. Vachon. *COALA: a design language for reliable distributed systems*. PhD thesis, Swiss Federal Institue of Technology, Lausanne, Switzerland, 2000.

[27] M. Koutny and G. Pappalardo. The ERT model of fault-tolerant computing and its applicaton to formalisation of coordinated atomic actions. Technical Report 636, Department of Computing Science, Newcastle upon Tyne, UK, 1998. http://www.cs.ncl.ac.uk/research/trs.

[28] S. Veloudis and N. Nissanke. *Modelling coordinated atomic actions in timed CSP*, volume 1926 of *Lectures Notes in Computing Science*, pages 228–239. Springer Verlag, Berlin, Germany, 2000.

[29] A. F. Zorzo and R. J. Stroud. A distributed object-oriented framework for dependable multiparty interactions. In *14th ACM Conference on Object-Oriented Programming Systems, Languages and Applications - OOPSLA'99*, pages 435–446, Denver, CO, USA, 1999. ACM Press.

[30] A. F. Zorzo, A. Romanovsky, B. Randell J. Xu, R. J. Stroud, and I. S. Welch. Using coordinated atomic actions to design safety-critical systems: A production cell case study. *Software: Practice and Experience*, 29(8):677–697, 1999.

[31] A. Romanovsky and A. F. Zorzo. Coordinated atomic actions as a technique for implementing distributed GAMMA computation. *Journal of Systems Architecture - Special Issue on New Trends in Programming*, 45(9):79–95, 1999.

Chapter 4

COMPONENT BASED DEPENDABLE SYSTEM MODELLING FOR EASIER VERIFICATION

Didier Buchs

Software Engineering Laboratory, Swiss Federal Institute of Technology Lausanne

Sandro Costa

Software Engineering Laboratory, Swiss Federal Institute of Technology Lausanne
Universidade Federal da Paraíba, Campina Grande - Brazil

David Hurzeler

Software Engineering Laboratory, Swiss Federal Institute of Technology Lausanne

Abstract: The aim of this Chapter is to present an example of incremental modelling in CO-OPN that allows easier verification. We show how to build the crossroads specification by "cleanly" integrating physical and logical modelling of the system by means of the CO-OPN component and context notions. We take the example of the crossroads controller, and proceed to "observe" it, i.e., to check some basic properties we might expect from such a system. We also incrementally include failure behaviours, and show how we then barely need to modify the observing apparatus.

Keywords: modelling, modularity, component, observation, verification

P. Ezhilchelvan and A. Romanovsky (eds.), Concurrency in Dependable Computing, 61–83.

1.   INTRODUCTION

Developing dependable embedded software systems needs modelling tools that can capture the properties of the system to develop as well as the structure of the interactions between the software and its environment. Moreover, if we want to guarantee some good properties of the system, we need to introduce the right level of abstraction in the specification as well as the mean to detect anomalies in the system behaviour. This last point will be explored, and we will show that failure detectors can easily be introduced at the specification level if we use the synchronous mechanisms of the CO-OPN language (CO-OPN stands for Concurrent Object-Oriented Petri Nets [3][1]). This will not produce undesired interferences with the basic specification behaviour.

In this chapter, we use a formal framework for the development of embedded systems from the modelling to the verification phase. The approach we propose has adopted the object-oriented paradigm as a structuring principle. We have devised a general formalism which can express both abstract and concrete aspects of systems.

The situation considered here is as follows. Given a concrete system, we implement some embedded software components and check some properties of the resulting system. Therefore, our approach consists of first modelling the existing components, then implementing the embedded compoutside worldonents models, and finally checking properties on the resulting model. We will also model possible system failures, and check that the properties mentioned above still stand in the failure situations.

We will first briefly explain how to start from a diagram establishing the interconnection of the software system (including that which we implement) to the outside world elements and how to produce, step by step, a model that will be used to define the failure modes of the system. The idea of these refinements is to preserve as much as possible the verification principles that were designed in the early stages of the development process. The modelling strategy is obviously completely determined by the kind of properties we want to check in the end. We shall only model useful (verification-wise) entities. Our final goal is to provide a context in which we can very simply apply existing verification tools and have relevant and useful results for our particular problem. Figure 1 shows the global principle: we first model the functions of the system and the detectors which signal problems to the outside world, and then design and apply our "verification entities". The modelling phase is distinct from the verification phase. What we call "verification phase" is in fact more of a "preparation for verification" phase. Our goal in this chapter is to provide techniques which are semantically transparent: our verification apparatus does not modify the semantics of the system (the application functions). We reach this transparency by designing some *observers*, entities used just for verification purposes. Thus, properties proved on the "observed" system (i.e. the system plus the observer) still stand for the original. The verification itself resides in the "verify" circles and is not treated in this chapter.

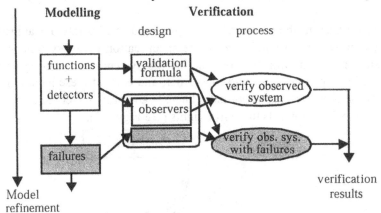

Figure 1 . The modelling and verification process

An example of a crossroads controller will illustrate our approach. The complete specification and supporting tools can be found at: http://lglwww.epfl.ch/Conform/CO-OPNTools.

The chapter is organized as follows. Section 2 presents the functional aspect of the crossroads and discusses the models that we can produce using CO-OPN. Section 3 presents the principles of observation that can be used for verification purposes. Section 4 presents how to introduce system failures into the model. Section 5 deals with verifying the specification in presence of failures.

2.   MODELLING FUNCTIONAL ASPECTS

CO-OPN is an object-oriented modelling language, based on Algebraic Data Types (ADT), Petri nets, and IWIM (Idealized Worker Idealized Manager) coordination models [5]. Hence, CO-OPN concrete specifications are collections of ADT, class and context (i.e. coordination) *modules* [10] (these concepts shall be further detailed below). Structurally, each module has the same overall structure; it includes an *interface section* defining all elements accessible from the outside, and a *body section* including the local aspects private to the module. Moreover, class and context modules have convenient graphical representations which are used in this chapter, showing their underlying Petri net model. Low-level mechanisms and other features dealing specifically with object-orientation, such as sub-classing and sub-typing, are out of the scope of this chapter, and can be found in [1] [3].

2.1   The Crossroads Example

Here, we present the crossroads example, used to illustrate our approach. We first show how to build a complete specification of the system we are interested in. Let us first briefly describe the system itself. The system is composed of two roads crossing each other, and each of these have a traffic light. These roads are one-way roads. There is an entity, called `CrossController`, which controls the traffic lights (see Figure 2).

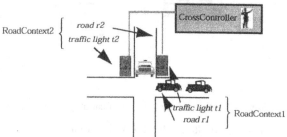

Figure 2 . The Crossroads system

To construct the model, we consider the existing system as being composed of three distinct subsystems: the controller, the machinery (traffic lights) and the car behaviour control (not detailed here). Then, to model the controller -the embedded system we are interested in- we have to model abstractions of the other subsystems -which, when implemented, will be parts of the embedded system responsible for the interaction with the outside world: they will be connected to the real components stated above.

First of all, we will explain the steps that can lead to the CO-OPN model of the crossroads controller.

Therefore, we shall describe the components and the way they are interconnected. The main concepts used to express the structure and the behaviour of the system are:
- a coordination model to describe the relations between the system components,
- object orientation for the structure and content of the system,
- causality relations for the dynamic aspects that must be reflected with non-deterministic and concurrent behaviours.

The controller is a program that coordinates the activities of the traffic lights, depending on the number of cars waiting to pass on each road. The controller sends commands to the traffic lights.

We consider that the controller can detect the presence and the absence of cars on the roads by the means of some magnetic sensor. The controller works as follows. As soon as one of the roads is empty, it switches the traffic lights in order to let the other road start emptying itself. It stops when both roads are empty. For fairness reasons, when five cars have crossed one road, even if the road is not empty, the controller turns the traffic light of that road to red and the traffic light of the other road to green.

2.2 Principles of Modelling Strategy

In this part the various concepts of CO-OPN will be introduced in the necessary order for the modelling of the system. As we use a kind of top-down strategy for modelling, we will first start by presenting the interface of the system simulator (which is in fact what we implement) given by the top-level coordination entity called CarCross context.

A useful approach for building systems composed of many computing entities is to use the high-level concept of *coordination programming* [13]. The term *coordination theory* refers to theories about how coordination can occur in various kinds of systems. We state that coordination is the *management of dependencies* among activities.

Taking a step further in this direction, it appeared that *coordination patterns* are likely to be applied since the beginning of the *design phase* of the software development. This fact gave birth to the notion of *coordination development* [5]. This process involves the use of specific coordination models and languages, adapted to the specific needs encountered during the design phase.

Due to their intrinsic nature, IWIM (*Idealized Workers, Idealized Managers*) coordination models [14] are particularly well suited for the coordination of software elements during the design phase [4]. The coordination layer of CO-OPN [5] [3] [4] is a coordination language based on a IWIM model, suited for the formal coordination of object-oriented systems. CO-OPN context modules define the *coordination* entities [12], while CO-OPN classes (and objects) define the basic *coordinated* entities of a system. CO-OPN allows one to cover the formal development of concurrent software from the first formal specification up to the final distributed software architecture [1].

We shall first quickly give an outline of the way values can be defined in CO-OPN, using algebraic data types. Then, we shall describe the class and context modules, which are the "components" of our formalism. Finally, we shall give a quick formal description of these components, and of how we can compose them.

2.3   ADT Modules

CO-OPN ADT modules define data types by means of algebraic specifications. Each module describes one or more sorts (i.e. names of data types), along with generators and operations on these sorts. The properties of the operations are given in the body of the module, by means of positive conditional equational axioms. For instance, Figure 3 describes the ADT defining the car sort, defined by several generators. Figure 4 describes the more complex Fifo ADT (the sequence sort is implicitly assumed). Having the ADT, it is possible to describe the dynamic components of a CO-OPN specification: the classes. Please note that in the following specifications, module names are different from sort names (a module may have several sorts). Hence the case differences.

```
ADT Car;
Interface
   Sort    car;
   Generators
      c1 , c2 , c3 : -> car;
End Car;
```

Figure 3 .The Car ADT

```
Generic Abstract Adt Fifo(Elem);
Interface
   Use Elem; Naturals;
   Sort fifo;
   Generators
      [] : -> fifo;
      _'_ : elem, fifo -> fifo;
   Operations
      insert _ to _ : elem, fifo -> fifo;
      next of _ : fifo -> elem;
      remove from _ : fifo -> fifo;
Body
   Axioms
   insert elemVar1 to fifoVar1 =  elemVar1'fifoVar1;
   next of (elemVar1'[]) = elemVar1 ;
   next of (elemVar1'elemVar2 'fifoVar1)= next of (elemVar2'fifoVar1);
   remove from (elemVar1'[]) = [] ;
   remove from (elemVar1'elemVar2 'fifoVar1)=elemVar1'(remove from
(elemVar2'fifoVar1));
   Where
   fifoVar1 : fifo;   elemVar1, elemVar2 : elem;
End Fifo;
```

Figure 4 .The Fifo ADT

2.4   Class Modules

In this subsection, we will show more detail on the basic structures equivalent to what we call component: classes. We will give some examples in the

`Crossroads` system, and using this example explain the main elements of a CO-OPN model.

CO-OPN classes are described by means of modular algebraic Petri nets with particular parameterised external transitions which are *methods* (provided services) and *gates* (required services) of the class. The behaviour of transitions are defined by *behavioural axioms*, similar to axioms in an ADT. A method call is achieved by synchronizing external transitions, according to the fusion of transitions technique. The axioms have the following shape:

`Cond => eventname With synchro : pre -> post`

in which the terms have the following meaning:

- `Cond` is a set of equational conditions, similar to a guard;
- `eventname` is the name of a method with the algebraic term parameters;
- `synchro` is the synchronization expression defining the policy of transactional interaction of this event with other events, the dot notation is used to express events of specific objects and the synchronization operators are sequence, simultaneity and non-determinism.
- `Pre` and `Post` are the usual Petri net flow relation determining what is consumed and what is produced in the object state places (which correspond to what was called "component attribute" above).

CO-OPN provides tools for the management of graphical and textual representations. We can see both the graphical and the textual representation of a class in Figure 5 and Figure 6 respectively. Please note that in the graphical representations, for each method, we have one black rectangle for the interface, and one for the component Petri net. So two side-by-side rectangles are in fact representations of one method.

For example, let us examine the seventh axiom in Figure 6:

`(n<5) = true => inc5counter::5counter n -> 5counter (n+1);`

The interpretation is the following: if the place `5counter` contains the integer n with `(n<5)` then the method `inc5counter` increases this integer by one. This axiom has no synchronization expression.

The fourth axiom is:

`pass With(this.takecar..this.inc5counter)..this.pass::->`

This time there is no condition, but we do have a synchronization expression: the `pass` method requires the execution of the `takecar` method of the object, followed by its `inc5counter` internal method, and its `pass` method. So there is a recursive call to the method. The execution of this method if and only if all methods can sequentially be executed. There is no pre or post condition, meaning that this method does not directly modify (or require anything from) the object's places' contents.

In our example, the basic classes are: `Road`, `TrafficLight`, and

`Crosscontroller.`

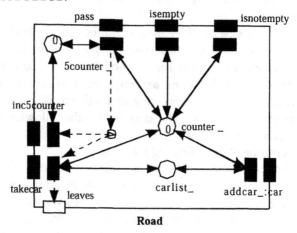

Figure 5 .The Road class graphical description

```
Class Road;
Interface
  Use
    Naturals;Car;FifoCar;
  Type
    road;
  Gate
    leaves;
  Methods
    isempty; isnotempty; pass;
    addcar _ : car;    takecar;
Body
  Methods
    inc5counter;
  Places
    counter _ ,5counter _ : natural;
    carlist _ : fifo;
  Initial
    counter 0; 5counter 0; carlist [ ];
  Axioms
    isempty::counter 0 -> counter 0;
    (n>0)=true => isnotempty::counter n -> counter n;
     pass With ((this.takecar)..(this.inc5counter))..(this.pass)::->;
      (m>0)=true => pass::5counter m,counter 0 ->5counter 0,counter 0;
    pass::5counter 5 -> 5counter 0;
     addcar c::counter n,carlist f->counter(n + 1),carlist(insert c to f);
    (n<5)=true => inc5counter::5counter n -> 5counter (n+1);

    ((n>0)=true) => takecar With this.leaves:: counter n, carlist f ->
      counter(n-1), carlist(remove from f);
  Where
       c : car; n,m : natural;  this : road; f : fifo;
End Road;
```

Figure 6 . The Road class textual description

As we can see in Figure 5, the Road class provides methods (black rectangles, gates being the white rectangles) to modify, in different ways, the state representation of the roads. For instance, the method `addcar` increments the value in the place `counter` by one and modifies the FIFO buffer in the `carlist` place. A corresponding class `TrafficLight` (Figure 7) is used to model the traffic lights associated with each road. This class simply has two states indicating whether the light is red or green.

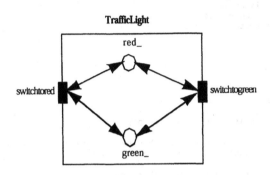

Figure 7.The TrafficLight class graphical description

In Figure 8, the reader can see the textual description of the `CrossController` Petri net. The `control` method empties one road, giving the traffic lights the correct commands. If it is called several times, it will alternate between emptying roads `r1` and `r2`. In real life, this method must be kept called, for instance by a time triggered component. It could have been possible to use a recursive method to empty the roads in only one call, but this has several disadvantages: first of all, when both roads are empty, if new cars arrive, the method must be called again, so we are back to the case where we have to assist the system by regularly calling the method. Also, as we will see, observation-wise, the adopted solution is far better, because it allows to decompose the execution into many steps, and to detect and locate potential problems with more ease.

This example also illustrates the transactional semantics of CO-OPN (all-or-nothing policy of synchronization) expressed in the `(r1.isempty)..(r2.isempty)` synchronization that can succeed if and only if both methods sequentially succeed.

2.5   Coordination with Contexts

Let us now describe more complex CO-OPN structures (still equivalent to the "components" described below) which result of composition: contexts.

In Figure 9 we can see the `Crossroads` system including the `CrossController` and a model of the physical components

```
Class CrossController;
Interface
 Use
    Naturals; TrafficLight; Car; Road;
 Type
    crosscontroller;
 Gates
    pass1;          pass2;
    isempty1;       isempty2;
    isnotempty1;    isnotempty2;
    switchtogreen1;switchtogreen2;
    switchtored1;   switchtored2;
 Methods
    control;
Body
Methods
    controlplace : natural;
Initial controlplace 1;
 Axioms
    control With this.isempty1..this.isempty2::->;

    control With (this.isnotempty1..((this.switchtogreen1 ..this.switchtored2)
    ..this.pass1)):: controlplace 1 -> controlplace 2

    control With (this.isnotempty2..((this.switchtogreen2..
    this.switchtored1)..this.pass2)):: controlplace 2 ->controlplace 1
 Where
    this : crosscontroller;
End CrossController;
```

Figure 8 . The CrossController class textual description

Roadcontext1, Roadcontext2, and Car, with the input events (methods) and output events (gates). Please note that in this case Car is an ADT, and thus does not have a graphical representation. It rather acts as a parameter.

The Crossroads context contains sub-components that interact to provide the controller behaviour. The Crossroads sub-components are: an instance of the class CrossController, the abstract data type Car, plus two contexts Roadcontext1 and Roadcontext2 which represent the road entities with their traffic lights. These two contexts have instances of the Road and TrafficLight classes as components. The abstract data types have not been represented in the picture. The oriented arcs between methods (black rectangles) or gates (white rectangles) are used to define strong synchronization between events. In CO-OPN, it means that the firing of synchronized events is strongly synchronous and atomic. The synchronization of entities in a context is an oriented couple of synchronization expressions of the form: synchro With synchro.

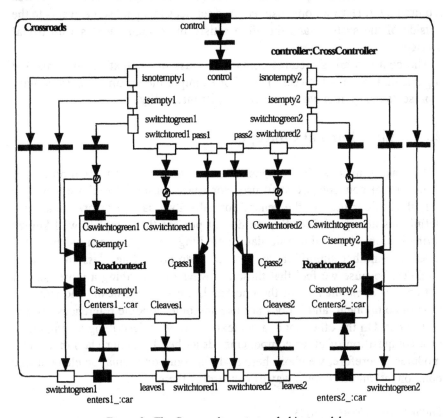

Figure 9. The Crossroads context and object model

Synchronisation expressions, as shown in our general component-based formalism, are built with the simultaneity (//), the sequence (..) and the non-determinist (+) operators. The `CrossController` component is devoted to managing the traffic lights. The `Road` objects, each containing its cars, have `TrafficLights` objects associated to them. This is why we have grouped the corresponding instances in contexts `Roadcontext1` and `Roadcontext2`.

Figure 9 shows what the outside world can see from the system: the `enters1` and `enters2` methods and `leaves1`, `leaves2`, `switchtored1`, `switchtored2`, `switchtogreen1` and `switchtogreen2` gates. The first methods allow for real time behaviour: cars may be added during "road-emptying" time. The `control` method is the "time triggered" method. Is must be called regularly for the controller to do its job. The gates tell the outside world when a car leaves one of the two roads or when the trafficlights change state. Basically, the methods of a system are the services it provides, and the gates of a system are the services required by it. Here we only use required services to signal some events to the outside of the system (and therefore satisfy these requirements with trivial services).

The contexts are structures containing class or context components and organising the links between them. For example the `Crossroads` context represents the system we are studying in its integrality.

2.6   Some Formal Concepts

To make things as clear as possible, this section gives the definitions of some formal concepts we shall use. For space reasons, we chose to define only the basic entities of the general formalism we base our work on, and the definitions are simplified. So, we do not present the complete well known formalisation of the algebraic data modelling concepts -such as the *ADT* modules. Another simplification is that we do not define *class* and *context* modules, because we feel that these are ways of describing a more general notion, i.e. *components*. On the one hand, a class is basically the simplest kind of component, and it does not use any other module references -except ADT ones. On the other hand, a context is a way of describing a component as a composition of other components -described by either class or context modules. Therefore, we chose here to define only one semantic element -the component- and to show a way of connecting them [18].

DEFINITION: COMPONENTS

Let **C** be a set of (component) names. A *component* is a tuple $\{c, I_c, B_c, \text{Trans}_c\}$, in which:

- $c \in C$, where c is the component identifier.
- $I_c = \{M_c, G_c\}$ is its interface, with M_c and G_c two sets of method and gate names. At this point, we assume that $\text{Events}_{\{c\}, M_c, G_c}$ is the set of all possible event expressions written on the methods and gates in M_c and G_c. We do not give details here on how these expressions are written, but examples of this can be seen in the CO-OPN examples above (for instance in Section 2.4).
- B_c is a set of attribute names. Again, without getting into the details, we say that $\text{States}(B_c)$ is the set of all possible states based on the states of each attribute.
- $\text{Trans}_c \subseteq \text{States}(B_c) \times \text{Events}_{\{c\}, M_c, G_c} \times \text{States}(B_c)$ is the labelled transition system that defines the semantics of the component. A triple $\{s, e, s'\} \in \text{Trans}_c$ is noted $s \xrightarrow{e} s'$.

We call *closed semantics* of a component c the labelled transition system

Sem_c; this semantics is the result of the closure of Trans_c with respect to both the multisets of states and the occurrence of parallelism (//), sequence (..), and non-determinism (+) of events. The completion is done by adding to the basic semantics of the component behaviours corresponding to its synchronization closure by the //, .., and + operators. For instance, simultaneous occurrence of one method requires the presence of the sum of resources in the precondition, this behaviour will be added by the closure process.

Component composition has a set of components as parameters, a set of synchronisation expressions -expressions that describe the way the components' interfaces are connected- and a new interface. The result is a new component. The process used to obtain the semantics of this new component is composed of three steps. Again, we shall give general ideas, and not define each operator precisely. Each of these steps is the result of a computation of one of the following operators on the semantics of the components to compose:

- *Union*: simply puts the individual behaviours of each component into the semantics of the new component;
- *Synchronisation Expression Solution* (SESolution): solves the synchronisation among the source components, i.e. finds the new possible behaviours resulting from the connections between the components (as stated in the synchronisation expression);
- *Interface Filter* (IFilter): eliminates behaviours associated to elements not in the new specified interface (in order to promote encapsulation).

DEFINITION: COMPOSITION

Let $C = \{(c_1, I_{c_1}, B_{c_1}, \text{Trans}_{c_1}), ..., (c_n, I_{c_n}, B_{c_n}, \text{Trans}_{c_n})\}$ be a set of components, where $I_{c_i} = \{M_{c_i}, G_{c_i}\}$. Let $I_{new} = \{M_{new}, G_{new}\}$ be an interface, such that $M_{new} \subseteq \biguplus_i M_{c_i}$ and $G_{new} \subseteq \biguplus_i G_{c_i}$.

Let *Expr* be a set of synchronisation expressions, and c be a component identifier. The composition of the set of components C w.r.t. the interface I_{new}, the set of synchronisation expressions *Expr* and the identifier c is the component $\text{Comp}(C, I_{new}, \text{Expr}, c) = \{c, I_c, B_c, \text{Trans}_c\}$ such that:

$$I_c = I_{new}, \; B_c = \biguplus_i B_{c_i}, \; \text{Trans}_c = \text{IFilter}_{I_{new}}\left(\text{SESolution}_{\text{Expr}}\left(\bigcup_{i=1}^{n} \text{Sem}_{c_i}\right)\right)$$

EXAMPLE: COMPOSITION OF TWO COMPONENTS

We shall now try to present an example to illustrate our formalism. Let $\{c1, \{m1, m2, g1, g2\}, B_{c1}, \text{Trans}_{c1}\}$ and $\{c2, \{m3, m4, g3\}, B_{c2}, \text{Trans}_{c2}\}$ be two components. Let us suppose that we want to compose them under the synchronisation expressions {`c1.g1 with c2.m3`, `c1c1.g2 with c2.m4`}. The result of the composition is a new component

$\{c3, \{m1, m2, g3\}, B_{c3}, Trans_{c3}\}$. Figure 10 and Figure 11 show the two steps of the composition. The right part of the figures shows a relevant piece of the transition system of each component.

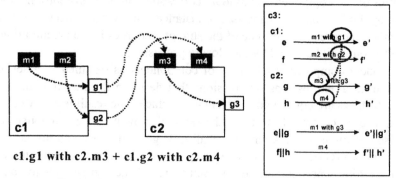

Figure 10. An example (1): first part of composition, semantics.

In Figure 10, we can see the first part of the composition process: on the right side of the picture, we have first part of the separate semantics of c1 and c2 and then below, what we can deduce from it for the composed component (c3) semantics. So, for instance, if:

- c1.m1 with c1.g1 takes the component c1 from a state e to a state e'.
- c2.m3 with c2.g3 takes the component c2 from a state g to a state g'.
- c1.g1 with c2.m3 is in the synchronization expression set.

then:

- c3.m1 with c3.g3 takes the component c3 from a state $e//g$ to a state $e'//g'$.

Please note that the $\|$ operator (different from the $//$ operator) is the reunion, or simultaneous availability of state resources. $e//e'$ means that the resources of e and e' are simultaneously available.

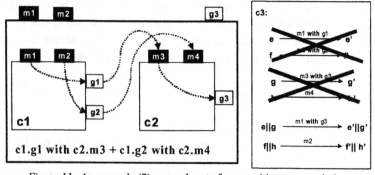

Figure 11. An example (2): second part of composition, encapsulation.

Figure 11 details the second part of the composition, where we encapsulate the two components composed into the new one, give it its new interface, and "hide" in the semantics the method and gate names which do not appear in the latter interface. We do not eliminate any behaviour, only delete the transition labels elements which are not in the interface. For example, m2 with m4 becomes m2, because m4 is not in the new interface.

These semantics will be used to provide CO-OPN with a simple formal framework (compatible with the semantics given in [3]): components translate into classes and contexts -components resulting from composition-, component attribute translate into CO-OPN places, and composition gives composition into contexts with synchronization (composition synchronization translates into axiom synchronization).

3. OBSERVATION AND VERIFICATION

As explained before the purpose of modelling is not only to produce the controller, but also to be able to study the behaviour of the machine that will be produced. We shall first give a small example of analysis using the notion of observation.

3.1 Concepts on Observation

In this subsection, we shall try to give general ideas on the concepts used, basing ourselves on the component-based formalism described very briefly in Section 2. Again, the complete formal description can be found in [18].

The general idea here is to constrain the system behaviour to be checked by the means of an *observer*, and then to evaluate a *validation formula* -which describes the property we are checking- on the resulting behaviour. The developer checking the system, (and/or the verification tool) will only interact with the observer. So this observer is a filter through which we can trigger the system. But we might only be interested in some of the system semantics, so this observer has some behaviour constraints: we cannot trigger it in any way we want, but only in some predefined fixed ways. Therefore, the system semantics to be checked will be reduced by these first behavioural restrictions, thus making verification simpler. A consequence of this is that for each system method we might want to call, we have a corresponding method in the observer's interface. In what follows we chose to give these methods the same name for the system as for the observer (see Figure 12).

Now let $\{o, I_o, B_o, \text{Trans}_o\}$ be a component, with $I_o = (M_o, G_o)$. Suppose that we are interested in proving a property p on some behaviour of o. Let us assume that given a behaviour s on some sets $M \subseteq M_o$ of methods and $G \subseteq G_o$

of gates, we are able to build a component $\{obs, I_{obs}, B_{obs}, Trans_{obs}\}$ s.t:

- $I_{obs} = \{M, G\}$
- $Sem_{obs} = s$

Then we compose *obs* with *o* into a new observation system $Comp(\{o, obs\}, \{M_o, G_o\}, Expr, obssys)$, connecting the corresponding methods and gates the following way: $Expr = \{\text{"}p \text{ with } p\text{"}, p \in M \cup G\}$.

We must then prove: $IFilter_{(M_o, G_o)}(Sem_{obssys}) \models p$. (where $S \models p$ means:"*S* satisfies *p*")

The process (of verification) described is that of *observation*, the *obs* component is called the *observer*, and *p* is called the validation formula. The idea is that it is "through" the observer component that we "observe" the component we wanted to verify in the first place. The observer constraints the behaviour of the first component on which we want to prove our property.

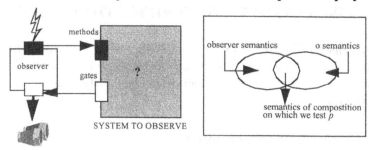

Figure 12 .Observation concepts

We believe the observation process is valid because the observation system's semantics is included in the original system's semantics: the observer component does not add, modify, or hide behaviours of the system. The observation system is a pure abstraction of the original system. In Figure 13, we illustrate the main motivation of the observation process: From the system, we design an observation system. We are interested in proving a property *p* (for example: "the lights are not simultaneously green") included in a set of properties *P*. So we first give a formal abstraction of this property *Abs(p)* (for example "*t* not fireable") and prove that the observation system satisfies *Abs(p)*. Our claim is that the system satisfies *p*:

Hypothesis of Abstraction correctness $\Rightarrow$ (Obs Sys $\models$ Abs(p) $\Rightarrow$ Sys $\models$ p)

Note that in practice, we do not formally verify the abstraction correctness, but try to find several arguments in its favour during the verification process design; for instance, in the crossroads example, we trust that the observer class does not mask possible wrong behaviours. This is in some case easy to verify, because the CO-OPN synchronization mechanism generates limited interferences between the observer and the original system.

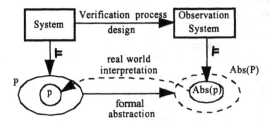

Figure 13. Semantic constraints of the observation process

3.2 Observation in CO-OPN

Let us now give a more detailed example of observation in the crossroads problem. The property we are going to observe is the following: "if traffi- clight t1 is in the green (red) state, then trafficlight t2 is not, and con- versely".

3.2.1 Detecting the State of the Traffic Lights

First of all, we define a Detector class (Figure 14), which has a test method that may only fire when both traffic lights are in the green state. This is because as such, the system does not allow us to see the colour of the traffic lights; we need something that shows them to us. We insist that we do not create a detector, we just chose to model it now; indeed, before, we did not need to model it. If a system does not contain a detector of some kind for some events validating a property, there is no way we can verify it.

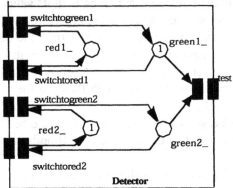

Figure 14. The Detector class

The new system, called here ObservContext, is shown in Figure 15.

```
Context ObservContext;
Interface
 Use
    CrossController; Car; Naturals; Detector;
 Methods
    empty; testTL;
    carenters1 _, carenters2 _:car;
 Gates
    carleaves1; carleaves2;
Body
 Use Context Crossingcontext;
 Object
    2greendetector : detector;
 Axioms
    switchtored1 With 2greendetector.switchtored1;
    switchtored2 With 2greendetector.switchtored2;
    switchtogreen1 With 2greendetector.switchtogreen1;
    switchtogreen2 With 2greendetector.switchtogreen2;
    empty With control;
    carenters1 c With enters1 c;
    carenters2 c With enters2 c;
    testTL With 2greendetector.test;
    leaves1 With carleaves1;
    leaves2 With carleaves2;
 Where
       c : car;
End ObservContext;
```

Figure 15. The Observer context description

3.2.2   Observing the System

As we have seen, the process of observation decomposes into two phases. First, one has to design an observer class synchronized on the class to observe (which is considered as a black box). This observer class's purpose is to constrain the behaviour of the observed class on which we want to observe/test properties.

Second, we build the observer class along with its validation formula. The description of this observer class is given in Figure 16. As the reader can see, as for the buffer previously examined, we constrain the behaviour on which we want to observe the property, because here the empty method is always called after any carenters1 or carenters2 method call. The observer's methods are synchronized with those of the Observcontext (Figure 17) that have the same name.

In this example's case, the validation formula could be "testTL is dead", because the testTL method can only be fired if both traffic lights are in the green state.

As for the verification of the validation formula itself, it is clear that the problem is in the general case undecidable. Here for example, deciding whether a method is live or not would be undecidable. In real-life problems however, we can often reduce the problem to a finite state problem where we can decide it. If not, we can sometimes reduce the problem to a simpler Petri-net problem where we have some results: if we can reduce it to a one-to-one-labelled Petri net, then we know we can decide some hard problems (like bisimulation) [16]. This is what we are currently working on.

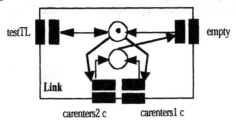

Figure 16. The Observer class graphical description

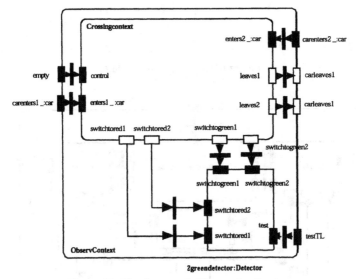

Figure 17. The Crossroads Observation Context

4. MODELLING FAILURES

4.1 Example of Failure: Link Failure

We shall now model failures in the system. These will for instance be failures in the connections between the controller and the traffic lights (Figure 18).

We shall see that this addition is done very simply (incrementally, thanks to the modular component modelling support of CO-OPN). In Figure 19, we have a schematic class model for the new system. Two new classes have been introduced: the Link class, which represents the connection between the traffic light and the controller, and the `FailureManager` class, which is basically an additional controller for the case where we have a connection failure. A slightly more detailed representation of the `Link` class is given in Figure 20.

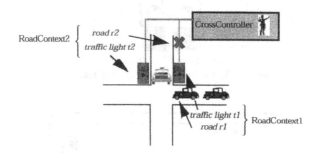

Figure 18. The connection failure

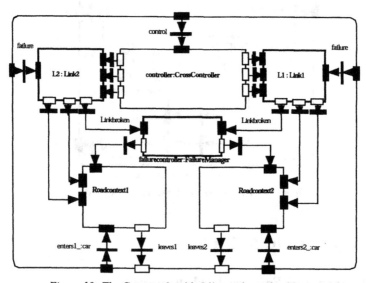

Figure 19. The Crossroads with failure schematic object model

In Figure 20 we have only given the class structure for the `pass` method. In fact we have a similar structure for every method call from the controller class to the traffic lights components, but for clarity reasons, we have chosen not to represent these on Figure 20. The idea here is that there is only one connection between the controller and a traffic light, and that all commands use this connection. The interpretation of the schema is very simple. Controller calls the `pass` method. Then, depending on whether the link is in "ok" or "broken" state, the call is passed on to the RoadContext or a "link broken" signal is sent to the failurecontroller. We have the same for every method of the class, and for each one, we need a place describing the state of the connection. The reason for this is that two methods might be called concurrently, and having only one "ok" resource in a unique place would obviously create problems. The idea is that when the connection is "ok", the behaviour of the Carcross with failure system is the same as the Carcross system. But of course we have only one failure method, and every place of the class always contain the same tokens.

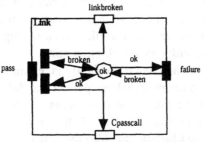

Figure 20 . The Link class brief graphical description

The failurecontroller class is not detailed here. What it basically does is to set a traffic light to "red" when it receives the "link broken" signal from the link to the other traffic light.

4.2 Verification of the System with Failures

Let us now observe the newly built system, i.e. the one that has potential connection failures. As before, we need to create an observation context, as we have seen in Figure 15. In fact, the context is pretty much the same, but now we have two new methods called failure1 and failure2, which cause respectively link1 and link2 to fail, and of course, the Crossingcontext is now modified by the new connection structures. The observer class is the same as before apart from two methods called failure1 and failure2, because we are interested in the same safety property. Also, the validation formula is the same, even with failures.

5. RELATED WORK AND CONCLUSIONS

5.1 Properties Preservation Principles and Related Work

This work is part of a more ambitious project on behavioural subtyping definition and verification that began in [3] (where strong behavioural sub-typing was defined). Our aim is to define a subtype relation based on property preservation, and observation is used as a tool to compare two components under certain behavioural constraints. Instead of using object-orientation and defining classes to create component templates, we chose to use observation and focus on some properties of isolated components.

Other approaches, such as Liskov's [17], define an equivalence relation based on the restriction of observed states. Also, most of the work on bisimulation techniques [20] concerns definition of an equivalence relation preserving properties related to concurrency aspects, and is usually not about trying to restrict the observed behaviour of a particular component. Ideas of taking into account client needs in a server client relationship is also defined with process algebra in [6] with type checking in mind.

These approaches are not able to explicitly take into account their environment to restrict the components taking part in the definition of the equivalence relation. With the definition of observation we are able to see the system through an entity that filters any behaviour we are not interested in. The presented example illustrate this idea for a specific safety property.

5.2   Conclusion and Future Work

We have presented an example of modelling in CO-OPN that allows for easier verification. We have seen that we can fairly simply model a realistic system. Our specification language's modularity makes incremental modelling easier: after having built a first basic system model, we have been able to add elements and behaviours we had not modelled before without any major change in the existing components: for example, a detector component, a failure manager, and failure behaviours.

We have introduced the concept of observation (further detailed in [18]) through the definition of an observer component and validation formula; we have shown how this concept constitutes a simple pleasant platform on which verification of properties in general can be conducted. Given a use context of a component to be checked, it allows us to reduce the semantics of this component. We can then connect a verification tool (or a test tool) to the observer component, and check/test a simpler semantics. This may be very useful in contexts where a general component is used by a system in a very specific manner, and where we need to check a property of the component when it is used in that manner.

We are currently working on the implementation of the verification and testing of a variety of validation formulae based on our previous work [16].

REFERENCES

[1]   D. Buchs and N. Guelfi, A Formal Specification Framework for Object-Oriented Distributed Systems, IEEE TSE, Vol. 26, no. 7, July 2000, pp. 635-652.

[2]   G. Weikum, "Principles and Realization Strategies of Multilevel Transaction Management", ACM Transactions of Database Systems, Vol 16, No 1, pp 132-180, 1991.

[3]   O. Biberstein, D. Buchs, and N. Guelfi. Object-oriented nets with algebraic specifications: The CO-OPN/2 formalism. In G. Agha, F. De Cindio and G. Rozenberg, editors, Advances in Petri Nets on Object-Orientation. Springer-Verlag, LNCS 2001, pp. 70-127.

[4]   D.Buchs and M. Buffo. Rapid prototyping of formally modelled distributed systems. In FrancesM. Titsworth, editor, *Proc. of the Tenth International Workshop on Rapid System Prototyping RSP'99*. IEEE, june 1999.

[5]   M. Buffo. Experiences in coordination programming. In *Proceedings of the workshops of DEXA'98 (International Conference on Database and Expert Systems Applications)*. IEEE Computer Society, aug 1998.

[6]   F. Puntigam. Dynamic type information in process types. In David Pritchard and J. Reeve, editors, Proceedings EuroPar '98, number 1470 in Lecture Notes in Computer Science, Southampton, England, September 1998. Springer-Verlag.

[7]   C. Choppy and S. Kaplan. Mixing abstract and concrete modules: Specification, development and prototyping. In *12th International Conference on Software Engineering*, pages 173–184, Nice, March 1990.

[8]   D. Buchs and J. Hulaas. Evolutive prototyping of heterogeneous distributed systems using hierarchical algebraic Petri nets. In *Proceedings of the Int. Conf. on Systems, Man and Cybernetics*, Beijing, China, October 1996. IEEE.

[9]   Ph. Schnoebelen. Refined compilation of pattern-matching for functionnal languages. *Science of Computer Programming*, pages 11:133-159, 1988.

[10] O. Biberstein and D. Buchs. Structured algebraic nets with object-orientation. In *Proc.of the first int. workshop on "Object-Oriented Prog. and Models of Concurrency"*, *16th Int. Conf. on Application and Theory of Petri Nets*, Torino, Italy, June 26-30 1995.

[11] Sun Microsystems: JavaBeans specification Version 1.01 (July, 1997).

[12] M. Buffo and D. Buchs. A coordination model for distributed object systems. In *Proc. of the Second Int. Conf. on Coordination Models and Languages COORDINATION'97*, Volume 1282 of *LNCS*, pages 410–413. Springer Verlag, 1997.

[13] N. Carriero and D. Gelernter. *How to Write Parallel Programs*. MIT Press, Cambridge and London, 1990.

[14] J. Kramer, J. Magee, M. Sloman, and N. Dulay. Configuring object-based distributed programs in rex. *IEEE Software Engineering Journal*, 7(2):139–149, 1992.

[15] Lego Web site, http:\\mindstorms.lego.com

[16] D. Hurzeler, "Subtype relations verification for the CO-OPN/2 formalism", DEA report, July 2000, EPFL.

[17] B. Liskov and J. M. Wing, A behavioral notion of subtyping, ACM Transaction on Programming Languages and Systems, 16(6):1811--1841, November 1994.

[18] S. Costa, D. Buchs, D. Hurzeler, "Observers for substitutability in CO-OPN", EPFL, technical report (to appear).

[19] R. Milner, A Calculus of Communicating Systems, Lecture Notes in Computer Science 92, Springer-Verlag, 1980

[20] W. Leal and A. Arora. State-level and value-level simulations in data refinement. Inf. Proc. Letters 77(2-4), 2001. Special issue on the retirement of prof. Edsger W. Dijkstra.

II

APPLICATION SPECIFIC MODELLING FOR DEPENDABLE DESIGN AND ANALYSIS

Chapter 5

DIGGING INTO CONCURRENCY

Angie Chandler, Serena Patching, Lynne Blair
Computing Department, Lancaster University, Lancaster,UK
{angie or lb @comp.lancs.ac.uk, serena.patching@virgin.net}

Abstract. The topic of this paper is the design and implementation of an interacting Lego digger and dumper truck through the use of Petri nets. The focus of this is primarily on the use of Petri nets in the developing of dependable systems, an area of particular concern in the full-size equivalent of our experiment. The content of this paper will discuss the progression of the Petri net model of these two Lego robots, from design to implementation, and finally evaluation. The paper also features an optional plug-in Petri net, intended to allow the dumper to authenticate the digger for added security.

Keywords: Petri nets, Kerberos, Lego, synchronisation, robotics.

1 Introduction

This paper discusses the design and implementation of a model representing a digger and dumper truck interacting on a building site with the use of formal, concurrent modelling methods. The idea owes a degree of its conception to the previous work completed on an autonomous excavator at Lancaster University, as discussed briefly in section 2, but here focuses more on the interaction between a digger and a dumper truck, rather than solely on the details of the digger's execution. To this end, a model digger and dumper truck were

P. Ezhilchelvan and A. Romanovsky (eds.), Concurrency in Dependable Computing, 87–104.
© 2002 *Kluwer Academic Publishers. Printed in the Netherlands.*

constructed with the use of the Lego Mindstorms [10] [1] kit in order to emulate the sense of the excavator itself, and an accompanying dumper truck, without the difficulties associated with larger scale models.

The primary modelling method discussed in this paper is the Petri net. The Petri net is a directed bipartite graph where each node is a member of a set of transitions, or a set of places. The definition of a Petri net must show the set of places, the set of transitions, and the bag of arcs between the two. This can be represented by $C=(P,T,I,O)$ where P is the set of places, T is the set of transitions, I is the bag of inputs from a place p_i to a transition t_j, and O is the bag of outputs from the transition t_j to the place p_i.

Coloured Petri nets extend this definition to include a colouring of tokens, which will regulate which tokens are permitted through each transition, and the colour of each token output from that transition given the input colour.

Here, coloured Petri nets are used to describe the tasks which the digger and dumper truck must perform, and later used to generate software directly equivalent to the Petri net model, in the sense that the structure of the Petri net remains intact. This equivalence provides a great deal of assurance about the software being used as it has been mathematically verified.

Petri nets are generic enough to provide the capacity for application to a wide variety of applications, although due to their asynchronous nature they are more commonly used for distributed systems [3] and other similar processes. However, their uses in distributed systems by no means exclude applications to the field of robotics. In fact, robots can themselves form part of a distributed system, as can be seen through the example of an orange-picking robot with point-to-point communications [5], and even the application demonstrated here. Other areas of robotics can also find use for Petri net modelling as a method of eliminating deadlock and other temporal inconsistencies [19] [4], although these properties require testing through timed Petri nets, an extension which has yet to be made to the analysis system used here. There are also examples of use of Petri nets to facilitate co-operation between multiple robots [20], or between a human and a robot [12]. The range of applications for Petri nets is enormously diverse, and limited only by the range of tools available to implement these possibilities.

Our use of Petri nets as a modelling tool for mobile robots, was initially inspired by their ability to represent both the data flowing in the system and the state of the system, simultaneously, in addition to their capacity to represent concurrently executing program threads. This initial interest was then furthered by the ease with which the model could be translated into executable code, as required by the TRAMP toolkit discussed briefly in section 4, without the need to alter any of the components modelled.

The Petri net is put into use here as both a testable model and an eventual implementation device, but an extension to this is also discussed towards the end of the paper, revealing an optional Petri net plug-in which will be used to provide authentication for the dumper truck so that no foreign diggers are making use of it. This authentication procedure makes use of Kerberos [8], and is discussed in section 6.

2 Background

In recent years there have been a number of approaches taken towards the autonomous execution of the JCB801 mini excavator LUCIE (Lancaster University Computerised Intelligent Excavator) [2]. These have included research into the autonomous use of the digging arm, and also the navigation of the excavator using a GPS receiver [18][6]. These projects have also investigated various approaches to the safety of the excavator [15], particularly with the use of a safety manager as an overseer to the rest of the LUCIE software, which operates using three separate PC104 computers.

The approach discussed in this paper highlights an alternative approach, potentially complementary to the existing system on board LUCIE. With the concerns inherent to LUCIE's autonomous execution, the dependable execution of the software on board the excavator can be highlighted as an ideal area for a formal approach to dependable, safe computing to be taken.

For the purposes of formally modelling and ultimately executing code, Petri nets [16] were chosen, not only for their modelling capabilities and the mathematical methods available for testing, but also for the ability to model concurrent programs and allow for a switching of context, as the digger and dumper truck discussed in this paper synchronise and interact with one another.

With the use of Petri nets established as an exciting method of creating reliable software, it was also necessary to find an equivalent hardware implementation which would not become too expensive, in terms of both time and resources. The Lego Mindstorms kit, in conjunction with the legOS [14] operating system, proved both simple to put into use, and capable of providing the necessary functionality. The Lego Mindstorms RCX boasts not only an excellent interface to its three sensors and three actuators, but also the capacity to communicate with other RCX robots through an infra-red port. It also features a fully multi-threaded operating system in the form of legOS, a version of C written for the RCX.

3   Design

With the basis of the model's implementation determined, the Petri nets for the digger and dumper truck must then be built up. These were built up initially through the use of the simpler data flow diagram (Figure 1), which allowed for the visualisation of the required functions for the models, prior to establishing the more dynamic Petri net model. The Petri net models were then built up from the functions of the data flow diagram, with the functions translating directly into transitions, and the places generated from the implied states between each function.

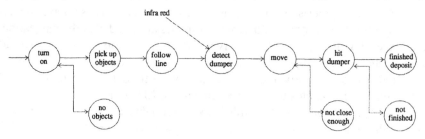

Figure 1 Digger Data Flow Diagram

The modelling process included two separate threads of execution. The first of these was the main Petri net which provided the digger and dumper truck with the means to follow their basic tasks, such as digging, dumping, and following the tracks laid out to get them to their required destinations.

This also included a second Petri net component, which was almost completely separate and only activated once the digger detected the dumper truck (and vice versa) and they had synchronised with one another. The second thread represented the infra-red receive function, a single transition which was required to check for any incoming messages in order to detect each model's counterpart, and looped continuously until a signal was detected. Once a signal was detected, the colouring of the token in "IR check" could be changed, and the secondary thread of the main Petri net could be activated.

A very simple colouring of the Petri net was added over the ordinary Petri net to allow the digger, for example, to act on the discovery of the object during the "find objects" state by entering the "pick up objects" transition instead of "no objects". Colouring of tokens was applied similarly throughout the Petri net, with the "meet dumper truck" transition able to accept *any* colour of token whenever the dumper truck was detected.

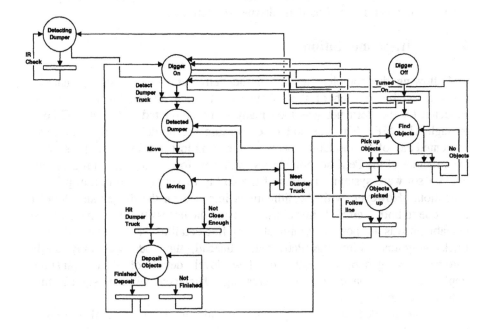

Figure 2 Digger Petri Net

Before any implementation of the models could be carried out, however, they first had to be thoroughly checked. This was done using the TRAMP

(Toolkit for Rapid Autonomous Mobile robot Prototyping) [7] toolkit, which would later be responsible for the automatic generation of the software to be executed on board the two robots. The Petri nets were primarily checked for simple reachability requirements, including any colouring restraints, ensuring that the eventual code would reliably reach its intended destination. It was also established that both Petri nets were reversible, where the net can reach its initial marking from any of its subsequent markings, ensuring that program could be exited satisfactorily, and it would not be necessary to essentially crash the program in the middle of Petri net execution. This may cause the software to develop memory leaks or become volatile. In fact, in this case it was unnecessary, as the Lego hardware provided adequate back up against these concerns but, reversibility was determined to be a desirable state in principle in the event of execution on board an alternative platform.

4   Implementation

Following the complete testing of the Petri net model, ensuring that the software on board each of the robots would reach all the functions it was expected to, the Petri net was then ready to be converted into legOS C code through TRAMP. This method of converting the model directly into code, prevented any of the model's aspects from getting lost in translation, preserving the structure of the Petri net completely in its new form and maintaining a fault-tolerant software system, in terms of the ability to verify the program prior to execution. However, with the limitations imposed on the digger and dumper truck due to both their real-time constraints and the necessity for the model to be readable, it was not possible to model every fine detail of the digger and dumper truck programs within the Petri net. Instead, the code was only partly automatically generated, with the low level detail of each transition implemented by hand, greatly increasing efficiency without significantly reducing reliability.

This hand-coded element may appear initially to re-introduce all the faults that the Petri net model was originally implemented to avoid, including any memory leaks and fatal errors which could occur. However, in fact, the remaining code is entirely segregated into code to be used within individual transitions, which are by definition atomic. It has no external references to any variables, and is restricted to locally defined variables and those passed into the transition as tokens. As such, this code is simple to thoroughly check; for most experienced programmers a simple glance would probably be enough to verify the code.

All details relevant to the transition are easily available through TRAMP, and selection of a button "More on Variables" will provide any details on the contents of incoming tokens instantly.

Although the implementation of hardware is not the subject of this paper, it is important to note at this stage a few key elements of the Lego hardware, used to execute the Petri net code produced by TRAMP.

Despite the adaptability of the Lego hardware it was important to make note of its inherent limitations, particularly the sensors available to it – in the form of touch, rotation and light sensors (a camera has since become available). With these limitations in mind, a simple track was devised to allow each robot to follow a line to a particular destination. Detection of the other robot through the infra-red was made as reliable as possible, by positioning the robots close together and facing one another. It was also important that each of the robots maintained certain elements of the behaviours of their real-life counterparts, without becoming too intent on producing precise replicas. For example, the digger performs its digging action with the use of a grabbing motion, producing the same effect for the purposes of this experiment, but completely unrealistic.

For the purposes of this experiment, the digger must travel around the circular line, picking up the object en route, then stopping when it detects a different colour on the line, signifying the end of its route. Meanwhile, the dumper truck must travel in a straight line along the other line until it detects a change in line colour and turns to face the digger. Once they detect one another through the infra-red detection/transmission, the digger will then turn and dump the object on the back of the dumper truck before restarting its Petri net. The dumper truck must then turn to continue back along the straight line, dumping the object to one side later.

5   Evaluation

Despite the efforts made to limit the impact of the hardware limitations on the overall experiment described above, it was difficult to ignore the main failings of the hardware implementation, by comparison to the software execution. Initial results highlighted the difficulties inherent in any physical simulation, in this case the unreliability of the light sensor on board the Lego

RCX, which was required to trace the line on the base, and the infra-red sensor. The infra-red sensor appeared to vary dramatically in its effectiveness, ranging from reflecting off every object in the room, to being unrecognisable from 10cms away. However, these problems were resolved, and the more critical issues of Petri net execution, and reliability of software were then considered.

In light of the numerous hardware problems faced, the software was an unqualified success. There were none of the unexpected and inconvenient problems produced even by this most simple hardware implementation. Instead the Petri net worked perfectly, the only problems within the programming being some early mistakes when setting the colours of tokens, causing transitions never to be enabled despite the availability of incoming tokens. This was in fact possible to test for within the TRAMP toolkit, but has yet to be automatically generated into the Petri net, perhaps an example of the full implications of the ability to automatically generate code from a Petri net without human interference.

It was only in the later stages of implementation that there were any serious software execution difficulties. These turned out to be due to the large increase in memory requirements placed on the RCX by storage of a complete Petri net structure, and gave rise to several instances where the RCX attempted to execute a program without the complete binary available. This was rectified through careful culling of the transition's handwritten code segments, but did successfully highlight one of the main problems with implementation of an automatically generated formal model, and the possibility of a completely dependable program failing despite all efforts.

To give an idea of the scale of the problem, table 1 shows the size of the binaries produced by the digger Petri net and a directly equivalent hand-coded version. It should be noted that the maximum program size permitted on the RCX is 32k, including an allocation for stacks for each thread. Clearly, the saving in removing the Petri net structure is highly significant.

Table 1 Binary Size

Type of Binary	Size of Binary (k)
Automatic digger.srec	31.4
Manual digger.srec	13.0

Traditionally, the other drawback to automatically generated code is the execution time required for all the necessary program management. Although there had been no signs of either the digger or dumper truck performing too slowly, it would be remiss to suggest that there were no overheads produced from the Petri net structure, particularly as the full-sized excavator may come to rely on the speed of the program implementation at some later stage [17]. To establish precisely the nature of the Petri net's overheads, an experiment was performed using a simple one place, one transition Petri net in a loop, against a hand-coded program, each simply adding one to a counter each time the function was entered, until the target was reached. The results in table 2 show the difference in response time between the two to be negligible over 1000 loops.

Table 2 Execution Times

Automatic (s)	Manual (s)
24.44	24.44
24.45	24.38
24.32	24.46
24.34	24.42

6   Extended Design

6.1   Introduction

In order to expand the concept of concurrency, fault tolerance and communication, an extended design is proposed to identify the area of authentication, to enhance the structure and actions performed within transitions of the Petri net as well as increase the tasks implemented by the digger and dumper truck themselves.

This concept involves the dumper truck authenticating the identity of the digger before allowing the digger to deposit its load. The authentication is based on the Kerberos protocol version 5, as will be seen in section 6.2. Although many different authentication or cryptography techniques could be used within this extended design, Kerberos is used in order to enable authentication of both the client and the server.

6.2   Background

Security and authentication play a very important role in society today. With the explosion of the Internet and other networked environments, information sent across networks must be protected from the attack of unauthorised personnel. Attacks could come in the form of, for example, eavesdropping, masquerading or tampering; therefore various forms of cryptography must be employed to act as a security mechanism to control the privacy and integrity of the data.

Kerberos is based on the key distribution model [13] and allows a client and server to authenticate themselves with each other, to verify their own individual identities.

Although authentication protocols were developed for use with both public and private (secret) keys, the Kerberos protocol, as discussed within this section uses only secret keys. The key is used to encrypt a *plaintext* message into *ciphertext*, which can then only be decrypted by the decryption key.

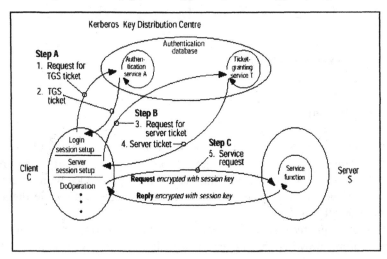

Figure 3 System Architecture of Kerberos [8]

Secret key cryptography is symmetric as the keys are only known to the authorised sender and receiver, who must share the knowledge of the key in order for the messages sent between them to be encrypted and decrypted securely, without the risk of attack.

In order to implement this concept the Kerberos protocol version 5 is used to act as an authentication service between the client and the server, which can be seen in Figure 3.

Further information on the Kerberos Protocol can be seen in [8].

Secret keys are used within the Kerberos protocol as the client and server, namely the digger and the dumper truck would only run on a local network as both the robots are contained within a specified area. This would therefore allow a secure key service to be used for key distribution to permit only an authorised digger to deposit its objects into the dumper truck. Only the digger and dumper truck will know the key, therefore the probability of attack is minimal.

Public keys, however do not require a secure key service, using two separate keys to encrypt and decrypt, and therefore are used in large-scale networks such as the Internet. Public keys also only allow one-way communication and are therefore unsuitable for this situation as two way communication must exist between the digger and the dumper truck in order for authentication to occur and the tasks to be completed by each robot to continue.

If multiple diggers were present in the area, each digger must be authenticated individually by the dumper truck using the Kerberos protocol, before the depositing of objects could be initiated.

6.3   Applying Kerberos to the digger and dumper truck

Initially encrypted messages are sent between the authentication server (AS) and the client (the digger) to allow a secret key to be sent to the client in order to begin to prepare for communication with the server (the dumper truck). The authentication server provides a secure means of obtaining shared keys to allow the communication of separate processes to begin.

The example shown in table 3 identifies the stages involved in authenticating the relationship between the digger and the dumper truck.

Table 3 Definitions of abbreviations used within Kerberos authentication

Identity	Key
Client	Digger (di)
Server	Dumper truck (du)
Key	K
Digger's secret key	Kdi
Dumper truck's secret key	Kdu
Secret key shared between digger and dumper truck	K(di du)
Authentication service	AS
Ticket granting service	TGS
Nonce	n
Timestamp	t
Start time of valid ticket	t1
Finish time of valid ticket	t2

Initially the digger receives a ticket and session key from AS to access the TGS, therefore a ticket for client digger (di) to access a server dumper truck (du) is defined as:

$$\{di, du, t1, t2, K_{(di\ du)}\}K_{du} \Rightarrow \{ticket_{(di,\ du)}\}\ K_{du}$$

Table 4 identifies the various stages involved in forming communication between the digger and dumper truck using the Kerberos protocol.

Any message encrypted in K(di du) is said to be secure and trustworthy as only the specified digger and dumper truck are able to decrypt the message, having used either the diggers or dumper trucks secret key during encryption. Each message has an expiration time and timestamp encrypted within it to ensure that client-server interaction is only available for a specified period. Each ticket has a lifetime of, in this case, one hour so can be used with other digger-dumper truck communication sessions, however authenticators must be regenerated with each new connection. This ensures that attackers can not impersonate the digger as the ticket becomes worthless after the specified time has expired.

Table 4 Stages involved in authentication of the digger by the dumper truck using the Kerberos Protocol

Header	Message	Notes
1) di → AS	di, TGS, n	Client, di request for the authentication server, AS to generate ticket to communicate with ticket granting service TGS
2) AS → di	{KdiTGS, n} Kdi, {ticket (di,TGS)} KTGS	AS replies with a message containing a ticket encrypted in its secret key along with a nonce in order to communicate with the TGS
3) di → TGS	{auth(du)} KduTGS, {ticket(du,TGS)} KTGS, du, n	di requests that the TGS replies by supplying a ticket for communication with a particular server, du
4) TGS → di	{Kdidu,n} KduTGS, {ticket(di,du)}Kdu	TGS verifies that the ticket initially generated by the AS is correct. If valid the TGS generates a new session key with a ticket encrypted in the server's secret key, Kdu, in order for communication between client and server to begin
5) di → du	{auth(di)} Kdidu, {ticket(di,du)} Kdu, request n	Client di sends the ticket to server du, along with an authenticator, used to confirm the identity of the client and a request encrypted in Kdidu. Authentication of the server is required by the client therefore a request for a nonce to be returned is made, to identify the freshness of the message
6) du → di (optional)	{n} Kdidu	As a request for authenticity is made by the client di, du sends the nonce to di encrypted in Kdidu

6.4   Construction of authenticating Petri nets

This process is then integrated within the Petri nets for both the digger and the dumper truck. Coloured, timed and hierarchical Petri nets are all used to ensure the main structure of the Petri net is not affected by this authentication and the actual process of authentication and communication does not exceed beyond a specified time period.

Coloured Petri nets are used to allow choices to be made about the authentication during the execution of the Petri net itself, for instance a "valid" and "invalid" coloured token coming from the place "request server ticket from TGS", as shown in Figure 9. If the "Not valid" transition is fired, the digger must begin the authentication process again, by requesting a TGS ticket from the Authentication Server.

Kerberos involves the use of timestamps to ensure the client-server session only lasts for a specified time period, after which the ticket request process must begin again. This is where t-timed Petri nets are used, not only to ensure the timestamp is not exceeded but also to ensure that the actual stages involved in requesting and receiving the tickets and authenticating the digger with the dumper truck are monitored.

The timings on the transitions as seen in Figures 9 and 10 respectively are set to (0.5, 2) seconds to represent the minimum and maximum length of time required before a transition can be fired. This ensures both that a transition does not take an excessive amount of time to fire and that enough time is allocated for tasks to be completed, therefore allowing tickets and messages to be sent and received between the digger, AS and TGS dumper truck. The timestamp is set to 60 minutes to allow the digger to deposit more than one load into the dumper truck, in addition to avoiding threats from attackers impersonating the digger.

Hierarchical Petri nets, as described in [9] are not directly implemented within the respective Petri nets. Instead a *plug in module* is inserted into the transitions of the Petri net, requiring a separate thread of execution to be implemented. This allows the actual stages involved during authentication to be identified, without increasing the complexity of the original Petri nets. The contents of the plug in module can be inserted or removed without affecting the structure of the Petri net itself.

The plug in module would be inserted between the transitions "detect_dumper" and "move" in the digger Petri net, as seen in Figure 3, to allow authentication between the robots to be implemented, a similar process will be carried out on board the dumper truck. These threads must begin and end with transitions. Separate tokens could be passed through this module so as not to interfere with the progression through the structure of the main Petri net and enable complete concurrency in the Petri nets.

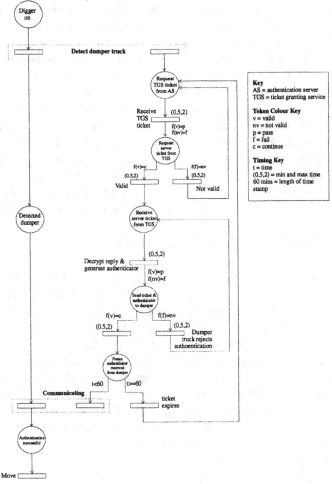

Figure 4 Inserting an authentication module within the digger Petri net

After authentication has occurred the digger is able to deposit its objects into the dumper truck, therefore allowing both robots to continue to completion of their own individual tasks.

To summarise, the Kerberos protocol is intended to allow the dumper truck to authenticate the digger, before the digger is able to deposit its load. Encrypted messages are initially sent between the *authentication server (AS),* situated within the *key distribution centre,* and the *client* (the digger) in order for tickets encrypted in the secret key to be sent to the various services within Kerberos. This enables communication between the digger and dumper truck to begin. After a new session key and ticket, encrypted in the *server's* (the dumper truck) secret key, has been generated by the *ticket granting service (TGS),* the digger may begin its communication with the dumper truck, provided authentication has been granted. This will be achieved by inserting a plug in module between the "detect_dumper" and "move", and "detect_digger" and "wait" transitions in the digger and dumper truck Petri nets, respectively.

After authentication and communication between the digger and dumper truck has occurred, each robot is able to continue with their specified tasks and complete the atomic actions described within the transitions of the Petri net.

7   Conclusions and Future Work

In terms of overall dependability, it can be concluded that the concurrent program, generated through the Petri net for both the digger and the dumper truck was for the most part successful. It completed the tasks set before it with only minor difficulties, largely caused through mechanical failure, and demonstrated the use of the software adequately. The execution of the Petri net was also efficient enough that the real-time requirements of the system can be considered to have been met, further encouraging the development of the methods involved. Despite this, there is still a way to go before the system could be considered completely dependable. The few minor problems, such as the failed colouring of the tokens could be catastrophic should they occur on board a full-size excavator, or even a larger model, and it is by these terms that any ultimate success or failure must be measured.

It should also be noted, that the legOS C language was chosen over any versions of java [11] in part because of the additional memory that running a Java virtual machine and writing object-oriented code requires. This system was intended to be useable on board systems with limited memory requirements and as such a degree of failure must be accepted due to the huge excess of memory taken up by the Petri net structure and management.

It is in these two areas, of token colouring and memory usage, that any future work should be targeted. For the purposes of colouring the tokens, the TRAMP toolkit is already in a position to simulate this colouring, and so the option of partially automating the final executable code is already a possibility. However, the difficulties faced with memory usage remain, and without further work in this area, it will soon be impossible to run code of any complexity on board an RCX, or equivalent system. This is a problem which must be faced in the immediate future, and, if necessary, a decision taken on whether to maintain complete Petri net structure, or to minimise the cost to memory.

Finally, it would be of interest to fully implement the Kerberos protocol within the Petri net plug-in. This implementation of this extension, whilst verified, is as yet some time away, but the mechanisms are in place to provide for this addition to the Petri net, so in the future this is likely to emerge.

8 References

[1] D. Baum, "Dave Baum's Definitive Guide to Lego Mindstorms." Apress 1999.

[2] D.A. Bradley and D.W. Seward "Developing real-time autonomous excavation – the LUCIE story." *Proceedings of the IEEE Conference on Decision and Control*, 1995, vol 3, pp 3028-3033

[3] P. Buchholz. "A hierarchical View on GCSPNs and its Impact on Qualitative and Quantitative Analysis." *Journal of Distributed Computing*, 1992, vol 15, pp 207 – 224

[4] A. Caloini, G. Magnani and M. Pezze. "A Technique for Designing Robotic Control Systems Based on Petri Nets." *IEEE Transactions on Control Systems Technology*, 1998, vol 6, no 1, pp 72-87.

[5] S. Cavalieri, A. DiStefano and O. Mirabella. "Impact of Fieldbus on Communication in Robotic Systems." *IEEE Transactions on Robotics and Automation*, 1997, vol 13, no. 1, pp 30-48

[6] A. Chandler. "An Object-Oriented Petri Net Toolkit for Mechatronic System Design." Ph.D. thesis, Dept. Engineering, Lancaster University, UK 1999.

[7] A. Chandler, A. Heyworth, L. Blair and D. Seward. "Testing Petri Nets for Mobile Robots Using Gröbner Bases." *21st International Conference on Application and Theory of Petri Nets: Software Engineering and Petri Nets Workshop Proceedings*, 2000, pp 21-34.

[8] G. Coulouris, J. Dollimore and T. Kindberg. "Distributed Systems Concepts and Design." (3rd Edition) Addison-Wesley Publishing Company, 2000.

[9] K. Jensen. "Coloured Petri Nets: Basic Concepts, Analysis Methods and Practical Use." Volume 1. Spring-Verlag. 1997.

[10] "Lego Mindstorms." http://www.legomindstorms.com/, 2001

[11] "LeJOS." http://lejos.sourceforge.net/, 2001

[12] S. Mascaro. And H.H. Asada. "Hand-in-Glove Human-Machine Interface and Interactive Control: Task Process Modelling Using Dual Petri Nets." *Proceedings - IEEE International Conference on Robotics and Automation*, 1998, vol 2, pp 1289-1295

[13] R.M. Needham and M.D. Schroeder. "Using Encryption for Authentication in Large Networks of Computers." *Comms, ACM*, 1978, vol 21, pp 993-9.

[14] M. Noga. "LegOS." http://www.noga.de/legOS/, 1999

[15] C. Pace and D.W. Seward. "Development of a Safety Manager for an Autonomous Mobile Robot," *Proceedings of the 29th International Symposium on Robotics* (ISR98), 1998 pp 277-282

[16] J.L. Petersen. "Petri Net Theory and the Modelling of Systems." Prentice-Hall 1981.

[17] D. Pilaud. "Efficient Automatic Code Generation for Embedded Systems." *Microprocessors and Microsystems*, 1997, v20, no.8, pp 501-504

[18] D. Seward and F. Margrave. "LUCIE the robot excavator – design for system safety." *Proceedings – IEEE International Conference on Robotics and Autonomy*, 1996, pp 963-968

[19] D. Simon, E.C. Castaneda and P. Freedman. "Design and Analysis of Synchronisation for Real-Time Closed-Loops Control in Robotics." *IEEE Transactions on Control Systems Technology*, 1998, vol 6, no. 4, pp 445-461

[20] I.H. Suh, H.J. Yeo, J.H. Kim, J.S. Ryoo, S.R. Oh, C.W. Lee and B.H. Lee. "Design of a Supervisory Control System for Multiple Robotic Systems." *IEEE International Conference on Intelligent Robots and Systems*, 1996, vol 1, pp 332-339

Chapter 6

DEADLOCK FREE CONTROL IN AUTOMATED GUIDED VEHICLE SYSTEMS

Maria Pia Fanti

Dipartimento di Elettrotecnica ed Eletteronica- Politecnico di Bari -Italy

Abstract   Automated Guided Vehicle Systems (AGVSs) are material handling devices playing an important role in modern manufacturing. This paper presents a control strategy to avoid deadlock and collisions in AGVSs. A coloured Petri net modelling method allows a simple synthesis of a real-time closed loop control policy managing the path selection and the movement of vehicles in the AGVS. The proposed control scheme manages the AGVS traffic by avoiding deadlocks and undesirable situations (restricted deadlocks), which inevitably evolve to a deadlock in the next future.

Key words   Automated Guided Vehicle Systems, deadlock avoidance, Coloured Petri nets.

1.   INTRODUCTION

Material handling devices are one of essential components of Automated Manufacturing Systems (AMSs). Among different employed equipments, Automated Guided Vehicle Systems (AGVSs) are regarded as an efficient and flexible alternative for material handling [12], [22]. Each vehicle follows a guide-path under the computer control that assigns route, tasks, velocity, etc.. The AGVS programming capability for path selection and reconfiguration easily accommodates changes in production volume and mix of AMSs. However, the design of AGVSs has to take into account some management problems such as collision and deadlock [12], [26]. In particular, for AGVS control there are two kinds of deadlocks [14], [25]: the

P. Ezhilchelvan and A. Romanovsky (eds.), Concurrency in Dependable Computing, 105–126.

first one is caused by limited buffers and can be eliminated by adding a central buffer; the second deadlock is caused by sharing the same guidepath.

This paper focuses on the second type of deadlock problem and uses a standard technique for vehicle management of AGVS, i.e., zone control. More precisely, in this type of traffic management, the guidepaths are separated in disjoint zones and deadlock occurs when a set of AGVs competes for a set of zones detained by vehicles of the same set.

Deadlock has been widely studied for AMS and the most used approaches to describe interactions between parts and resources are Petri nets [1], [3], [10], [21], [24], automata [13], [18], [19]) and digraphs [2], [5], [6], [7], [23]. Following these approaches, Lee and Lin [14] face deadlock in AGVSs using high-level Petri nets and Yeh and Yeh [25] introduce a deadlock avoidance algorithm based on a digraph approach. The first paper proposes a deadlock avoidance policy based on a look-ahead procedure on the complete path of vehicles and the second applies a strategy based on a one-step look ahead. However, such algorithms do not prevent some situation, known in the literature as "restricted deadlock" [1], [2], [5], [23]. When a restricted deadlock occurs, the system is not in deadlock condition but some vehicles remain permanently in circular wait, partly because some of them are blocked and partly because the control prevents them from moving. In a recent paper [20], Reveliotis solves deadlock problems in AGVS using a variation of Banker's algorithm and a dynamic route planning that performs the route selection in real-time.

This paper presents a procedure to control the assignment of new paths and the acquisition of next zone. The proposed control scheme is able to avoid collisions and deadlocks in AGVSs with unidirectional paths and some lanes with bidirectional paths. Indeed bidirectional paths are used to gain efficiency and flexibility in manufacturing systems, but they can frequently incur deadlock and restricted deadlock. So we introduce a control scheme able to avoid every type of circular wait conditions. The starting point of the control procedure is the graph-theoretic analysis of the interactions between parts and resources for AMS [5], [6]. The obtained control policies are slightly modified to be applied to AGVSs in which paths change dynamically and the number of vehicles in the system is fixed. Moreover, we propose Petri nets (PNs) and coloured Petri nets (CPNs) to model the AGVS and to implement the control strategies working on the basis of the knowledge of the system state. To this aim, following the approach proposed by Ezpeleta and Colom [4], the AGVS is modelled considering two main elements: the set of paths that the travelling vehicles have to follow and the movements of vehicles in the system. The vehicle paths are modelled in a modular way by ordinary finite capacity PNs that give the skeleton of the

CPN. On the other hand, the CPN models the dynamics of the AGVS: tokens are vehicles and the path that each AGV has to complete gives the token colour. The CPN peculiarities guarantee two benefits to the controller synthesis. First, as several authors point out [4], [8], [16], the CPNs allow a concise modelling of dynamic behaviour in industrial applications and are graphically oriented languages for design specification and verification of systems. Second, the deadlock avoidance policies proposed by Fanti et al. [5], [6] are synthesized without building digraphs but using the PN and the CPN incidence matrices.

In this framework, the proposed control structure consists of two levels. The first level (*route scheduler*) focuses on the vehicle route planning i.e., it proposes paths to assign to each vehicle mission. The second level (*real-time controller*) manages vehicle traffic and it is in charge of making decisions on path assignments and vehicle moves so that collisions and deadlocks are avoided. The paper focuses on the second level: the real time controller specification. Even if the algorithms to synthesize the real-time controller are obtained by means of digraph tools that efficiently describe interactions between zones and vehicles, such digraphs are not suited to model the dynamic of the whole AGVS. On the contrary, CPNs represent a powerful tool capable of modelling AGVS dynamics and implementing the discrete event control strategies.

The organization of the paper is the following. Section 2 describes the proposed AGVS control architecture, Sections 3 and 4 model the vehicle paths and the system dynamics respectively. Moreover, Section 5 recalls previous results and defines the relations between Petri nets and digraphs. Finally, Section 6 introduces the controller synthesis and Section 7 draws the conclusions.

2. THE AGVS DESCRIPTION AND CONTROL STRUCTURE

We consider an AGVS layout involving unidirectional guidepaths and some lanes with bidirectional guidepaths. The AGVS is divided into several disjoint zones and each zone can represent a workstation that a vehicle can visit, an intersection of several paths and a straight lane (see Figure 1). Moreover, the AGVS possesses a docking station where idle vehicles park. The set of zones of the AGVS is denoted by $Z=\{z_i \ i=1,...,N_Z\}$ where z_i for $i=2,..., N_Z$ represents a zone and z_1 denotes the docking station. Besides, the set $V=\{v_j: j=1,..., N_V\}$ represents the set of vehicles available in the system.

Since each zone can accommodate only one vehicle at a time, zones z_i for $i=2,\ldots,N_Z$ have unit capacity. On the contrary, the docking station can detain all the vehicles of the system and it is modelled by zone z_1 with capacity equal to N_V.

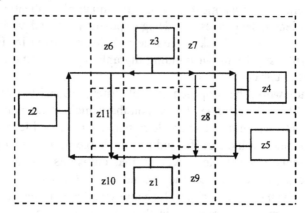

Figure 1. A zone-control AGVS where lines denote guide paths and sketched squares denote zones.

Example 1. The AGVS shown by Figure 1 connects four workstations (denoted in the figure by z_2, z_3, z_4 and z_5) and the docking station z_1. The load/transfer stations located close the workstations represent five zones (z_1, z_2, z_3, z_4 and z_5) and other six zones denote the intersections of the paths and the parts of lanes (z_6, z_7, z_8, z_9, z_{10}, and z_{11}). Let us suppose that the paths z_6-z_3, z_3-z_7, z_{10}-z_1, and z_9-z_1 are bidirectional and the others are unidirectional. We consider five vehicles in the system, so that the docking station has capacity equal to 5.

Each vehicle starts its travel from a zone z_i, it reaches a designed zone z_j where it loads a part, and then it unloads the part in the destination zone z_k and concludes the travel to the docking station. Even if the route of an AGV may change dynamically, we suppose that the route $r(v)$ assigned to the vehicle $v \in V$ ends to the docking station, i.e. it is of the following form: $r(v)=(z_i \ldots z_j \ldots z_k \ldots z_1)$. As Reveliotis [20] points out, this formal assumption is useful to guarantee that, starting from any configuration reached by the AGVS, each idle vehicle is able to go back to the docking station, so that it does not remain blocked or starved in a zone. Indeed, a new routing can be assigned to an AGV waiting for destination in the docking station or to a vehicle performing its route to return to the docking station. In the sequel, rr(v) denotes the residual route that v∈ *V* has to visit to complete its travel starting from a system configuration. Obviously it is a sub sequence of r(v).

A control structure is proposed to manage the AGVS traffic avoiding deadlock and collisions (see Figure 2).

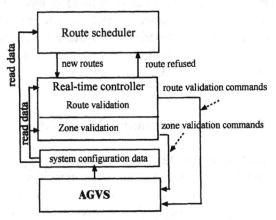

Figure 2. The AGVS control architecture

Specifically, the control scheme is constituted of two levels. The first higher level (*route scheduler*) determines the paths to assign to each AGV and selects the situations in which it is necessary to alter the routing of a vehicle. More precisely, the route scheduler proposes a new path to a vehicle waiting for destination in the docking station or travelling in the system and informs of the potential path the second level (*real-time controller*) that proceeds to the first type of its decisions, i.e. the *route validation*. If the path is validated on the basis of the knowledge of the system configuration data, then the real-time controller assigns the route to the vehicle. On the contrary, the controller refuses the path and sends a message to the route scheduler that can propose a new path. Moreover, when a vehicle has to move to next zone, the AGVS requires the move permission to the real-time controller that performs its second decision, i.e., the *zone validation*. More precisely, an appropriate algorithm validates the zone to prevents deadlock and collisions, by enabling or inhibiting the AGV zone acquisition. Both levels perform decisions in closed loop on the basis of the system state knowledge.

In this paper, we deal with the second control level, i.e., the real time controller. In particular, a first strategy verifies if a path can be assigned to a vehicle (route validation) without incurring a restricted deadlock and a second strategy checks if a zone can be acquired (zone validation) so that the AGVS behaviour is deadlock and collision free.

3. THE PETRI NET MODELLING THE AGVS

The controller decisions are based on the system configuration knowledge. Hence it is necessary to formally describe and model the AGVS. In this section we propose a method to build in modular way the Petri net modelling all the paths assigned to each vehicle travelling in the system. This procedure does not describe the system layout but the routes that, starting from an AGVS condition, are assigned to the vehicles. So, if the route scheduler changes a path, then the Petri net must be consequently built again.

3.1 Overview of Ordinary Petri Nets

An ordinary (marked) Petri net is a bipartite digraph $PN=(P, T, F, m)$ where P is a set of places and T is a set of transitions [15]. The set of arcs $F\subset(P\times T) \cup(T\times P)$ is the flow relation. Given a PN and a node $x\in P\cup T$, the set $\bullet x=\{y\in P\cup T : (y,x)\in F\}$ is the preset of x while $x\bullet=\{y\in P\cup T : (x,y)\in F\}$ is the post-set of x.

The state of a PN is given by its current marking that is a mapping m: $P\to\overline{N}$ where $\overline{N}$ is the set of non-negative integers. m is described by a $|P|$-vector and the i-th component of m, indicated with m(p) represents the number of tokens pictured by dots in the i-th state place $p\in P$. Note that $|(.)|$ stands for the cardinality of the set (.).

The structure of the PN can be described by two matrices **O** and **I** of non-negative integers of dimension $|P|\times|T|$. The typical entries of **O** and **I** for an ordinary Petri net are given by:

$O(p,t)=1$ if $(t,p)\subset F$ else $O(p,t)=0$

$I(p,t)=1$ if $(p,t)\subset F$ else $I(p,t)=0$

Matrix **I-O** is called the incidence matrix of the Petri net. A transition $t\in T$ is enabled at a marking m if and only if (iff) for each $p\in \bullet t$, $m(p)>0$: this fact is denoted as $m[t>$. When fired, t gives a new marking m': this will be denoted as $m[t>m'$.

Petri nets fall in two classes: infinite and finite capacity PNs. The former allows each place to hold an unlimited number of tokens while the latter limits at least a place to a finite number of tokens it can hold. So the function K(p) with $p\in P$ denotes the capacity of p and it is the maximum number of token that place p can hold at a time. A transition $t\in T$ in a finite capacity PN is enabled in a marking m if for each $p\in P$ it holds:

$$m(p)\geq I(p,t) \tag{1}$$

and

$$K(p) \geq m(p) - I(p,t) + O(p,t) \qquad (2)$$

Firing an enabled transition t∈ T at m changes m in m' according to the equation:

$$m'(p) = m(p) - I(p,t) + O(p,t) \qquad (3)$$

3.2   The PN Modelling the AGV Paths

In our model the ordinary finite capacity Petri net $PN_v = (P_v, T_v, F_v, m_{ov})$ describes the path assigned to the vehicle v∈ V. The elements of PN_v are defined as follows. A place $z_i \in P_v$ denotes the zone $z_i \in Z$ and a token in z_i represents a vehicle that is in zone z_i. The transition set T_v models the moving of v∈ V between consecutive zones. Moreover, the set of arcs $F_v \subset (P_v \times T_v) \cup (T_v \times P_v)$ is defined as follows: if z_i and z_m are two consecutive zones in the route r(v), then transition t_{im} belongs to T_v and it is such that $t_{im} \in \bullet z_m$ and $t_{im} \in z_i \bullet$.

If $r(v) = (z_i ... z_j ... z_l)$ is the route of v∈ V, then the associated Petri net PN_v begins with $z_i \in P_v$ and ends with z_l. When v∈ V is waiting for destination in the docking station, then the associated Petri net is formed by only one place z_l and no transitions. Besides, the initial marking m_{ov} is such that $m_{ov}(z_i) = 1$ and $m_{ov}(z_j) = 0$ for each $z_j \in P_v$ such that $z_j \neq z_i$.

The model of the whole AGVS describing the travelling processes of all vehicles in the system is obtained by merging the defined Petri nets PN_v for $v = 1, ..., N_V$. The merged $PN = (P, T, F, m_0)$ is a net such that:

$$P = \bigcup_{v \in V} P_v \qquad (4)$$

$$T = \bigcup_{v \in V} T_v \qquad (5)$$

$$F = \bigcup_{v \in V} F_v \qquad (6)$$

For each $z_j \in P$ $m_0(z_j) = 1$ if there exists v∈ V such that z_j is the first zone (7) of r(v) else $m_0(z_j) = 0$
$m_0(z_1) = |\{v : v \in V$ and z_1 is the first zone of $r(v)\}|$

We remark that the defined PN is self loop free and that there is one to one relation between zones and places. Moreover, there is just one transition between an ordered couple of places.

In our model, the introduction of the capacity leads to a very simple condition to enable the transitions. Since $K(z_1) = N_V$ and $K(z_i) = 1$ for each

$z_i \in P$ with $z_i \neq z_1$, a transition t_{ij} is enabled in a marking m if the following conditions hold:

$m(z_i)=1$ and $m(z_j)=0$ for z_i, $z_j \in P$ with $z_i \neq z_j$ and $z_j \neq z_1$ (8)

$m(z_i)=1$ for $z_j=z_1$ (9)

Example 2. Let us consider the AGVS described in Example 1 and the following routes assigned to the AGVs:

$\mathbf{r}(v_1)= (z_{10}, z_2, z_6, z_{11}, z_{10}, z_1)$, $\mathbf{r}(v_2)=(z_2, z_6, z_{11}, z_{10}, z_1)$,

$\mathbf{r}(v_3)=(z_3, z_6, z_{11}, z_{10}, z_1)$, $\mathbf{r}(v_4)= (z_{11}, z_{10}, z_1)$, $\mathbf{r}(v_5)= (z_1)$.

We remark that v_5 is a vehicle waiting for destination in the docking station. Figure 3 depicts the Petri net modelling the routes assigned to the vehicles travelling in the system.

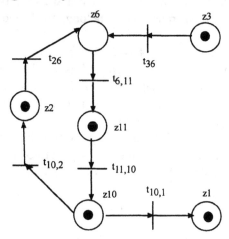

Figure 3. The Petri net PN modelling the vehicle routes for example 1.

4.   MODELLING THE AGVS DYNAMICS

A Coloured PN that integrates the PN modelling zones and paths with the model of the vehicles travelling in the system describes the AGVS behaviour. Moreover, the CPN model allows us to implement the discrete-event control system to manage the AGVS traffic.

To enlighten on the role of the Coloured PN, let us consider example 2 and a token in z_{10}. It enables either $t_{10,2}$ if the token represents v_1 or $t_{10,1}$ if the token represents v_2. The ordinary PN does not distinguish the vehicle, so to model this feature colours must be introduced.

4.1   Overview of Coloured Petri Nets

A marked coloured Petri net is a 7-tuple $CPN=(P, T, Co, \mathbf{C}^+, \mathbf{C}^-, \Omega, M_0)$ where P is a set of places, T is a set of transitions, Co is a colour function defined from $P \cup T$ to a set of finite and not empty sets of colours [4], [11]. Co maps each place $p \in P$ to a set of possible token colours $Co(p)$ and each transition $t \in T$ to a set of possible occurrence colours $Co(t)$. $\mathbf{C}^+$ and $\mathbf{C}^-$ are the post-incidence and the pre-incidence $|P| \times |T|$ matrices respectively, so that $\mathbf{C}^+(p,t)$ associates to each set of colour of $Co(t)$ a set of colour of $Co(p)$. $\mathbf{C}^+(p,t)$ ($\mathbf{C}^-(p,t)$) is represented by means of an arc from t to p (from p to t) labelled with the function $\mathbf{C}^+(p,t)$ ($\mathbf{C}^-(p,t)$). The set Ω is defined as follows: $\Omega = \cup_{x \in P \cup T}\{C(x)\}$.

A marking M is a mapping defined over P so that $M(p)$ is a set of elements of $Co(p)$, also with repeated elements (i.e., a multiset) corresponding to token colours in the place p. M_0 is the initial marking of the net. As in the ordinary Petri nets, we can define the matrix $\mathbf{C}=\mathbf{C}^+-\mathbf{C}^-$ as the flow matrix.

A transition $t \in T$ is enabled at a marking M with respect to a colour $c \in Co(t)$ iff for each $p \in \bullet t$, $M(p) \geq \mathbf{C}^-(p,t)(c)$: this fact is denoted as $M[t(c)>$. When fired, this gives a new marking M': this will be denoted as $M[t(c)>M'$. For what concerns the definition of multisets and operations on multisets, the reader can refer to [11].

4.2   The Coloured Petri Net Model

In our model P and T are respectively the sets of places and transitions previously defined. Indeed, the introduced ordinary PN represents the skeleton of the CPN. Each vehicle $v \in V$ is modelled by a coloured token and its token colour is $<rr(v)>$ where $rr(v)$ is the residual path that the vehicle has to follow to reach the docking station.

The state of the AGVS is represented by the marking of the CPN, i.e., if $M(z_i)=<rr(v)>$ then vehicle v is in zone z_i and its colour $<rr(v)>$ is the sequence of zones that v has to visit starting from the current marking. Consequently, the colour domain of place $z_i \in P$ is:

$Co(z_i)=\{<rr>$ where rr is a sequence of zones and z_i is the first zone of $rr\}$.

Moreover, *Co* associates with each transition t_{im} a set of possible occurrence colours:

$Co(t_{im})=\{<rr>$ such that **rr** is a sequence of zones and z_i and z_m are respectively the first and the second element of **rr**$\}$.

Here, the CPN is represented by the incidence matrix **C** that contains a row for each place $z_i \in P$ and a column for each transition $t \in T$. Each element $C(z_i,t)$ is a function that assigns an element of $Co(t)$ with $t \in T$ to an element of $Co(z_i)$ with $z_i \in P$. The incident matrix is computed as $\mathbf{C}=\mathbf{C}^+-\mathbf{C}^-$ where the pre- and the post-incidence matrices $\mathbf{C}^-$ and $\mathbf{C}^+$, respectively, are defined as follows:

1. for each $(z_i,t_{im}) \in F$ $\mathbf{C}^-(z_i,t_{im})="I_D"$ where I_D stands for "the function makes no transformation in the elements", otherwise $\mathbf{C}^-(z_i,t_{im})=0$. This definition means that each token leaving a zone $z_i \in P$ is not modified;

2. for each $(t_{im},z_m) \in F$, $\mathbf{C}^+(z_m,t_{im})=UP$ where UP is a function that updates the colour $<rr>$ with the colour $<rr'>$, otherwise $\mathbf{C}^+(z_m,t_{im})=0$. More precisely, **rr'** is the residual sequence of zones obtained from **rr** by cutting the first element z_i, When a token leaves z_i and reaches z_m, its colour, i.e., its residual path, is updated.

The set Ω is defined by $\Omega=\{Co(x) : x \in P \cup T\}$. Finally, considering that at the initial marking M_0 a route $r(v)$ is assigned to each $v \in V$, M_0 is defined as follows: if $z_i \in P$ is the first zone of a route $r(v)$ for some $v \in V$ then $M_0(z_i)=<r(v)>$ else $M_0(z_i)=<0>$.

Now, let us suppose that a vehicle $v \in V$ has to leave zone z_i to reach next zone z_m. In such a case transition t_{im} of the CPN at marking M is enabled if two conditions are verified:

C1) $M(z_m)=<0>$ if $m \neq 1$.

C2) $M(z_i) \geq \mathbf{C}^-(z_i,t_{im})(<rr(v)>)$ with $M(z_i)=<rr(v)>$ and $rr(v)=(z_i\ z_m, ...z_1)$.

The first condition refers to the conditions (8) and (9) of the ordinary finite capacity PN that can be verified by using the marking of the CPN. The second one represents the enabling condition of the CPN at marking M. Now, if $t_{im} \in T$ is enabled and fires, then the new marking M' such that $M[t_{im}(rr)>M'$ is the following:

$M'(z_i)= M(z_i)-\mathbf{C}^-(z_i,t_{im})(<rr(v)>)=<0>$,

$M'(z_m)=M(z_m)+\mathbf{C}^+(z_m,t_{im})(<rr(v)>)=<rr'(v)>$,

where $rr'(v)=(z_m, ...z_1)$ is obtained by applying function "UP" to $rr(v)=(z_i\ z_m, ...z_1)$.

An important information to implement the real time controller is the cardinality of the set of vehicles, which possess a route to follow at marking M and do not wait for destination in the docking station. This number is indicated by n(M) and is defined as follows: $n(M)=|\{v \in V \mid rr(v) \neq (r_1)\}|$

Example 3. Now, let consider the system described by Examples 1 and 2. Figure 4 represents the corresponding CPN model at the initial marking M_0 defined as follows: $M_0(z_{10})=<\mathbf{rr}(v_1)>=<(z_{10}, z_2, z_6, z_{11}, z_{10}, z_1)>$, $M_0(z_2)=<\mathbf{rr}(v_2)>=<(z_2, z_6, z_{11}, z_{10}, z_1)>$, $M_0(z_3)= <\mathbf{rr}(v_3)>=<(z_3, z_6, z_{11}, z_{10}, z_1)>$, $M_0(z_{11})= <\mathbf{rr}(v_4)>=<(z_{11}, z_{10}, z_1)>$, $M_0(z_1)=<\mathbf{rr}(v_5)>=<(z_1)>$.

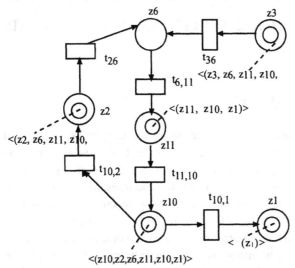

Figure 4. The CPN at marking M_0 for Example 3.

Note that the token colour in z_{10} enables $t_{10,2}$ and does not enable $t_{10,1}$. However, since $M_0(z_2)\neq<0>$, transition $t_{10,2}$ is inhibited by condition C1). For this example we obtain $n(M_0)=|\{v_1, v_2, v_3, v_4\}|=4$.

Before closing this section, we recall that two events can change the system state (i.e. the marking of the CPN) and trace the AGVS behaviour:
i) a new path **r** is assigned to a vehicle $v\in V$ (1-type event). This event is identified by the pair $\sigma_1=(v, \mathbf{r})$. Obviously, the first entry in the path **r** must be the zone currently held by v;
ii) a vehicle moves from a zone to another one (2-type event). This event is identified by the symbol $\sigma_2=v$.

The occurrence of a 1-type event $\sigma_1=(v_i, \mathbf{r})$ changes the skeleton of the CPN at the marking M. Indeed, a Petri net PN_{vi} is built to model the new path **r** assigned to vehicle v_i. Besides, the Petri nets PN_v with $v\in V$ and $v\neq v_i$ are built by considering the residual paths $\mathbf{rr}(v)$ for each $v\in V$. Hence, the

new merged net is obtained by equations (1)-(4) and it models the future
path of each vehicle after the occurred event.

On the other hand, when a 2-type event $\sigma_2 = v$ happens with $\mathbf{rr}(v) = (z_i \, z_m, \ldots z_1)$, transition t_{im} fires in the CPN and the marking M is updated
accordingly.

5.   DEADLOCK CONDITIONS, DIGRAPHS AND PETRI NETS

5.1   Previous Results

The approach used here to avoid deadlock and collisions is based on
some theoretical results obtained in the context of deadlock avoidance in
AMS, where parts in progress compete to acquire resources [5] [6]. More
precisely, in this context zones substitute resources and vehicles stand for
jobs. Moreover, the output of the system is represented by the zone z_1 that
can accommodate all the vehicles. So, following the mentioned results, all
the possible and current interactions between vehicles and zones can be
respectively described by means of two digraphs named *Route digraph* and
Transition digraph. The former digraph $D_R = (N, E_R)$ shows the specific order
in which zones appear in all the paths assigned to the vehicles in the AGVS.
Each vertex in N corresponds to a zone z_i, so that the same symbol is used
for vertices and zones, i.e., $N = Z$. An edge e_{im} directed from z_i to z_m, belongs
to E_R iff z_m immediately follows z_i in some $\mathbf{r}(v)$ with $v \in V$. Clearly, digraph
D_R describes a "static" situation and is not able to show the move of
vehicles. So to represent the dynamic interaction between vehicles and
zones, we introduce the Transition Digraph $D_T = (N, E_T)$ that is a subdigraph of
D_R. In particular, while the vertex set still coincides with the zone set, the
edge set is defined as follows: $e_{im} \in E_T$ iff there exists a vehicle $v \in V$ holding
z_i and requiring z_m as next zone. As proven by Fanti, et al. [5], the Transition
Digraph allows an easy detection of deadlock states according to the
following proposition:

Proposition 1. The AGVS is in deadlock condition in the current state iff
there exists a cycle in the transition digraph that does not contain the zone z_1.

Example 4. Let us consider the system of Example 1 where five vehicles
perform the following travels: $\mathbf{r}(v_1) = (z_2, z_6, z_{11}, z_{10}, z_1)$, $\mathbf{r}(v_2) = (z_6, z_{11}, z_{10},$

z_1), $r(v_3)=(z_3, z_6, z_{11}, z_{10}, z_1)$, $r(v_4)=(z_{10}, z_1)$, $r(v_5)=(z_1, z_{10}, z_2, z_6, z_3, z_7, z_8, z_9, z_1)$. Figure 5 shows the corresponding route digraph that exhibits two cycles not including z_1: $\gamma_1=(\{z_6,z_3\},\{e_{63},e_{36}\})$, $\gamma_2=(\{z_6, z_{11}, z_{10}, z_2,\},\{e_{6,11}, e_{11,10}, e_{10,1}, e_{1,6}\})$. Finally, considering the system in a state with $rr(v_i)=r(v_i)$ for $i=1,...,5$, the current interactions between vehicles and zones are described by the transition digraph exhibited by Figure 6.

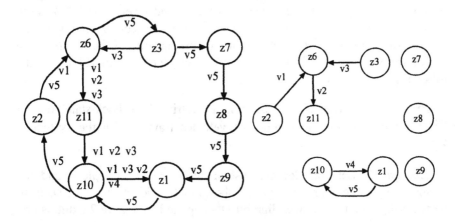

Figure 5. Digraph D_R for Example 4   *Figure 6.* Digraph D_T for Example 4.

The control actions to avoid deadlock consists of inhibiting or enabling the occurrence of some 1-type or 2-type events, depending on the current state of the AGVS. Starting from Proposition 1, a simple deadlock avoidance policy can be defined, based on a look-ahead procedure of only one step. More precisely, when an event has to occur, the policy builds the new transition digraph D_T and inhibits the event iff such a digraph contains a cycle not including z_1. As shown in Fanti et al. [5] this control algorithm might lead the system to a situation that is called *restricted deadlock*. More precisely, although the system is not in a deadlock state, it inevitably incurs a permanent blocking caused by the control inhibition. As it is proven, a restricted deadlock can happen only if the cycles of D_R enjoy a particular property that can be exhibited using a further digraph, $D^2_R=(N^2, E^2_R)$, named Second level digraph and obtained from D_R as follows. Denoting by $\{\gamma_1, \gamma_2, ..., \gamma_M\}$ the complete set of the cycles of D_R not including r_1, we associate a vertex $\gamma_k \in N^2$ to each cycle γ_k. Moreover, an edge e^2_{kh} is in E^2_R iff the following two conditions hold true: a) γ_h and γ_k have only one vertex in common (say z_m); b) there exists a path r requiring zones z_i, z_m and z_p in strict order of succession and e_{im} is an edge of cycle γ_h while e_{mp} is an edge of cycle γ_k.

Now let γ^2 be a cycle from $D^2{}_R$ (second level cycle) and let Γ^2 be the subset of second level cycles enjoying the following property: $\gamma^2 \in \Gamma^2$ iff the cycles associated with the vertices of γ^2 are all disjoined but for one vertex, common to all of them. Moreover, let the capacity of a cycle γ (denoted by $C(\gamma)$) be defined as the number of zones involved in such a cycle. Analogously, let us define the capacity of a second level cycle $C(\gamma^2)$ as the number of distinct zones involved in all the cycles corresponding to the vertices of γ^2. Finally, let $C^2{}_0$ be the minimum capacity of the second level cycles from Γ^2 ($C^2{}_0 = \infty$ if Γ^2 is empty). Now, Fanti et al. [5] prove the following proposition:

Proposition 2. The AGVS can be in a "restricted deadlock state" only if Γ^2 is not empty and the number of vehicles travelling in the system is $\geq (C^2{}_0 - 1)$.

Example 5. Let consider the system described in example 4 and the correspondig route dugraph. Figure 5 shows that cycles γ_1 and γ_2 of D_R have vertex z_6 in common. Hence, digraph $D^2{}_R$ depicted by Figure 7 exhibits one cycle pertaining to Γ^2 and the minimum second level cycle capacity is $C^2{}_0 = C(\gamma_1) + C(\gamma_2) = 5$. By proposition 2, since five vehicles travel in the AGVS, the system is not restricted deadlock free.

Figure 7. Digraph $D^2{}_R$ for Example 5

5.2   Relations between Petri Nets and digraphs

In this section we establish the relation between the described Petri net model and the introduced basic digraph tools to detect deadlocks. To this aim, we remind that a digraph containing N nodes is completely characterized by its (N×N) adjacency matrix [9]. We assume that the (j,i)-entry of the adjacency matrix is equal to one iff the digraph contains an arc from the i-th node to the j-th one.

Modelling the AGVS by the CPN, it is possible to implement the procedures avoiding deadlock without building D_R and D_T. Indeed we show that the incidence matrices of the PN and the CPN modelling the AGVS behaviour allow us to obtain the adjacency matrix of D_R and D_T.

Now let consider the $(|P| \times |P|)$ matrix $\mathbf{A_R} = \mathbf{O} \ \mathbf{I}^T$ obtained by a Boolean product. It is easy to show that $\mathbf{A_R}$ is the adjacency matrix of D_R. In fact, if there exists $t \in T$ such that $\mathbf{O}(z_i,t)=1$ and $\mathbf{I}(z_j,t)=1$, i.e., $t \in z_i \bullet$ and $t \in \bullet z_j$, then $\mathbf{A_R}(j,i)=1$. On the other hand, by the construction of D_R, we obtain $e_{ij} \in E_R$.

The transition digraph depends on the marking of the CPN. So to build the adjacency matrix of D_T, we define the $(|P| \times |T|)$ matrix $\mathbf{I_M}$ such that $\mathbf{I_M}(z_i,t_{ij})=1$ if there is a coloured token in $z_i \in P$ enabling $t_{ij} \in T$, otherwise $\mathbf{I_M}(z_i,t_{ij})=0$. Clearly, $\mathbf{I_M}$ depends on the marking M of the CPN and can be built by the following algorithm:

Algorithm 1

Step 1   Set i=1

Step 2   If $M(z_i) \neq <0>$ and z_j is the second resource of $<rr>=M(z_i)$ then
$\mathbf{I_M}(z_i,t_{ij})=1$

Step 3   If i<|P| then i=i+1, go to step 2

Step 4 $\mathbf{A_T} = \mathbf{O} \ (\mathbf{I_M})^T$ (Boolean product).

The $(|P| \times |P|)$-matrix $\mathbf{A_T} = \mathbf{O} \ (\mathbf{I_M})^T$ has a clear meaning. Namely, the (j,i)-entry of $\mathbf{A_T}$ is unit iff there exists a coloured token in z_i enabling the acquisition of zone z_j. But this is equivalent saying that $e_{ij} \in E_T$ and it leads to the conclusion that $\mathbf{A_T}$ is the adjacency matrix of the transition digraph.

6.   REAL-TIME CONTROLLER SYNTHESIS

This section describes the two activities of the real time controller: the *route validation* and the *zone validation*.

6.1   Zone Validation

Implementing the zone validation requires that any transition (2-type event) of the CPN be enabled according to an exogenous logical condition based on a one-step look ahead procedure. To this aim, we introduce a control place set P_C and an arc set $F \subset (P_C \times T)$. A place $p_{im} \in P_C$ is added for each transition $t_{im} \in T$ so that $p_{im} \in \bullet t_{im}$, $p_{im} \notin t \bullet$ if $t \neq t_{im}$, while $\bullet p_{im}$ is empty. Note that transitions $t_{i1} \in T$ do not require any control because their occurrence do not determine deadlocks and collisions.

A control function sets the marking of the control place as follows:

$m(p_{im})=1$ if the firing of t_{im} does not determine a deadlock in the new marking M' of the CPN such that $M[t_{im}>M'$; $m(p_{im})=0$ otherwise.

So let us suppose that the CPN is at the marking M and that transition t_{im} is colour enabled, i.e. $M(z_i)=<(z_i\ z_m, \ldots z_1)>$. In such a case, the controller executes the following Zone Validation Algorithm (ZVA).

ZVA

A1 If $M(z_m)\neq<0>$ by C1) the transition can not fire, the zone is not validated. Go to step A5.

A2 If $M(z_m)=<0>$ then the controller determines the new marking:
$M'(z_i)=<0>$
$M'(z_m)=<z_m, \ldots z_1>$
$M'(z)=M(z)$ for each $z\in P$ with $z\neq z_m$, and $z\neq z_i$

A3 Algorithm 1 provides matrices $I_{M'}$ and A_T.

A4 A depth-first search algorithm [17] is applied to A_T: if the search finds a cycle not including z_1 then $m(p_{im})=0$ and go to step A5 else $m(p_{im})=1$ and go to step A6.

A5 the zone is not validated, the behaviour of the AGVS continues with the CPN at marking M.

A6 the zone is validated and t_{im} fires, the behaviour of the AGVS continues with the CPN at marking M'.

We remark that Step A1 allows us to avoid collisions and step A4 tests whether marking M' is a deadlock state or not.

6.2   Route Validation

The route validation consists in enabling or inhibiting 1-type events in order to avoid immediate deadlocks and restricted deadlocks as long as a new path is assigned to some vehicle. Let **r** be the path that the scheduler proposes for vehicle v_k and let M be the current marking of the CPN.

The real time controller has to validate the proposed route by using the Route Validation Algorithm (RVA) which consists of two phases. The first phase checks whether the new path causes a deadlock in the next state and the second phase verifies if a restricted deadlock can occur. The RVA works according to the following steps:

RVA

B1 Build the Petri net PN_{vk} associated with $r(v_k)=r$ and the Petri nets PN_v associated with each $r(v)=rr(v)$ with $v\in V$ and $v\neq v_k$.

B2 Build the new merged net PN' as defined by equations (1), (2), (3) and (4).

B3 Build the new coloured PN CPN' such that PN' is its skeleton and M'_0 is its initial marking. More precisely, the marking M' is defined as follows: $M'_0(z_i)=<rr(v)>$ if z_i is the first resource of $rr(v)$ for some $v \in V$, else $M'_0(z_i)=<0>$.

Phase 1

B4 Algorithm 1 provides matrices $I_{M'0}$ and A_T.

B5 A depth-first search algorithm [17] is applied to A_T: if the search finds a cycle not including z_1 then go to step B9 else go to Phase 2.

Phase 2

B6 Build matrix A_R

B7 Determine C^2_0.

B8 If $n(M'_0)<C^2_0-1$ then $r(v_k)$ is validated and the evolution of CPN' continues starting from M'_0 else go to B9.

B9 $r(v_k)$ is not validated and the evolution of the old CPN continues starting at marking M

By proposition 1, test B5 guarantees that the new marking M'_0 does not correspond to a deadlock state. On the other hand, test B8 assures that, as long as a new path is assigned, no restricted deadlock can occur when vehicles advance in their paths.

We conclude this section by presenting an example, which shows the two activities of the real-time controller.

Example 6. Once again let us consider the system of Example 1 described by the CPN at marking M_0 shown by Figure 4. Transition t_{36} is colour enabled, i.e., $M_0(z_3)=<rr(v_3)>=<(z_3, z_6, z_{11}, z_{10}, z_1)>$. Now, if event $\sigma_2=(v_3)$ has to occur, then the controller applies the ZVA:

A1 $M_0(z_6)=<0>$ then t_{36} is enabled by condition C1).

A2 $M'(z_3)=M_0(z_3)-C^-(z_3,t_{36})(<(z_3, z_6, z_{11}, z_{10}, z_1)>)=<0>$,
$M'(z_6)=M_0(z_6)+C^+(z_6,t_{36})(<(z_3,z_6,z_{11},z_{10},z_1)>)=<z_6, z_{11}, z_{10}, z_1>$
$M'(z)=M_0(z)$ for each $z \in P$ with $z \neq z_3$ and $z \neq z_6$.

A3 Algorithm 1 gives $I_{M'}$ and A_T

A4 The depth search algorithm applied to A_T finds the cycle $\gamma=(\{z_6,z_{11},z_{10},z_2\},\{e_{6,11}, e_{11,10}, e_{10,2}, e_{26}\})$ shown by the Transition digraph of Figure 8. So, we put $m(p_{36})=0$: the zone is not validated and t_{36} does not fire.

A5 The behaviour of the AGV continues modelled by the CPN at marking M_0.

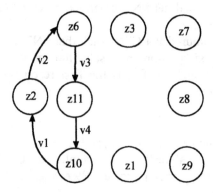

Figure 8. Digraph D_T for Example 6.

Now let us suppose that the previous CPN is at the following marking M shown by Figure 9: $M(z_1)=<rr(v_5)>=<(z_1)>$, $M(z_2)=<rr(v_1)>=<(z_2, z_6, z_{11}, z_{10}, z_1)>$, $M(z_3)=<rr(v_3)>=<(z_3,z_6,z_{11},z_{10},z_1)>$, $M(z_6)=<rr(v_2)>=<(z_6, z_{11}, z_{10}, z_1)>$, $M(z_{10})= <rr(v_4)>=<(z_{10}, z_1)>$, $M(z_{11})=<0>$. The route scheduler tries to assign a new route to v_5 waiting in the docking station: $r(v_5)=<(z_1, z_{10}, z_2, z_6, z_3, z_7, z_8, z_9, z_1)>$. Since event $\sigma_1=(v_5,r)$ has to occur, the real time controller applies the RVA.

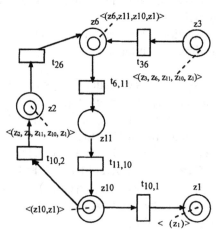

Figure 9. The CPN at marking M.

The algorithm builds the new PN' and the CPN' obtained considering $r(v_i)=rr(v_i)$ for $i=1,\dots,4$ and $r(v_5)=r$ (see Figure 10). The marking is updated at the new marking M' with $M'(z_1)=<r(v_5)>$, $M'(z_i)=M(z_i)$ for each $z_i \in P$

with $z_i \neq z_1$. The corresponding digraphs D_R, D_T and $D^2{}_R$ are depicted by Figures 5, 6 and 7, respectively.

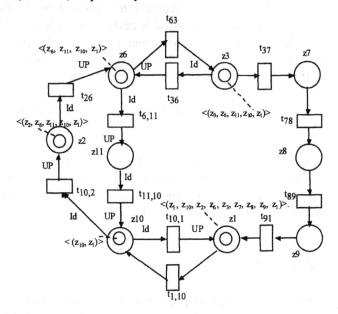

Figure 10. The CPN at marking M' built by the route validation controller for Example 6.

Performing Phase 1, Step B4 provides matrices $\mathbf{I}_{M'}$ and $\mathbf{A}_T$ and Step B5 finds that D_T contains just a cycle including z_1 (see Figure 6). So the algorithm proceeds to phase 2. Step B6 builds matrix $\mathbf{A}_R$. As Figure 7 shows, the second level digraph contains a cycle and $C^2{}_0 = 5$. Since $n(M') = 5 > 3$ the route is not validated, $\mathbf{r}(v_5)$ is not assigned to v_5 and the system continues its behaviour modelled by the old CPN starting at marking M.

6.3   Some Remarks about the Computational Complexity

The computational complexity of the deadlock avoidance control laws must be low to be efficient. Now, the on line computation of the zone validation activity has the complexity of the depth-first search algorithm [17]. This search can be easily performed in polynomial time with complexity $O(N_Z)$.

Implementing the route validation requires a first phase having the same computational complexity of ZVA. On the contrary, the second phase computes the bound $C^2{}_0$ by generating all cycles of D_R and of $D^2{}_R$. Such a computation requires $O(c_1, c_2)$ operations where c_1 and c_2 indicate the number of cycles of D_R and D^2_R respectively. So determining C^2_0 is possible in real time if the values of c_1 and c_2 are low, i.e. if the AGVS layout contains a low number of bidirectional paths. To overcome this difficulty, we propose a second version of phase 2 where the bound is obtained in polynomial time, by avoiding the cycle determination. In particular, the phase 2 determines the minimum capacity C_0 of cycles in D_R. Since it is easy to prove that $(2C_0-1) \leq C^2_0$, step B8 of the RVA can be replaced by the following step:

B8'   If $n(M'_0) < 2C_0 - 2$ then v_k is validated and the evolution of CPN' continues starting from M'_0 else go to step B9.

We remark that the condition of B8' is more severe than the one used in B8. However, it involves efficient computation because the algorithm to compute C_0 is performed in $O(N_Z^3)$ operations. So B8' is suitable for real time implementation even if D_R has many cycles.

7.   CONCLUSIONS

This paper proposes a closed loop control scheme that manages route assignment and vehicle movements in the Automatic Guided Vehicle Systems (AGVSs) to avoid deadlock and collisions. Coloured Petri nets (CPNs) model the system and describe in a modular and concise way the paths that vehicles have to follow and the move of AGVs among zones. Besides, the CPN is an excellent tool that facilitates the synthesis of the discrete event controller managing the vehicle traffic. The proposed control strategy is obtained using a graph theoretic approach that is very effective to solve deadlock in Automatic Manufacturing Systems. Such a control scheme pursues two aims: i) avoiding deadlocks and collisions by enabling or inhibiting the acquisition of next zone (*zone validation*), ii) accepting or refusing new paths to be assigned dynamically to the vehicles (*path validation*) to avoid undesirable situations called "restricted deadlocks". The CPN model is a suitable framework where the proposed policies can be applied by using the incidence matrices and avoiding the construction of digraphs. A peculiarity of the proposed approach is its generality. Indeed a different control strategy can be applied to menage a generic AGVS in the defined PN framework. Moreover, the CPN model is a tool suited to perform a simulation of the AGVS behaviour to test the developed real time controller and to compare different control strategies managing vehicle traffic.

REFERENCES

[1] Z.A. Banaszak and B.H. Krogh, "Deadlock Avoidance in Flexible Manufacturing Systems with Concurrently Competing Process Flows," *IEEE Trans on Robotics and Automation*, vol.6, no.6, Dec. 1990, pp. 724-734.

[2] H. Cho, T.K. Kumaran, and R.A. Wysk, "Graph-Theoretic Deadlock Detection and Resolution for Flexible Manufacturing Systems," *IEEE Trans. on Robotics and Automation*, vol. 11, no.3, June 1995, pp. 413-421.

[3] J. Ezpeleta, J.M. Colom, and J. Martinez, "A Petri Net Based Deadlock Prevention Policy for Flexible Manufacturing Systems," *IEEE Trans. on Robotics and Automation*, vol.11, no. 2, Apr. 1995, pp. 173-184.

[4] J. Ezpeleta, J. M. Colom, 1997, "Automatic sysnthesis of Colored Petri Nets for Control of FMS." *IEEE Trans. on Robotics and Automation*, vol. 13, n. 3, 1997, pp.327-337.

[5] M.P. Fanti, B. Maione, S. Mascolo, and B. Turchiano, "Event Based Feedback Control for Deadlock Avoidance in Flexible Production Systems," *IEEE Trans. on Robotics and Automation*, vol. 13, no. 3, June 1997, pp. 347-363.

[6] M.P. Fanti, B. Maione, and B. Turchiano, "Event Control for Deadlock Avoidance in Production Systems with Multiple Capacity Resources," *Studies in Informatics and Control*, vol.7, no.4, December 1998, pp.343-364.

[7] M.P. Fanti, B. Maione, and B. Turchiano, "Comparing Digraph and Petri Nets Approaches to Deadlock Avoidance in Petri Nets," *IEEE Trans. on Sistems, Man, and Cybernetics,-Part B: Cybernetics*, vol. 13, no. 3, June 1997, pp. 347-363.

[8] K. Feldmann, A.W., Colombo, "Material Flow and Control Sequence Specification of Flexible Systems Using Coloured Petri Nets," *Int. J. Adv. Manufacturing Technology*, vol. 14, 1998, pp. 760-774.

[9] F. Harary, *Graph Theory*, Addison-Wesley Publishing Company, Reading, MA, April 1971.

[10] F. Hsieh and S. Chang, "Dispatching-Driven Deadlock Avoidance Controller Synthesis for Flexible Manufacturing Systems," *IEEE Trans. on Robotics and Automation*, vol. 10, no. 2, Apr. 1994, pp. 196-209.

[11] K. Jensen *Colored Petri Nets, Basic Concepts, Analysis methods and Practical Use*, vol I EATS Monography and Theoretical Computer Science, Springer Verlag, New York:, 1992.

[12] C. W. Kim, and J.M.A. Tanchoco, "Conflict-free shortest bi-directional AGV routing," *International Journal of Production Research*, vol. 29,no. 12, 1991, pp. 2377-2391.

[13] M.A. Lawley, "Deadlock Avoidance for Production Systems with Flexible Routing," *IEEE Trans. on Robotics and Automation*, vol. 15, no.3, June 1999, pp. 497-509.

[14] C. C. Lee, and J.T. Lin, "Deadlock prediction and avoidance based on Petri nets for zone-control automated guided vehicle systems," *International Journal of Production Research,*vol.33, 1995, pp. 3249-3265.

[15] T. Murata, "Petri Nets: Properties, Analysis and Applications," *Proceedings of the IEEE*, vol. 77, no. 4, Apr. 1989, pp. 541-580.

[16] M. Nandula, and S.P. Dutta, "Performance evaluation of an auction-based manufacturing system using coloured Petri nets,". *International Journal of Production Research*, vol. 38, no. 9, **38,** 2000, pp. 2155-2171.

[17] E.M. Reingold, J., Nievergelt, and N. Deo, *Combinatorial Algorithms: Theory and practice*. Prentice Hall, Englewood Cliffs, N. J., 1977.

[18] S.A. Reveliotis and P.M. Ferreira, "Deadlock Avoidance Policies for Automated Manufacturing Cells," *IEEE Trans. on Robotics and Automation*, vol. 12, no.6, December 1996, pp. 845-857.

[19] S.A. Reveliotis, M.A. Lawely, and P.M. Ferreira, "Polynomial-Complexity Deadlock Avoidance Policies for Sequential Resource Allocation Systems," *IEEE Trans. on Automatic Control*, vol.42, no.10, October 1997, pp.1344-1357.

[20] S.A. Reveliotis, "Conflict resolution in AGV Systems," *IIE Transactions*, vol. 32, 2000, pp. 647-659.

[21] N. Viswanadham, Y. Narahari, and T.L. Johnson, "Deadlock Prevention and Deadlock Avoidance in Flexible Manufacturing Systems Using Petri Net Models," *IEEE Trans. on Robotics and Automation*, vol. 6, no.6, Dec. 1990, pp. 713-723.

[22] N. Viswanadham, and Y. Narahari, *Performance Modeling of Automated Manufacturing Systems*. Englewood Cliff, NJ: Prentice Hall, 1992.

[23] R.A. Wysk, N.S. Yang, and S. Joshi, "Detection of Deadlocks in Flexible Manufacturing Cells," *IEEE Trans. on Robotics and Automation*, vol.7, no.6, December 1991, pp.853-859.

[24] N. Wu, 1999, "Necessary and sufficient Conditions for deadlock-free operation in Flexible Manufacturing Systems using Colored Petri Net model." *IEEE Transaction on Systems, Man,and Cybernetics – Part C: Applications and Reviews*, vol. 29, no. 2, pp. 192-204.

[25] M.S. Yeh, and W.C.Yeh, "Deadlock prediction and avoidance for zone-control AGVS," *Int. Journal of Production Research*, vol. 36, n. 10, 1998, pp. 2879-2889.

[26] L. Zeng L., H.P. Wang, H.P., S: Jin S, "Conflict detection of Automated Guided Vehicles *International Journal of Production Research*, vol. 29, no. 5, 1991, pp. 865-879.

Chapter 7

QUALITY ANALYSIS OF DEPENDABLE INFORMATION SYSTEMS

Apostolos Zarras and Valerie Issarny

INRIA UR Rocquencourt
Domaine de Voluceau
78153 Le Chesnay
France
{Apostolos.Zarras, Valerie.Issarny}@inria.fr

Abstract   Large industrial organizations strongly depend on the use of enterprise information systems for the application of their complex business processes. Typically, an enterprise information system (EIS) consists of a set of autonomous distributed components providing basic services. Business processes can be realized as workflows consisting of: (1) tasks combining basic services provided by EIS components and (2) synchronization dependencies among tasks. EIS users have ever-increasing non-functional requirements (e.g. performance, reliability, availability, etc.) on the quality of those systems. To satisfy those requirements, EIS engineers must perform quality analysis and evaluation, which involves analytically solving, or simulating quality models of the system (e.g. Markov chains, Queuing-nets, Petri-nets etc).

Good quality models are hard to build and require lots of experience and effort, which are not always available. A possible solution to the previous issue is to build automated procedures for quality model generation. Such procedures shall encapsulate previous existing knowledge on quality modeling and their use shall decrease the cost of developing quality models. In this paper, we concentrate on the performance and reliability of EISs and we investigate the automated generation of quality models from EIS architectural descriptions comprising additional information related to the aspects that affect the quality of the EIS.

Keywords: Performance, Quality, Reliability, Software Architecture, Workflow.

P. Ezhilchelvan and A. Romanovsky (eds.), Concurrency in Dependable Computing, 127–145.

1.   Introduction

Today's industrial organizations use large scale enterprise information systems for performing and managing their complex business processes. An enterprise information system (EIS) typically is built of numerous, disparate, autonomous subsystems, named EIS components hereafter. Business processes can then be realized as workflows. A workflow consists of: (1) tasks combining basic services provided by EIS components and (2) synchronization dependencies among tasks [10, 9]. The business processes that need to be supported by an EIS serve as the primary functional requirements for developing and maintaining the EIS. However, nowadays, non-functional requirements on the quality of the EIS (e.g. performance, reliability, availability) are also of significant importance. EIS architects, designers and developers are supposed to design, implement and maintain the EIS while taking into account the user's non-functional requirements. Consequently, quality analysis is required during the life-cycle of the EIS.

The analysis of certain quality attributes (e.g. performance, reliability, availability) is not a new challenge since a variety of techniques have been proposed and used for several years [4, 5]. Those techniques are supported by an underlying modeling formalism, which allows to specify structural and behavioral aspects of the inspected system that affect the system's quality. Well known examples of such formalisms are block diagrams, graphs, Markov chains, Petri-nets, Queuing-nets, logics, etc. The resulting models are then analytically solved, or simulated. Based on the above, the challenge nowadays becomes to make existing techniques more tractable to the end users. The main problem today is that building good quality models, which when solved or simulated, give accurate predictions on the quality of the system, requires lots of experience and effort. EIS architects, designers and developers use architecture description languages (ADLs) and object oriented notations (e.g. OMT, UML) to design the EIS architecture. It is a common case that they are not keen on building quality models using Markov chains, Petri-nets, Queuing-nets etc.

Hence, the ideal approach would be to provide the EIS architects, designers and developers with an environment, which enables the specification of EIS architectures and further provides adequate tool support for the automated generation of models suitable for the quality analysis of the system. In this paper, we investigate this issue. More specifically, we focus on the automated performance and reliability analysis of EIS and our main objectives are summarized in the following two points:

- The provision of support for modeling at the architectural level, aspects that affect the performance and reliability of EIS.

- The design and realization of automated procedures for generating traditional performance and reliability models starting from EIS architectural descriptions. The key to achieve this point is to formally specify the mapping between EIS architectural models and traditional models for performance and reliability analysis.

The remainder of this paper is structured as follows. Section 2 presents previous work related to the quality analysis of systems and identifies problems that are addressed by the approach proposed in this paper. Section 3 provides the definition of a base architectural style for specifying EIS architectures. Sections 4 and 5 detail the automated procedures for the generation of traditional performance and reliability models. Finally, section 6 concludes this paper with a summary of our contribution.

2.   Background and Related Work

Pioneer work on modeling and analyzing the quality of software systems at the architectural level includes attribute-based architectural styles proposed in [3]. In general, an architectural style includes the specification of types of basic architectural elements (e.g. pipe and filter) that can be used for specifying a software architecture. Moreover, an architectural style includes the specification of constraints on using those basic architectural elements and patterns describing the data and control interaction among them. An attribute-based architectural style (ABAS) is an architectural style, which additionally provides modeling support for the analysis of a particular quality attribute (e.g. performance, reliability, availability). More specifically, an ABAS provides support for specifying:

- *Quality attribute measures* characterizing the quality attribute (e.g. the probability that the system correctly provides a service for a given duration, mean response time).

- *Quality attribute stimuli*, i.e., events affecting the quality attribute of the system (e.g. failures, service requests).

- *Quality attribute parameters*, i.e., architectural properties affecting quality attribute of the system (e.g. faults, redundancy, thread policy).

- *Quality attribute models*, i.e., traditional models that formally relate the above elements (e.g. a Markov model that predicts reliability based on the failure rates and the redundancy used, a Queuing network that enables predicting the system's response time given the rate of service requests and based on the performance parameters).

In [2] the authors propose an architecture tradeoff analysis method (ATAM) where the use of an ABAS is coupled with the specification of a set of scenarios, which roughly constitutes the specification of a service profile. ATAM has been tested for analyzing qualities like performance, availability, modifiability, and real-time. In all those cases, quality attribute models (e.g. Markov models, queuing networks etc.) are manually built given the specification of a set of scenarios and the ABAS-based architectural description. However, in [2], the authors recognize the complexity of the aforementioned task. Moreover, it is our opinion that the need to manually produce quality attribute models significantly decreases the benefits of using a disciplined method such as ATAM for analyzing the quality of software systems. ATAM is a promising approach for doing things right. Nowadays, however, there is a constant additional requirement for doing things fast and easy. Asking EIS engineers to build performance and reliability models from scratch is certainly a drawback towards achieving this objective. To deal with this drawback, this paper proposes automating the generation of quality attribute models from architectural descriptions. To accomplish this goal, there is a need for specifying the mapping between architectural descriptions and quality attribute models. Hence, we need more formal definitions of ABAS. Indeed, it is not feasible to generate traditional quality attribute models starting from scenarios described in natural language and architectural descriptions within which the relationships among basic architectural elements and quality attribute measures, parameters and stimuli are not precisely defined.

Based on the previous remarks, in the following section we present the definition of a base architectural style for the specification of EIS architectures. Then, in sections 4 and 5 we detail the mapping between EIS architectural models and performance and reliability quality attribute models.

3.   A Base EIS Architectural Style

Figure 1(a) gives the UML definitions of the meta-elements used for the specification of EIS architectural models. The semantics and the use of those elements are further discussed in the remainder of this section. Moreover, Figure 1(b) gives the graphical representations of the EIS meta-elements.

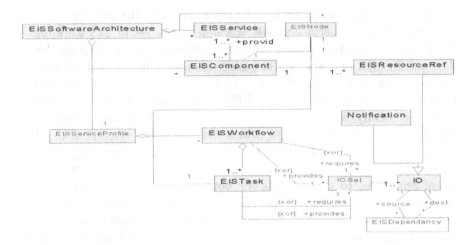

(a) UML definitions of meta-elements for the specification of EIS architectures.

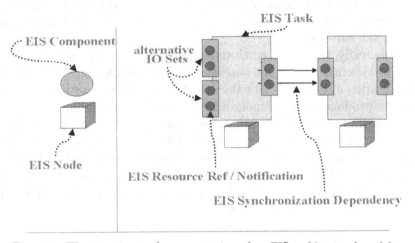

Figure 1. The structure and representation of an EIS architectural model.

3.1.   Basic EIS architectural elements

An EIS software architecture comprises the specification of a non empty set of EIS components and the specification of a non empty set of EIS services. An EIS component provides one, or more of the EIS services, and an EIS service is provided by at least one EIS component. Every EIS component is associated with an EIS node, representing the execution platform on top of which it is deployed. Technically, EIS components and services are specified textually using Darwin-like notations. Darwin is among the first and most popular ADLs (for more information see [7]).

An EIS architectural description further includes the specification of a service profile. A service profile is a non-empty set of EIS workflows describing how the EIS is used. An EIS workflow is a model that specifies the coordination of a set of EIS tasks. The workflow model we use is inspired by the one proposed in [10], which has recently become an OMG standard [9]. Tasks combine basic EIS services provided by components. More specifically, a task requires using a set of alternative input-sets. An input-set consists of inputs, which may be either references to EIS components, or notifications from other tasks. While executing, a task uses one of the alternative input-sets to produce an output-set (i.e. a set of references to components, or notifications to other tasks). By definition, a set of alternative output-sets may be produced by the task. Task coordination is specified in terms of synchronization dependencies among inputs and outputs. A task may be compound representing a workflow model. More specifically, a compound task consists of sub-tasks and synchronization dependencies between sub-tasks. The input and output sets of a compound task are mapped on input and output sets of the sub-tasks.

Technically, tasks and synchronization dependencies among them are specified textually using the language detailed in [10]. Moreover, textual specification of tasks describe the way different alternative input sets are used to produce the corresponding alternative output sets.

To facilitate the specification and quality analysis of EIS architectures, we developed a prototype tool whose use is demonstrated in the following subsection. The tool allows both the graphical and textual specification of EIS architectures. Already existing parsers for the Darwin and the workflow specification languages are then used for verifying the correctness of those specifications.

3.2.   Example

The use of the tool for the specification and quality analysis of EISs has been tested with a real world case study, part of which we use here as an example. The goal of case study is the quality analysis of an EIS used for managing the Bull SA organization. The basic EIS architecture consists of a variety of autonomous and disparate components including:

- The Log component, which provides access to log files produced by a firewall system used by Bull.

- The Billing component, which provides billing services for Bull employees and customers.

- The **Department** component, which provides access to the personal records of Bull employees and customers.

The EIS service profile includes, among others, a workflow which combines services provided by the aforementioned EIS components into a complex billing service. The workflow consists of the following tasks:

- The **Bill** task, which uses services of the **Log** and the **Department** server to produce per-customer bills.

- The **Payment** task, which takes as input a bill produced by the **Bill** task and a reference to the **Department** server, and checks whether the bill is accepted, or not.

- The **Transfer** task, which is activated for all accepted bills and eventually uses the **Billing** server to transfer money from the account of the customer to a bank.

- The **Claim** task, which is activated for all rejected bills and uses the **Billing** server to cancel them.

Figure 2, gives a snapshot of the tool we developed showing the specification of the complex billing service workflow.

4. Automated Performance Analysis

The basic performance measures used to characterize the execution of EIS workflows and tasks are given in Table .1. Moreover, the basic stimuli that causes changes on the values of those measures is the initiation of workflows. Hence, an EIS workflows is further associated with an attribute whose value gives the statistical pattern by which the workflow is initiated. Finally, EIS components are characterized by their thread and scheduling policies, their capacity and the work demands needed for providing the associated EIS services. In the remainder, we present how EIS architectural descriptions including the specification of the previous properties can be mapped to traditional performance models.

4.1. Mapping EIS models on traditional performance models

For EIS performance analysis, we use a tool-set, called QNAP2 [1], providing a variety of both analytic and simulation techniques. QNAP2 accepts as input a queuing network model of the system that is to be analyzed.

The general structure of a queuing network model is given in Figure 3. A queuing network model consists of a set of stations providing services

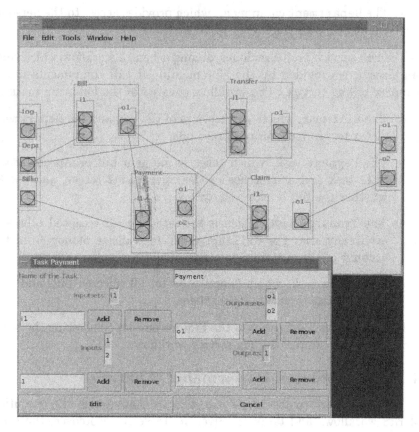

Figure 2. The specification of the complex billing service.

requested by customers. A service is associated with a set of transition rules describing what happens to a customer after the customer is served. A station is further associated with queues that store requesting customers. In a queuing network, we may have special stations, called source stations, whose purpose is to create new customers. Those stations are characterized by a statistical pattern according to which they generate customers.

Given an EIS architectural description the steps for mapping it to the corresponding queuing network are the following. First, a set of stations is generated, corresponding to EIS nodes on top of which EIS components and workflows are deployed. Moreover, for every workflow specified in the EIS service profile, a source station, characterized by the corresponding statistical pattern, is generated. Formally, the following OCL [2] constraint gives the post condition of the first step of the generation procedure.

Measure	Type
mean-service-time	Real
mean-waiting-time	Real
mean-execution-time	Real
mean-system-throughput	Real

Stimuli	Type
statistical-pattern	Real |
	exp : Real -> Real |
	hexp : Real, Real -> Real |
	erlang : Real, Integer -> Real

Parameter	Type
thread-policy	Enum{single, multi, pool}
scheduling-policy	Enum{fifo, lifo, quantum, priority, order-preserving, sharing}
capacity	Integer | infinite
work-demands	Real |
	exp : Real -> Real |
	hexp : Real, Real -> Real |
	erlang : Real, Integer -> Real

Table .1. EIS performance measures, stimuli and parameters

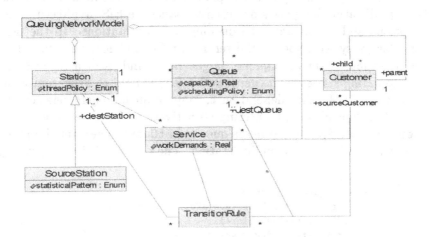

Figure 3. Basic meta-elements used for the specification of queuing networks.

```
EISSoftwareArchitecture:
  self.eisNode->forall(
   node |self.queuingNetworkModel.station->exists (
   st |st.name = node.name)) and
  self.eisServiceProfile.eisWorkflow->forall(
   wf |self.queuingNetworkModel.station->exists (
   st |st.name = wf.name->concat('SourceStation') and
   st.statistical-pattern = wf.statistical-pattern)
```

Then, for every EIS component, a queue is generated and associated
with the appropriate station. Performance parameters related to the
capacity and scheduling policy of the component are used to define the
corresponding properties that characterize the queue. In addition, a
service is generated for every EIS service provided by the component.
The generated service is characterized by the work-demands required for
the corresponding EIS service. Formally, the post condition of this step
is:

```
EISSoftwareArchitecture:
  self.eisComponent->forall(
   res |self.queuingNetworkModel.station->select(
   st | st.name = res.eisNode.name).queue->exists(
   q | q.name = res.name and q.scheduling-policy =
      res.scheduling-policy and q.capacity = res.capacity
   ) and
   res.eisService->forall(
    eisserv |self.queuingNetworkModel.station->select(
    st | st.name = res.eisNode.name
   ).service->exists(
     serv | serv.name = eisserv.name and
      serv.work-demands = eisserv.work-demands)))
```

Technically, up to this point, the parsers for the Darwin and the workflow specification languages are used to parse the EIS architectural descriptions and to generate the queuing network stations. In the next
step, for every workflow in the service profile and for every task t in
this workflow, a queue, tQueue, is generated and associated with the
corresponding station. The generated queue is used to synchronize the
execution of tasks that depend on t. tQueue queues customers sent by
tasks that depend on t, requesting t's activation. Moreover, the service
tService provided to customers queued in tQueue is generated and associated with the corresponding station. The post condition of this step
is:

```
EISSoftwareArchitecture:
  self.eisServiceProfile.eisWorkflow->forall(
   wf | wf.eisTask->forall(
   t |self.queuingNetworkModel.station->select(
    st | st.name = t.eisNode.name).queue->exists(
    q | q.name = t.name->concat('Queue'))) and
   wf.eisTask->forall(
   t |self.queuingNetworkModel.station->select(
    st | st.name = t.eisNode.name
   ).service->exists(
    serv | serv.name = t.name->concat('Service'))))
```

The code of tService follows the pattern described below:

- The initiation of the workflow causes the creation of customers initc sent to the queue of each task t.

- Serving initc causes the generation of new sets of customers, one per alternative input set required by task t. Each new set of customers is sent to the stations that host queues of the tasks providing the corresponding outputs.

- initc waits until one of the new customer sets is served. Then, another set of customers is created and sent to the queues that correspond to the EIS components used by t. The exact code generated here depends on the way tasks use EIS services provided by EIS components.

- initc remains blocked until all of the created customers are served by the EIS components. Then, an output set is produced and customers waiting on stations for this particular output set are unblocked. Finally, customer initc is unblocked and destroyed.

Technically, to generate the queues and the services, used for the synchronization of tasks, we use the parsers for the Darwin and the workflow specification languages.

4.2.   Example

Getting back to our example, the three components used by the tasks of the BillingServiceWorkflow are multi-threaded and are modeled to have an unlimited capacity. The policy according to which they serve requests is FIFO. Finally, the work demands for providing the EIS services associated with them are constant (we do not provide further details here due to the lack of space). Hence, for all three components we have:

```
EISComponent:
  self.thread-policy = multi and
  self.scheduling-policy = fifo and
  self.capacity = infinite
```

The BillingServiceWorkflow is initiated regularly at the end of each month. Hence we have:

```
BillingServiceWorkflow:
  self.statistical-pattern = 30*24*3600
```

A queuing network for QNAP2 is then generated simply, using the tool functionality, and according to the mapping defined in the previous subsection. In particular, the following elements are generated: 3 stations and the corresponding queues representing the components; 4 stations

```
 1  /STATION/
 2  NAME = PaymentQueue;
 3  TYPE = INFINITE;
 4  SERVICE =
 5  BEGIN
 6  IF(Payment-H(CUSTOMER.wfid, 4).STATE <> TRUE) THEN
 7  BEGIN
 8      SET(Payment-H(CUSTOMER.wfid, 4));
 9      PRINT("Payment serving workflow", CUSTOMER.wfid);
10      tmp-Bill(1):= NEW(CUSTOMER);
11      tmp-Bill(1).wfid:= CUSTOMER.wfid;
12      tmp-Bill(1).Bill-IOS :=1;
13      tmp-Bill(1).all-avai:= NEW(FLAG);
14      TRANSIT(tmp-Bill(1), BillStation, Payment-CL);
15      WAITOR(tmp-Bill(1).all-avai);
16      TRANSIT(NEW(CUSTOMER), Department);
17      JOIN;
18      res_H := HISTOGR(s_pay, (0.33333334,0.33333334,0.33333334));
19      IF ((res_H >0.0) AND (res_H <= 0.33333334)) THEN
20      BEGIN
21          SET(pay_H(CUSTOMER.wfid, 1));
22      END
23      ELSE
24      IF ((res_H >0.33333334) AND (res_H <= 0.6666667)) THEN
25      BEGIN
26          SET(pay_H(CUSTOMER.wfid, 2));
27      END
28      ELSE
29          IF ((res_H >0.6666667) AND (res_H <= 1.0)) THEN
30          BEGIN
31              SET(pay_H(CUSTOMER.wfid, 3));
32          END;
33      TRANSIT(OUT);
 &................................
56      IF(OK-fin AND OK-Transfer AND OK-Payment AND OK-Bill AND OK-rec AND OK-Claim) THEN
57          SET(CUSTOMER.all-avai);
58  END; & of ELSE CLAUSE
59  END; & of service
```

Figure 4. Part of the code of the service provided to customers used for the synchronization of task Payment with task Bill.

hosting queues used for the synchronization of tasks; a source station whose statistical pattern equals to the one of the BillingServiceWorkflow.

Figure 4 gives part of the model of the station that hosts the queue used to synchronize the Payment task with the rest of the tasks of the BillingServiceWorkflow workflow. During the initiation of the workflow, an initiation customer is sent to the PaymentQueue. As shown in Figure 2, the Payment task depends on the completion of the Bill task. Consequently, serving the initiation customer results in the creation of a synchronization customer, which is sent to BillQueue requesting the initiation of the Bill task (Figure 4, lines 10-14). The initiation customer is blocked until the newly created synchronization customer is properly served (Figure 4, line 15). Then, a new customer is sent to the station that hosts DepartmentQueue, asking for a basic service. Once this customer is served, Payment completes and the initiation customer is destroyed (Figure 4, lines 16-33).

To give an idea of the complexity of the resulting model, its total size for the complex billing service workflow is 490 lines.

Measure	Type	
reliability	0..1	

Stimuli	Properties	
Failure	domain	Enum{time, value}
	perception	Enum{consistent, inconsistent}

Parameter	Properties	
Fault	nature	Enum{intentional, accidental}
	phase	Enum{design, operational}
	causes	Enum{physical, human}
	boundaries	Enum{internal, external}
	persistence	Enum{permanent, temporary}
	arrival-rate	Real

Table .2. EIS reliability measures, stimuli and parameters

5. Automated Reliability Analysis

The basic reliability measure for EIS is the probability that a workflow successfully completes during the lifetime of the EIS. Getting to the reliability parameters, EIS components, tasks and nodes may fail because of faults causing errors in their state. The manifestations of errors are failures [5]. Hence, faults are the basic parameters that affect the reliability of an EIS, while failures are the stimuli causing changes in the value of the reliability measure. Faults and failures are further characterized by properties given in Table .2. Different combinations of the values of those properties lead to the definition of fault and failure taxonomies (e.g. see [5]), facilitating the automated generation of traditional reliability models. Except for faults and errors, another parameter affecting reliability is design diversity. Frequently, more than one components provide similar services, which can be exploited towards achieving a particular objective. Such cases can be specified using the workflow specification language. In particular, EIS tasks may require one, or more alternative input-sets and may provide one, or more alternative output-sets. Hence, tasks representing N-Version-Parallel (NVP) and Recovery Block (RB) schemas [6] can be defined and taken into account for the generation of traditional reliability models.

5.1. Mapping EIS models on traditional reliability models

Reliability analysis techniques are typically based on state space models whose overall structure is given in Figure 5. A state space model consists

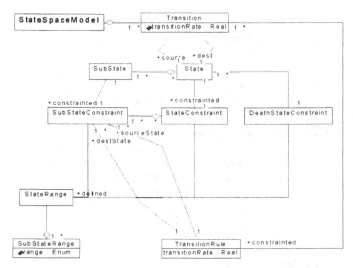

Figure 5. Basic meta-elements used for the specification of state space models.

of a set of transitions between states of the system. A state describes a situation where either the system operates correctly, or not. In the latter case the system is said to be in a *death state*. The state of the system depends on the state of its constituent elements. Hence, it can be seen as a composition of sub states, each one representing the situation of a constituent element. A state is constrained by the range of all possible situations that may occur. A state range can be modeled as a composition of sub state ranges, constraining the state of the elements that constitute the system. A transition is characterized by the rate by which the source situation changes into the target situation. If, for instance, the difference between the source and the target situation is the failure of a component, the transition rate equals to the failure rate of the component.

The specification of large state-space models is often too complex and error-prone. The approach proposed in [1] alleviates this problem. In particular, instead of specifying all possible state transitions, the authors propose specifying the state range of the system, a death state constraint, and transition rules between sets of states of the system. In a transition rule, the source and the target set of states are identified by constraints on the state range (e.g. if the system is in a state where more than 2 components are operational, then the system may get into a state where the number of components is reduced by one). Given the previous information, a complete state space model can be generated using the algorithm described in [1]. Briefly, the algorithm takes as input an initial state and recursively applies the set of the transition rules. During a recursive step, the algorithm produces a transition to a state derived from the initial one. If the death state constraint holds for the resulting state, the recursion stops.

Based on the above, in the remainder we detail how to exploit the EIS architectural description to generate the information needed for the generation of a corresponding complete state space model. The first step towards that goal is to generate a state range definition for each workflow belonging to a given service profile. The state of a workflow is composed of the states of the tasks making up the workflow and the states of the nodes on top of which tasks and components are deployed.

The state of a task consists of a state representing the situation of the task itself and states representing the situations of the task's alternative input and output sets. The situation of a task depends on the kinds of faults that may cause the failure of this task. For instance, if the task fails due to permanent faults, its state may be `Waiting`, `Busy`, `Complete`, or `Failed`. If the task fails due to intermittent faults, its state may be `Waiting`, `Busy`, `Complete`, `FailedActive`, or `FailedPassive`.

The state of an input (resp. output) set, `ioset`, is composed of the states of the individual inputs `io` (resp. outputs) included in the set. If `io` is a notification, its state may be either `Available`, `NotYetAvailable`, or `NeverAvailable`; `io` is `NeverAvailable` if the task that provides it has failed, or completed by producing an output set that does not include `io`. If `io` is a reference to a component `c`, its state depends on the kind of faults that may cause the failure of `c`.

Based on the previous, the post condition of the generation of a state range is given below:

```
EISSoftwareArchitecture:
self.eisServiceProfile.eisWorkflow->forall(
  wf |wf.eisTask->forall(
   t | wf.stateRange.subStateRange->exists(
     str, strNode | strNode.name =
       t.eisNode.name->concat('StateRange') and
     str.name = t.name->concat('StateRange') and
     t.requires->union(t.provides)->forall(
       ioSet |str.stateRange.subStateRange->exists(
       str' |str'.name = ioSet.name->concat('StateRange') and
       ioSet->forall(
       io | str'.subStateRange->exists(
       str'', strNode'' | str''.name =
         io.name->concat('StateRange') and
       strNode''.name = io.eisNode.name->concat('StateRange')
     )))))))
```

After generating the state range definition for a workflow `wf`, the step that follows comprises the generation of transition rules for every task `t` of wf and for the EIS nodes. Those rules depend on the kind of faults that may cause the failure of t. For permanent faults, the rules for task t follow the pattern below:

- If wf is in a state where t is Waiting then:

    - If an alternative input set ioset is available then wf may get into a state where t is Busy.

    - If none of the alternative input sets ioset may eventually become available then wf may get into a state where all tasks depending on t are aware about the fact that its output sets will never be available.

    The previous are, typically, fast transitions, i.e. the probability that they take place is close to 1.

- If wf is in a state where t is Busy due to the availability of ioset then wf may get into a state where:

- t is Complete. Again, this is a fast transition.

- t is Failed and all tasks depending on t are aware about the fact that its output sets will never be available. The rate of getting into this state equals to the arrival rate of the fault that caused the failure of t, i.e. t.fault.arrival-rate.

- t is Waiting and io belonging to ioset is Failed. All EIS references io' used by other tasks of wf, for which io'.eisComponent = io.eisComponent holds, get into a Failed state. The rate of this transition equals to the arrival rate of the fault that caused the failure of io, i.e. io.eisComponent.fault.arrival-rate.

The rules for a node n are more obvious, and are not given here due to the lack of space. Finally, a death state constraint must be generated. In general, wf is in a death state if none of its output sets may eventually become available due to the unsuccessful termination of the tasks providing the corresponding outputs.

Technically, the generation of the information discussed in this section requires using the parsers for the Darwin and the workflow specification languages.

5.2.   Example

Getting back to our example, from the workflow specification given in Figure 2 we can generate the necessary information that serves as input to the algorithm presented in [1]. More specifically, both the tasks of the `BillingServiceWorkflow` and the components used by those tasks may fail due to permanent faults. Hence,

```
BillingServiceWorkflow:
  self.eisResource->forall(
  res | res.fault.persistence = permanent
  ) and
  self.eisServiceProfile.eisTask->forall(
  res | res.fault.persistence = permanent
  )
```

The state of the workflow is composed of the states of the `Bill`, `Payment`, `Transfer`, and `Claim` tasks, and the states of the nodes on top of which tasks and components are deployed. The range of each of those states is `Enum{Waiting, Busy, Complete, Failed}`.

Figure 6 gives the transition rules generated for the `Payment` task and used as input to the realization of the algorithm [1]. In particular, if the workflow is in a state where `Payment` is `Waiting` and its input set is available, then the workflow may get to a state where `Payment` is `Busy` (lines 1-4). If the workflow is in a state where `Payment` is in a `Busy` state, the workflow may get into a state where `Payment` is `Complete` (lines 18-29). Alternatively, the workflow may get into a state where `Payment` is `Failed` and the `Claim` and `Transfer` tasks are aware about the fact that the `Payment` outputs will never become available. (lines 30-37). The workflow reaches a death state if neither of its output sets may eventually become available.

The overall size of the model used as input for the algorithm [1], is 325 lines of code. Moreover, the generated Markov model contains 616 states. 282 out the 616 are death states. Finally, the model contains 2092 transitions.

6. Conclusion

In this paper, we presented an approach for automating the performance and reliability analysis of EIS systems. The approach is based on the formal definition of mappings between EIS architectural models and traditional performance and reliability models. The benefits of the proposed approach are both qualitative and quantitative. In particular, the quality of traditional performance and reliability models is assured since the required experience for building them is encapsulated in automated model generation procedures. Moreover, the cost of performing performance and reliability is minimized since the development of the corresponding traditional models is achieved automatically. It is worth-noticing that according to the authors of [2], 25% of the time required for performing architecture tradeoff analysis of software systems is actually

```
1 IF (Payment = WAITING) THEN
2   IF (PaymentInset00 = AVAILABLE AND
3       PaymentInset01 = AVAILABLE) THEN
4       TRANTO Payment = BUSY BY INPUT_AVAILABLE;
5   ELSE
6       IF (PaymentInset00 = NEVERAVAILABLE OR PaymentInset00 = FAILED OR
7 PaymentInset01 = NEVERAVAILABLE OR PaymentInset01 = FAILED) THEN
8       TRANTO
9       Payment = COMPLETE ,
10      PaymentOutset00 = NEVERAVAILABLE,
11      PaymentOutset10 = NEVERAVAILABLE,
12      TransferInset02 = NEVERAVAILABLE,
13      ClaimInset01 = NEVERAVAILABLE BY
14      INPUT_AVAILABLE;
15   ENDIF;
16   ENDIF;
17 ENDIF;
18 IF (Payment = BUSY) THEN
19  TRANTO Payment = COMPLETE,
20      PaymentOutset00 = AVAILABLE,
21      TransferInset02 = AVAILABLE BY
22      INPUT_AVAILABLE;
23 ENDIF;
24 IF (Payment = BUSY) THEN
25  TRANTO Payment = WAITING,
26      PaymentInset00 = FAILED BY
27      LAMBDA;
28 ENDIF;
29 IF (Payment = BUSY) THEN
30  TRANTO Payment = WAITING,
31      PaymentInset01 = FAILED BY
32      LAMBDA;
33 ENDIF;
34 IF (Payment = BUSY) THEN
35  TRANTO Payment = COMPLETE,
36      PaymentOutset10 = AVAILABLE,
37      ClaimInset01 = AVAILABLE BY
38      INPUT_AVAILABLE;
39 ENDIF;
40 IF (Payment = BUSY) THEN
41  TRANTO Payment = FAILED,
42      PaymentOutset00 = NEVERAVAILABLE,
43      PaymentOutset10 = NEVERAVAILABLE,
44      TransferInset02 = NEVERAVAILABLE,
45      ClaimInset01 = NEVERAVAILABLE BY
46      LAMBDA;
47 ENDIF;
```

Figure 6. Transition rules for the Payment task, used for the generation of a complete state space model for the BillingServiceWorkflow.

spent on building traditional quality models. The approach proposed in this paper enables decreasing this cost.

The approach presented here can be applied for automating the quality analysis of EISs regarding several other attributes. More specifically, the case of availability is pretty similar to the one of reliability. From our point of view, an interesting perspective is to extend this work towards the analysis of EISs regarding qualities attributes like openness and scalability.

Acknowledgments. The work presented in this paper was partially funded by the C3DS ESPRIT [3] and the DSoS IST [4] projects.

Notes

1. www.simulog.com

2. OCL is a first order logic notation used for specifying constraints on UML models. OCL supports the basic logical operators (e.g. `and`, `or`, `forall`, `exists`, `implies`). Moreover, the `.` operator allows to navigate through associations defined in the UML model. For more details see [8]

3. http://www.newcastle.research.ec.org/c3ds/

4. http://www.newcastle.research.ec.org/dsos/index.html

References

[1] S. C. Johnson. Reliability Analysis of Large Complex Systems Using ASSIST. In *Proceedings of the 8th Digital Avionics Systems Conference*, pages 227–234. AIAA/IEEE, 1988.

[2] R. Kazman, S. J. Carriere, and S. G. Woods. Toward a discipline of scenario-based architectural engineering. *Annals of Software Engineering*, 9:5–33, 2000.

[3] M. Klein, R. Kazman, L. Bass, S. J. Carriereand M. Barbacci, and H. Lipson. Attribute-Based Architectural Styles. In *Proceedings of the First Working Conference on Software Architecture (WICSA1)*, pages 225–243. IFIP, Feb 1999.

[4] H. Kobayashi. *Modeling and Analysis : An Introduction to System Performance Evaluation Methodology*. Addison-Wesley, 1978.

[5] J-C. Laprie. Dependable Computing and Fault Tolerance : Concepts and Terminology. In *Proceedings of the 15th International Symposium on Fault-Tolerant Computing (FTCS-15)*, pages 2–11, 1985.

[6] J-C. Laprie, J. Arlat, C. Béounes, and K. Kanoun. Definition and analysis of hardware and software fault-tolerant architectures. *IEEE Computer*, 23(7):39–51, July 1990.

[7] J. Magee, N. Dulay, S. Eisenbach, and J. Kramer. Specifying Distributed Software Architectures. In *Proceedings of the 5th European Software Engineering Conference (ESEC'95)*, number 989 in LNCS, pages 137–153. Springer Verlag, 1995.

[8] OMG. *Object Constraint Language Specification*, 1.1 edition, Sept 1997.

[9] OMG. UML Profile for Enterprise Distributed Object Computing. Technical report, OMG, 2000.

[10] S.M. Wheater, S.K. Shrivastava, and F. Ranno. A CORBA Compliant Transactional Workflow System for Internet Applications. In *Proceedings of MIDDLEWARE'98*, pages 3–18. IFIP, September 1998.

III

EVENT ORDERING AND ITS APPLICATION

Chapter 8

FAULT-TOLERANT SEQUENCER

Specification and an Implementation

Roberto Baldoni
Carlo Marchetti
and Sara Tucci Piergiovanni
Dipartimento di Informatica e Sistemistica
Università di Roma "La Sapienza"
Via Salaria 113, 00198 Roma, Italia
{baldoni,marchet,tucci}@dis.uniroma1.it

Abstract   The synchronization among thin, independent and concurrent processes in an open distributed system is a fundamental issue in current architectures (e.g. middlewares, three-tier architectures etc.). "Independent process" means no message has to be exchanged among the processes to synchronize themselves and "open" means that the number of processes that require to synchronize changes along the time. In this paper we present the specification of a sequencer service that allows independent processes to get a sequence number that can be used to label successive operations (e.g. to allow a set of independent and concurrent processes to get a total order on these labelled operations). Moreover, we propose an implementation of the sequencer service in the timed asynchronous model along with a sketch of the correctness proof.

Keywords: Synchronization, Open Distributed Systems, Timed Asynchronous model.

Introduction

Since the middle of 80s, the abstraction of process group has been of primary importance in designing fault-tolerant distributed applications

P. Ezhilchelvan and A. Romanovsky (eds.), Concurrency in Dependable Computing, 149–167.

[1]. A group is a set of cooperating processes able to order events (such as message receipts, failures, recoveries etc.) identically by using specific group operations and mechanisms such as broadcast communication primitives, views operations, state transfer, failure detection mechanisms etc. [2]. This approach, which actually *tightly couples* the processes of a group, has shown to work quite well on-the-field when facing small and closed groups.

Recently, distributed systems are moving towards *open* distributed architectures in which *loosely coupled* and *independent* entities cooperate in order to meet a common goal. In particular, these environments generally assume very thin clients (embedding at most a redirection/retransmission mechanism) that interact with more thick entities. *Three-tier architectures* (e.g. [3, 4]) and open *middleware platforms* (e.g. [5]) are examples of such open distributed systems.

Independently from the nature of a distributed architecture, a basic issue like the *synchronization* among processes spread over the computer network has to be faced. Synchronization in the presence of failures is the fundamental building block for the solution of many important problems in distributed systems such as mutual exclusion and replication (for nice surveys about these topics refer to [6] and [7] respectively). Synchronization in mutual exclusion is needed to get a total order on critical section accesses while in replication to get the same total order of updates at each replica[1].

In the context of a closed group, the solutions proposed for this class of problems are mainly either based on a virtual synchronous environment fully distributed [1] or token-based [8]. Both solutions do not fit well open architectures as clients should implement functionalities much more complex than a simple retransmission/redirection mechanism becoming, thus, thick entities. These reasons make appealing the service approach for synchronization in such architectures.

which independent processes can obtain a sequence number to globally order successive events they generate

In this chapter we first present the specification of a sequencer service that allows thin client processes which implement a rudimentary time-out based retransmission mechanism to get a sequence number that can be used to globally order successive relevant events they generate. Such a specification allows different processes to get a different sequence number for each distinct relevant events despite, for example, multiple receipts of the same request by the sequencer. Moreover, the sequence number associated by the sequencer to each request has to be consecutive.

Then, we provide a fault-tolerant implementation of the sequencer service. Such implementation adopts a primary-backups (passive) replication scheme where replicas interact with clients through asynchronous channels and among them through a timed asynchronous datagram service [9]. This model captures the interesting application scenario in which replicas are on a LAN while clients are thin applications (e.g. browsers) spread over the Internet. Finally, due to lack of space, we provide a sketch of the correctness of our implementation with respect to the sequencer specification. The interested readers can refer to [10] for the formal correctness proof.

1. Specification of the sequencer service

A sequencer service receives requests from clients and assigns an integer positive sequence number, denoted $\#seq$, to each *distinct* request. Each client request has a unique identifier, denoted req_id, which is a pair $\langle cl\_id, \#cl\_seq \rangle$ where cl_id is the identifier of the client and $\#cl\_seq$ represents the sequence number of the requests issued by cl_id.

As clients implement a simple retransmission mechanism to cope with possible sequencer implementation failures or network delays, the sequencer service maintains a state A composed by a set of assignments $\{a_1, a_2 \ldots a_{k-1}, a_k\}$ where each assignment a is a pair $\langle req\_id, \#seq \rangle$, in which $a.req\_id$ is a client request identifier and $a.\#seq$ is the sequence number returned by the sequencer service to client $a.req\_id.cl\_id$.

A sequencer service has to satisfy the following five properties:

(P1) Assignment Validity. If $a \in A$ then there exists a client c that issued a request identified by req_id and $req\_id = a.req\_id$.

(P2) Response Validity. If a client c delivers a reply $\#seq$, then $\exists a = \langle req\_id, \#seq \rangle \in A$.

(P3) Bijection. $\forall a_i, a_j \in A : a_i.\#seq \neq a_j.\#seq \Leftrightarrow a_i.req\_id \neq a_j.req\_id$

(P4) Consecutiveness. $\forall a_i \in A : a_i.\#seq \geq 1 \wedge a_i.seq > 1 \Rightarrow \exists a_j : a_j.\#seq = a_i.\#seq - 1$

(P5) Termination. If a client c issues a request identified by req_id, then, unless the client crashes, it eventually delivers a reply $\#seq$.

Properties from (P1) to (P4) define the safety of the sequencer service while (P5) defines its liveness.

More specifically, (P1) expresses that the state of the sequencer does not contain "spurious" assignments. i.e., each assignment has been executed after having received a request from some client. (P2) states that the client cannot deliver a sequence number that has not been assigned by the sequencer to a *req_id*. The predicate "(P1) and (P2)" implies that each client delivering a sequence number has previously issued a request.

Property (P3) states that there is an one-to-one correspondence between the set of *req_id* and the elements of the set A. i.e., the sequencer has to assign a different sequence number to each distinct client request. Property (P4) says that numbers assigned by the sequencer to requests do not have "holes" in a sequence starting from one. Property (P5) expresses the fact that the service is live.

2.   System model

We consider a distributed system in which processes communicate by message passing. Processes can be of two types: clients and replicas. The latter form a set $\{r_1, \ldots, r_n\}$ of processes implementing the fault-tolerant sequencer. A client c runs in an asynchronous distributed system and communicates only with replicas using *reliable asynchronous channels*. Replicas exchange messages among them by using a *timed asynchronous datagram service*[11, 9].

2.1   Client Processes

A client process sends a request to the sequencer service and then waits for a sequence number. A client performs (unreliable) failure detection of replicas using only local timeouts and cope with replica failures using a simple retransmission mechanism. A client may fail by crashing.

Communication between clients and replicas are *asynchronous* and *reliable*. Therefore, (i) there is no bound on message transfer delay and process speeds (asynchrony) and (ii) messages exchanged between two non-crashing processes are eventually delivered (reliability). More specifically, clients and replicas use the following communication primitives to exchange messages:

- **A-send**(m, p): to send an unicast message m to process p;

- **A-deliver**(m, p): to deliver a message m sent by process p.

The client pseudo-code is shown in Figure 1. To label a generic event with a sequence number generated by the sequencer service, a client invokes the GETSEQ() method (line 3). Such method blocks the client process and invokes the sequencer replicas. Once an integer sequence number has been received from a replica, the GETSEQ() method returns it as output parameter. In particular, the GETSEQ() method first assigns to the ongoing request a unique request identifier $req\_id = \langle cl\_id, \#cl\_seq \rangle$ (line 7-8), and then enters a loop (line 9). Within the loop, the client (i) sends the request to a replica (line 10) and (ii) sets a local timeout (line 11). Then, a result is returned by GETSEQ() if the client process receives within the timeout period a sequence number for the req_id request (line 14). Otherwise another replica is selected (line 15) and the request is sent again towards such a replica (line 12).

```
CLASS CLIENT
  1   rlist := ⟨r₁, ..., rₙ⟩;
  2   INTEGER #cl_seq := 0;
  3   INTEGER GETSEQ()
  4     begin
  5       INTEGER i := 0;
  6       REQUEST req_id;
  7       #cl_seq := #cl_seq + 1;
  8       req_id :=< cl_id, #cl_seq >;
  9       loop
 10         A-send ["getSeq", req_id] to rlist[i];
 11         t.setTimeout := period;
 12         wait until ((A-deliver ["Seq", seq, req_id] from r ∈ rlist) or (t.expired()))
 13         if (not t.expired())
 14           then return (seq);
 15           else  i := (i + 1) mod |rlist|;
 16       end loop
 17     end
```

Figure 1. Protocol Executed by a Client c

2.2 Replica Processes

Each replica r_i has access to a hardware clock with bounded drift rate with respect to other replicas' clocks. Replicas can fail by crashing. However they can also become "slow" with respect to their specification: a time-out σ is introduced to define a replica performance failure. A replica with a scheduling delay greater than σ suffers a performance failure. A process is *timely* in a time interval $[s, t]$ iff during $[s, t]$ it neither crashes nor suffers a performance failure. For simplicity, a process that fails by crashing cannot recover.

Communications among replicas occur through channels that are subject to two kind of failures: a message can be omitted (dropped) or can be delivered after a given timeout δ (performance failure). A message whose transmission delay is at most δ is *timely*. Two replicas are *connected* in a time interval $[s, t]$ iff they are *timely* in $[s, t]$ and each message exchanged between the two replicas in $[s, t]$ it timely. A subset of replicas form a *stable* partition in $[s, t]$ if any pair of replicas belonging to the subset is connected. Timed asynchronous communications are achieved through a *datagram service* [9] which filters out non-timely messages to the above layer. In the following we assume replicas communicate through the following primitives:

- **TA-send**(m, r_i): to send an unicast message m to process r_i;

- **TA-broadcast**(m): to broadcast m to all replicas including the sender of m;

- **TA-deliver**(m, r_j): upcall initiated by the datagram service to deliver a *timely* message m sent by process r_j.

We assume replicas implement the leader election service specified by Cristian and Fetzer [12]. The leader election service ensures that:
• at every physical time there exists at most one *leader*, a *leader* is a replica in which the *Leader?()* boolean function returns *true*;
• the leader election protocol underlying the *Leader?()* boolean function takes at least 2δ for a leader change;
• when a majority of replicas forms a stable partition in a time interval $[t, t + \Delta t]$ $(\Delta t >> 2\delta)$, then it exists a replica r_i belonging to that majority that becomes leader in $[t, t + \Delta t]$.

Note that the leader election service cannot guarantee that when a replica becomes leader it stays connected to all other replicas of its stable partition for the duration of its leadership.

In order to cope with asynchronous interactions between clients and replicas, to ensure the liveness of our sequencer protocol, we introduce the following assumption, i.e.:

• **eventual global stabilization**:there exists a time t and a set $\mathcal{S} \subseteq \{r_1, ...r_n\} : |\mathcal{S}| \geq \lceil \frac{n+1}{2} \rceil$ such that $\forall t' \geq t$, $\mathcal{S}$ is a *stable* partition.

The eventual global stabilization assumption implies (i) only a minority of replicas can crash[2] and (ii) there will eventually exist a leader replica in $\mathcal{S}$.

3. The Sequencer Protocol

In this section we present a fault-tolerant implementation of the sequencer service. A primary-backup replication (or passive replication) scheme is adopted [13].

Backup failures are transparent to clients while, when a primary fails (either by crashing or by a performance failure), a main problem has to be addressed: *the election of a new primary whose internal state verifies the sequencer specification properties described in Section 1.*

In our implementation, the election of a primary lies on:

1. The availability of the leader election service running among replicas (see Section 2). To be a leader is a necessary condition firstly to have the chance to become the primary and, secondly, to stay as the primary.
2. A "reconciliation" procedure (namely "*computing_sequencer_state*" procedure) that allows a newly elected leader to remove possible inconsistencies from its state before becoming a primary. These inconsistencies if kept in the primary state could violate sequencer service properties defined in Section 1.

In our implementation we exploit the *computing_sequencer_state* procedure, in order to enhance performance of the update primitives during failure-free runs. More specifically, an update primitive (denoted WRITEMAJ()) issued by a primary successfully returns if it timely updates at least a *majority* of replicas. As a consequence during the reconciliation procedure a newly elected leader, before becoming a primary, has to read at least a majority of states of other replicas (this is done by a READMAJ() primitive). This allows a leader to have a state containing all the successfully updates done by previous primaries. Then the leader removes from such state all possible inconsistencies caused by unsuccessful primary updates.

3.1   Protocol Data Structures

Each replica r_i endows:
- *primary* boolean variable, which is set according to the role (either primary or backup) played by the replica at a given time;
- *seq* integer variable, which represents the sequence number assigned to a client request when r_i acts as a primary;
- *state* consisting of a pair $\langle TA, epoch \rangle$ where TA is a set $\{ta_1, ...ta_k\}$ of *tentative assignments* and *epoch* is an integer variable.
- *state.epoch* represents a value associated with the last primary seen by r_i. When r_i becomes the current primary, *epoch* has to be greater than any *epoch* value associated with previous primary. *state.epoch* is set when a replica becomes primary and it does not change during all the time a replica is the primary.
- A *tentative assignment ta* is a triple $\langle req\_id, \#seq, \#epoch \rangle$ where $ta.\#seq$ is the sequence number assigned to the client request $ta.req\_id$

and *ta.#epoch* is the epoch number of the primary that executed the assignment *ta*.

The set *state.TA* is ordered by the field *TA.#seq* and ties are broken using the field *TA.#epoch*. Then the operation *last(state.TA)* returns the tentative assignment with greatest epoch number among the ones, if any, with greatest sequence number. If *state.TA* is empty, then *last(state.TA)* returns *null*.

3.2   Basic Primitives and Definitions

The pseudo-codes of the WRITEMAJ() and the READMAJ() functions are respectively shown in Figures 2 and 3. Moreover, Figure 4 shows the pseudo-code of the LISTENER() thread handling message receipts at each replica.

WriteMaj().   The WRITEMAJ() function (Figure 2) takes as input argument m and returns a boolean b. m can be either a tentative assignment *ta* or an epoch e. In both cases, upon invocation, the WRITEMAJ() function first checks if the replica is the leader, then it executes **TA-broadcast**(m) and then sets a timer of duration[3] $T = 2\delta(1 + \rho)$ to count the number of timely received acknowledgement messages (lines 5-10). Each replica sends an acknowledgement upon the delivery of m (see Figure 4, line 8). When the timer expires (line 11) the function checks if a majority of timely acknowledgments has been received (line 12). In the affirmative, m is put into the replica state according to its type (line 15-16), then the function returns $\top$ (i.e. it *successfully* returns) if the replica is still leader at the end of the invocation (line 17).

Let us finally present the following observations that will be used in Section 4 to show the correctness of our protocol:

Observation 1. *Let ta be a tentative assignment, if r_i successfully executes* WRITEMAJ(*ta*) *then*
$\exists maj : maj \subseteq \{r_1, ..., r_n\}, |maj| \geq \lceil\frac{n+1}{2}\rceil, \ r_i \in maj, \ r_j \in maj \Rightarrow ta \in state_{r_j}.TA$.

Observation 2. *Let ta be a tentative assignment, if r_i executes without success* WRITEMAJ(*ta*) *then ta $\notin state_{r_i}.TA$.*

Observation 3. *Let e be an epoch number, if r_i successfully executes* WRITEMAJ(*e*) *then*
$\exists maj : maj \subseteq \{r_1, ..., r_n\}, |maj| \geq \lceil\frac{n+1}{2}\rceil, \ r_i \in maj, \ r_j \in maj \Rightarrow state_{r_j}.epoch = e$.

```
1   BOOLEAN WRITEMAJ(MSG msgtosend)
2     begin
3       BOOLEAN succeeded := ⊥;
4       INTEGER i := 0;
5       if (Leader?())
6         then TA-broadcast (["Write", msgtosend]);
7              alarmclock.setalarm(T); % T = H() + 2δ(1 + ρ) %
8              loop
9                when (TA-deliver (["Ack"](sender))) do
10                  i := i + 1;
11               when (alarmclock.wake(T)) do
12                 if (i ≥ ⌈n+1/2⌉)
13                   then succeeded := ⊤;
14                     if (recmsg is Assignment)
15                       then state.TA := state.TA ⋃ recmsg;
16                       else  state.epoch := recmsg;
17                   return (succeeded and Leader?())
18               end loop
19    end
```

Figure 2. The WRITEMAJ() Function Pseudo-code Executed by r_i

Such properties trivially follow from the WRITEMAJ() function and LISTENER() thread pseudo-codes (Figure 2 and Figure 4).

Definitive and Non-definitive Assignments. We are now in the position to introduce the notion of *definitive assignment* that will be used in the rest of the paper:

Definition 1. *A tentative assignment ta is a* definitive *assignment iff exists a primary p such that p executed* WRITEMAJ(*ta*)= ⊤.

Therefore, a definitive assignment is a tentative one. The viceversa is not necessarily true. A tentative assignment which is not definitive is called *non-definitive*.

Non-definitive assignments are actually inconsistencies due to unsuccessful WRITEMAJ() executions. If the state of a primary would contain non-definitive assignments, it could violate the bijection property (Section 1). However, by filtering out non-definitive assignments during the *computing_sequencer_state* procedure, we let the state of a primary contain only definitive assignments. Thus we enforce the bijection property only on definitive assignments (Theorem 3 in Section 4).

ReadMaj( ). This function does not have input arguments and returns as output parameter a pair $\langle b, s \rangle$ where b is a boolean value and s is a state as defined in Section 3.1. If READMAJ() returns $b = ⊤$, then (i) $s.TA$ contains the union of the tentative assignments contained in the states of a majority of replicas, denoted maj_state and (ii) $s.epoch$ equals the greatest epoch number contained in states of the replicas belonging to maj_state.

As shown in Figure 3, this function executes a **TA-broadcast**() (line 6) which causes the LISTENER() thread running in every replica r_i to send its replica state ($state_i$) as the reply to the broadcast (Figure 4, line 9). After executed the broadcast, the READMAJ() function sets a time-out (line 7) to count timely replies. Then it enters a loop where handles two types of events, i.e. the arrival of a timely reply and the elapsing of the timeout. In the first case (lines 9-12) the function (i) merges the tentative assignments contained in the just received state ($state_{sender}$) with the one contained in the $maj\_state.TA$ variable (initially empty), (ii) sets the $maj\_state.epoch$ value to the maximum between the current $maj\_state.epoch$ value and $state_{sender}.epoch$ and (iii) increases the counter of the timely reply.

In the second case (i.e., when the timeout elapses, line 13), the function checks if at least a majority of timely replies has been received (line 14). In the affirmative, if the replica is still the leader it returns a pair $\langle b, s \rangle$ with $b = \top$ and $s = maj\_state$ (line 17).

Let us introduce the following observations that will be used in Section 4 to show the correctness of our protocol:

Observation 4. *If r_i successfully executes* READMAJ()*, then* $maj\_state.TA$ *contains all the definitive assignments previously executed.*

Observation 5. *If r_i successfully executes* READMAJ()*, then* $maj\_state.epoch \geq max\{e' : some\ replica\ executed\ \mathrm{WRITEMAJ}(e') = \top\}$.

Such properties trivially follow from the READMAJ() function and LISTENER() thread pseudo-codes (Figure 3 and Figure 4) and from Definition 1.

3.3   Introductory Examples and Descriptions

Let us present in this section two introductory examples and a preliminary explanation of the sequencer protocol before getting through the pseudo-code executed by each replica (shown in Figure 7).

The "*computing_sequencer_state*" procedure.   The first action performed by a newly elected leader r_i is to invoke READMAJ(). If READMAJ() returns false and r_i is always the leader, r_i will execute

```
 1   <BOOLEAN,STATE> READMAJ()
 2   begin
 3      BOOLEAN succeeded := ⊥;
 4      INTEGER i := 0;
 5      STATE maj_state := (∅ 0);
 6      TA-broadcast (["Read"]);
 7      alarmclock.setalarm(T); % T = H() + 2δ(1 + ρ) %
 8      loop
 9         when (TA-deliver (["State", state_sender](sender))) do
10            maj_state.TA := maj_state.TA ∪ state_sender.TA;
11            maj_state.epoch := max(maj_state.epoch, state_sender.epoch);
12            i := i + 1;
13         when (alarmclock.wake(T)) do
14            if (i ≥ ⌈(n+1)/2⌉)
15               then succeeded := ⊤;
16            return (succeeded and Leader?(), maj_state)
17      end loop
18   end
```

Figure 3. The READMAJ() Function Pseudo-code Executed by r_i

```
 1   THREAD LISTENER()
 2   begin
 3      when (TA-deliver ([typemsg, recmsg](sender))) do
 4         case typemsg
 5         {"Write"} : if (recmsg is Assignment and r_i ≠ sender)
 6                        then state.TA := state.TA ∪ recmsg;
 7                        else state.epoch := recmsg;
 8                     TA-send (["Ack" ]) to sender;
 9         {"Read"} : TA-send (["State", state]) to sender;
10         end case
11   end
```

Figure 4. The LISTENER() Thread Pseudo-code Executed by r_i

again READMAJ(). If r_i is no longer leader, the following leader will execute READMAJ() till this primitive will be successfully executed.

Once the union of the states of a majority of backup replicas, denoted *maj_state*, has been fetched by READMAJ(), the *computing sequencer state* procedure executed by r_i has three main goals:

1. to transform the tentative assignment *last(maj_state.TA)* in a definitive assignment *on behalf of a previous primary* that issued WRITEMAJ(*last(maj_state.TA)*), as there is no way for r_i to know if that WRITEMAJ() was executed with success by the previous primary.

2. to remove from *maj_state.TA* all non-definitive assignments. Non-definitive assignments are filtered out using the epoch field of a tentative assignment. More specifically, our sequencer implementation enforces the bijection property (Section 1) by guaranteeing that when *there are* *multiple assignments with the same sequence number, the one with the greatest epoch number is a definitive assignment.* The filter is shown in Figure 7 from line 23 to line 25.

3. to impose a primary epoch number e by using a WRITEMAJ() function. Epoch number e is greater than the one returned by READMAJ() in $maj\_state.epoch$. From Observation 5, it also follows that e is greater than all previous epoch numbers associated to primaries.

If r_i executed with success all previous points it sets $state$ to maj_state and starts serving client requests as primary.

In the following we introduce two examples which point out how the previous actions removes inconsistencies (i.e., non-definitive assignments) from a primary state during the *computing_sequencer_state* procedure.

Example 1: Avoiding inconsistencies by redoing the last tentative assignment. Figure 5 shows a protocol run in which a primary replica r_1 starts serving client requests. In particular r_1 accepts a client request req_id_1, creates a tentative assignment $ta_1 = \langle req\_id_1, 1, 1 \rangle$, performs WRITEMAJ($ta_1$)$= \top$ (i.e. ta_1 is a definitive assignment) and finally sends back the result $\langle 1, req\_id_1 \rangle$ to the client. Then r_1 receives a new client request $req\_id_2 \neq req\_id_1$, invokes WRITEMAJ($ta_2 = \langle req\_id_2, 2, 1 \rangle$) and crashes during the invocation. Before crashing it updated only replica r_3. The next leader r_2 enters the sequencer state computation: it executes READMAJ(), which returns in $maj\_state.TA$ the union of states of r_2 and r_3 (i.e., $\{ta_1, ta_2\}$) and in $maj\_state.epoch$ the epoch number of the previous primary r_1 (i.e., 1). Therefore, as $last(maj\_state.TA)$ returns ta_2, r_2 executes WRITEMAJ(ta_2)$= \top$ on behalf of the previous primary (r_2 cannot know if ta_2 is definitive or not).

Replica r_2 then executes WRITEMAJ($maj\_state.epoch + 1$) to notify its epoch number as last action of the "*computing sequencer state*" procedure. Finally, when r_2 receives the request req_id_2, it founds ta_2 in its state and immediately returns $ta_2.\#seq$ to the client.

Example 2: Avoiding inconsistencies by filtering out non-definitive assignments. The example is shown in Figure 6. Primary r_1 successfully serves request req_id_1. Then, upon the arrival of a new request req_id_2, it invokes WRITEMAJ(), exhibits a performance failure and updates only replica r_3 (ta_2 is a non-definitive assignment). As a consequence r_i looses its primaryship and another leader r_2 is elected. r_2 executes READMAJ() which returns in maj_state the union of as-

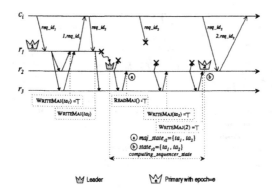

Figure 5. Example of a Run of the Sequencer Protocol

signments belonging to r_1 and r_2 states (i.e., $\{ta_1\}$). Then r_2 ends its reconciliation procedure by executing WRITEMAJ(ta_1)= ⊤ and by notifying its epoch.

Upon the arrival of a new request req_id_3, primary r_2 executes WRITEMAJ($ta_2' = \langle req\_id_3, 2, 2\rangle$) with success (i.e. ta_2' is a definitive assignment) and sends back the result $\langle 2, req\_id_3\rangle$ to the client.

Note that r_1 and r_3 contain two distinct assignments (i.e., ta_2 and ta_2') with a same sequence number and different epoch numbers ($ta_2.\#epoch = 1$ and $ta_2'.\#epoch = 2$). The $maj\_state.TA$ of a successive leader r_i (r_1 in Figure 6) includes, from Observation 4, the definitive assignment ta_2'. If ta_2 is also a member of $maj\_state.TA$, r_i is able to filter ta_2 out from $maj\_state.TA$ as $ta_2.\#epoch < ta_2'.\#epoch = 2$. After the filtering, the state of the primary r_1 is composed only by definitive assignments. Note that without performing such filtering the bijection property would result violated, as the state of a primary could contain two assignments with a same sequence number.

Then, when r_1 receives the client request req_id_2 (due to the client retransmission mechanism) previously associated to ta_2, it performs WRITEMAJ($ta_3 = \langle req\_id_2, 3, 3\rangle$) and if it returns with success, r_1 returns the sequence number 3 to the client.

3.4 Behaviour of Each Replica

The protocol executed by r_i consists in an infinite loop where three types of events can occur (see Figure 7):

1. Receipt of a client request when r_i acts as a primary (line 6);

2. Receipt of a "no leadership" notification from the leader election service (line 14);

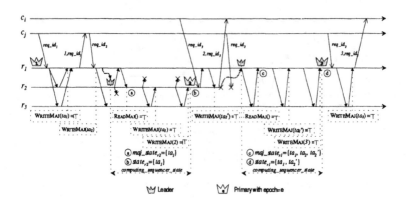

Figure 6. Example of a Run of the Sequencer Protocol

CLASS SEQUENCER
```
1   TENTATIVE ASSIGNMENT ta;
2   STATE state := (∅, 0);
3   BOOLEAN primary := ⊥; connected := ⊥;
4   INTEGER seq := 0;
5   loop
6     when ((A-deliver ["GetSeq", req_id] from c) and primary) do
7       if (∃ta' ∈ state.TA : ta'.req_id = req_id)
8       then A-send ["Seq", ta'.#seq, req_id] to c;
9       else  seq := seq + 1;
10            ta.#seq := seq; ta.req_id := req_id; ta.#epoch := state.epoch;
11            if (WriteMaj (ta))
12            then A-send ["Seq", seq, req_id] to c;
13            else  primary := ⊥;
14    when (not Leader?()) do
15      primary := ⊥;
16    when ((Leader?()) and (not primary)) do
17      (connected, maj_state) := ReadMaj ();   % computing_sequencer_state %
18      if (connected)
19      then ta := last(maj_state.TA);
20            if (ta ≠ null)
21            then connected := WriteMaj (ta);
22                  if (connected)
23                  then for each ta_j, ta_ℓ ∈ maj_state.TA :
24                        (ta_j.#seq = ta_ℓ.#seq) and (ta_j.#epoch > ta_ℓ.#epoch)
25                        do maj_state.TA := maj_state.TA − {ta_ℓ};
26                  state.TA := maj_state.TA; seq := last(state.TA).#seq;
27            if (WriteMaj (maj_state.epoch + 1) and connected)
28            then primary := ⊤;
29  end loop
```

Figure 7. The Sequencer Protocol Pseudo-code Executed by r_i

3.Receipt of a "leadership" notification from the leader election service when r_i is not primary (line 16).

Receipt of a client request *req_id* **when** r_i **acts as a primary.**

r_i first checks if the client request is a retransmission of an already served request (line 7). In the affirmative, p_i simply returns to the client the global sequence number previously assigned to the requests (line 8). Otherwise, p_i (i) increases by 1 the *seq* variable (line 9) and (ii) generates a tentative assignment *ta* such that $ta.\#seq = seq; ta.req\_id = req\_id; ta.\#epoch := state.epoch$ (line 10). Then p_i executes WRITEMAJ(*ta*) (line 11). If it successfully returns *ta* becomes a definitive assignment and the result is sent back to the client (line 12). Otherwise, the primary sets *primary* $= \perp$ (line 13) as WRITEMAJ(*ta*) failed and r_i stops serving client requests.

Receipt of a "leadership" notification when r_i **is not primary.**

A *computing_sequencer_state* procedure (lines 16-29) is started by r_i to become primary. As described in the previous section, r_i has to execute with success all the following four actions to become a primary:

A1. r_i invokes the READMAJ() function (line 18). If the invocation is successful it timely returns a majority state in the *maj_state* variable[4].

A2. r_i extracts the last assignment *ta* from *maj_state.TA* (line 19) and invokes WRITEMAJ(*ta*) (line 21) to make definitive the last assignment of *maj_state.TA* (see the examples in the previous section).

A3. r_i eliminates from *maj_state.TA* any assignment ta_ℓ such that it exists another assignment ta_j having the same sequence number of ta_ℓ but greater epoch number (lines 23-25). The presence of such a ta_j in *maj_state* implies that ta_ℓ is not definitive. This can be intuitively justified by noting that if an assignment ta_j performed by a primary p_k is definitive, no following primary will try to execute another assignment with the same sequence number. After the filtering, *state.TA* is set to *maj_state.TA* and *seq* to $last(state.TA).\#seq$ as this is the last executed definitive assignment (line 26).

A4. r_i invokes WRITEMAJ(*maj_state.epoch* + 1) at line 27 to impose its primary epoch number greater than any previous primary. Then, r_i becomes primary (line 28).

If any of the above actions is not successfully executed by r_i, it will not become primary. Note that if r_i is still leader after the unsuccessful execution of the *computing_sequencer_state* procedure, it restarts to execute the procedure.

Receipt of a "no leadership" notification. r_i sets the *primary* variable to $\perp$ (line 15). Note that a notification of "no leadership" imposes READMAJ() and WRITEMAJ() to fail (i.e. to return $\perp$, see Figure 2, line 17 and Figure 3 line 16). As a consequence if r_i was serving a request and executing statement 11, it sets *primary* to $\perp$ (line 13) upon a leadership loss.

4.   Sketch of the Correctness Proof

In this section, due to lack of space we show a sketch of the correctness proof. The formal correctness proof can be found in [10]. This sketch shows that our sequencer implementation satisfies the properties defined in Section 1. Let us remark that the state of the sequencer service A corresponds to the set of tentative assignments, denoted $state_{p_i}.TA$, contained in the state of the current primary p_i.

Definition 2. *A primary sequence* $\mathcal{P} = \langle p_1, ...p_k \rangle$ *is a sequence of replica identifiers* r_i *where* p_i *represents the i-th replica executing statement 28.*

Theorem 1 (P1). *If* $ta \in state_{p_i}.TA$ *then there exists a client c that issued a request identified by* req_id *and* $req\_id = ta.req\_id$.

Proof. The existence of a tentative assignment $ta \in state_{p_i}.TA$ implies that a WRITEMAJ(ta) has been executed at line 11 by a primary p_j, $(j \leq i)$. The latter statement is executed by a primary only after the receipt of a client request (line 6) identified by req_id and after $ta.req\_id$ has been set to req_id at line 10.   □

Theorem 2 (P2). *If a client c delivers a reply* $\#seq$, *then it exists a primary* $p_i \in \mathcal{P}$ *and a tentative assignment ta such that ta =* $\langle req\_id, \#seq \rangle \in state_{p_i}.TA$.

Proof. By contradiction. Suppose a client c delivers a reply $\#seq$ and $\nexists p_i \in \mathcal{P} : ta \in state_{p_i}.TA$ and $ta.\#seq = \#seq$. If c delivers a reply $\#seq$, from channel reliability assumption, it has been sent by a primary p_j that executed either statement 8 or statement 12. In both cases $ta \in state_{p_j}.TA$ (either ta already belongs to the p_j's state, statement 7, or from Observation 1 as p_j executed WRITEMAJ(ta)= ⊤ at statement 11). Therefore in both cases $ta.\#seq = \#seq$. This contradicts the initial assumption.   □

Theorem 3 (P3). *Let* p_i *be the current primary*
$\forall ta_i, ta_j \in state_{p_i}.TA : ta_i.\#seq \neq ta_j.\#seq \Leftrightarrow ta_i.req\_id \neq ta_j.req\_id$

Proof. As ta_i and ta_j are two assignments belonging to $state_{p_i}.TA$, they are definitive assignments as informally shown in the two examples of section 3.3. As $ta_i, ta_j \in state_{p_i}.TA$ then two primaries exist such that executed respectively $\text{WRITEMAJ}(ta_i) = \top$ and $\text{WRITEMAJ}(ta_j) = \top$. Without loss of generality, we assume $\text{WRITEMAJ}(ta_i) = \top$ is executed before $\text{WRITEMAJ}(ta_j) = \top$ by a primary p. As p increases the *seq* variable (statement 9) each time it executes a new assignment it follows that two assignments with the same sequence number have never been executed. Moreover p contains in its state ta_i (Observation 1). This implies that when p receives a client request such that $req\_id = ta_i.req\_id$, it will execute always lines 7-8. It follows that it never executes a new assignment with the same req_id.

As ta_i is definitive, if p stops serving client requests the successive primaries contain ta_i in their states before they start serving requests. This derives from Observation 4 and from the fact that a definitive assignment is never filtered out at the statement 25 as we shown in example 2 section 3.3. As a consequence any primary successive to p never executes a new assignment ta with $ta.req\_id = ta_i.req\_id$ or $ta.\#seq = ta_i.\#seq$. $\qquad\square$

Theorem 4 (P4). *Let p_i be the current primary*
$$\forall ta_i \in state_{p_i}.TA : ta_i.\#seq \geq 1 \land ta_i.seq > 1 \Rightarrow \exists ta_j \in state_{p_i}.TA :$$
$$ta_j.\#seq = ta_i.\#seq - 1$$

Proof. As at line 5 the *seq* variable is initialized to 0 and each primary before executing a tentative assignment (statement 10) executes an increment of *seq* (statement 9), it follows that for each assignment executed by a primary $ta_i.\#seq \geq 1$.

The existence of an assignment $ta_i \in state_{p_i}.TA$ implies that a $\text{WRITEMAJ}(ta_i)$ has been executed at line 11 by a primary p_j, $(j \leq i)$. We have two cases:

(p_j executes statement 11 for the first time). Being primary, p_j completed *computing_sequencer_state* procedure (lines 17–29). This implies that it has previously executed a $\text{WRITEMAJ}(ta_j) = \top$ with a given $ta_j.\#seq$ (line 21). As p_j, before executing line 11, executes line 9, it increases *seq* by one, hence $ta_j.\#seq = ta.\#seq - 1$.

(p_j already executed statement 11 at least one time). In this case p_j has previously executed $\text{WRITEMAJ}(ta_j = \top)$ at statement 11 with a given $ta_j.\#seq$. When p_i executes $\text{WRITEMAJ}(ta_i)$ at statement 11, from line 9, it follows $ta.\#seq = ta'.\#seq + 1$.

As $\text{WRITEMAJ}(ta_j) = \top$ from Definition 1 it follows that is a definitive assignment. From Observation 4 and from the fact that a definitive assignment is never filtered out at the statement 25 as we shown in example 2 section 3.3, it follows that $ta_j \in state_{p_i}.TA$. $\qquad\square$

Theorem 5 (P5). *If a client c issues a request identified by req_id, then, unless c crashes it eventually delivers a reply $\#seq$.*

Proof. By contradiction. Let us assume that c does not crash and invokes the GETSEQ() method of class CLIENT (Figure 1 at page 5) and never receives a reply. c eventually sends the request identified by *req_id* to every replica $r_i \in \{r_1, ..., r_n\}$. From the channel reliability assumption and the global stabilization assumption, it will eventually exist a primary p_k which will receive the *req_id* request, generate a reply *#seq* and send the reply back to the client. From channel reliability, the reply will eventually reach the client. Contradiction.   □

5.   Conclusions

In this paper we presented the specification of a sequencer service which allows thin, independent clients to get a unique and consecutive sequence number in order to globally order successive relevant events they generate. We have then shown a fault-tolerant sequencer implementation based on a primary-backup replication scheme which uses a timed asynchronous datagram service to communicate among replicas. The implementation shows good performance in failure free runs as only a majority of replicas needs to receive primary updates. A sketch of the correctness proof of the implementation, with respect to the specification, has been also given.

Notes

1. In an asynchronous distributed system where processes can crash this problem cannot be solved (unless a minimum degree of synchrony is added to the system) as it is equivalent to solve the consensus problem [14].

2. Note that at any given time t' (with $t' < t$) any number of replicas can simultaneously suffer a performance failure.

3. 2δ is the maximum round-trip time for timely messages in timed asynchronous model and $2\delta(1 + \rho)$ is the timeout to set in a replica with the clock with maximum positive drift (ρ) to measure a 2δ time duration.

4. Due to the time taken by the the leader election protocol [12] (at least 2δ) to select a leader (see Section 3), it follows that any READMAJ() function starts after the arrival of all the *timely* messages broadcast through any previous WRITEMAJ().

References

[1] K. Birman and T. Joseph. Reliable Communication in the Presence of Failures. *ACM Transactions on Computer Systems*, 5(1):47–76, February 1987.

[2] K. Birman, A. Schiper, and P. Stephenson. Lightweight Causal and Atomic Group Multicast. *ACM Transactions on Computer Systems*, 9(3):272–314, August 1991.

[3] R. Baldoni and C. Marchetti. Software replication in three-tiers architectures: is it a real challenge? In *Proceedings of the 8th IEEE*

Workshop on Future Trends of Distributed Computing Systems (FT-DCS'2001), pages 133–139, Bologna, Italy, November 2001.

[4] R. Guerraoui and S. Frolund. Implementing E-Transactions with Asynchronous Replication. *IEEE Transactions on Parallel and Distributed Systems*, 12(2):133–146, 2001.

[5] Object Management Group (OMG), Framingham, MA, USA. *The Common Object Request Broker Architecture and Specifications. Revision 2.4.2*, OMG Document formal edition, February 2001. OMG Final Adopted Specification.

[6] M. Raynal. *Algorithms for Mutual Exclusion*. MIT Press, 1986.

[7] R. Guerraoui and A. Schiper. Software-Based Replication for Fault Tolerance. *IEEE Computer - Special Issue on Fault Tolerance*, 30:68–74, April 1997.

[8] L.E. Moser, P.M. Melliar-Smith, D.A. Agarwal, R.K. Budhia, and C.A. Lingley-Papadopoulos. Totem: A Fault-Tolerant Multicast Group Communication System. *Communications of the ACM*, 39(4):54–63, April 1996.

[9] C. Fetzer and F. Cristian. A Fail-aware Datagram Service. *IEE Proceedings - Software Engineering*, 146(2):58–74, April 1999.

[10] R. Baldoni, C. Marchetti, and S. Tucci-Piergiovanni. Fault Tolerant Sequencer: Specification and an Implementation. Technical Report 27.01, Dipartimento di Informatica e Sistemistica, Universitá di Roma "La Sapienza", http://www.dis.uniroma1.it/~baldoni/publications, november 2001.

[11] C. Fetzer and F. Cristian. The Timed Asynchronous Distributed System Model. *IEEE Transactions on Parallel and Distributed Systems*, 10(6):642–657, 1999.

[12] C. Fetzer and F. Cristian. A Highly Available Local Leader Election Service. *IEEE Transactions on Software Engineering*, 25(5):603–618, 1999.

[13] N. Budhiraja, F.B. Schneider, S. Toueg, and K. Marzullo. *The Primary-Backup Approach*, chapter 8, pages 199–216. Addison Wesley, 1993.

[14] M. Fischer, N. Lynch, and M. Patterson. Impossibility of Distributed Consensus with One Faulty Process. *Journal of the ACM*, 32(2):374–382, April 1985.

Chapter 9

QoS ANALYSIS OF GROUP COMMUNICATION PROTOCOLS IN WIRELESS ENVIRONMENT*

Andrea Bondavalli
Univ. of Firenze, 50134 Firenze, Italy
a.bondavalli@dsi.unifi.it

Andrea Coccoli
Univ. of Pisa, 56126 Pisa, Italy
a.coccoli@guest.cnuce.cnr.it

Felicita Di Giandomenico
IEI-CNR, 56124 Pisa, Italy
digiandomenico@iei.pi.cnr.it

Abstract QoS analysis is a necessary step for the early verification and validation of an appropriate design, and for taking design decisions about the most rewarding choice, in relation with user requirements. The area of distributed applications, whose development is increasing more and more, favoured by the high connectivity provided by advanced Internet and Web technologies, poses special challenges in this respect. In this chapter, we describe an analytical approach for the evaluation of the QoS offered by two group communication protocols in a wireless environment. Experimental data are used both to feed the models and to validate them. Specific performance and dependability related indicators have been defined and evaluated. To improve the utility of our study, we analysed the protocols taking into account relevant phenomena affecting the environment in which such protocols are called to operate. Specifically, the fading phenomenon and the user mobility have been explicitly introduced in our models, to evaluate their impact on the correlation among successive packet transmissions. Also, in order to enhance the correctness of the derived models, a formal description of the protocols has been performed, adopting the timed asynchronous system model. The aim of this work is to provide a fast, cost effective, and formally sound way to analyse and understand protocols behaviour and their environment.

* This work has been partly performed in the framework of the DECOR project, involving GMD (Germany) and CNR (Italy).

P. Ezhilchelvan and A. Romanovsky (eds.), Concurrency in Dependable Computing, 169–188.
© 2002 *Kluwer Academic Publishers. Printed in the Netherlands.*

1 INTRODUCTION

The advances of the Internet and the Web technologies, as well as those of the mobile networks infrastructures, have greatly favoured the development of distributed applications by providing high connectivity. To properly account for the different users requiring such applications, it is important to have suitable computational and structural models to represent the point of view of the specific user, and appropriate methods to evaluate the system quality of service (QoS). QoS can be defined as a set of qualitative and quantitative characteristics of a distributed system, which are necessary for obtaining the required functionality of an application [1]. Therefore the term QoS encompasses many aspects including reliability, availability, fault tolerance and also properties such as the atomicity or reliability of broadcast/multicast services.

It is clear that the usefulness and practical utilisation of such (sub)system designs depend on the possibility to provide a QoS analysis of their offered features, in terms of properly defined indicators. When building a system, this is a necessary step for the early verification and validation of an appropriate design, and for taking design decisions about the most rewarding choice, in relation with user requirements. Our approach for contributing towards these objectives is through analytical modelling and experimental evaluation. In this paper, we concentrate on two group communication protocols in wireless environment, used as reference systems to which the QoS analysis is applied. The protocols defined in [2] provide real-time reliable group communication by extending the IEEE 802.11 standard for wireless local area networks [3].

In this paper, we analyse the two protocols and their environment, focusing our attention on typical performance indicators and on the coverage of the assumptions the correctness of the protocol is based on. To improve the understanding of the protocols behaviour, necessary to a correct analysis, a formal description of the protocols is first provided, using the timed asynchronous system model [4]. Based on this formal description, the analysis is carried on, resorting to an analytical approach adopting Stochastic Activity Networks (SAN) [5, 6]. Experimental data, previously collected in a representative experimental context [7], are used both to provide parameters values for the model and to validate the analytical model itself, thus raising the confidence on the accuracy of the (more complex) final figures derivable from the analytical model. To keep adherence with reality, the *fading channels* phenomenon and the user mobility are considered, and their influence on the correlation on messages losses is analysed. Previous work based on the simplistic assumption of independence among message failures had, in fact, shown deficiencies when comparing the obtained results with others experimentally derived.

The rest of the paper is organised as follows. Section 2 is devoted to the introduction of the considered communication protocols, and to their formal description in the timed asynchronous system model. The definition of relevant metrics representative of the QoS in the selected environment is also presented. In Section 3, our approach to modelling and the assumptions made are described. Section 4 is devoted to the models description. Parameters settings and results of the models' evaluation are discussed in Section 5. Finally, concluding remarks are outlined in Section 6.

2 A FAMILY OF GROUP COMMUNICATION PROTOCOLS FOR WIRELESS LANS

2.1 Definition of the protocols

A basic means for supporting the co-operation of autonomous mobile systems is their ability to communicate via wireless links. To achieve a real-time reliable group communication [8] in wireless local area networks is a hard task: the mobility of the system components has a direct effect on the definition of a co-operative group and the hostility of the environment produces a great loss of messages. The protocol presented in [2], based on extending the IEEE 802.11 standard for wireless local area networks, allows reliable and efficient group communication services.

The IEEE 802.11 [3] standard has the great advantage of providing the basic means for the implementation of a real-time communication protocol via the "Contention Free Period" (T_{CFP}) a phase in which the medium access control is centralised and performed by a central station, denoted as the "Access Point" (AP). The problem of message losses shows a relevant phenomenon, because the wireless medium is unshielded and exposed to external interference. Broadcast messages are just unreliable datagrams sent on a best effort basis, neither order nor atomic delivery of broadcast messages is considered.

The protocols in [2] are developed following these fault assumptions:

1) Messages delivered during the T_{CFP} are delivered correctly within a fixed time-bound (t_m).
2) Messages may be lost (omission faults). Furthermore, the losses may be asymmetric; i.e., some stations may receive a broadcast message and some may not. We assume that the number of consecutive message losses is bounded by the so-called *omission degree OD*.
3) Stations may suffer crash failures or leave the reach of the access point.
4) The access point is stable; i.e., it is not subject to any kind of error.

A first developed version aims at providing a reliable group communication protocol satisfying the properties of

i) *validity*: a message broadcast by a correct station is eventually delivered by every correct station;

ii) *agreement*: a message delivered by a station is eventually delivered by any other correct station;

iii) *integrity*: for any message m, every correct station delivers m at exactly once and only if m has been broadcast;

iv) *total order*: if the messages m_1 and m_2 are delivered by stations s_1 and s_2, then station s_1 delivers message m_1 before message m_2 if and only if station s_2 delivers message m_1 before m_2.

Using the AP as the central co-ordinator, the communication of the group has been structured into rounds. During each round, the AP polls each station of the group exactly once. Upon being polled, a station returns a *broadcast request message* to the access point, which assigns a sequence number to that message and broadcasts it to the stations group. The broadcast request message is also used to acknowledge each of the preceding broadcasts by piggybacking a bit field on the header of the request message. Each bit is used to acknowledge one of the preceding broadcasts. By this, one round after sending a *broadcast message*, the access point is able to decide whether each group member has received the message or not. In the latter case, the access point will retransmit the affected message. By the assumptions made above, a message is successfully transmitted after at most $OD+1$ rounds. If the AP does not receive the request message within a certain delay after polling the station, it considers the request message (or polling message) to be lost, and transmits again the last broadcast message of the not responding station, if such message has not yet been acknowledged by all stations. If the AP does not receive the request message from a station for more than OD consecutive times, it considers that station to have left the group and broadcasts a message indicating the change in the group membership.

In order to improve the timing guarantees, a variant of the protocol has been developed, that allows the user to specify the maximum number of retransmissions of the messages. This user-defined bound on message retransmissions (called *resiliency degree, res(c)*) may be varying for different message classes c. Obviously, it is not useful to choose $res(c)$ greater than OD. Choosing $res(c)$ smaller than OD, however, allows trading reliability of message transmission for shorter transmission delays. If a message m is acknowledged by all stations within $res(c)+1$ rounds, the AP issues the decision to deliver m to the applications, through the broadcast of a *decision message* (retransmitted $OD+1$ consecutive times to guarantee reception by all the correct stations under assumption 2) above). If, however, this is not the case, a decision not to deliver m is issued, again through the broadcast of a *decision message*. To make the implementation efficient, the access point piggybacks its decisions on the messages it broadcasts, by properly extending their headers. In this version of the protocol, the shorter delivery time for a message, obtained by allowing at most *res(c)* retransmissions, is paid in terms of violation of the validity property (point i) above). In fact, a message broadcast by a correct station may not be delivered. However, the agreement and integrity properties are retained, which is enough for significant application scenarios.

2.2 Formalisation

We proceed here with a formalisation of the protocols and of their supporting system, using the timed asynchronous system model introduced by Cristian and Fetzer in [4]. In fact, the protocols under analysis rely on a synchronous system model where messages can be lost; the mentioned timed asynchronous system model is shown to be adequate and even appropriate to expose such characteristics, as well illustrated in the following. The benefits of such an effort are twofold. First, it determines a rigorous description of the protocols characteristics so as to enhance the correctness of the models defined for QoS evaluation purposes. Second, expressing the protocols in terms of a general system model, as the timed asynchronous system is, allows to simplify the definition of a family of protocols (obtained through modifying individual predicates), leading to identify the protocol variant more adequate for QoS requirements of specific applications. In this paper we adopt the results of the formalisation for improving QoS evaluation models, postponing a full discussion on a family of such protocols to better fit disparate application requirements to a next development of this study.

At the basis of the timed asynchronous model is the consideration that existing fault-tolerant services for asynchronous distributed systems are timed. The specification of the services describes not only the states transitions and the outputs in response to invocations of operations, but also the time interval within which these transitions have to be completed [4].

The timed asynchronous system model is characterised by a set of assumptions on the behaviour of processes, communications and hardware clocks:

1) all services are timed (the temporal characteristics of the events are specified), so it is possible to associate some time-outs whose expiration produces a performance failure;
2) communication between processes is obtained via an unreliable datagram service with omission/performance failure semantics;
3) processes have crash/performance failure semantics [9];
4) all non-crashed processes have access to private hardware clocks that run within a linear envelope of real-time;
5) no bound exists on the rate of communication and process failures.

The timed asynchronous system model does not require the existence of upper bounds for message transmissions and scheduling delays. However, the access to local hardware clocks and the definition of time-outs allow de-

fining the performance failure as that failure which occurs when an experienced delay is greater than the associated time-out delay. For the datagram
service the following assumptions hold:
i) there are no assumptions on the physical network topology;
ii) it permits to transmit messages either via unicast and broadcast;
iii) it univocally identifies every message;
iv) there is no upper bound on the message transmission delay;
v) it permits the definition of a time-out on the message transmission whose
    value influences the failures rate and, consequently, the system stability;
vi) it transmits the messages with a time proportional to their dimension;
vii) it has a crash/omission failure semantics (the possibility of message cor-
    ruption is negligible).
   It can be easily recognised that these assumptions cover the characteristics of the wireless LAN the analysed protocols are based on. We now proceed to the definition of our system with the concepts introduced so far.

   We assume to have a timed asynchronous system with omission failures.
The access point is assumed to be stable, i.e. to suffer no kind of failure.
   As a first step, we need to define several predicates that allow refining
the notion of a *correct* station.
   (P1) A station is within an *(OD,t_m) broadcast range* of the access point if
it receives at least one message with delay $\leq t_m$ out of *OD*+1 broadcasts of
the same message from the access point.
   (P2) A station is within an *(OD_{cons},t_m) broadcast range* of the access
point if it receives at least one message with delay $\leq t_m$ out of *OD*+1 consecutive broadcast messages of the access point.
   (P3) A station is within an *(OD,t_{PR}) request-reply range* of the access
point if at least one polling-request pair out of *OD* +1 pairs exchanged between them is successful with delay $\leq t_{PR}$.
   (P4) A station is within a *(res(c),t_m) broadcast range* of the access point
if it receives at least one message with delay $\leq t_m$ out of *res(c)*+1 broadcast
of the same message from the access point.

   On the basis of the behaviour of the first protocol, the following predi-
cates can be defined for the system:
   (P5) A station is said to be *correct* if it has not crashed, it is in an
(OD,t_{PR}) *request-reply range* and in an *(OD,t_m) broadcast range*.
   We recall that the aim of the protocol is to ensure that all the stations that
belong to the group deliver the same messages to their application level.
   Assuming that in the group there are correct stations, the protocol has the
following properties:
   (Pr1) A station that is part of the group will not be excluded from the
group as long as it is correct.

(Pr2) A non correct station will be eventually excluded from the group.

(Pr3) *Validity*: a message broadcast by a correct station is eventually delivered by every correct station.

(Pr4) *Agreement*: a message delivered by a station is eventually delivered by every correct station.

(Pr5) *Integrity*: For any message m, every correct station delivers m exactly once and only if m has been broadcast.

(Pr6) *Total Order*: If the messages m_1 and m_2 are delivered by stations s_1 and s_2, then station s_1 delivers m_1 before m_2 if and only if station s_2 delivers m_1 before m_2.

(Pr7) *Timeliness*: If all stations belonging to the group are within a *(OD, t_m) broadcast range* of the access point, a message broadcast by a correct station at real time t either is delivered to all the stations before real-time $t+\Delta t$, or not at all, for some known constant Δt.

Let's analyse first why we need such a definition for a correct station.

The *(OD,t_{PR}) request-reply range* condition ensures that the pair of messages poll-request is, at least once over OD times, successfully exchanged between the AP and the station itself. This gives the AP the knowledge of the participation of the station to the group. If the condition *(OD,t_{PR}) request-reply range* is not respected, the station is excluded from the group. As we can see, this condition is essential for guaranteeing properties Pr1 and Pr2 and, therefore, the *liveness* of the protocol.

The *(OD,t_m) broadcast range* condition is necessary for the *safety* of the protocol; in fact, the AP retransmits the same message at most OD+1 times: the case where a message is not received after all these transmissions is not explicitly considered.

Properties Pr3..Pr7 describe the characteristics of the broadcast, which is de facto an atomic broadcast. By definition, if a station is correct it will successfully exchange a couple of poll-request messages with the AP, so the AP will be 'in possess' of the message to be broadcast. The OD broadcast range condition mentioned earlier ensures *validity* and *agreement*. *Integrity* and *Total Order* are easily guaranteed by the use of the global and local sequence numbers attached to each message.

As already discussed, the second variant has been developed to improve on the protocol execution time: OD might have a very pessimistic value, while in most cases a lower number of retransmissions could be enough for all the stations to receive the broadcast. The supposed performance improvement has a cost in terms of assumptions on the system. The definition of correct station is now the following:

(P6) A station is said to be *correct* if it has not crashed, it is in an *(OD,t_{PR})-request reply range* and in an *(OD_{cons}, t_m) broadcast range*.

Also in this case, the *safety* and *liveness* of the protocol rely on the existence of correct stations. Differently from the first protocol, the (OD, t_m) *broadcast range* condition is no more necessary for the safety of the protocol; it is instead necessary that a station do receive one out of OD+1 consecutive messages, to guarantee that *decision messages* issued by the AP be received by each correct station. For this protocol, however, correctness alone is not satisfactory: guaranteeing that *progress* is made by the correct stations is required. The following predicate on progress is therefore defined:

(P7) The protocol is said to make *progress* if each correct station are in a $(res(c), t_m)$ *broadcast range*.

The properties guaranteed by the second version of the protocol slightly differ from the previous one. Specifically, properties Pr1, Pr2, Pr4, Pr6, Pr7 remain the same, while the others change as follows:

(Pr3) *"Probabilistic" Validity*: the probability that a message broadcast by a correct station will be delivered by every correct station increases with the resiliency degree res(c).

(Pr5) *Integrity*: For any message m, every correct station delivers m at *most* once and only if m has been broadcast.

Properties Pr1, Pr2, Pr4, Pr6 and Pr7 do not change with respect to the previous protocol because of the presence of the (OD, t_{PR}) *request-reply range* and (OD, t_m) *broadcast range* conditions in the definition of correctness and to the presence of sequence numbers. Property Pr4 is still the same but it is ensured by the (OD_{cons}, t_m) *broadcast range* condition (in the first protocol it was thanks to the (OD, t_m) *broadcast range* condition).

By reducing the number of retransmissions, property Pr3 cannot be anymore deterministic as before: the AP can decide for a message not to be delivered even if all the stations are correct. For this reason, an evaluation of the coverage of the assumption can give also an information on the QoS provided by this protocol.

3 APPROACH TO MODELLING

Based on the formal description of the protocols, we defined Stochastic Activity Networks (SAN) [10] models, to analyse their QoS indicators. Instead of just one single model for all the analysed measures, we defined some models, each one tailored for the evaluation of specific indicators. This allows limiting both the complexity and the size of the resulting models, with obvious benefits. The analysis has been conducted under the following assumptions:

1) the time-bound for sending a message over the network is fixed and denoted with t_m. It represents a bound for both a) the time to exchange a message between two agents in the network (namely, the AP and any other mobile station), and b) the time to broadcast a message from the AP

to all the other stations;

2) each message exchanged among system components has the same marginal probability of failure PE;

3) the couple of actions "AP polls station$_i$ - station$_i$ sends a request to broadcast" (indicated as poll-request) is managed as a single event. In fact, it is of minor importance in our study whether the access point does not receive an answer because of a lost polling- or a lost broadcast-request message. The probability of failure for the couple poll-request is constant and equal for each station; it is indicated as q_{pr};

4) failures considered are only those affecting the messages, which may fail to be received by the mobile stations and/or by the AP (omission failure). Mobile stations are therefore reliable. However, a station may migrate from the group; this event is taken into account by the protocol, through counting the number of poll-request messages towards the station that leaves the group. Although the probability of this event is not of interest per-se in the derived models, it contributes to the probability of failure of a message. The AP is assumed to be stable and reachable by all the stations belonging to the group;

5) correlation between successive transmissions of messages by the same station due to the fading channels phenomenon is considered. However, message failures among different stations are independent (the failure of a message transmitted by station$_i$ does not influence the message transmission by any other station$_j$);

6) the value of res(c) is the same for all the messages;

7) the models for the evaluation of the dependability-related figures assume that the group membership remains the same during the whole T_{CFP} interval, that is, no station misses OD+1 consecutive poll-requests, the condition for the AP to consider that station as migrated from the group.

We concentrate in the following on the analysis of two groups of figures of interest, namely dependability and performance related measures. Based on the formal description introduced, the dependability-related figures for the first variant are related to the definition of correctness and in particular to the conditions of (OD, t_m) *broadcast range* and (OD, t_{PR}) *request-reply range*. For the second variant, the dependability indicators are related to the concept of (OD_{cons}, t_m) *broadcast range* and to the probabilistic nature of property Pr4 (*"Probabilistic" Validity*). A measure $P_{R>OD}$ is defined and evaluated for the first version of the protocol, indicating the probability that a *broadcast message* is not received by at least one of the receiving stations after OD+1 transmissions, in the time interval T_{CFP} (i.e., the timing window during which the protocol operates). A corresponding measure $P_{D>OD}$ is defined and evaluated for the second protocol, indicating the probability that a *decision message* misses to be received by at least one station, again evaluated in the T_{CFP} time interval. So, both $P_{R>OD}$ and $P_{D>OD}$ represent the probability, for the protocols, to fail in an undetected way, a very undesirable event with possibly catastrophic consequences on the system and its users (*catastrophic failure* of the protocol).

Knowing such a measure is very important at design phase, in order to take appropriate actions to avoid or limit such undesirable failure event. For example, should $P_{R>OD}$ result too high, a possible recovery could be to use higher values for OD, properly trading higher probability of delivering a message to all the stations within OD retransmissions with the consequent diminishing of throughput. Alternatively, the protocol could be slightly modified, by disconnecting the stations which did not acknowledge the receipt of the message (they are known to the AP), so as to maintain a consistent view of the received messages by all the active stations.

Moreover, evaluated is also the probability P_{UM} that, in the second protocol, the AP does not receive acknowledgements on a message by all the stations in *res(c)* retransmissions. P_{UM} gives an indication of the extent of the probabilistic validity condition discussed in subsection 2.2; to get desired values of P_{UM} implies proper tuning of the protocol parameter *res(c)*.

The performance analysis is intended to determine the technical limitations imposed by the communication system and the way the protocol behaves according to them. Representative figures to evaluate are: i) the average number R_m of retransmissions for a single message; and ii) the throughput, determined as the number of delivered messages per second. These metrics are typical performance indicators, with R_m also useful to properly tune the protocol parameter *res(c)*.

4 THE MODELS

4.1 The fading phenomenon

Fading is caused by interference between two or more versions of the transmitted signal which arrive at the receiver at slightly different times following several different paths. In urban areas, fading occurs because there is no single line-of-sight path between a mobile antenna and the base station (e.g. because of the difference of height between the mobile antenna and the surrounding structures). Even when a line-of-sight exists, the reflections from the ground and the surrounding structures cause the fading phenomenon. Another cause of the fading is the relative motion between the transmitting and the receiving antennas which originates a different shift in the received signal frequency called Doppler shift [11].

We considered the model proposed in [12] for the representation of data transmission on fading channels. This model considers the so-called *flat fading* channel with relatively high data-rates (hundreds of kbit/s) and data blocks of hundreds of bits. In the literature this channel is modelled as a Gaussian random process and its correlation properties depend only on the normalized Doppler frequency F_D*T where:

F_D = Doppler Frequency = (speed of the antenna) / (signal wave-length);

T = packet size / Data rate.

If F_D*T is < 0.1 then the process is very correlated. If F_D*T is > 0.2 then the correlation is practically negligible. The fading channel can be approximated by a first-order Markov model, depicted in Figure 1.

The transition matrix $M(x) = M(1)^x$ that describes the Markov process is:

$$M(x) = \begin{pmatrix} p(x) & 1-p(x) \\ 1-q(x) & q(x) \end{pmatrix}; M(1) = \begin{pmatrix} p & 1-p \\ 1-q & q \end{pmatrix} \quad (1)$$

where p(x) (q(x)) is the probability that the ith transmission is successful (unsuccessful) given that transmission $(i-x)^{th}$ was successful (unsuccessful).

Figure 1. Markov Model of a Fading Channel

Note that $1/(1-q)$ is the average length of error bursts, while the steady state probability that an error occurs (i.e. that the process is in state F) is given by $PE=(1-p)/(2-p-q)$. Parameters p and q depend on the fading model and on the characteristics of the communication scheme. This kind of correlation has been included in the protocols models, and appropriate values for p and q have been derived using experimental data, as shown later on.

Using the SAN formalism, the alternation between the two states can be modelled by a place (called "SUCCESS") and by an activity whose case probabilities depend on the marking of this place. The marking of SUCCESS (0 or 1 in our models) represents the state of the channel (F and S, respectively). The probabilities to be associated to the cases of the activity representing the reception of a message are derived from the probabilities associated to the transitions of the Markov Model in Figure 1. Once the outcome of the activity is determined, the subsequent action consists in changing the marking of SUCCESS in a consistent way.

4.2 Model for evaluating $P_{D>OD}$, $P_{R>OD}$ and P_{UM}

We have defined a single model for the evaluation of $P_{D>OD}$, $P_{R>OD}$

and $P_{U}M$, from which the three indicators can be obtained by simply changing the value of some parameters.

Taking advantage of the features offered by the tool UltraSAN (used to solve the models), the whole model is obtained by defining the sub-model for a single station$_i$, and then using the REP operator to replicate such sub-model for the number of stations in the system [13]. Of course, common places among the sub-models are identified, through which the evolution of the protocol is captured. The structure of the model for $P_{D>OD}$, $P_{R>OD}$ and $P_{U}M$ is in Figure 2.

Let's start considering the evaluation of $P_{D>OD}$. Since we are interested in *decision messages* (i.e., messages broadcast by the AP to commit or abort the delivery of a *broadcast message*), we have to consider the reception of consecutive messages by each station.

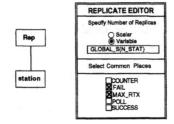

Figure 2. Structure of the SAN model for $P_{D>OD}$, $P_{R>OD}$ and $P_{U}M$.

In Figure 3, the sub-model representing the reception of a message by one generic station is detailed. The place common to all the sub-models when connecting them through the REP operator is FAIL.

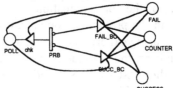

Figure 3. Sub-model station$_i$ used to evaluate $P_{D>OD}$, $P_{R>OD}$ and $P_{U}M$

The activity PRB represents the execution of the three actions: i-ii) the exchange of the poll-request messages between the AP and the station iii) the broadcast of the received message. These actions require the exchange of messages, which may be affected by the fading phenomenon. The "poll" message is shorter than the "broadcast request message" and the "broadcast message" (these last two being of the same length). Define M' as the transition matrix for the "poll" message and M the transition matrix for the other messages (as previously explained in subsection 4.1). We obtain the state transition probabilities after the three actions, as the product of the matrices M'*M*M. These probabilities are associated to the cases of the activity PRB. If a failure occurs (case1) the output gate FAIL_BC will add one to the marking of COUNTER (this place traces the number of consecutive failures) and, unless the new marking exceeds OD, it also sets the marking of POLL to 1. If COUNTER exceeds OD, a token is put in FAIL and this event will stop any further action in the sub-model. Moreover, since FAIL is in common with all the sub-models, and since the input gate CHK enables the activity PRB only when one token is in POLL and no tokens are in FAIL, all the sub-models will stop their activity. When a success occurs, the marking of COUNTER is set to zero, and a new poll can be executed. From this model, $P_{D>OD}$ is obtained through a transient analysis at time T_{CFP},.

The evaluation of $P_{R>OD}$ shifts our attention to the reception of messages broadcast once per round. In fact, the event we are now interested in is the reception by the generic station$_i$ of the same broadcast message, relative to station$_j$, broadcast by the AP once per round (in correspondence to the polling of station$_j$). The model in Figure 3 can be used to evaluate the occurrence of this event, by properly setting the rate of the activity PBR to a round duration (i.e., $3t_m*N$). Accordingly, keeping into account the fading phenomenon, the state transition probabilities after the three actions "poll-request-broadcast" have to be determined on the basis of a round interval. Therefore, the transition matrix which determines such probabilities is given by the product M'*M*M performed N times, that is, $[M'*M*M]^N$.

P_{UM} can be determined exactly as $P_{R>OD}$, but considering res(c) instead of OD as the threshold for COUNTER to put a token in FAIL.

4.3 Model for the evaluation of R_m

The model for the evaluation of R_m is obtained following the same approach illustrated at the previous section: identification of the sub-model for a generic station$_i$, and the replication of such sub-model through the REP operator. The sub-model station$_i$ is derived from that used to evaluate $P_{R>OD}$. In fact, we are still interested in what happens to a specific broadcast message, so the related events occur once per round.

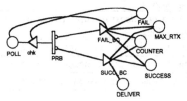

Figure 4. Sub-model station$_i$ used to evaluate R_m

Figure 4 shows the sub-model relative to the generic station$_i$ used to evaluate R_m. The places MAX_RTX and DELIVER are in common to all the sub-models when combining a (parametric) number of them through the REP operator. As in the previous model, the place COUNTER contains information on the number of retransmissions a message is subject to. If the number of retransmissions is greater than OD+1, a token is put in FAIL indicating a catastrophic failure of the protocol. To evaluate R_m, we have to compute the maximum value reached by COUNTER for each broadcast message. Thus the place MAX_RTX has been introduced, which is updated by both the output gates FAIL_BC and SUCC_BC by replacing its marking with that of COUNTER, if this last is higher. When all the sub-models terminate their execution (the marking of DELIVER is equal to the number of stations), the marking of MAX_RTX is the actual number of retransmissions needed by the message, and will give the number of average retransmissions.

5 EVALUATION RESULTS

A numerical evaluation of the SAN models presented in section 4 has been carried out, by using the tool UltraSAN [13]. Table 1 reports the parameters of the models, and the values used in the numerical evaluation.

Table 1. Notation, definitions and numerical settings

Notation	Description	Value
PE	probability of failure of a broadcast message	[1.6E-4, 1E-2]
q_{pr}	probability of failure of the couple *poll-request*	6.041E-04
N	mobile stations in the group	4
t_m	time-bound for a message transmission (μsec)	7646
1-q	transition probability from the F state to the S state	f(PE, F_D*T)
1-p	transition probability from the S state to the F state	f(PE, F_D*T)
F_D*T	Normalized Doppler Frequency	{3E-3, 3E-1}
OD	omission degree	[2, 10]
res(c)	resiliency degree (second version of the protocol)	[0, 10]
t_p	Time-bound for a poll message transmission	2380 μsec
T	duration of a Contention Free Period (in msec)	{600, 2400}
$P_{D>OD}$	probability that a *decision message* is lost by a station after OD+1 retransmissions	
$P_{R>OD}$	probability that a *broadcast message* is lost by a station after OD+1 retransmissions	
R_m	number of retransmissions for a *broadcast message* (average)	
T_{hr}	throughput (number of delivered messages per second)	
P_{UM}	probability that a broadcast message is not delivered	

Most of the values adopted in this setting have been directly derived through experimental measurements performed in [7]. In fact, an implementation of the second version of the protocol was set up on a system of Windows NT 4.0 Workstations and Laptops connected by an IEEE 802.11 Standard compliant wireless network. The settings were as follows:

Carrying frequency: 2.4 GHz

Packet size: 100-1000 bytes

Data Rate: 2 Mbit/sec

Some experiments have been carried out in an office environment under good physical conditions providing the following results:

Marginal probability of packet loss (PE): 1,60E-04

Upper-bound for messages: 7646μsec (1000bytes), 2843μsec (100bytes)

From the experimental data it has been possible to derive values for those parameters related to the correlation of packet loss (p and q of Figure 1). A commonly adopted approximation in the presence of coding for data block transmission [14] considers the success determined by comparing the signal power to a threshold: if the received power is above a certain threshold the block is successfully decoded with probability 1, otherwise it is lost with probability 1. This threshold is sometimes called *fading margin F*. When a Rayleigh fading channel is considered, PE and q can be calculated as in [15]:

$$P_E = 1 - e^{-1/F}; \qquad 1 - q = \frac{Q(\theta, \rho\theta) - Q(\rho\theta, \theta)}{e^{1/F} - 1} \qquad (2)$$

Where $\rho = J_0(2\pi F_D{}^*T)$ and

$$\theta = \sqrt{\frac{2/F}{1 - \rho^2}} \qquad (3)$$

$Q(.,.)$ is the Marcum Q function. J_0 is the modified Bessel function of 0-th order.

Recalling the equations for F_D and T from section 4.1, given the packet size, the speed of the mobile stations and the marginal error probability, one can compute $F_D{}^*T$, p and q. A few values for p and q are reported in Table 2 (1000byte packets). Note that when $F_D{}^*T$ is equal to 3E-01 $p=1-q$, thus reproducing the case of independence among message failures.

Table 2. Derivation of $F_D{}^*T$ and of the correlation parameters p and q.

Speed (m/s)	PE	$F_D{}^*T$	p	q
0.05	1.6E-04	3.0E-03	0.99991	0.45318
0.5	1.6E-04	3.0E-02	0.99984	0.00898
5	1.6E-04	3.0E-01	0.99984	0.00016

5.1 Dependability-related indicators

Figures 5.a and 5.b show the values of the probability $P_{D>OD}$ as a function of PE, of OD, of T, and for two different values of F_D*T.

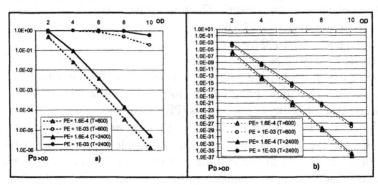

Figure 5.a) $P_{D>OD}$ for $F_D*T = 3.0E-3$ *5.b)* $P_{D>OD}$ for $F_D*T = 3.0E-01$

When PE increases, $P_{D>OD}$ increases, whereas for the same PE higher values of F_D*T determine lower values for $P_{D>OD}$. When $F_D*T = 3E-3$ (Figure 5.a), the fading is quite strong with strong correlation between message failures, thus resulting in a higher probability of protocol failure. The effects of the fading decreases as F_D*T increases, as it can be observed in Figure 5.b, resembling independence. The influence of the marginal probability of message failure PE and that of the contention free interval T are not surprising. The higher is PE, the higher is $P_{D>OD}$; similarly, the longer is T and the higher is $P_{D>OD}$.

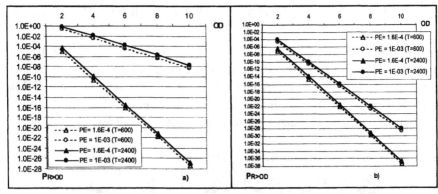

Figure 6.a) $P_{R>OD}$ with $F_D*T = 3.0E-3$ *6.b)* $P_{R>OD}$ with $F_D*T = 3.0E-1$

Figures 6.a and 6.b report the values obtained for $P_{R>OD}$. It can be noted that values of $P_{R>OD}$ are lower than values of $P_{D>OD}$ with the same settings. This is due to the different time interval between retransmissions of two consecutive decision messages and broadcast messages; as already discussed in Section 4, the influence of fading on message losses depends on the time interval between two message transmissions. For the comparison with the case of independence among message failures (performed in Figure 6.b), comments similar to those already discussed for $P_{D>OD}$ apply.

Figures 7.a plots P_{UM}, using res(c)=[0, 3], PE={1.6E-4, 1E-2}, T={600, 2400} and F_D*T=3E-03. Since P_{UM} is obtained from the model used for $P_{R>OD}$ by simply substituting the parameter res(c) with OD, the same considerations already made for $P_{R>OD}$ apply.

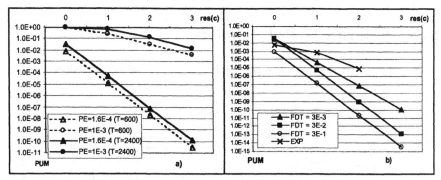

Figure 7.a). P_{UM} at varying res(c), for $F_D*T = 3.0E-3$

7.b). P_{UM} at varying res(c) and F_D*T, including experimental results.

Figure 7.b plots the curves representing P_{UM} as derived experimentally together with a few curves analytically derived for PE = 1.6E-04, T = 2400 and res(c) = [0,3]. From the comparison, it can be observed that the correlation in the environment during the experiment was higher than that modelled. This reinforces the necessity to consider correlation in this context.

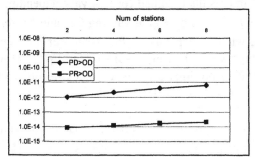

Fig. 8. $P_{D>OD}$ and $P_{R>OD}$ for varying number of stations.

As a final observation on dependability indicators, we report together, in Figure 8, the values of $P_{D>OD}$ and $P_{R>OD}$ on a system with the same stations (2, 4, 6, and 8) and parameter setting: $F_D*T = 3E-2$; OD = 5; PE = 5E-4. It is apparent that correlation makes the second protocol less resilient than the first. The higher probability of failure shown by such protocol version is due to the higher influence of the fading on consecutive messages (i.e., decision messages, on which the $P_{R>OD}$ measure is defined) than on cyclic messages (i.e., broadcast messages, on which the $P_{D>OD}$ measure is defined).

Moreover, it can be also observed the influence of the varying number of mobile stations N on both measures. It does not appear that much relevant; in the figure, it amounts to a maximum of one order of magnitude in the case of $P_{R>OD}$, when moving from N=2 to N=8. This is mainly due to the fact that failures of messages transmitted by different stations are kept independent, according to the assumptions in Section 3.

5.2 Performance-related indicators

R_m and the throughput have been determined in presence of fading.

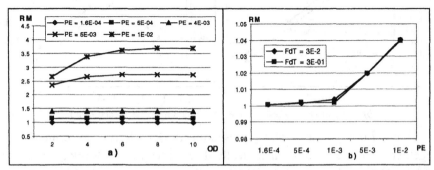

Figure 9.a) R_m at varying PE and OD with $F_D*T = 3E-03$
9.b) R_m at varying PE and F_D*T with OD=4

In our setting, the results obtained for R_m vary depending on F_D*T. Figure 9.a shows the variations on R_m at varying OD and PE for $F_D*T=3E-03$. We observe that, while it depends on PE, some dependence on OD is observed only for high PE. When $F_D*T=3E-02$ and $F_D*T=3E-01$, as depicted in Figure 9.b, OD does not impact on the obtained results (and their range of variation is very narrow [1.002, 1.04]).

*Table 3:*Comparison of Throughput, as a function of res(c)

res(c)	FD*T = 3E-3		FD*T = 3E-1		Exp.
	PE=1.6E-04	PE=1.E-03	PE=1.6E-04	PE=1.E-03	
1	56.949	47.272	57.107	57.018	57.71
2	56.950	47.378	57.107	57.018	57.87
3	56.950	48.276	57.107	57.018	57.97

Finally, the evaluation of the throughput is based on R_m and the average message delay t_m. In our settings, the throughput depends only on R_m, since we assumed a constant message delay. The values for the throughput are given by the formula $1/((t_p+2t_m)*R_m)$. Table 3 reports the values of the throughput T_{hr} as determined by the analytical and experimental evaluation.

Interestingly, changing res(c) has a negligible impact on the throughput in both cases. Actually, message losses are a small fraction of the total number and the number of retransmissions is low, this explains why the impact of res(c) is minor. This result suggests that using the (more complex) protocol version with both *res(c)* and *OD* is not worthwhile if only throughput considerations matter; however, if real-time requirements have to be accounted for, restricting to *res(c)* retransmissions allows meeting the timing guarantees. The fading, instead, has significant impact on T_{hr}: when $F_D*T=3.0E-3$ (high fading), the throughput changes significantly at varying the probability of message loss. However, such influence decreases at decreasing values of the fading, becoming negligible for $F_D*T=3.0E-1$.

8 CONCLUSIONS

The work presented in this paper is concerned with QoS analysis of group communication protocols in an experimental setting. This study contributes to the QoS analysis of distributed systems, being group communication protocols basic mechanisms for the co-operation among the distributed entities. QoS analysis is being more and more recognised as an important step for the early verification and validation of system designs, also providing precious feedback for the refinement process.

The identified QoS metrics relate to both dependability and performance. Specifically, the dependability-related figures aim at giving an estimate of the coverage of the assumptions on which the protocols rely, while the performance figures can be used as indicators of the technical limitations imposed by the communication system.

In order to improve the correct representation of the protocols, their formal description has been provided using the timed asynchronous model. The QoS analysis has been developed through an analytical approach based on the SAN formalism. The derived models closely represent the system and the environment, by accounting for physical characteristics such as the *fading channel* phenomenon, and for user mobility. In fact, both of them affect a wireless communication and cause time correlation among successive messages, captured by our models. We used experimental data previously collected in a representative experimental context to provide parameters values. Then we performed several evaluations to highlight the behaviour of the protocols depending on their settings and on the environment characteristics.

Although shown through two group protocols, the work presented can be applied to other distributed contexts. First, the formalisation of group communication properties can be exploited to generate a number of variants of group communication protocols, to find the "best fit" among performance, delay time, reliability and formal properties of the broadcast, in accordance with user requirements. Second, the basic approach to QoS analysis defined here can be successfully applied to other distributed protocols/mechanisms with proper adaptation to the specific characteristics of the new context.

REFERENCES

[1]   B. Teitelbaum, J. Sikora, and T. Hanss, "Quality of Service for Internet2," presented at First Internet2 Joint Applications/Engineering Workshop: Enabling Advanced Applications Through QoS, Santa Clara, CA, 1998.

[2]   M. Mock, E. Nett, and S. Schemmer, "Efficient Reliable Real-Time Group Communication for Wireless Local Area Networks," presented at 3rd European Dependable Computing Conference, Prague, Czech Republic, 1999.

[3]   IEEE_802.11, IEEE 802.11: Wireless LAN Medium Access Control (MAC) and Physical Layer (PHY) speci-fications, 1997.

[4]   F. Cristian and C. Fetzer, "The Timed Asynchronous Distributed System Model," presented at 28th Int. Symp. On Fault-Tolerant Computing (FTCS-28), Munich, Germany, 1998.

[5]   W. H. Sanders and W. D. Obal II, "Dependability Evaluation Using UltraSAN," presented at 23rd Annual International Symposium on Fault-Tolerant Computing, Toulouse, France, 1993.

[6]   W. H. Sanders, W. D. Obal, M. A. Qureshi, and F. K. Widjanarko, "The UltraSAN Modeling Environment," Performance Evaluation, vol. 24, pp. 89-115, 1995.

[7]   A. Coccoli, S. Schemmer, F. D. Giandomenico, M. Mock, and A. Bondavalli, "Analysis of Group Communi-cation Protocols to Assess Quality of Service Properties," presented at HASE00, Albuquerque, NM, USA, 2000.

[8]   V. Hadzilacos and S. Toueg, "Fault-tolerant Broadcasts and Related Problems," in Distributed Systems, S. J. Mullender, Ed. Reading: Addison-Wesley, 1993, pp. 97-145.

[9]   F. Cristian, "Understanding Fault-tolerant Distributed System," Communications of ACM, vol. 34, pp. 56-78, 1991.

[10] W. H. Sanders and J. F. Meyer, "A Unified Approach for Specifying Measures of Performance, Dependability and Performability," in Dependable Computing for Critical Applications, vol. 4 of Dependable Computing and Fault-Tolerant Systems, H. K. A. Avizienis, and J. Laprie, Ed.: Springer-Verlag, 1991, pp. 215-237.

[11] T. S. Rappaport, Wireless Communications - Principles and Practice, 1996.

[12] M. Zorzi, R. R. Rao, and L. B. Milstein, "On The Accuracy Of A First-Order Markov Model For Data Block Transmission On Fading Channels," presented at IEEE ICUPC'95, 1995.

[13] W. H. Sanders, W. D. Obal II, M. A. Qureshi, and F. K. Widjanarko, "UltraSAN Version 3: Architecture, Features, and Implementation," presented at AIAA Computing in Aerospace 10 Conference, San Antonio, TX, 1995.

[14] L. F. Chang, "Throughput Estimation Of Arq Protocols For A Rayleigh Fading Channel Using Fade- And Interfade-Durations Statistics," IEEE Trans. Veh. Tech., vol. VT-40, pp. 23-229, 1991.

[15] K. S. Miller, Multidimensional Gaussian Distributions. New York, 1964.

Chapter 10

SEMANTICALLY RELIABLE BROADCAST

*Sustaining High Throughput
in Reliable Distributed Systems*

José Pereira
U. do Minho
jop@di.uminho.pt

Luis Rodrigues
U. de Lisboa
ler@di.fc.ul.pt

Rui Oliveira
U. do Minho
rco@di.uminho.pt

Abstract   Replicated services are often required to sustain high loads of multiple concurrent requests. This requirement is hard to balance with strong consistency. Typically, to ensure inter-replica consistency, all replicas should receive all updates. Unfortunately, in this case, a single slow replica may degrade the performance of the whole system. This paper proposes a novel reliable broadcast primitive that uses semantic knowledge to weaken reliable delivery guarantees while, at the same time, ensuring strong consistency at the semantic level. By allowing some obsolete messages to be dropped, the protocol that implements this primitive is able to sustain a higher throughput than a fully reliable broadcast protocol. The usefulness of the primitive and the performance of the protocol are illustrated through a concrete example.

Keywords: Reliable broadcast, high throughput, semantic reliability.

P. Ezhilchelvan and A. Romanovsky (eds.), Concurrency in Dependable Computing, 189–207.

Introduction

Replication is a widely used technique to implement reliable services. One of the most important primitives to support replication is reliable broadcast [6]. Intuitively, reliable broadcast ensures that all replicas receive the same messages and, therefore, have the information required to reach a consistent state. Unfortunately, reliable broadcast is also an expensive primitive, since messages need to be stored to ensure recovery in the case of network omissions. In systems with many concurrent clients, the replicated servers have to cope with a high throughput of requests, and this may quickly exhaust the memory available for storing messages. Therefore, it is a hard task to balance the need to sustain a high input of concurrent requests and the need to keep the replicas consistent.

This paper proposes a novel reliable broadcast primitive to address this problem. This primitive offers a weak form of reliability, as it allows some messages to be dropped by the protocol. This eases the task of sustaining high throughput by alleviating the memory requirements imposed by stored messages. However, instead of simply dropping messages at random, a strategy that would compromise the consistency of the replicated service, our primitive uses semantic knowledge on the contents of the message, to selectively drop only messages that have became obsolete while in transit. The primitive ensures that, at the semantic level, all replicas receive the same up-to-date information and are therefore guaranteed to have the information needed to preserve inter-replica consistency.

The new primitive is called FIFO Semantic Reliable Broadcast (FIFO-SRB), and it is an extension to our previous work with semantic reliability [9]. While our previous work motivated the need for semantic reliability in point-to-multipoint streams by showing that in some applications it cannot be avoided that many messages become obsolete while still in transit, without concern for inter replica consistency, in this paper we make the following contributions: We present a specification of the FIFO-SRB primitive, present a protocol to implement FIFO-SRB and, finally, show using a concrete example how FIFO-SRB can be used to support the replication of services with many concurrent clients.

The rest of the paper is structured as follows: Section 1 motivates the need to weaken reliability to sustain high throughput. Section 2 introduces the formal definition of the broadcast primitive and an algorithm implementing it. Section 3 shows how to apply the primitive in strongly consistent replication and illustrates the benefits with performance measurements. Section 4 concludes the paper.

1.   Weakening Reliability to Sustain High Throughput

This section motivates our work by presenting the problem of throughput stability in applications based on reliable broadcast communication protocols.

Then we briefly examine existing proposals and outline intuition underlying semantic reliability.

1.1   Throughput Stability

The difficulty with sustaining high throughput has been identified as one of the limiting factors for the scalability of reliable broadcast protocols [11]. This is unfortunate as throughput stability is a requirement for many demanding applications that would benefit from reliable broadcast primitives [2]. In the following paragraphs we explain why this feature is inherent to any fully reliable broadcast protocol.

A reliable broadcast protocol must ensure the delivery of a message to all correct recipients, despite the occurrence of faults. Typical faults to be considered are omissions in the links and crashes of processes. For instance, a sender may crash while transmitting a message. This may cause a message to be delivered to some of the recipients but not to the others. To ensure recovery, processes need to store messages for the case retransmissions are needed. These messages must not be discarded until one is sure the message has been received by all processes (at that point, the message is said to be *stable*). Furthermore, messages need also to be stored until consumed by the application.

To sustain a high input rate from senders, one must ensure that: *i)* enough memory is available to store incoming messages until previous messages have been delivered; *ii)* messages are consumed at the same pace new messages arrive. If these conditions are not verified, memory is quickly exhausted and clients are prevented from obtaining further service. Unfortunately, in order for a message to be discarded from buffers, it has to be acknowledged by all replicas. This means that if a single replica is slower (for instance, due to a transient overload of the hosting node) all the group is affected.

The typical solution to cope with a replica that is continuously slower than the remaining replicas is to consider that the replica is faulty, and exclude it from the group of replicas. However, if one wants to preserve a given replication degree, a new replica needs to be added to the group in order to replace the excluded replica, and this typically requires the execution of an expensive integration procedure. Due to the costs of excluding a replica, it is advisable to not exclude replicas that are subject to transient overloads. On the other hand, even if no single replica is continuously slow, different replicas may exhibit transient overloads at different moments always impacting all the group, preventing the replicated service from sustaining a high throughput of requests.

1.2   Relaxing Reliability

One approach to address the throughput problem described above is to weaken the reliability requirements of the broadcast primitive, such that slower recipients are not required to deliver all messages. This would allow messages to be purged earlier from the retransmission buffers and would prevent a single process from slowing down the entire group of replicas.

Two examples of this approach can be found in literature. Bimodal multicast [3] offers probabilistic reliability guarantees which do not hold for slower processes that fail to meet performance assumptions. Application Level Framing (ALF) [5] does not perform automatic retransmissions, and requires the receivers to explicitly request retransmissions of lost messages that are considered relevant.

Both these approaches introduce a significant complexity to be managed by the application. If a message loss compromises the correctness of a server, and the message is no longer available for retransmission, the server may be forced to exclude itself from the group and rejoin later in order to get a correct copy of the state. Notice that even if some mechanism is implemented to notify the receiver that some messages have been dropped, the application might be unable to take any corrective measure since it has no knowledge of that message's content and thus cannot evaluate whether the unknown message is relevant. This last problem can be circumvented by the use of two multicast protocols in parallel [12]: An unreliable protocol used for payload and a reliable protocol used to convey meta-data describing the content of data messages sent on the payload channel. Using information from the control channel, the receiver may evaluate the relevance of lost messages in the payload channel and explicitly request retransmission when needed.

Our work is also inspired in the Δ-causal [1] and deadline constrained [13] causal protocols. These protocols allow real-time constraints to be met at the cost of discarding delayed messages.

1.3   Message Obsolescence

Our goal is to avoid the increased complexity qof the previous approaches while retaining the assumption that some messages do not need to be retransmitted if lost. The approach derives from the observation that some messages implicitly convey or overwrite the content of other messages sent in the past, therefore making these old messages irrelevant. Obsolete information can be then safely purged from re-transmission buffers as soon as newer messages, that overwrite the contents of obsolete messages, are safely available.

By immediately purging obsolete messages, the freed resources can be allocated to the remaining messages. Thus it is possible to accommodate receivers with different capacities within the same group. The resulting reliability criterion is *semantic reliability*, as all current information is delivered to all receivers, either implicitly or explicitly, without necessarily delivering all messages.

In order to provide information to the communication protocol about which messages are related, the application has simply to tag each message with a label that conveys information about the obsolescence relation. For instance, a label can be associated with each data item managed by the application: Two messages that overwrite the value of the same data item would carry the same label. Using simple labeling schemes it is possible for the protocol to manage purging tasks in an efficient manner.

The notion of semantic reliability has been previously proposed in [9]. In that paper we have studied the performance of message obsolescence relations in point-to-multipoint channels. As it is expected, the performance of the approach is mostly dependent of the degree of obsolescence of the traffic generated by the application. Fortunately, applications exhibiting high throughput due to rapidly changing data tend to exhibit meaningful obsolescence rates as recent values make older ones obsolete. Such applications range from multiplayer games to distributed control, and on-line transaction processing. We have also considered the semantic reliability in the context of probabilistic multicast protocols [10]. However, we have not addressed previously applications with inter-replica consistency requirements. Such requirements are taken into account only in FIFO-SRB and associated protocol that are presented in the following sections.

2. Semantically Reliable Broadcast

In this section we present and discuss the specification of FIFO-SRB. Then we introduce an algorithm and its correctness proof. Finally we discuss how this algorithm is mapped to protocol implementation techniques.

2.1 Specification

We consider an asynchronous message passing system [4]. Briefly, we consider a set of sequential processes communicating through a fully connected network of point-to-point reliable channels. The system is asynchronous, which means that there are no bounds on processing or network delays. Processes can only fail by crashing and do not recover (a correct process does not crash). We assume that at most f processes may crash.

The definition of FIFO-SRB is based on obsolescence information formalized as a relation on messages. This relation is defined by the application program and encapsulates all the semantics ever required by the protocol. This way the FIFO-SRB protocol can be developed independently of concrete applications. The fact that m is *obsoleted* by m' is expressed as $m \sqsubseteq m'$. The obsolescence relation is a strict partial order (*i.e.* anti-symmetric and transitive) coherent with the causal ordering of events. The intuitive meaning of this relation is that if $m \sqsubseteq m'$ and m' is delivered, the correctness of the application is not affected by omitting the delivery of m. $m \sqsubseteq m'$ is used as a shorthand for $m \sqsubset m' \lor m = m'$.

FIFO Semantically Reliable Broadcast (FIFO-SRB) is defined by the following properties:

Validity: If a correct process broadcasts a message m and there is a time after which no process broadcasts m'' such that $m \sqsubset m''$, then eventually it delivers some m' such that $m \sqsubseteq m'$.

Agreement: If a correct process delivers a message m and there is a time after which no process broadcasts m'' such that $m \sqsubset m''$, then all correct processes eventually deliver some m' such that $m \sqsubseteq m'$.

Integrity: For every message m, every process delivers m at most once and only if m was previously broadcast by some process.

FIFO Order: If a process broadcasts a message m before it broadcasts a message m', no process delivers m after delivering m'.

FIFO Completeness: If a process broadcasts a message m before it broadcasts a message m' and there is a time after which no process broadcasts m''' such that $m \sqsubset m'''$, no correct process delivers m' without eventually delivering some m'' such that $m \sqsubseteq m''$.

The intuitive notion that a message can be substituted by another that makes it obsolete is captured in the previous definitions by the statement "deliver some m' such that $m \sqsubseteq m'$". When compared with the specification of reliable broadcast [6], our definition has two interesting differences: *i)* if there is an infinite sequence of messages that obsolete each other, the implementation may omit all of these messages; and *ii)* it requires the implementation to ensure FIFO order and completeness. We will address each of these differences in turn.

The possibility of omitting all messages that belong to an infinite sequence is captured by the statement "there is a time after which no process broadcasts m'' such that $m \sqsubset m''$". It may seem awkward at first that such occurrence is allowed. However, it should be noted that the application, by an judicious use of the labels that capture the obsolescence relation, can easily prevent infinite sequences from occurring. Actually, the application can decide exactly which is the most appropriate length of any sequence of messages from the same obsolescence relation. On the other hand, if the protocol was forced to deliver messages from an infinite sequence (by omitting the statement above from the specifications), the protocol designer would be forced to make an arbitrary decision of which messages to choose from that infinite sequence (e.g. one out of every k messages). It is clearly preferable to leave this decision under control of the application.

The FIFO completeness property ensures that full consistency at the semantic level is always guaranteed to be eventually reached, even if FIFO-SRB allows for temporary inconsistency of replicas. This happens because the specification enforces that, if a message is delivered, then all previous messages have already been delivered or have been made obsolete by subsequent messages whose delivery has been guaranteed.

2.2 Algorithm Overview

At first glance, it may seem that an implementation of FIFO-SRB can be obtained directly from an implementation of a Reliable Broadcast protocol. A naive implementation would just delete from the buffers messages made obsolete by the reception of a subsequent message. However, purging alone does not implement FIFO-SRB.

Consider for instance the following scenario: *i)* a process p broadcasts two unrelated message m_1 and m_2 ($m_1 \not\sqsubseteq m_2$); *ii)* the same process p broadcasts an infinite sequence of messages $m_3, m_4, \ldots$ such that $m_1 \sqsubseteq m_3$ and $\forall_{i \geq 3}$: $m_i \sqsubseteq m_{i+1}$. Consider that p purges m_1 from its buffer before sending both m_1 and m_2 to another process q. Since m_2 was sent after m_1, q will not deliver m_2 before m_1 arrives (which would never occur) or until it realizes that m_1 was purged because it was made obsolete by some other message m_i. However, since m_i belongs to an infinite sequence, it may never arrive at q. Therefore, the protocol must incorporate some mechanism to ensure that q is informed about the purging of m_1.

There is another more subtle issue regarding the implementation of FIFO-SRB. Even if information about purged messages is propagated, it is possible to show that the naive implementation would not ensure both Validity and FIFO Completeness in the case of failures. Consider the same scenario as above and the following sequence of events: *i)* process p broadcasts m_1, m_2 and m_3; *ii)* p purges m_1 due to m_3 and informs the remaining processes that m_1 was purged; *iii)* p sends m_2 which is delivered by some process q; *iv)* p crashes. Clearly, this sequence violates FIFO Completeness. The problem is that m_1 was purged before ensuring the delivery of m_3. A message is guaranteed to be eventually delivered as soon as it has been received by $f + 1$ processes, where f is the maximum number of processes that may fail. When this condition holds, we say that the message is *safe*. In the particular sequence above, violation of FIFO Completeness could be avoided if purging of m_1 was delayed until m_3 was known to be safe.

Given these observations, our protocol is based on the following principles:

- As in any reliable protocol, processes forward all the messages they received to mask the failure of the sender.

- In a retransmission buffer, a message m may be purged only if there is another message m' such that: $m \sqsubseteq m'$ and m' is safe.

- When a message is purged, enough information is stored to inform the remaining processes that the message has been purged.

The protocol is presented in detail in the next section.

2.3   Algorithm Specification

We describe the algorithm using an abstract specification. The use of this level of abstraction simplifies the proof of correctness and highlights the fundamental aspects of the solution. Later in Section 2.5 we show how a practical implementation can be obtained form this specification.

The system execution is modeled as a sequence of states. Each state is a mapping from state variables to values. A next state relation is a predicate on pairs of states. A specification is a set of executions, which can be defined by a next state relation which is true for consecutive states in legal executions, plus fairness assumptions written in temporal logic.

The state describes both the algorithm and the environment. Processes and channels are not explicit: A process state is a portion of system state and channel operations are modeled as copying elements between the state of two processes [7]. Process crash is denoted explicitly by state variables. A process is considered correct if its crashed state is forever false.

We use the common notation for sets. For tuples, we use the usual notation π_n to denote projection of element n. This notation is extended for sets of tuples with Π_n to denote the set of projections. For sequences, we use $\langle m \rangle$ to denote a sequence with one element m and $\circ$ to denote concatenation. $elems(S)$ denotes the set of elements of a sequence S. A message broadcast by process i is expressed as $m \in elems(B_i)$ and a message delivered by process i is expressed as $m \in elems(D_i)$. Likewise, order of broadcast and delivery are expressed as ordering in sequences B_i and D_i.

The variables used by each process i are listed in Figure 1. Variable B_i simply keeps the messages that have been broadcast by the process. The variable c_i records the state of the process (false if the process is correct and true if the process is crashed). Each process keeps a pair of buffers $I_{i,j}$ and $O_{i,j}$ for each process j. $I_{i,j}$ are incoming buffers, where messages waiting to be ordered are stored. $O_{i,j}$ stores messages waiting to be transmitted. Messages ordered are copied to a local delivery queue Q_i and messages that have been delivered are recorded in D_i. Messages in $O_{i,j}$ and Q_i can be purged. Purging is modeled by changing an attribute that is associated with each message in a given queue. This attribute can have one of two values: D (the message contains data) or P (the message has been purged).

State for each process i:

    B_i: messages broadcast, initially empty sequence

    D_i: messages delivered, initially empty sequence

    c_i: boolean, initially false

    $O_{i,j}$: outgoing toward j, initially empty

    $I_{i,j}$: incoming via j, initially empty

    Q_i: queued for delivery, initially empty

Figure 1. State variables.

TE1: $transmit_{j,i}(m,o)$

  Pre-condition:

    $(m,o) \in O_{j,i} \wedge \neg c_j \wedge$

    $m \notin \Pi_1(I_{i,j}) \wedge \neg c_i$

  Effect:

    $I_{i,j} := I_{i,j} \cup \{(m,o)\}$

TE2: $crash_i$

  Pre-condition:

    $|\{j : c_j\} \cup \{i\}| < f$

  Effect:

    $c_i := true$

Figure 2. Transitions associated with the environment.

Figure 2 depicts the transitions of the environment. Transition TE1 simply specifies that messages in output buffers are eventually inserted in the corresponding input buffers from the destination processes (this models the transmission of messages in the links). Transition TE2 specifies that a process may crash as long as the maximum number of faulty processes has not been reached.

Figure 3 depicts the transitions for each process i.

- Transition TP1 corresponds to the broadcast of a message m. In this transition the fact that m has been broadcast is stored in B_i and the message is sent to self by inserting it in $O_{i,i}$ (note that the environment will eventually move the message to $I_{i,i}$). Notice that the predicate $next(m, S)$, which ensures that all predecessors of message m are available in set S, is used to enforce that the message being broadcast has the right sequence number.

- Transition TP2 captures the forwarding procedure executed by every node. When a message is received for the first time and it is the next message in the sequence, as enforced by $next(m, S)$, it is copied to all output buffers and inserted in Q_i for delivery.

- Transition TP3 captures the delivery of messages (note that, in practice, when a purged message is delivered the application is not disturbed).

TP1: $broadcast_i(m)$
  PRE-CONDITION:
    $next(m, O_{i,i}) \wedge \neg c_i$
  EFFECT:
    $B_i := \langle m \rangle \circ B_i$
    $O_{i,i} := O_{i,i} \cup \{(m, D)\}$

TP2: $enqueue_i(m, o)$
  PRE-CONDITION:
    $\exists j : (m, o) \in I_{i,j} \wedge m \notin \Pi_1(Q_i) \wedge$
    $next(m, Q_i) \wedge \neg c_i$
  EFFECT:
    for all $k \neq i$:$O_{i,k} := O_{i,k} \cup \{(m, o)\}$
    $Q_i := Q_i \cup \{(m, o)\}$

TP3: $deliver_i(m)$
  PRE-CONDITION:
    $(m, D) \in Q_i \wedge m \notin elems(D_i) \wedge \neg c_i$
  EFFECT:
    $D_i := \langle m \rangle \circ D_i$

TP4: $purge\_q_i(m)$
  PRE-CONDITION:
    $\exists m' : (m, D), (m', D) \in Q_i \wedge$
    $m \sqsubset m' \wedge \neg c_i$
  EFFECT:
    $Q_i := (Q_i \setminus \{(m, D)\}) \cup \{(m, P)\}$

TP5: $purge\_r_i(m)$
  PRE-CONDITION:
    $\exists m' : (m, D), (m', D) \in O_{i,j} \wedge$
    $m \sqsubset m' \wedge safe_i(m') \wedge \neg c_i$
  EFFECT:
    $O_{i,j} := (O_{i,j} \setminus \{(m, D)\}) \cup \{(m, P)\}$

$safe(m, i) =$
    $|\{j : m \in I_{i,j}\}| > f$

$next(m, S) =$
    $\forall s < seq(m), \exists m \in \Pi_1(S) :$
      $snd(m) = snd(m') \wedge seq(m') = s$

Figure 3. Transitions associated with process i.

- Transition TP4 specifies that a message m, waiting to be delivered, can be purged as long as in the same queue there is a subsequent message m' that makes m obsolete.

- Finally, transition TP5 specifies that a message m in an output buffer can only be purged if in the same queue there is a subsequent message m' that makes m obsolete *and* m' is safe. This is ensured by predicate $safe(m, i)$, which checks that process i has received m from more than f processes.

The fairness assumptions for the algorithm are the following. No fairness assumptions for $broadcast_i(m)$, $purge\_q(m)$, $purge\_r(m)$ and $crash$, thus allowing them to be forever enabled but never executed. Weak fairness is assumed for $transmit_{j,i}(m, o)$, for all i, j, m, o, and for $enqueue_i(m, o)$ and $deliver_i(m)$, for all i, m, o. This requires them to be eventually executed if forever enabled. Notice that there is no fairness imposed on purging operations, thus allowing reliable executions where no message is discarded.

2.4 Proof Sketch

We focus on proving liveness properties of the specification because these are the ones that make the difference to strict reliability and are those that can be compromised by losing messages.

Of the remaining properties, Integrity is trivially satisfied. The correctness of FIFO Order derives from *i)* Q_i containing a complete prefix and *ii)* a message which is purged in Q_i is never available as data after that in Q_i.

The proof of each of the liveness properties of the specification requires that if some condition on a message m is true, then some message m' such that $m \sqsubseteq m'$ is eventually delivered. This is split in two steps:

1 We prove that if for a pair of correct processes j, i, $m \in \Pi_1(O_{j,i})$ and there is a time after which no process broadcasts m'' such that $m \sqsubset m''$, then eventually exists some $m' \in elems(D_i)$ such that $m \sqsubseteq m'$.

2 For each specification property, we prove that the condition it imposes on m implies that for some pair of correct processes j, i, $m \in \Pi_1(O_{j,i})$.

This makes the proof associated with the first step in Lemma 3 the only eventuality proof required. This proof uses the results of two auxiliary lemmata which summarize interesting aspects of the protocol. The proofs use some additional notation: The *path* to a process i, denoted H_i, is defined as $H_i = \bigcup_{\neg c_j} (O_{j,i} \cup I_{i,j})$. The *world* W is $\bigcup_{i=0,j=0}^{n,n} (I_{i,j} \cup O_{i,j})$. The predecessors of a message m are $Pred(m) = \{m' \in M : snd(m') = snd(m) \wedge seq(m') < seq(m)\}$.

Lemma 1 *If* $(m, \mathrm{P}) \in H_i$ *then there is some* m' *such that* $m \sqsubset m'$ *and for every process* j *(correct or not)* $m' \in \Pi_1(H_j)$.

PROOF: If $(m, \mathrm{P}) \in H_i$ then for some process k, $(m, \mathrm{P}) \in O_{k,i}$ or $(m, \mathrm{P}) \in I_{i,k}$. Moreover, if $(m, \mathrm{P}) \in I_{i,k}$ then $(m, \mathrm{P}) \in O_{k,i}$. This is true as *i)* (m, P) is never removed from $O_{k,i}$ and *ii)* the only action that inserts elements in $I_{i,k}$ is only enabled if the same element is in $O_{k,i}$.

Trivially if $(m, \mathrm{P}) \in O_{k,i}$ then $(m, \mathrm{P}) \in W$. If $(m, \mathrm{P}) \in W$ then there is some m', $m \sqsubset m'$, and a set of processes L with $|L| > f$, such that for any $l \in L$, $m' \in I_{k,l}$. This is true as *i)* the only action that inserts (m, P) in W is only enabled when m' is in more than f incoming queues and *ii)* if $m' \in \Pi_1(I_{k,l})$ once, then it is forever true. Therefore, for any process $l \in L$, $m' \in O_{l,k}$ and there is at least one $l \in L$ that is correct, as crash is enabled only for f processes.

If $m' \in \Pi_1(O_{l,k})$ then for all j, $m \in O_{l,j}$. This is true as *i)* transition $enqueue_j(m, o)$ always inserts m in all $\Pi_1(O_{l,j})$. Therefore, for any j, $m' \in \Pi_1(H_j)$.$\square$

Lemma 2 *Any path* H_i *contains a complete sequential prefix of the message ordering: For all* $m \in \Pi_1(H_i)$, $Pred(m) \subset \Pi_1(H_i)$.

PROOF: For all i, $\Pi_1(Q_i)$ is a prefix of the ordering. This is true as the only action that changes it is only enabled when the new message is the next in the sequence. Moreover, $\Pi_1(O_{j,i} \cup I_{i,j})$ is always equal to $\Pi_1(Q_j)$. The only actions that change $\Pi_1(O_{j,i} \cup I_{i,j})$ also change $\Pi_1(Q_j)$ accordingly. Therefore, as the union of prefixes is still a valid sequential prefix, any path H_i contains a prefix. $\square$

Lemma 3 *If forever* $m \in \Pi_1(H_i)$ *then eventually* $m' \in elems(D_i)$ *such that* $m \sqsubseteq m'$.

PROOF: We define a set of tuples $Stat(m) \subseteq P \times M \times 2^M \times 2^M \times 2^M \times 2^M$ such that $(r, x, s_0, s_1, s_2) \in Stat(m)$ iff $m \sqsubseteq x$; $\bigcup_{i=0}^{3} s_i = Pred(x) \cup \{x\}$ and $\forall i \neq j : s_i \cap s_j = \emptyset$.

We define a relation $\prec$ in $Stat(m)$ such that $t \prec t'$ iff either $\pi_1(t) \subset \pi_1(t')$; or $\pi_1(t) = \pi_1(t')$ and $\pi_1(t) \sqsubset \pi_1(t')$; or $\pi_1(t) = \pi_1(t')$ and $\pi_1(t) \not\sqsubseteq \pi_1(t')$ and for some a for all $3 \leq a < b \leq 5$, $\pi_a(t) = \pi_b(t')$ and $\pi_a(t) \subset \pi_b(t')$. If the set of messages that make m obsolete is finite, then $Stat(m)$ is also finite. $(Stat(m), \prec)$ is a strict partial order because both strict set inclusion and obsolescence are strict partial orders. Thus $(Stat(m), \prec)$ is well-founded.

We now define a function $f_{i,m}$ from system state to $Stat(m)$ defined for states in which process i has not crashed and $m \in \Pi_1(H_i)$. Let $f_{i,m} = (r, x, s_0, s_1, s_2)$ such that:

- $r = \{i : \neg c_i\}$

- choose $x \in \Pi_1(H_i)$ such that $m \sqsubseteq x$ and $\forall m' \in \Pi_1(H_i) : x \not\sqsubseteq m'$;

- $s_0 = \Pi_1(\bigcup_{k \in c} O_{k,i}) \setminus \Pi_1(\bigcup_{k \in c} I_{i,k}) \cap Pred(x)$

- $s_1 = \Pi_1(\bigcup_{k \in c} I_{i,k}) \setminus \Pi_1(Q_i) \cap Pred(x)$

- $s_2 = \Pi_1(Q_i) \setminus D_i \cap Pred(x)$

Assuming that $m \in \Pi_1(O_{j,i})$ such that j is correct (forever $\neg c_j$), we prove that eventually $m' \in elems(D_i)$ by ensuring that *i)* if $m \in O_{j,i}$ then $f_{i,m} \in Stat(m)$, which is true by definition; *ii)* for some helpful transitions either $f_{i,m} \prec f'_{i,m}$ or $m' \in elems(D_i)$ and at least one is enabled or $m' \in D_i$; and *iii)* for the remaining transitions, never $f'_{i,m} \prec f_{i,m}$.

The transitions considered helpful and respective resulting values for $f_{i,m} = (r, x, s_0, s_1, s_2)$ are:

- $transmit_{j,i}(m', o)$ if $m' \in s_0$, leads to $(r, x, s_0 \setminus \{m'\}, s_1 \cup \{m'\}, s_2)$.

- $enqueue_i(m', o)$ if $m' \in s_1$, leads to $(r, x, s_0, s_1 \setminus \{m'\}, s_2 \cup \{m'\})$.

- $deliver_i(m')$ if $m \not\sqsubseteq m' \wedge m' \in s_2$, leads to $(r, x, s_0, s_1, s_2 \setminus \{m'\})$. Notice that $m' \not\sqsubseteq m$ implies $m' \neq x$.

- $deliver_i(m')$ if $m \sqsubseteq m'$. Goal reached with $m' \in elems(D_i)$.

At least one of these is enabled: If $transmit_{j,i}(m, o)$ is not enabled for all j, then at least $m \in \Pi_1(I_{i,j})$ for some j as $m \in \Pi_1(H_i)$. If $enqueue_i(m, o)$ is also not enabled, then $m \in \Pi_1(Q_i)$. Otherwise, with $m \in \Pi_1(H_i)$ and H_i containing complete prefixes (by Lemma 2), transmission would have to be enabled. If $delivery_i(m), m \not\sqsubseteq m'$ is also not enabled then $s_2 = \{x\}$, as Q_i contains x. Otherwise $delivery_i(x)$ is enabled as x must be tagged with D. Otherwise (by Lemma 2) it would not be a maximal element.

There are transitions which help but are not guaranteed to occur. Either because there is no fairness, namely in $broadcast_i(m')$ if $x \sqsubset m'$ and $crash_j$ if $\neg c_j$, or are fair but may never be enabled, namely $enqueue_k(m')$ if $x \sqsubset m'$. Other actions leave $f_{i,m}$ unchanged. Notice that $crash_i$ does not happen by assumption that i is correct. $\square$

Theorem 1 (Validity) *If a correct process broadcasts a message m and there is a time after which no process broadcasts m'' such that $m \sqsubset m''$, then eventually it delivers some m' such that $m \sqsubseteq m'$.*

PROOF: It is trivially true that if $m \in B_i$ then $m \in O_{i,i}$ and process i is correct by assumption. Proof follows immediately by Lemma 3. $\square$

Theorem 2 (Agreement) *If a correct process delivers a message m and there is a time after which no process broadcasts m'' such that $m \sqsubset m''$, then all correct processes eventually deliver some m' such that $m \sqsubseteq m'$.*

PROOF: By a simple invariance proof, if i delivers m then $m \in O_{i,j}$ for all j and process i is correct by assumption. Proof follows immediately by Lemma 3. $\square$

Theorem 3 (FIFO Completeness) *If a process broadcasts a message m before it broadcasts a message m' and there is a time after which no process broadcasts m''' such that $m \sqsubset m'''$, no correct process delivers m' without eventually delivering some m'' such that $m \sqsubseteq m''$.*

PROOF: By a simple invariance proof (same as Agreement), if i delivers m' then $m' \in O_{i,j}$ for all j. By Lemma 2, the same $O_{i,j}$ contains m. Thus either m is delivered or by Lemma 1 some m'' such that $m \sqsubseteq m''$ exists. $\square$

2.5   Deriving an Implementation

The abstract specification of the algorithm makes several simplifications, such as assuming that information about past messages indefinitely accumulates in the variables at each process. The specification also requires that information about purged messages is always explicitly sent on the network. We now argue how a practical implementation can be derived from the specification. For clarity, we address first the case where no purging occurs before discussing how purging can be implemented.

In the algorithm, sets $O_{j,i}$, $I_{i,j}$ and Q_i represent a point-to-point FIFO reliable channel as follows: Messages currently in transit (sent but not yet received), are $O_{j,i} \setminus Q_i$. Messages available only at the sender side are $O_{j,i} \setminus I_{i,j}$. Messages available at the receiver side waiting to be ordered are $I_{i,j} \setminus Q_i$. Notice that operations *transmit* and *enqueue* never refer to the content of messages in Q_i but need only the knowledge of which is the sequence number of the last message delivered.

In practice, this can be implemented using a pair of buffers (one on each side of the channel) and a sequence counter on the receiver: *i)* messages sent are placed in the outgoing buffer, being eventually sent and if necessary repeatedly resent to the network (this is first line of *enqueue*); *ii)* upon reception, an acknowledgment is sent back and if necessary, repeatedly resent; *iii)* upon reception of acknowledgment the message is removed from the sender buffer (this implements *transmit*); *iv)* when a message bearing the next sequence number is available at the receiver, it is removed from the buffer and the sequence number is incremented (this implements the second line of *enqueue*).

Therefore, it is possible to implement the abstract specification of a channel using a window-based protocol. Since in the proposed algorithm there is symmetric connection (*i.e.* $O_{i,j}$, $I_{j,i}$ and Q_j), acknowledgments can be piggy-backed on messages traveling in the opposite direction as happens in TCP/IP in which acknowledgments are implicit in the lower bound of the window.

When purging happens in $O_{j,i}$, (m, D) is replaced by (m, P). In practice, for purging to be useful this must be implemented as freeing all resources (memory and bandwidth) consumed by m. That this can be done in the sender's buffer, thus preventing network resources from being wasted. However, the receiver has to be notified that m has been purged in order to advance the sequence counter without receiving m.

This can be done using the following strategy: *i)* assume a fixed window of size w: the sender never puts sequence $s + w$ in the network without previously receiving an acknowledgment to s; *ii)* the sender knows that it has not received an acknowledgment s if some m such that $seq(m) = s$ is in the buffer; *iii)* if m is purged, it is removed from the buffer thus allowing $s + w$ to be put in the network and eventually received. When the receiver gets $s + w$ without ever getting s it must conclude that the message with sequence s has been purged. This implements (m, P) being inserted in $I_{i,j}$. Notice that no message labeled with P is in the algorithm ever used for anything besides inspecting its sequence number, which in practice translates to it not occupying space. Note also that if there are no further messages to send, a message indicating that the window is empty needs to be explicitly sent.

Likewise, Q_i and D_i abstract a FIFO queue holding messages $Q_i \setminus D_i$ ordered by sequence number. Messages are inserted by *enqueue* and removed by *deliver*. Purging in this buffer is implemented by removing the purged message.

If broadcast links are available, it is also possible to optimize the message forwarding procedure that, in the abstract specification, requires each message to be transmitted on the network n^2 times. Two optimizations are possible:

- As a message is always simultaneously inserted in all outgoing channels $O_{i,j}$, a network level broadcast mechanism can be used to transmit it, thus reducing the complexity to n.

- As soon as a message is received in some $I_{i,j}$ it can be acknowledged in all incoming channels: the receiver advances the lower bound of the window thus allowing the sender to immediately remove the message from its buffers. This also reduces the complexity to n.

Using both optimizations simultaneously, a message can be transmitted only once in the network. In addition, as in conventional reliable broadcast protocols, the explicit point-to-point acknowledgment mechanism can be replaced by a global stability tracking mechanism thus further improving performance and scalability.

3. Applying FIFO-SRB

This section illustrates the use of FIFO-SRB. For that we consider a set of replicated servers that store the current value of a set of data items. These values are updated by a stream of requests from one or more concurrent clients.

3.1 Defining the Obsolescence Relation

To make the presentation clearer, we concentrate on a single stream of updates from a client to the set of servers. Note that this simplification does not make our simulation less relevant: The studied scenario is characteristic of one of the main techniques to implement dependable servers; the so called primary-backup replication. In a primary-backup system, requests from clients are executed at the primary that subsequently broadcasts an update to the backup replicas. Should the primary fail, it is required that replicas are consistent among them and with the primary so that any of them can be promoted to primary. When using FIFO-SRB, this translates to ensuring that all backups have the most recent version of all items.

It is assumed that each request modifies at most one data item of the state. The obsolescence relation is determined by the identification of the item carried by each message, thus $m \sqsubseteq m'$ if both m and m' refer to the same item and m is broadcast prior to m'. As we want the state of clients strongly consistent with the server's, we expect that:

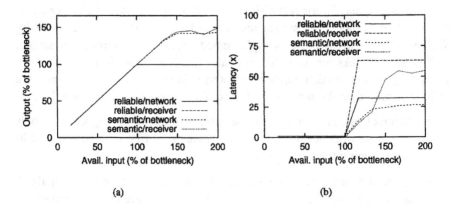

Figure 4.   Performance of FIFO-SRB and a slow network link or a slow receiver.

- If the server stops to modify its state then eventually the same state is reached by all correct clients.

- If the server crashes then eventually the state of all correct clients is the same and equal to the state of the server at some point in time.

In the first scenario, we know that the last update to each item never becomes obsolete. Therefore, by Semantic Validity the last update is always delivered back to sender. By Semantic Agreement and Integrity, each other correct process delivers the same set of last updates. By FIFO Order, each of the last updates is delivered after other updates to the same item thus resulting in the same state as in the sender.

In the second scenario, consider the last update message to each item delivered by some process. By Integrity, Semantic Agreement and FIFO Order, all other correct processes deliver the same messages as last updates as they never become obsolete. Therefore the state among receivers is consistent. Consider the last messages delivered by receivers. By FIFO Completeness, we know that for every message broadcast by the sender prior to the last message delivered, at least one message that makes it obsolete has been delivered. Thus the state is the same as the state of the sender at the moment in time when it broadcast the last message delivered.

3.2   Performance

The impact of purging in the performance of a protocol without inter-replica consistency concerns has been extensively explored in [9]. Therefore we are here concerned only with the impact of the protocol mechanisms used to ensure inter-replica consistency, such as the necessity to ensure safety prior to purging a message from retransmission buffers. This is done using an high-level discrete event simulation allowing us to isolate performance degradation due to slower receivers and network links from other aspects of group performance and to directly compare the results with our previous work.

The network is modeled as $n \times n$ queues fully connecting all processes. We model network latency by adjusting the delay of messages in the queue and network bandwidth by using a simple leaky-bucket scheme. The capacity of receivers is determined by the time required to consume each message. Each process implements the FIFO-SRB protocol by managing local bounded buffers. When its delivery queue fills up, it ceases to accept further messages from the network. Eventually, this will cause the outgoing buffers of the sender to be exhausted which, in turn, prevents further messages from the application from being accepted. This degrades throughput to all the remaining group members. Consumers are attached to all nodes. A single producer injects traffic in one of the nodes according to item access pattern described in the previous section. Item access frequency is generated using the distribution observed in a stock-trading application [8]:

Number of Stocks:	25	100	750	Total:	875
Frequency:	50%	40%	10%		100%

The fact that some items are accessed much more frequently than others (*e.g.* 25 of 875 items are accountable for 50% of total accesses) increases the probability of messages containing updates to the same item being near in the message stream. Such access patterns are common in high throughput applications.

The results from the simulations obtained for a configuration with 5 processes, and for all combinations of reliable and semantically reliable protocols with bottlenecks in the network and in the receiver are depicted in Figure 4. The relation between the sustained output and the desired input in the presence of a bottleneck (such as when the aggregate bandwidth of network links to a node is reduced or when the processing capacity of a receiver is limited) is illustrated in Figure 4(a). When the available input is less than the capacity of the bottleneck, all messages can be transmitted and consumed and thus the output equals the input as shown by the 45 degree slope in the graphic. It is also possible to observe that a reliable protocol is unable to sustain a output larger than the limit of the bottleneck, as shown by the horizontal line in the graphic for input greater than 100%. On the other hand, with FIFO-SRB, the remaining receivers are unaffected by the bottleneck as long as purging remains effective. As noted before, the purging rate depends on the buffer size and on traffic profile: in the simulated scenario purging remains effective with loads up to 150% of the bottleneck throughput. In addition, purging also improves latency by reducing average buffer usage as presented in Figure 4(b). Notice that when the bottleneck is the network, messages queue only on the sender's buffer thus cutting latency in half regardless of semantic purging. In both situations, the observed purging rates are similar to those observed under the same circumstances without consistency concerns [9].

4.   Conclusions and Future Work

Achieving stable high throughput in large and heterogeneous networks supporting reliable distributed systems is a challenging task. In this paper we address this challenge using the notion of message obsolescence, a technique that uses semantic knowledge about the contents of messages to discard old information from buffers.

The paper has proposed a new primitive, FIFO Semantic Reliable Broadcast (FIFO-SRB) that makes use of the obsolescence relation. FIFO-SRB is particularly useful for applications that have to disseminate updates to a collection of data items: It ensures that all correct processes are guaranteed to receive the last update to each item, even if they do note receive exactly the same set of updates. An algorithm to implement FIFO-SRB has been specified and proved.

The performance of FIFO-SRB was evaluated through simulation. For our experiences we have use the reported obsolescence pattern of stock-trading applications. The results show that a FIFO-SRB protocol can prevent a slow process or link from becoming a bottleneck for the complete group.

In this paper we have considered systems using a fixed set of processes. The work on FIFO-SRB can be combined with a membership service to offer a generalization of View Synchronous communication that takes message obsolescence into account. It is also possible to define different coding techniques to capture more complex obsolescence relations.

References

[1] R. Baldoni, A. Mostefaoui, and M. Raynal. Causal delivery of messages with real-time data in unreliable networks. *J. Real-time Systems*, 10(3), 1996.

[2] K. Birman. A review of experiences with reliable multicast. *Software Practice and Experience*, 29(9):741–774, July 1999.

[3] K. Birman, M. Hayden, O. Ozkasap, Z. Xiao, M. Budiu, and Y. Minsky. Bimodal multicast. *ACM Trans. Computer Systems*, 17(2):41–88, 1999.

[4] T. Chandra and S. Toueg. Unreliable failure detectors for reliable distributed systems. *J. ACM*, 43(2):225–267, March 1996.

[5] D. Clark and D. Tennenhouse. Architectural considerations for a new generation of protocols. In *SIGCOMM Symp. on Communications Architectures and Protocols*, pages 200–208, Philadelphia, PA, September 1990. ACM.

[6] V. Hadzilacos and S. Toueg. A modular approach to fault-tolerant broadcasts and related problems. Technical Report TR94-1425, Cornell Univ., Computer Science Dept., May 1994.

[7] L. Lamport. Processes are in the eye of the beholder. *Theoretical Computer Science*, 179(1–2):333–351, 1997.

[8] P. Peinl, A. Reuter, and H. Sammer. High contention in a stock trading database: A case study. *ACM SIGMOD Record*, 17(3):260–268, September 1988.

[9] J. Pereira, L. Rodrigues, and R. Oliveira. Semantically reliable multicast protocols. In *Proc. 19th IEEE Symp. Reliable Distributed Systems*, pages 60–69, October 2000.

[10] J. Pereira, L. Rodrigues, R. Oliveira, and A.-M. Kermarrec. Probabilistic semantically reliable multicast. In *Proc. IEEE Int'l Symp. Network Computing and Applications (NCA)*, February 2002.

[11] R. Piantoni and C. Stancescu. Implementing the Swiss Exchange Trading System. In *Proc. 27th Annual Int'l Symp. Fault-Tolerant Computing (FTCS'97)*, pages 309–313. IEEE, June 1997.

[12] S. Raman and S. McCanne. Generalized data naming and scalable state announcements for reliable multicast. Technical Report CSD-97-951, Univ. of California, Berkeley, June 1997.

[13] L. Rodrigues, R. Baldoni, E. Anceaume, and M. Raynal. Deadline-constrained causal order. In *3rd IEEE Int'l Symp. Object-oriented Real-time distributed Computing*, March 2000.

Chapter 11

EXCEPTION HANDLING IN TIMED ASYNCHRONOUS SYSTEMS

Robert Miller

Department of Computer Science
University of Minnesota, Minneapolis, MN 55455
mill0376@tc.umn.edu

Anand Tripathi

Department of Computer Science
University of Minnesota, Minneapolis, MN 55455
tripathi@cs.umn.edu

Abstract: Recent research on exception handling in concurrent systems has progressed along two dimensions: conversation-based approaches for structuring, and global exception handling for program design separation. Although that research has made significant strides, there are still two open problems: current exception models do not adequately support global faults, and how should a mechanism support global exception handling To address these problems, this paper presents the *guardian model* for exception handling in synchronous and timed asynchronous concurrent systems. Characteristics of the model are global exception handling, timed asynchrony, an extended fault model, and separation of concurrent exception handling from program flow.

Key words: Exception handling, distributed systems, concurrent systems, fault model.

1. INTRODUCTION

One of the major problems in distributed systems is the inability to handle exceptional conditions properly [11]. Distributed systems are of three types [2]: *synchronous* (all messages are within time bounds), *timed*

P. Ezhilchelvan and A. Romanovsky (eds.), Concurrency in Dependable Computing, 209–227.
© 2002 *Kluwer Academic Publishers. Printed in the Netherlands.*

asynchronous (messages are within a time bound with high probability), and *asynchronous* (messages may not be time bounded). (Timed asynchronous systems are similar to *partially synchronous* systems [8].)

Research has progressed along two dimensions: programming structures and methodologies. Many models have been proposed by researchers, and popular models in each dimension are *open multithreaded transactions* (OMTT) [6] and *coordinated atomic* (CA) actions [14] for structures, and *citizens* [3] for global exception handling.

CA actions are based on *conversations*. A conversation [1] is a method of structuring system activities, and has some similarities to transactions. Conversations have a synchronized entry and exit for all of the activity's participants, and all participants either commit or abort the activity together. When an exception is raised in one participant, it is either *internal* or *external*. An internal exception is handled locally within a participant, while an external exception is propagated to and raised in all other participants. If concurrent external exceptions are raised, then the exception that is raised in all participants is the root of an exception sub-tree of all concurrently raised exceptions (*exception resolution*). Conversations use synchronous messages for the communication of exceptions and their cooperative resolution. Generally, the resolution procedure is based on some predefined hierarchy of exceptions. However, there is no explicit global exception handling communication other than raising and resolving exceptions.

OMTT uses transactions as a structure and has similarities to conversations. Transactions provide the ACID property, and they may be nested. Threads can join an open transaction, or a new thread may be spawned within a transaction. The participant threads in a transaction can access shared transactional objects. A thread in a transaction can raise internal and external exceptions. An internal exception is handled by a thread within its current transaction context, but an external exception is communicated to other participants. However, unlike in CA actions, there is no cooperative exception resolution by the participants; an external exception in OMTT aborts the transaction in which it was raised, and raises a *Transaction_Abort* exception to the enclosing transaction.

Exception handling patterns have been proposed by [7] to separate exception handling from a program's main flow, and to allow a knowledge-base outside of a program to determine what actions to take in case of complex exception conditions. The *citizens* paradigm is a methodology that is based on human citizens in society. A human citizen will have some knowledge on how to handle exceptional conditions (e.g., attempt to treat oneself for an illness), but if the condition is too severe, the citizen goes to an established institution for assistance (see a doctor). A citizen is a participant in an action, and has simple exception handling rules. If the condition exceeds what the citizen can do, then the citizen contacts a problem handling agent, which uses a knowledge-base to find an exception handling pattern to deal with the situation. The problem-solving agent may be quite sophisticated, while the citizen is relatively simple.

Conversation models are useful in a variety of applications. However, conversation models are application level structures, and so can only handle application level faults; environment or system faults are not readily handled. Conversations also rely on local exception handling. Other than exception resolution, there is no global coordination of exception handling, nor is there a separation of exception handling from the application code. Lastly, exception resolution cannot distinguish independent concurrent exceptions.

The research in exception handling patterns has focused on the knowledge-base, and not as much on the underlying mechanism. For example, the *citizen model* is based on the *contract net protocol* (CNET) [12]. However, [3] notes that CNET has "serious shortcomings" that includes being a heavy protocol, timeout followed by retry which may cause a cascading effect with subtasks, a limited number of exceptions that CNET can detect, and that some exception handling actions require a global view (such as monitoring resource constraints) that CNET does not provide. This suggests that current fault models are not sufficient for global exception handling.

To improve exception handling models requires re-evaluation of three issues. First is the set of assumptions as to what kinds of faults the exception handling is expected to detect (the fault model). The second issue is related to the semantics of what an exception means and what actions can occur (the exception model). Third is the syntax of the exception model (the programming model). Not part of the exception handling model is how the model is used (the methodology). A given model may have many methodologies applied to it.

This paper proposes an exception model based on *guardians*. Guardians can be used in either synchronous or timed asynchronous systems. Guardians have an inherent separation of exception handling from a program's main flow, which makes them a good candidate for paradigms that support separation. Lastly, guardians can complement conversations. Conversations are a structure, while guardians are a mechanism. Guardians can detect environment-related and system-level faults, as well as handle application-level exceptions. Guardians use globally coordinated exception handling, yet can also be used in local exception handling. Guardians also have considerable flexibility with the exceptions that are raised globally. During global exception handling, it does not require that the same exception is to be raised in all participants of a distributed application. The guardian model can be used as an implementation level mechanism for exception handling in a conversation based approach. With that, one can extend the exception handling model of a conversation scheme using global exception handling supported through guardians.

There are many fault models, and for this paper one is chosen to be representative of them, and is called the *standard fault model*. That model, along with its limitations, is discussed in Section 2 of this paper. Section 3 discusses several unresolved issues in distributed exception handling. Section 4 proposes the *guardian exception handling model* for synchronous and timed asynchronous systems. This model uses an enhanced fault model called the *guardian fault* model, and a global exception handler called a *guardian*. Section 5 shows how guardians can be used in two examples, and lastly, Section 6 provides conclusions and outlines the direction of our future work in this area.

2. THE STANDARD FAULT MODEL

A *distributed activity* consists of a set of cooperating processes. Each of the cooperating processes is a *participant* of the activity. An activity defines a *process group,* which is a set of cooperating processes with time bounds on message communication and processing. A *member* is a process in this group.

Though there are several current fault models, they share many characteristics. A representative fault model is chosen from [5], which this paper calls the *standard fault model* (SFM). SFM defines the following faults:

1. *Crash.* A participant has failed or halted. There are three variants. *Fail-silent* is when other participants do not know of the failure. *Fail-stop* is when other participants do know of the failure. *Fail-safe* occurs when a participant has arbitrary behaviour before it halts, but has no effect on other participants.
2. *Omission.* A participant fails by randomly not receiving or sending a message. A communication channel or process could have failed, and such failures can be intermittent.
3. *Byzantine.* A participant can have arbitrary incorrect behaviour, which may affect other participants.
4. *Timing.* A participant has the correct behaviour, but it has exceeded a time bound. This may be due to message delivery delays, overload conditions, or scheduling delays.
5. *Response.* An error has occurred that is local to a participant.

Recall that the purpose of a fault model is to identify faults that an exception handling system is expected to handle. Several authors have noted the inadequacy of SFM and similar models. For example, in [13], environment faults due to security and configuration, and crash faults that affect participant membership in synchronous operations such as barriers, are discussed. This paper expands that work, and notes that SFM does not model well the classes of faults pertaining to the following aspects of distributed systems:

1. *Fail-Partition.* A type of crash in which it is unknown if a participant is failed or not. This occurs when there is a loss of communication between participants, such as in a network partition. The participants that are partitioned cannot be assumed to be alive, and there are no mechanisms that a participant can use to verify if a partitioned participant has failed. Fail-partition is not necessarily fail-safe because the partitioned participant's actions may not be benign to the other partition.

2. *Concurrent.* Multiple faults that occur concurrently. There are two kinds, *causal* and *non-causal.* Causal faults are related, either due to the same cause or that one is a direct consequence of another. Non-causal faults are independent of each other. Current research tends to consider concurrent faults to be causal.

3. *Membership.* A fault in the membership of an activity, such as the failure of one or more members in a group which are all required to synchronize at a barrier. A crash may or may not affect the membership, and so the exception handler action for a crash may be different depending on whether the crashed participant is a member of the activity or not.

4. *Environment.* These are faults due to configuration, security, or resource constraints. A *configuration fault* occurs when a participant is supposed to have access to a resource but does not, while a *security fault* is when a participant tries to access a resource it is not supposed to. A *resource constraint fault* is due to insufficient resources or resource contention, for example a deadlock condition. These could be considered as special cases of response faults, but unlike other response faults, environment faults are not due to program logic errors or invalid inputs. Rather, they are due to either a malicious user, or the run-time environment for the participant is not configured correctly.

5. *Compatibility.* This fault is rarely mentioned, yet it is pervasive in distributed computing. What computer user using the Internet has not come across an error in which a web-page can only be displayed properly using a certain browser? With machine-independent programming, such as Java applications or mobile agents, the host environment between participants may be different due to the evolution of the environment in terms of its functionality, underlying mechanisms, or addition of new exception classes [10]. The same code libraries and mechanisms cannot be assumed to be identical on all participants, and neither can the faults that can be signalled.

Separation of exception handling implies separation of faults, i.e., faults are local or global. As noted in [3], simply having a global exception handler is not sufficient. The additional faults listed above are not easily identifiable with SFM. SFM cannot distinguish between a crash where a participant eventually stops, and when a participant does not stop (fail-partition). SFM cannot determine if two concurrent exceptions are related or not, or whether a crash is a membership fault. SFM considers environment faults to be response faults that may not be correctable (such as a participant cannot change its authorities). Lastly, compatibility faults are generally beyond what a participant can even detect because they are not expected by the participant.

3.   ISSUES IN SYSTEM EXEPTION HANDLING

There are five significant issues related to exception handling in concurrent systems: contextual exceptions, causal exception resolution, unhandled exceptions, global exception handling, and support of exception handling program separation, or what may be called exception handling methodology.

3.1   Contextual Exceptions

Exceptions are raised within a *context*, which is the program state that has meaning for the exception. If the exception and its data refers to valid program state or a current operation, then the exception is *contextual*, otherwise it is *non-contextual*. In sequential programs, at the point that an exception is raised, it is always contextual because the exception is being raised by a direct program action.

In concurrent exception handling, a participant may receive an exception that is raised from another participant. The exception may be non-contextual unless the participants are synchronous, not only with message communication but also in the processing steps.

3.2   Causal Exception Resolution

In a concurrent system, distributed or not, there is the possibility that multiple participants raise an exception simultaneously. If the exceptions are related or dependent on each other, either due to the same fault or from a cascading effect, then the exceptions are *causal*. Otherwise, the exceptions are independent or unrelated, and are *non-causal*.

Current research has approached this issue with *exception resolution*, which was proposed in [1]. Exception resolution takes all concurrent exceptions, and creates one exception out of them. That one exception is then signalled to all participants. There are several ways to resolve the exception, such as [1]. All exceptions are assumed to form a hierarchy, and thus form a singly rooted tree that may have many sub-trees. The resolved exception is the exception at the root of the smallest sub-tree formed by all concurrently raised exceptions.

The assumption made by exception resolution is that all concurrent exceptions are causal. What makes exceptions causal is when the exceptions are raised in the same context. The broader the context, the less specific is the exception data, and the more difficult it is to recover. Because existing exception handling systems have a loose notion of context, it is difficult to determine causality because the context may be broad.

This inhibits using exception resolution in systems that have independent subsystems. The concurrent exceptions cannot be handled distinctly because it appears they are in the same context. A sensible recovery action cannot be easily determined, so the alternative is often to halt. For example, it is common in many programs that if a fault occurs while handling a fault, the activity is aborted or the system halted. This is partly due to the difficulty in programmatically determining if the second fault is related to the first one, or if the second fault can be handled separately.

3.3 Global Exception Handling

The next issue is the coordination of participant exception handling to achieve a global action, or *global exception handling*. Each participant is in its local handler, and to achieve a global action the participant handlers coordinate together. Global exception handling is needed when the exception handling action is beyond a participant's context, or a participant cannot make a decision because it does not have sufficient information.

As an example, consider an environment fault representing a deadlock condition that occurs during a system activity. Without global exception handling, it may be difficult to determine an action to get out of the deadlock because any one participant does not know what any other participant is doing about the deadlock, or even if another participant has detected the deadlock yet. In the worst case, each participant detects the deadlock and releases its resource allocation, thus all participants release their resources. However, the deadlock occurs again when all participants try to do the activity again. Current systems tend to provide no explicit mechanism for global handling, but rather use local exception handling instead.

3.4   Unhandled Exceptions

A pervasive problem with exception handling is unhandled exceptions. The consequences may be dramatic, such as detonating a rocket while it still has its payload [4]. The research on unhandled exceptions has focused on verifying they do not happen programmatically, i.e., explicitly raised by the program.

Unfortunately, as noted in the Gypsy system [9], that means a handler has to be active during most operations, including simple arithmetic, unless it is known beforehand what the guaranteed bounds of the operands are. The explosion of paths makes it infeasible for complete verification of all possible exceptions. In distributed systems, there is an even greater number of paths since exceptions from remote systems may also be raised in addition to the exceptions mentioned above. Additionally, with machine-independent programs (e.g., Java programs), it cannot even be guaranteed what exceptions the run-time environment can generate.

Having a generic handler active does not solve the issue since the typical action for an unhandled exception is to terminate the process. There is little else the handler can do since the exception was unexpected, which implies the program has provided no recovery for this situation.

3.5   Exception Handling Methodology

One of the key cornerstones of structured programming, including object-orientation, is the encapsulation and separation of functions. Most researchers agree that the complexity of exception handling requires a separation of exception handling from the main program flow. There is significant research on separating the handler from the program flow (e.g., *catch* blocks in C++ and Java), and that is considered to be well-understood. However, it is not as well understood on separating the handling from the program. The issue is that the exception handling mechanism needs to be able to support that separation.

The methodology, or the way the exception handling system is used, to achieve the separation has proceeded along two paths: explicit handler coordination, and *exception handling patterns* [8]. Explicit handler action requires the program to have the handling actions. Though handlers achieve separation of the handler from the main program flow, they do not separate exception handling from the program. Thus, each program would need to have its own exception handling. This is a brute force methodology that is error-prone, repetitive, and not easily extendable.

Another methodology that allows for program separation is *exception handling patterns*. Handlers query a knowledge-base to determine a pattern that matches the raised exceptions, with the result being an appropriate handler action.

4. THE GUARDIAN MODEL

The *guardian exception handling model* is an attempt to overcome the issues described above. The model is based on a timed asynchronous computation model, global exception handlers, separation of exception handling, and an extended fault model. The model provides a separation between program execution and exception handling paths, allowing modular high-level exception handlers that can be changed with few changes to application programs.

The basic elements of this model are shown in Figures 1 and 2. The model uses a *guardian*, which is a distributed global exception handler that is associated with an activity. The guardian is logically replicated at all participants' environments. A *guardian member* is a co-process in a participant's environment. The guardian members of an activity form a logical group implementing the global abstraction for its guardian. The members in this group communicate with each other using reliable group communication primitives.

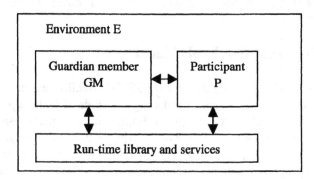

Figure 1. A Participant and its Guardian Member at a Node

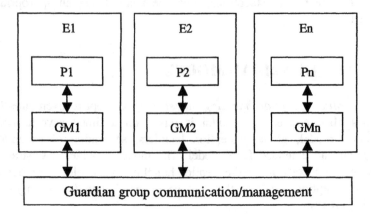

Figure 2. Conceptual View of a Guardian Group

A participant raises global exceptions through its local guardian member, which then uses the group communication primitives of the guardian fault model (described in the next section) to determine a global exception handling action. Each guardian member communicates the action locally to its local participant as an exception, perhaps deferring it until its associated participant is ready for it. A guardian member also has access to the run-time environment (e.g., Java virtual machine) so it can query the state of the environment.

4.1   The Guardian Fault Model

The goal of the *guardian fault model* (GFM) is to allow easier separation between local and global faults by reducing the kinds of faults a participant needs to handle locally that have global implications. A participant should need to raise global faults explicitly only if the participant's program needs to raise one based on program semantics. Conditions that are outside the context of a program, such as deadlock, do not have to be detected by the program. Also, the global recovery actions are orchestrated by the handlers that are encapsulated in the guardian.

GFM uses group communication based on the timed asynchronous model. Group messages are delivered and processed within time bounds; if the bound is not met then the message is considered lost. Groups allow for reliable and ordered messaging within the bounds. From the fault model view, there is no difference between synchronous and timed asynchronous systems. Synchronous systems simply have no messages lost due to a time bound being exceeded. Thus, the guardian approach is suitable for tightly coupled systems, as well as distributed systems.

GFM has the following assumptions:

1. Group communication. Each participant has a corresponding group member called a *guardian member*. The group as a whole is a *guardian*. All messages are reliable and ordered: a message is either delivered to all the non-failed intended recipient members that are in the group or is delivered to none, and messages are delivered in the same order to all members.

2. Virtual synchrony. Group communication monitors group membership, and sends ordered messages to all members when the membership changes. This implies that membership faults are detectable within the limits of the time bound for a message, including fail-partition. Fail-partition is necessary in timed asynchronous systems since messages may exceed time bounds, giving a false indication of crash.

3. Causal and totally ordered messages. Group communication assures that all messages are received in the same order on all members, including membership messages, and are FIFO ordered with respect to a sender.

4. Each participant has a liveness self-check that is reliable and correct. The liveness is sent to the participant's guardian member periodically.

5. Security, configuration, environment, and compatibility faults are detectable. In most cases, a participant has limited recovery for these kinds of faults. For malicious participants, it may try to mask faults, especially security ones, to avoid detection. GFM assumes that these faults are not maskable by a participant.

6. A participant notifies its guardian member when it is performing an operation that is in a global context. For example, if a participant is to perform a barrier operation, it informs its guardian member that it is going into a barrier.

7. A participant and its local guardian member have a consistent view of the network connectivity and communication link status to other nodes.

8. Participant Byzantine faults that are not detectable by the security model or liveness check are assumed to not occur.

The purpose of group communication is to allow a guardian to be notified when faults outside the context of a participant occurs, and not necessarily a replacement for participant communication. Thus, GFM's fault separation is using the guardian group to monitor the participants and their environments for faults that require global recovery. GFM does this by having the guardian group detect the following faults on behalf of a participant:

a) Network omission faults, within the timing constraints of group communication. With Assumptions 6 and 7, when a participant is engaged in communication with other participants, the guardian is aware of it. If a network omission occurs, then by Assumptions 1 and 3, the loss will be detected by group communication. If a participant does not send a

message or does not process one correctly, than that is detected by
Assumption 4.

b) Participant timing faults due to message delivery time bounds being
exceeded. The reasoning is similar to above.

c) Participant crash faults. Whenever a participant halts (fail-silent or fail-
stop), it is detected by its liveness check, which in turn is detected by its
guardian member. For node crashes, the guardian member fails along
with the participant, so the guardian group detects the failed participant.
Fail-safe crashes are eventually detected by the liveness check. Fail-
partition crashes are detected by the guardian group by Assumption 7.

The expense of GFM is a security model, reliable participant liveness
checks, and group communication. In a distributed environment, a security
model and liveness checking are typically already used. Thus, the extra cost
of GFM is in the use of group communication.

GFM is one way that the use of guardians may enhance conversation
approaches. Conversation based exception handling approaches typically are
concerned primarily with application level faults, while GFM is concerned
with faults at both the system as well as the application level. A conversation
approach using guardians can get the additional system-level fault checking
of GFM as part of the guardian mechanism.

4.2   The Guardian Exception Model

The purpose of the guardian exception model is twofold: to allow global
exception handling actions, and to separate global exception handling from a
participant's exception handling. Global exception handlers are meant to be
modular with little effect to participants, provide default exception handling,
and provide sophisticated exception handling.

When a participant wishes to send a global exception to other participants,
it notifies its guardian member with the exception it wishes to raise. The
guardian member uses its group to broadcast the exception to the desired
members. If concurrent exceptions are raised, then the group orders the
exceptions. When a global exception is broadcast through the group, then all
guardian members process the exception to determine what action to take.

The processing is in three steps: diagnose, analyse, and decide. Diagnosis
is with the raised exception, and allowing a guardian member to query the
state of its participant or run-time environment. Analysis may be a variety of
methods, but the one suggested here is exception handling patterns, such as
the *citizen* approach. The guardian members cooperatively decide on an
action, and each member communicates the action to its local participant via
an exception. The required actions are, *suspend, terminate,* or *query.* It is not
necessary that a participant be able to perform all these actions, though it

must have a handler for them. If a participant cannot perform the action, then it informs its guardian member. Along with the global exception is optional exception data. A participant may raise a global exception along with exception-specific data by sending a notification to its guardian member for broadcast. The exception has an attribute that indicates if the exception is to be analyzed through the guardian, or if the exception is to be globally raised and each participant has a specific handler for it. Alternatively, a participant-raised global exception may be raised directly in all intended participants. The global exception handling policy the guardian accesses has actions for the types of global faults it wishes to analyze, including ones detectable by GFM as well as explicitly raised by the participants. If a guardian is trusted and secure, it may be able to change a participant's environment to allow recovery for certain security, configuration, and environment faults. In the cases where the policy determines that only a local action is needed, then only the guardian member that needs to signal the exception to the affected participant need do so. In this way, guardians could also be used for local exception handling. Lastly, the policy could be updated independently of guardians, which further separates participant exception handling from global exception handling.

4.3 The Guardian Programming Model

The programming model assumes an object-oriented language such as C++ or Java. For convenience, this paper will use Java-like syntax and exceptions. Local and global exceptions are distinct sub-trees in the exception object hierarchy, named *LocalException* and *GlobalException*, respectively. Other than the predefined global exceptions explained below, there are no restrictions on what user-defined global exceptions may be. Each exception object has required and optional user data.

For a participant to have a guardian member, it inherits from the *Guardian* class if it wishes to specialize a guardian. The *Guardian* class is instantiated with the name of the group and other information that describes the participant. For example, the data may specify that the participant is a primary or a backup. The instantiated object creates a thread that represents the guardian member for the participant. The guardian member either creates or joins the guardian group.

A participant raises a global exception by invoking the *Raise* method of its guardian. The method sends a local message to its guardian member, and waits for an exception response back from the guardian. The exception object includes a *named context*, which is a user-defined name that represents the participant context that all guardian members can use to determine if participants are in the same context. A named context is not the context itself, just a unique name or handle for it. When a global activity is to begin, a participant informs its guardian member of its named context (described below). Since this is a global activity, all participants in the activity also inform their respective guardian members with the same named context. Thus, though it is a local context that is being named, a named context represents a global context composed of participant local contexts.

Named contexts are application specified, and so may have different meanings based on the application. This provides the flexibility for the guardian mechanism to be used in a wide variety of exception handling paradigms. For example, a named context may be used to represent a number of different abstractions such as checkpoint, a recovery block, a transaction or conversation context, a barrier synchronization point, an assert point, or the stage that an application execution is at. Global exceptions can be deferred until all participants are at a certain context, or a global exception may be handled by a specific context.

The exception object also has a list of the participants that are to be in the context. In synchronous operations, such as barriers, it is assumed that all group members are to participate, and so the exception object need not specify them. If only a subset of participants are in the operation, then the list of participants can be specified in the exception object.

The guardian response is either a *Command* exception derived from *GlobalException* that the participant is expected to have a handler for, or an explicitly raised global exception from a participant. *Command* exceptions are used when the guardian is expected to provide an action. Derived from *Command* are the three commands a guardian may issue: *Suspend, Terminate, or Query*. Optional data in the exception object may be used to pass information to participants, which may be used to modify a participant's action. The data is supplied by whoever raises the exception: the guardian group or a participant.

A participant enables a top-level exception handler to catch all unhandled exceptions. The handler only invokes *Raise* with the predefined *Unhandled* global exception. *Raise* blocks until the guardian sends a *Command* back to the participant. Whenever a participant ends, it notifies its guardian member by invoking *Raise* with a predefined *ThreadEnd* global exception. Crashes raise a *Crash* global exception in all participants.

A participant uses named contexts and notifications to let its guardian know when it is ready to accept a *GlobalException*. A participant invokes the *Accept* method of its guardian for the notification, and the method is passed the named context the participant is in. A guardian can now determine when a participant can accept exceptions for a given named context by checking if its local participant has entered the context. Activities, and so named contexts, may be nested.

Similar to *Accept*, whenever a participant enters a synchronization operation, such as a barrier, it invokes the *SyncOp* method of its guardian with a list of the other participants it is waiting for, along with the context name. *SyncOp* is a wrapper around *Accept*, setting some state that allows easier use of *Accept* in synchronization operations. *SyncOp* differs from *Accept* in that *SyncOp* will automatically be aware via the guardian if any participant in the specified list fails. Each *Accept* and *SyncOp* have unique named contexts, and so may be nested to any depth or order. When a participant is done with a context, it invokes the *EndContext* method of the *Guardian* class. Thus, it is straightforward for a guardian member to keep track of context relationships.

Whenever a participant invokes *Accept* or *SyncOp*, it is assumed the participant also has handlers for *GlobalException*. When a *Command* is raised to a participant, *Command* has the named context that raised the exception, and the context that is to handle the exception. A named context could specify an application-defined program context that the exception is raised in, allowing a participant to perform local recovery in its corresponding local context. Crash exceptions can be delivered in any named context.

The implementation of the command *Terminate* may be as in [13]. The implementation of *Suspend* may be that the handler waits for a predefined exception to continue. *Suspend* can be used to temporarily halt a participant, such as for debugging, checkpointing, or retrieving a participant state. *Query* requires the participant to send information back to its guardian about its state relative to a specified context. *Query* is similar to *Suspend*, except it retrieves the query information and automatically continues. The query information could be local state information, such as the current named context, and status of state variables that the guardian could use for determining its actions.

Guardians can address the five issues mentioned above. The first issue of identifying contextual and non-contextual exceptions is addressed by the exception's raising context. Each guardian knows when a participant is in the target context. The target context can either be the smallest context among all participants that subsumes all of them, or each guardian member waits for its participant to enter the target context (a *deferred exception*), at which time the guardian signals the exception to the participant. This is similar to exception resolution, but rather than using an exception hierarchy, a context hierarchy is used instead.

Another way of considering contextual exceptions is that a global exception is only raised at well-defined points in a participant's execution. The points are when a participant informs its guardian that it is ready to accept an exception, and the participant environment allows an exception to be signaled to it. In the case of Java, remote exceptions are only raised when the thread is blocked. If the thread is in an infinite loop, then an exception is never signaled to it. The only known ways out of this are the loop polls for an exception, the code stream checks for pending exceptions, or the participant's liveness check includes periodic wait times that allow the timer handler to determine if the participant is making progress. GFM assumes a reliable liveness check that would detect such conditions.

The second issue is causal or non-causal exceptions. The guardian knows of previous *GlobalExceptions*, and each participant's context. If an exception is not contextual or deferred, then the guardian can diagnose further with *Query*, and analyze it using the guardian's policy. The analysis determines exception causality.

The third issue of global exception handling is addressed by the guardian itself. The fourth issue of unhandled exceptions is addressed with the *Unhandled* method. Using the diagnosis and analysis similar to exception causality, an action can be determined by the guardian while the participant with the unhandled exception has not ended yet (because the participant is blocked in *Raise* until a *Command* is sent to it). Finally, the last issue of exception handling methodology is addressed with the inherent separation guardians provide.

5.   APPLICATIONS OF THE GUARDIAN MODEL

This section illustrates the use of the guardian model using two examples of distributed computing: a primary-backup system, and a process control system involving a conveyor belt.

5.1   Primary-Backup System

In a client-server system, the service is implemented as a group of server processes. One of the processes in this group acts as the primary. The backup servers are replicas of the primary. Client requests are sent to all members of this group using a reliable and total ordered broadcast. All member processes execute the request using the local copy of the data; however, only the primary sends a response message to the client. If the primary fails, then one of the backups becomes the primary. Let us consider the following failure conditions:
- The primary fails silently or its node environment crashes.
- The primary encounters an environment exception such as its local file system being full, preventing it from completing the processing of the current request.

Consider the same situation with the guardian model. The primary and backup have associated guardian group members. When the primary fails silently, then either the environment the primary is in failed, or the primary participant failed. If the environment failed, then eventually the backup guardian member will receive a membership fault from group communication indicating the loss of the primary guardian member (since the member is in the same environment, if the environment fails so does the member). The loss of the primary member implies the loss of the primary participant. The guardian members at all backup servers would be delivered a global exception indicating the primary server's failure. The global handler would select one of the backup servers as the new primary. A new exception, indicating a configuration change due to the new primary, would be now delivered by the guardian to all backup participants. One of them would take over the functions of the primary. If only the primary participant failed silently, then eventually the liveness check for the primary participant will indicate the failure, and inform the primary guardian member. The member raises a global exception indicating primary failure, which gets raised to the backup participants. Once again, one of the backup servers becomes the primary. Similar kinds of recovery actions are initiated when the primary server communicates to its guardian member an occurrence of the "file system full" exception. In this case, the new primary determines from the context of the exception the request that was not completely processed by the previous primary. The new primary then takes over the function of sending a response message to the client.

5.2   Production Cell System

A simple production cell has a conveyor belt with an automatic input hopper that places metal parts on the conveyor from an input bin. A metal stamp removes the part from the conveyor, stamps it to form the part, and places the part back on the conveyor. Lastly, an output hopper removes the part from the conveyor and places it in an output bin. Assume that each of the four mechanical components (conveyor, input hopper, stamp, and output hopper) are software subsystems, and that there are sufficient sensors to indicate to each subsystem part placement necessary for the component's functioning, such as part detection, conveyor motion, and so on.

Suppose that the conveyor subsystem has a fault, and it has to halt. The conveyor fault is sent as a global exception to the other subsystems (stamp, input hopper, and output hopper), and the action is to halt them. However, the conveyor subsystem has a fault such that the conveyor belt could not be stopped. In this case a second global exception is raised at the stamp, indicating parts are still being delivered though the stamp is halted.

With the conveyor potentially full of parts, though no additional parts are placed on the belt, the parts could jam up at either the stamp or output hopper, perhaps damaging those mechanical components. The jamming could trigger safety alarms not directly associated with this production cell, such as device overheating, causing a much wider effect than just the production cell.

Typically, when the first global exception is raised during some activity, the activity aborts. While in the exception handler, the second global exception is raised. If the exception handling system ignores the second fault, or believes it is related to the first exception, then the second exception is ignored and a potential mechanical jam could occur.

Now consider using the guardian model. As above, the first exception is in an activity that aborts. The second exception is known to be non-causal, i.e., the exception is not due to the conveyor belt being halted, but it is due to the conveyor belt not being halted. This is due to the exception handler being in a different context than the activity, or alternatively the guardian's global exception handling policy could be involved. Suppose the action is to keep the stamp halted, but allow the output hopper to continue to remove parts from the conveyor and place them in the reject bin. The guardian sends a resume command only to the output hopper; keeping the other subsystems halted. Additionally, exception data in the output hopper command could direct the output hopper to place all parts in the reject bin.

6.   SUMMARY

Current research on concurrent exception handling has proceeded along two paths: structuring, typically using conversation-based approaches, and separating global exception handling from a program's main flow. Structuring works well in defining activities, but not as well in handling environment or system faults, globally coordinated exception handling other than exception resolution, or exception handling separation. The guardian model presented in this paper attempts to bridge the gap between structuring and separation by being a mechanism that is compatible with both.

The guardian model extends standard fault models with faults related to: fail-partition crash, membership, environment, and compatibility. Global exception handling is through a distributed handler called a guardian, which uses timed asynchronous group communication to coordinate and raise global exceptions. Named contexts offer application level flexibility in exception handling structures, including but not limited to conversation approaches. Guardians can use a global exception handling policy, perhaps patterns, to determine global actions. Future research will be in validating the guardian model. An experimental prototype of the model is in the planning stages, and once completed it will be used as a testbed to determine the usefulness of the model.

ACKNOWLEDGEMENTS

This research was partly supported by NSF grants 0082215 and 0087514.

REFERENCES

[1] R. H. Campbell and B. Randell, "Error Recovery in Asynchronous Systems," *IEEE Transactions on Software Engineering*, vol. 12, pp. 811-826, Aug 1986.

[2] F. Cristian and C. Fetzer, "The timed asynchronous distributed system model," *IEEE Transactions on Parallel and Distributed Systems*, vol. 10, pp. 642-657, June 1999.

[3] C. Dellarocas and M. Klein, "An experimental evaluation of domain-independent fault handling services in open multi-agent systems," in *Proceedings of the 4th International Conference on Multi Agent Systems*, 2000.

[4] M. Dowson, "The ARIANE 5 Software Failure," *Software Engineering Notes (ACM SIGSOFT)*, vol. 22, pp. 84, March 1997.

[5] V. Hadzilacos and S. Toueg, "A modular approach to fault-tolerant broadcasts and related problems," University of Toronto, Technical Report, 1994.

[6] J. Kienzle, A. Romanovsky, and A. Strohmeier, "Open multithreaded transactions: keeping threads and exceptions under control," *6th International Workshop on Object-Oriented Real Time Dependable Systems*, pp. 197-205, Jan 2001.

[7] M. Klein and C. Dellarocas, "Exception handling in agent systems," in Proceedings of the Third International Conference on Autonomous Agents (Agents '99), Seattle, Washington, 1999.

[8] N. Lynch, *Distributed Algorithms*: Morgan Kaufmann, 1996.

[9] J. McHugh, "Towards the Generation of Efficient Code from Verified Programs," University of Texas at Austin, Department of Computer Science, Technical Report 40, March 19841]

[10] R. Miller and A. Tripathi, "Issues with Exception Handling in Object-Oriented Systems," in *Proceedings of ECOOP'97*, pp. 85-103, June 1997.

[11] A. Romanovsky, C. Dony, J. L. Knudsen, and A. Tripathi, *Advances in Exception Handling Techniques - LNCS 2022*: Springer-Verlag, 2001.

[12] R. G. Smith, "The contract net protocol: high level communication and control in a distributed problem solver," *IEEE Transactions on Computers*, vol. 29, pp. 1104-1113, 1980.

[13] A. Tripathi and R. Miller, "Exception handling in agent-oriented systems," in *Advances in Exception Handling Techniques* LNCS 2022, Springer-Verlag, 2001, pp. 128-146.

[14] J. Xu, A. Romanovsky, and B. Randell, "Concurrent Exception Handling and Resolution in Distributed Object Systems," *IEEE Transactions on Parallel and Distributed Systems*, vol. 11, pp. 1019-1031, Oct 2000.

IV

TRANSACTIONS AND CONSISTENT CHECKPOINTING

Chapter 12

A recovery model for cooperative computations

Edgar Nett[1] and Michael Mock[2]

[1] University of Magdeburg:[2]Fraunhofer Institute for Autonomous intelligent Systems

Abstract: Fault-tolerance and concurrency are closely related issues to be addressed
when designing computer systems. The established theory of transactions with
the ACID-properties has solved the problem of integrating fault-tolerance and
concurrency control for classical database applications. In order to make the
benefits of transactions also applicable to other application domains, much
work has been invested in the development of extended transaction models and
atomic action concepts. These models all have in common that they aim at
supporting cooperation between different computations. Since the driving
force of the extension of the classical transaction model was providing more
flexible concurrency control, the further development of the transaction theory
focused on concurrency control and nesting. However, the formal basis of the
recovery aspects has not yet been extended to the new situation in which cooperation between individual computations is allowed. The traditional way of
formalizing the notion of commit only considers the commit of individual actions and leads to the criterion of "recoverability" that, in the end, prevents actions from cooperating with each other. This chapter provides a formal model
extending the notion of commit to the notion of commit-correctness that reflects the possibility of interactions between different actions by enabling them
to commit together. By this, it extends previous formal work on the reliability
of database transactions to the world of cooperative computations. It explicitly
does not address concurrency control, which is inherently more application
dependent, but provides a formal recovery model as basis for any concurrency
control concept or action model that supports cooperative computations.

Key words: Fault tolerance, recovery, formal model, atomic actions, cooperative computing

P. Ezhilchelvan and A. Romanovsky (eds.), Concurrency in Dependable Computing, 231–251.
© 2002 Kluwer Academic Publishers. Printed in the Netherlands.

1.   INTRODUCTION

Fault-tolerance and concurrency are closely related issues to be addressed when designing computer systems. Typical problems of fault-tolerance such as error detection, locating faults, damage assessment and recovery are much easier to design and implement in a purely sequential system than in a concurrent system. The most complex part of recovery schemes such as recovery blocks, checkpointing and message logging schemes, or conversation schemes deal with problems caused by the concurrency of the considered processes. Similarly, concurrency control algorithms, that are designed to preserve some consistency criteria in the presence of concurrent processes, are much more complex when they must be fault-tolerant with respect to some defined fault-model. The concept of transactions with the ACID-properties [6,7] has solved the problem of fault-tolerance and concurrency for classical database applications. Based on the premise that individual computations should be "isolated", i.e., not interact with each other, solid theories of concurrency [19,2] and reliability [9] have been developed. The benefits of transactions are: 1) they handle concurrency by guaranteeing serializable executions of concurrent processes, 2) they achieve fault-tolerance by the means of committing transactions such that they are no longer subject to transaction faults, site faults or media faults.

In order to make the benefits of transactions also applicable to other application domains, much work has been invested in the development of extended transaction models [4]. Also, atomic actions with transaction-like properties have been introduced at the system as generic primitives for the construction of robust distributed programs [11,22]. These models for extended transactions or atomic actions respectively, such as nested transactions [14], open transactions [5], group transactions [20], dynamic actions [15,13], coordinated atomic actions [24,25], to mention only a few of them, all have in common that they aim at supporting cooperation between different computations, that are then normally structured as (sub-)units of a global transaction. In other words, classic concurrency control that prohibits information flow between active transactions is considered to be too restrictive, and more flexible schemes are established. Still the same degree of fault-tolerance should be accomplished as provided by classical transactions. Since the driving force of the extension of the classical transaction model was providing more flexible concurrency control, the further development of the transaction theory focused on concurrency control and nesting. Besides the development of a number of more application-oriented formal consistency criteria [21], formalisms have been developed to describe and capture the effects of nesting [1,12] and of other new action constructs, such as split and join as described in the ACTA framework [3].

However, the formal basis of the recovery aspects of actions has not yet been extended to the new situation in which cooperation between individual computations is allowed. In order to explain this, let us consider the traditional way of formalizing the notion of commit. Since we will focus on the recovery aspects, which are valid for cooperative concurrency control concepts in various extended transaction or atomic action models, will use the neutral term "action" to denote an individual computation. An action is only characterized by the all-or-nothing property, i.e. it can either be successful (commit) or its effects are removed from the system (abort). An action is not subject to a specific kind of concurrency control. The traditional notion of commit is usually considered to be an event related to an individual action. This leads to the criterion of for recoverable schedules [2,9] as a prerequisite for commit. It requires that whenever an action reads information from another action, it must not commit before that other action is committed. Otherwise, the other action could be aborted later on, potentially making the state of the already committed action inconsistent. Hence, recoverability prevents invalid information from being committed in case of an abort of another action that has contributed to that state. The following example shows that the notion of recoverability fundamentally conflicts with the goal of cooperation between actions. We use the commonly adopted notion of a "schedule" (sometimes also termed "history") to denote the execution of a set of actions. Let S be the following schedule of the two actions A_1 and A_2:

$$S = W_{11}(x)R_{21}(x)W_{22}(y)R_{12}(y)$$

In this schedule, action A_1 performs a write operation $W_{11}(x)$ on the object x, which is then read by action A_2 with the read operation $R_{21}(x)$. After that, action A_2 writes on object y, which afterwards is read by A_1. A practical interpretation of this access pattern could be that both actions cooperate to write two chapters in a document. Action A_1 writes the first chapter represented by the object x, A_2 reads x and writes the second chapter y, which again is read by A_1. Both actions cooperate to come to a common decision on whether or not both chapters are acceptable and both would agree to commit the final result. But the notion of recoverability established in the classical theory requires that whenever an action reads information from another action, it must not commit before that other action is committed. Because in the example schedule each action reads information from the other action, i.e. there is a cyclic dependency between the two actions, none of them would be allowed to commit. The only possible extension of the schedule would be to abort both actions. Also, some kind of nesting concept could not solve the problem either, since there is no hierarchical relationship between the actions in the example. Hence, the traditional way of formalizing the notion of commit as an event belonging to individual actions, or to action trees, respectively, prevents actions from cooperating with each other.

This chapter provides a formal model extending the notion of commit to the notion commit-correctness that reflects the possibility of interactions between different actions. It extends the work of Hadcilacos [9] to the world of cooperative computations. It explicitly does not address concurrency control, which is inherently more application dependent, but provides a formal recovery model as basis for any concurrency control concept or action model that supports cooperative computations.

2.   THE FORMAL MODEL

The notion of schedules is the basis for the well-developed theory of concurrency [2,19]. Hadzilacos [9] introduces a **Herbrand semantics** [8] for schedules, that allows analyzing reliability properties of schedules. In the following, the approach of [9] is adopted to formalize how to commit cooperative computations. The formalism provided by the ACTA framework, however, [3] is designed for comparing different new transactional constructs at the syntactic level. In our work, rather than introducing new constructs, we analyze the effects of information flow on a formal semantics level. This work is part of a larger scientific effort that is reflected in various scientific publications and theses, e.g. [13,15,16,17]. Due to the space limitations of this chapter, only a few of the formal proofs can be incorporated in here. Those omitted follow the same line. Interested readers are referred to the above-mentioned literature.The proof of the main theorem 28 that presents a criterion for commit-correctness is given in the appendix. The basic definitions follow the well-known multi-step schedule based read/write model for concurrent computations. A computation is modeled as a partial order of read/write steps on objects.

DEFINITION 1: OBJECTSPACE
    An objectspace $D = \{ x, y, z, ... \}$ is a finite number of objects.

DEFINITION 2: OPERATION
    An operation is an element of $OP = \{ R,W \} \times D$. Instead of using tuples, operations are commonly denoted by $R(x)$ and $W(x)$ for $x \in D$. $R(x)$ denotes a read operation on the object x and $W(x)$ denotes a write operation on the object x.

DEFINITION 3: CONFLICT
    Two operations are conflicting with each other if they operate on the same object and if at least one of them is a write operation.
    The following definition introduces the basic concept of an action as a related set of operations that are either successful or aborted. As in the classic theory for transactions, this distinction expresses the all-or-nothing property

as a basic fault-tolerance property of actions. Faults, such as action faults incurred during the execution of an action, and site faults of a site on which the action is executing, lead to the abort of that action (media faults are handled by standard mechanisms and not considered further). However, since our model aims at supporting cooperation between different actions, a more fine-grained fault-model is needed. Cooperation implies that the model must be able to handle the effects of the dissemination of information that will become invalid if the respective action will be aborted later. In this case, having disseminated these results to other actions is equivalent to the effect of fault propagation. The classical transaction approach is to avoid fault propagation by enforcing isolation. Other approaches, e.g. [20, 25], still enforce isolation, but allow for cooperation between multiple threads of the same action by supporting application specific forward error recovery for exception handling. If, however, cooperation between actions is to be supported, fault propagation cannot be avoided (or ignored), but must be tolerated. This is, the model must allow for the propagation of uncommitted information, which in case of a later abort turns out to be a fault propagation. This fault-propagation must then be tolerated. On the system level, without referring to further application semantics, it must be handled by backward error recovery. Hence, besides the classical faults tolerated by action systems, namely action faults and site faults, a new type of fault must be introduced, namely the cascading action fault. As usual, action faults and site faults denote the exceptional termination of an action or a computing site, respectively. A site fault, which is assumed to be fail-stop, is mapped onto action faults of those actions which effects are lost due to that site fault. Introducing the cascading action fault reflects the above mentioned case of fault propagation meaning that an action is aborted caused by the use of input data which has become invalid by the abort of other actions. The usual notion of successful completion of an action, the commit, means that an action is safe with respect to all considered faults. We will maintain this important interpretation of commit, but will extend it to groups of actions. For individual actions, we will introduce a weaker termination, namely the *completion* of an action, meaning that it will no longer be affected by action faults, but still can be subject to site faults or cascading action faults.

DEFINITION 4: ACTION

An action is a pair $A_i = (OP^{(i)}, \prec^{(i)}), i \in IN$ with

1. $OP^{(i)} = \{o_{i1}, o_{i2}, \ldots, o_{im_i}\}, m_i \in IN$ the set of operations of A_i,

2. $\prec^{(i)} \subseteq (OP^{(i)} \cup \{a_i, t_i\}) \times (OP^{(i)} \cup \{a_i, t_i\})$, a precedence relation with the following properties:

2.1 $\prec^{(i)}$ is a partial order,

2.2 for any two conflicting operations o_{ik} and o_{il} holds:

$$o_{ik} \prec^{(i)} o_{il} \vee o_{il} \prec^{(i)} o_{ik} ,$$

2.3 The following condition holds:

$$(\forall o_{il} \in OP^{(i)} : o_{il} \prec^{(i)} a_i \wedge \neg(o_{il} \prec^{(i)} t_i \vee t_i \prec^{(i)} o_{il}))\vee$$

$$(\forall o_{il} \in OP^{(i)} : o_{il} \prec^{(i)} t_i \wedge \neg(o_{il} \prec^{(i)} a_i \vee a_i \prec^{(i)} o_{il}))\vee$$

$$(\forall o_{il} \in OP^{(i)} : o_{il} \prec^{(i)} t_i \wedge t_i \prec^{(i)} a_i)$$

Clauses 1) to 2.2) just define actions in the usual way as partially ordered set of operations on objects, possibly including so called termination operations a_i and t_i. The basic difference to traditional transaction models is how these termination operations *complete* t_i and *abort* a_i can be used, as expressed in clause 2.3). It basically says that an action is either terminated by an abort operation (and there is no complete operation), or by a complete operation (and there is no abort operation), or, and this extends the conventional model, by a complete operation that still can be followed by an abort operation (or by a commit operation as will be introduced in section 2.3). The usual commit and abort operations are mutually exclusive, i.e., a committed action cannot be aborted by any considered fault. As explained in the example in the introduction, models that only provide the commit event to denote the successful completion of an individual action only allow for the class of so-called recoverable schedules, which, roughly speaking, prohibits cooperation between different actions. If cooperation was supported, the commit cannot be decided upon autonomously by an individual action. What is the complete operation good for, given that a completed action can be aborted later on? It is used to indicate the willingness of an action involved in some cooperation to commit. An action that terminates in the additional state called "completed", indicates that it will execute no further operations and will not be subject of an action fault (but still can be affected by a cascading action fault or site fault if the eventual commit fails). It is ready to commit from its individual point of view. However, the real commit still depends on the agreement of other actions it has cooperated with. Modeling the commit event, which, therefore, can comprise more than one action, is dealt with in section 2.3. The concurrent execution of actions is modeled as a schedule. A schedule roughly is a prefix of a complete schedule, i.e., a schedule containing termination operations for all actions.

DEFINITION 5: TERMINATION OPERATIONS

The termination operations $T^{(i)}$ of an action A_i are defined as

$$T^{(i)} = \{a_i, t_i\} \cap \bigcup_{(a,b) \in \prec^{(i)}} pr_{2,1}(a,b)$$

whereby $pr_{m,n}$ denotes the projection of an m-tuple onto its n'th component.

DEFINITION 6: COMPLETE SCHEDULE

Let $A = \{A_1, A_2, \ldots, A_n\}, n \in IN$ be a set of actions. A complete schedule for A is a pair $S = (OP^S, \prec^S)$ with:

1. $OP^S = \bigcup_{i=1}^{n}(OP^{(i)} \cup T^{(i)})$ the set of steps in S,

2. $\prec^S \subseteq OP^S \times OP^S$ the (schedule-) precedence relation of S with the following properties:

2.1 $\prec^S$ is a partial order,

2.2 for any two conflicting operations of S, p and q, holds: $p \prec^S q \vee q \prec^S p$,

2.3 $\prec^S \supseteq \bigcup_{i=1}^{n} \prec^{(i)}$, i.e., the (schedule-) precedence relation conforms to all precedence relations of all actions in S

DEFINITION 7: SCHEDULE

$S' = (OP^{S'}, \prec^{S'})$ is a schedule for the actions $A = \{A_1, A_2, \ldots, A_n\}, n \in IN$, if there is a complete schedule $S = (OP^S, \prec^S)$ for A with:

1. $OP^{S'} \subseteq OP^S$,   the set of steps in S',

2. $\prec^{S'} \subseteq \prec^S$,   the (schedule-) precedence relation of S',

3. $p \in OP^{S'} \Rightarrow \forall q \in OP^S (q \prec^S p \Rightarrow q \in OP^{S'})$, i.e., with any step of S', all preceding steps (wrt. $\prec^S$) must be in S'.

Since the schedule is the basic formal notion of the model, the following definitions introduce some formal tools to make the handling of schedules easier.

DEFINITION 8: PROJECTION OF A SCHEDULE

Let $S = (OP^S, \prec^S)$ be a schedule for the actions $A = \{A_1, A_2, \ldots, A_n\}, n \in IN$. The projection $PR_{cond}(S) = (OP^{PR}, \prec^{PR})$ over the predicate *cond* (a total function over OP^S with range $\{t, f\}$, i.e. *true, false*) is a schedule with:

1. $OP^{PR} = \{o \in OP^S \mid cond(o) = t\}$

2. $\prec^{PR} = \prec_{|OP^{PR}}$, the restriction of $\prec^S$ on OP^{PR}.

The projection thus eliminates all steps that do not fulfill its condition. The following definition defines special cases for predicates over schedules:

DEFINITION 9: OPERATION PROJECTION

Let $S = (OP^S, \prec^S)$ be a schedule for the actions $A = \{A_1, A_2, \ldots, A_n\}, n \in IN$. Let $o \in OP^S$ be a step in S.

1. $S_{\leq o} = PR_{cond}(S)$ with $cond(o') = \begin{cases} t \text{ if } o' = o \text{ or } o' \prec^S o \\ f \text{ in any other case} \end{cases}$

denotes the projection of S on the steps equal to or before o.

2.
$$S_{<o} = PR_{cond}(S) \text{ with } cond(o') = \begin{cases} t \text{ if } o' \prec^S o \\ f \text{ in any other case} \end{cases}$$

denotes the projection of S on the steps before o.

DEFINITION 10: PREFIX AND EXTENSION OF A SCHEDULE

Let $S = (OP^S, \prec^S)$ and $S' = (OP^{S'}, \prec^{S'})$ be schedules for the actions $A = \{A_1, A_2, ..., A_n\}, n \in IN$. S' is a prefix of S ($S' \leq S$), if:

1. $OP^{S'} \subseteq OP^S$,

2. $\prec^{S'} \subseteq \prec^S$,

3. $p \in OP^{S'} \Rightarrow \forall q \in OP^S (q \prec^S p \Rightarrow q \in OP^{S'})$

S is called extension of S'.

So far, the operations executed in a schedule have no semantics. It is not yet expressed that a write operation produces a value that is input to the next read operations on that object. Since we want to introduce a new way of formalizing the semantics of "commitment", we refer to the established way of formalizing the reliability aspects of transactions as introduced in [9], which defines a **Herbrand-Semantics** for the read and write operations. This approach abstracts from the application semantics of the actions and captures the relationship between different operations by associating them with uninterpreted function symbols. Roughly speaking, the semantics of a read operation on a given object is determined by the semantics of the last write operation (belonging to a non-aborted action) on that object. The semantics of a write operation is defined as the application of an uninterpreted function symbol on the semantics of all read operation that so far have been executed within the corresponding action. To avoid "undefined" read operations (i.e., reading an object that never has been written), a special initializing action is introduced which writes on all objects.

DEFINITION 11: INITIALIZING ACTION

Let $S = (OP^S, \prec^S)$ be a schedule for the actions $A = \{A_1, A_2, ..., A_n\}, n \in IN$ on the objects $D = \{x_1, x_2, ..., x_{|D|}\}$. The initializing action of S, $A_0 = (OP^{(0)}, \prec^{(0)})$, has the following properties:

1. $OP^{(0)} = \{W_{oi}(x_i) \mid x_i \in D\}$, all objects are written,

2. $T^{(0)} = \{t_0\}$, the action completes and is not aborted,

3. $\forall o \in OP^S : t_0 \prec^S o$, the completion precedes all other steps in the schedule.

In the following, all schedules will be assumed to be extended by an initializing action. The following notion of a maximum of the schedule-precedence relation is useful to define the last preceding write operation.

DEFINITION 12: MAXIMUM WRT. THE SCHEDULE-PRECEDENCE RELATION

Let $S = (OP^S, \prec^S)$ be a schedule for the actions $A = \{A_0, A_1, A_2, ..., A_n\}, n \in IN$ and let $O \subseteq OP^S, O \neq \varnothing$ be a non-empty subset of the steps of S. The maximum wrt. $\prec^S$ of O is defined as:

$$\max_{\prec^S} O = \left\{ o \in O \middle| \forall o' \in O: \neg\left(o \prec^S o'\right) \right\}$$

Now we can define the Herbrand-Semantics of the operations as follows.

DEFINITION 13: SEMANTICS OF READ/WRITE OPERATIONS

Let $S = (OP^S, \prec^S)$ be a schedule for the actions $A = \{A_1, A_2, ..., A_n\}, n \in IN$ and let $R_{il}(x)$ and $W_{jk}(y)$ be steps in S. The Herbrand-Semantics of $R_{il}(x)$ and $W_{jk}(y)$ are defined recursively by:

1. $H_S(R_{il}(x)) = H_S(W_{gk}(x))$ with

$$W_{gk}(x) = \max_{\prec^S}\{W_{mn}(x) \in OP^S \mid W_{mn}(x) \prec^S R_{il}(x) \wedge a_m \notin OP^S\}$$

Due to the initializing action the set of preceding write operations is never empty. Since all write operations on x are conflicting with each other, the maximal write operation wrt. $\prec^S$ is well defined.

2. $H_S(W_{jk}(y)) = f_{jk}(H_S(R_{jk_1}(x_1)), H_S(R_{jk_2}(x_2)), ..., H_S(R_{jk_m}(x_m)))$ with

$R_{jk_t}(x_t), 1 \leq t \leq m$ are all those read operations of A_j with

$R_{jk_t}(x_t) \prec^{(i)} W_{jk}(x)$, and f_{jk} is an uninterpreted m-ary function symbol.

The following definition finally introduces the Herbrand-Universe as the smallest set of uninterpreted function symbols that is needed to define the semantics of all operations of a schedule.

DEFINITION 14: HERBRAND-UNIVERSE FOR ACTIONS

The Herbrand-Universe HU for the actions $A = \{A_1, A_2, ..., A_n\}, n \in IN$ on the objects $D = \{x_1, x_2, ..., x_{|D|}\}$ is the smallest set of uninterpreted function symbols for which holds:

1. $\forall x_i \in D: f_{oi}() \in HU$

with 0-ary function symbols $f_{oi}()$, therefore denoting constants,

2. $\forall i = 1, ..., n, \forall j = 1, ..., |D|, \forall W_{ik}(x_j) \in OP^{(i)}:$

$$\left(\begin{array}{c} \left| \left\{ R_{ij}(y) \middle| y \in D \wedge R_{ij}(y) \prec^{(i)} W_{ik}(x_j) \right\} \right| = m \\ \wedge v_1, \cdots, v_m \in HU \end{array} \right) \Rightarrow f_{ik}(v_1, \cdots, v_m) \in HU$$

with m-ary function symbols f_{ik}.

The semantics of a schedule is now defined by a mapping of objects onto values in the Herbrand-Universe. Roughly speaking, every object is assigned with the value of the last write operation executed on that object.

DEFINITION 15: SEMANTICS OF A SCHEDULE

Let $S = (OP^S, \prec^S)$ be a schedule for the actions $A = \{A_1, A_2, \ldots, A_n\}, n \in IN$ on the objects D and let HU be the corresponding Herbrand-Universe. The semantics of S is a mapping $H[S]: D \rightarrow HU$ with

$$x \mapsto H_S(W_{ik}(x)) \text{ with } W_{ik}(x) = \max_{\prec^S}\{W_{jl}(x) \in OP^S \mid a_j \notin S\}$$

2.1   Abort-Correctness

The semantics of schedules now gives us a means to formally capture the effects of aborting an action, which is the basic mechanism to provide the All-or-Nothing property. What are the effects for other, concurrent actions and under which circumstances can the concurrent execution be considered to be correct in the presence of aborts? The traditional approach is to restrict cooperation between actions in order to localize the effects of aborting an action within the action itself. This leads to the class of schedules that avoid cascading aborts [2,9]. If cooperation between actions is supported, cascading aborts cannot be avoided. Nevertheless, it is still possible to derive a useful notion of correctness that works in the presence of cascading aborts. This abort-correctness will be developed in the following, starting with some motivating examples. Note that the precedence relations will be implicitly given by the writing order from left-to-right.

The definition of the semantics of operations already includes that write operations of aborted actions have no effect. Note that the abort of an action subsequently can change the semantics of operations of other actions.

Example: Let S be the schedule:

$$S = W_{01}(x)t_0R_{11}(x)W_{12}(x)R_{21}(x)W_{22}(x)$$

Then, the semantics of $R_{21}(x)$ is defined by:

$$H_s(R_{21}(x)) = H_s(W_{12}(x))$$
$$= f_{12}(H_s(R_{11}(x)))$$
$$= f_{12}(H_s(W_{01}(x)))$$
$$= f_{12}(f_{01}(\ ))$$

Thus, the semantics of $W_{22}(x)$ is:

$$H_s(W_{22}(x)) = f_{22}(H_s(R_{21}(x)))$$
$$= f_{22}(f_{12}(f_{01}(\ )))$$

This means, the value produced by the action A_2 on the object x depends on the action A_1. Let S' be an extension of S, in which the action A_1 is aborted:

$$S' = W_{01}(x)t_0R_{11}(x)W_{12}(x)R_{21}(x)W_{22}(x)a_1$$

In S', the semantics of $R_{21}(x)$ is:
$$H_{s'}(R_{21}(x)) = H_{s'}(W_{01}(x)) \text{ as } a_1 \in S'$$
$$= f_{01}(\ )$$

Now, the semantics of $W_{22}(x)$ is:
$$H_{s'}(W_{22}(x)) = f_{22}(H_{s'}(R_{21}(x)))$$
$$= f_{22}(f_{01}(\ ))$$

Aborting A_1 subsequently has changed the semantics of the operations of A_2. In other words, the operations of A_2 had a different semantics at the time of their execution compared to resulting schedule. This would mean in real life, that its read operations get other values and that its write operations produce other values. This is not acceptable, if the operations have already taken place. However, the situation can be considered to be correct, if A_2 is aborted as well. This leads to the following definition of abort-correct schedules:

DEFINITION 16: ABORT-CORRECT SCHEDULE

Let $S = (OP^S, \prec^S)$ be a schedule for the actions $A = \{A_0, A_1, A_2, ..., A_n\}, n \in I\!N$ with the semantics H_S. S is abort-correct for an action $A_i \in A$, if:

$$\forall o_{ik} \in OP^{(i)} : \left(H_{S \le o_{ik}}(o_{ik}) \ne H_S(o_{ik}) \Rightarrow a_i \in OP^S \right)$$

S is abort-correct, if S is abort correct for each $A_i \in A$.

This definition says, that if an operation o_{ik} had some semantics $H_{S \le o_{ik}}(o_{ik})$ at the time of its execution and some other semantics $H_S(o_{ik})$ in the considered schedule, then the corresponding action A_i must be aborted. In other words, in an abort-correct schedule, all those actions are aborted that have executed operations that changed their semantics after the time of their execution..

In the following, we will develop a criterion to characterize abort-correct schedules. This criterion then allows to formally proving cascading aborts to be an appropriate means to implement abort-correctness. We start by citing a Lemma on the Herbrand-Semantics taken from [9].

LEMMA 17: PROPERTY OF THE HERBRAND-SEMANTICS

Let S, S' and S'' be schedules with $S \le S' \le S''$ and let $o \in OP^S$ a step in S. Then: $H_S(o) = H_{S''}(o) \Rightarrow H_S(o) = H_{S'}(o) = H_{S''}(o)$ i.e., if the semantics of an operation is the same at two different points in the schedule, than it has never changed in between.

Now, we introduce two further formal tools to develop the characterization.

DEFINITION 18: LAST WRITE OPERATION

Let $S = (OP^S, \prec^S)$ be a schedule for the actions $A = \{A_0, A_1, A_2, ..., A_n\}$, $n \in IN$ on the objects D. Let $o_{ik} \in OP^S$, $i \neq 0$ be an operation in S on the object $x \in D$ (i.e. $o_{ik} = R_{ik}(x)$ or $o_{ik} = W_{ik}(x)$) that does not belong to the initializing action of S. The last write operation wrt. $o_{ik} \in OP^S$ in S is defined as:

$$LSO_S(o_{ik}(x)) = \max_{\prec^S}\left\{W_{mn}(x) \in OP^S \mid W_{mn}(x) \prec^S o_{ik}(x) \wedge a_m \notin OP^{S_{\leq o_{ik}}}\right\}$$

Obviously, the last write operation determines the semantics of a read operation [13].

LEMMA 19: LAST WRITE OPERATION DETERMINES SEMANTICS

Let $S = (OP^S, \prec^S)$ be a schedule for the actions $A = \{A_0, A_1, A_2, ..., A_n\}$, $n \in IN$ and let $R_{ik}(x)$ be a read operation in S. Then

$$W_{jk'}(x) = LSO_S(R_{ik}(x)) \Leftrightarrow H_{S_{\leq R_{ik}(x)}}(R_{ik}(x)) = H_{S_{\leq R_{ik}(x)}}(W_{jk'}(x))$$

This motivates the definition of the reads-from relation and of the dependency set.

DEFINITION 20: READS-FROM RELATION OF A SCHEDULE

Let $S = (OP^S, \prec^S)$ be a schedule for the actions $A = \{A_1, A_2, ..., A_n\}$, $n \in IN$ on the objects D.

1. A_i reads $x \in D$ directly from A_j in S (formally

   $(A_j, x, A_i) \in LV_S(x), LV_S(x) \subseteq A \times D \times A)$ if:

   $i \neq j \wedge \exists k, k' : H_{S_{\leq R_{ik}(x)}}(R_{ik}(x)) = H_{S_{\leq R_{ik}(x)}}(W_{jk'}(x))$

2. A_i reads directly from A_j in S (formally $(A_j, A_i) \in LV_S, LV_S \subseteq A \times A$, notation $A_j \xrightarrow{LV_S} A_i$) if there is a $x \in D$, which is read directly by A_i from A_j in S.

3. Let $LV_S^* \subseteq A \times A$ the transitive closure of LV_S, i.e.

   $(A_j, A_i) \in LV_S^*$ iff $(A_j, A_i) \in LV_S \vee$

   $\exists m \in IN \exists A_{k_1}, ..., A_{k_m} \in A : (A_j, A_{k_1}) \in LV_S \wedge$

   $(A_{k_m}, A_i) \in LV_S \wedge \underset{l \in \{2, ..., m\}}{\forall} : (A_{k_{l-1}}, A_{k_l}) \in LV_S$

   A_i reads from A_j in S (notation $A_j \xrightarrow{LV_S^*} A_i$) if $(A_j, A_i) \in LV_S^*$.

4. Let for each action A_i in S be the **dependency set** defined by

   $AB_S(A_i) = \{A_j \in A \mid A_j \xrightarrow{LV_S^*} A_i\}$

The dependency set will be the central notion in the characterization of abort-correct schedules. The following lemma shows, that a subsequent change of the semantics of an operation can only be caused by an abort of either the action itself or an abort of an action in its dependency set.

LEMMA 21: ONLY ABORTS SUBSEQUENTLY CHANGE OPERATION SEMANTICS

Let $S = (OP^S, \prec^S)$ be a Schedule for the actions $A = \{A_0, A_1, A_2, ..., A_n\}, n \in IN$ and let $R_{ik}(x_m)$ a read operation in S. Then:

$$\left(\forall A_j \in \{A_i\} \cup AB_s(A_i) : a_j \notin OP^S\right) \Rightarrow H_{S_{\le R_{ik}(x)}}(R_{ik}(x_m)) = H_S(R_{ik}(x_m))$$

The proof is an induction over the order of read operations in S and can be found in [13]. Now we are ready to give the criterion for abort-correct schedules:

THEOREM 22: CRITERIA FOR ABORT-CORRECTNESS

Let $S = (OP^S, \prec^S)$ be a schedule for the actions $A = \{A_1, A_2, ..., A_n\}, n \in IN$. S abort-correct for an action $A_i \in A$, if and only if:

$$\forall j \in \{1, \cdots, n\}: A_j \in AB_S(A_i) \wedge a_j \in OP^S \Rightarrow a_i \in OP^S \qquad (1)$$

S is abort-correct, if and only if (1) holds for S each $A_i \in A$.

The proof is to be found in [13]. Theorem 22 is the formal basis of an algorithm to achieve abort-correctness. It shows that the knowledge of the reads-from relation is sufficient to guide a chasing algorithm along direct reads-from dependencies in order to guarantee abort-correctness. The set of actions that actually are aborted in the chasing algorithm is called abort set. Algorithms to compute the abort set in a distributed system are discussed in [18]. Note that so far no means has been introduced to prevent the so-called domino-effect [10,23], i.e., the uncontrolled roll back of system progress. In fact, every schedule trivially can be made abort-correct by aborting all of its actions. The next section introduces the commit event as a means to prevent this undesirable behavior.

2.2 Commit-Correctness

This section introduces the notion of commit into the formal model. To commit an action means to make sure that its results are not subject to any of the considered faults, i.e., a committed action can no longer be aborted. However, as shown in theorem 22, aborting dependent actions is the basic means to achieve abort-correctness. Thus, the goal is again to formalize conditions under which an action can be committed (given that the schedule remains abort-correct). Again, the classical approach taken in [2,9] rules out cooperation between different actions and leads to the class of so-called recoverable schedules in which each action can decide autonomously on its own commit. This approach is not feasible for cooperating actions where the agreement of different actions is needed for a commit. To model this behavior, we introduce a formal commit event for sets of actions. We start by defining the usual notion of partitioning taken from the theory of sets.

DEFINITION 23: PARTITIONING

Let M be a set. $I = \{I_1, ..., I_k\}, k \in IN$ is a (finite) partitioning of M, if:

1) $I \subset POT(M)$, 2) $\bigcup_{i \in \{1,...,k\}} I_i = M$, 3) $\forall i, j \in \{1,...,k\}, i \neq j : I_i \cap I_j = \emptyset$, i.e.,

I consists of subsets of M (1), that cover M (2) and are mutually disjoint (3).

The notion of a complete schedule with commit events now extends the definition 6:

DEFINITION 24: COMPLETE SCHEDULE WITH COMMIT EVENTS

Let $A = \{A_1, A_2, ..., A_n\}, n \in IN$ be a set of actions. A complete schedule with commit events for A is a pair $S = (OP^S, \prec^S)$ with:

0. $I = \{I_1, ..., I_k\}, k \in IN$ the subset of a partitioning of $\{1,...,n\}$, and

   $C^S = \{c_{I_1}, ..., c_{I_k}\}$ the set of commit events in S.

1. $OP^S = \bigcup_{i=1}^{n} (OP^{(i)} \cup T^{(i)} \cup C^S)$ the set of steps in S,

2. $\prec^S \subseteq OP^S \times OP^S$ the schedule-precedence relation with:

2.1 $\prec^S$ is a partial order,

2.2 for any two conflicting operations of S, p and q, holds $p \prec^S q \vee q \prec^S p$,

2.3 $\prec^S \supseteq \bigcup_{i=1}^{n} \prec^{(i)}$, i.e., the (schedule-) precedence relation conforms to all precedence relations of all actions in S.

3. The following condition holds

   $\forall i \in \{1,...,n\} \forall I' \in I : i \in I' \Rightarrow a_i \notin OP^S \wedge t_j \prec^S c_{I'}$

Definition 24 extends definition 6 by commit events. A commit event c_{I_k} holds for an action A_j, if $j \in I_k$. We call A_j committed. Condition 0) in definition 24 says that there is at most one commit event for each action. Condition 3) states that a committed action cannot be aborted and vice versa. It says furthermore, that only a completed action can be committed. Similar to definition 7, a schedule with commit events can be defined as prefix of a complete schedule with commit events. In the following, we will denote "schedule with commit events" simply as "schedules".

A committed action can no longer be aborted. This implies in an abort-correct schedule, that the semantics of its operations is not subject to subsequent changes. This nice property formally reflects that a committed action is safe with respect to all considered faults.

THEOREM 25: COMMIT EVENTS IN ABORT-CORRECT SCHEDULES

Let $S = (OP^S, \prec^S)$ be a schedule, S' with $S \leq S'$ an extension of S for the actions $A = \{A_1, A_2, ..., A_n\}, n \in IN$ and let c_I be a commit event for A_i in S. Then the following holds:

S' is abort-correct for $A_i \Rightarrow \forall o_{ik} \in OP^{(i)} : H_{S \leq o_{ik}}(o_{ik}) = H_{S'}(o_{ik})$

Proof: Assume there was a $o_{ik} \in OP^{(i)}$ with $H_{S \leq o_{ik}}(o_{ik}) \neq H_{S'}(o_{ik})$. Then, as S' is abort-correct for A_i, there must be $a_i \in OP^{S'}$. With $c_l \in OP^S$ and $S \leq S'$ follows $c_l \in OP^{S'}$, thus from condition 3) in definition 24 $a_i \notin OP^{S'}$. This is a contradiction to $a_i \in OP^{S'}$.

Theorem 25 says that in an abort-correct schedule, the semantics of any operation of a committed action cannot be changed by any fault. This shows that a commit event actually prevents system progress from being rolled-back, even if cascading aborts take place to achieve abort-correctness for non-isolated actions. Thus, it is very desirable to have commit events in abort-correct schedules. However, is it actually possible? The goal of achieving abort-correctness sometimes requires aborting actions. Committing disables to abort. Thus, a commit event only can take place if the abort-correctness of the schedule is not endangered. Such a schedule will be denoted as commit-correct in the following definition.

DEFINITION 26: PERMISSIBILITY OF COMMIT EVENTS, COMMIT-CORRECTNESS

Let $S = (OP^S, \prec^S)$ a schedule for the actions $A = \{A_1, A_2, ..., A_n\}, n \in IN$ and let c_l be a commit event in S. c_l is permissible in S, if:

$$\bigvee_{S' : S_{\leq c_l} \leq S'} \bigvee_{A_i \in A : i \in I} : \quad S' \text{ is abort-correct for } A_i$$

S is commit-correct, if each commit event in S is permissible in S.

In other words, a commit event for an action is permissible, if no possible extension of the schedule requires aborting that action for achieving abort-correctness. The definition of commit-correctness immediately implies that a schedule is abort-correct for all committed actions. Every commit-correct schedule can be extended to an abort-correct schedule by aborting all actions that are not committed.

Although the definition of commit-correctness makes a strong guarantee for the committed actions, it is not directly helpful in order to find out *at the time of the commit* whether the commit event is permissible or not. This is because the very definition 26 seems to require knowledge about all the possible future extensions of the schedule. In the following, we will develop a criterion for commit-correctness that can be evaluated at the time of the commit event. Not surprisingly, the reads-from relation and the dependency set will again play a central role in that criterion. We start by defining some formal abbreviations:

DEFINITION 27: COMMIT SET, COMMITTED PORTION

Let $S = (OP^S, \prec^S)$ be a schedule for the actions $A = \{A_1, A_2, \ldots, A_n\}, n \in IN$ with the commit events $C^S = \{c_{I_1}, \ldots, c_{I_k}\}$.

1. The commit set of a commit event $c_I \in C^S$ is: $CM(c_I) = \{A_i \in A | i \in I\}$
2. The committed portion of S is: $CA(S) = \bigcup_{c_I \in C^S} CM(c_I)$

We can now formulate the criterion for achieving commit-correct schedules (the proof is given in the appendix).

THEOREM 28: CRITERION FOR COMMIT-CORRECTNESS

Let $S = (OP^S, \prec^S)$ be a schedule for the actions $A = \{A_1, A_2, \ldots, A_n\}, n \in IN$ and let c^S be the commit events in S. S is commit-correct, if and only if:

$$\forall c_I \in C^S : \forall A_i \in CM(c_I): ABS_{S_{\leq c_I}}(A_i) \setminus CA(S_{<c_I}) \subset CM(c_I)$$

Similar to the case of abort-correctness, the knowledge of the reads-from relation and the dependency sets is essential for the criterion. It shows that all actions from the dependency set, which are not yet committed, must be included in the commit set. This condition gives a clear rule how to commit system progress, i.e., how to move forward the commit line of the system. Recall that, even if cascading aborts are used to achieve abort-correctness, they cannot roll back system progress beyond the commit line (theorem 25). Thus, theorem 28 gives us a basic means to prevent the domino-effect, even if communication among actions is allowed. Theorem 28 also clearly extends the traditional notion of recoverability, which only allows for commit sets containing exactly one element. Recoverability can be expressed by

$$\forall c_I \in C^S : \forall A_i \in CM(c_I): ABS_{S_{\leq c_I}}(A_i) \setminus CA(S_{<c_I}) \subset \{A_i\}$$

i.e., all actions in the dependency set of A_i must commit before A_i. The example from the introduction shows that the set of commit-correct schedules is a strict superset of the class of recoverable schedules. Again, let S be the following schedule

$$S = W_{11}(x)R_{21}(x)W_{22}(y)R_{12}(y)t_1 t_2$$

Now, we can use the complete operations to indicate the successful termination of each action. Both actions cooperate to come to a common decision and both of them announce via their complete operation that they agree upon the result of their common effort. So, there is no reason not to commit them. But, considering the conventional definition of commit that leads to the notion of recoverability, one notices that

$$AB_S(A_1) = AB_S(A_2) = \{A_1, A_2\} \wedge CA(S) = \emptyset$$

This is, none of the actions is committed and none of them can commit individually, because it depends on the commit of another action. Thus, the only possibility to extend the schedule to a "recoverable" schedule is to abort both actions. In our formal model however, a commit-correct extension of the schedule is possible by the means of committing them together in a single commit event, namely

$$S' = W_{11}(x)R_{21}(x)W_{22}(y)R_{12}(y)k_1t_2c_{\{1,2\}}$$

This example demonstrates that it is possible to commit together actions that have cooperated with each other and that we need a new semantics for commit in case of cooperating actions.

3. CONCLUSION

Committing system progress is an essential feature of any fault tolerant system. It protects a system state from being invalidated due to subsequent faults and establishes a firewall against the domino-effect. Sharing objects between concurrent computations, thus allowing for communication and co-operation, is a natural property of distributed systems. Structuring computations as actions with the all-or-nothing property is a clear basis for introducing fault tolerance into distributed systems. The desirable combination of these two major features raises the problem of how to commit system progress in case of cooperating actions. Our answer to that problem is an extension of the traditional formal model for actions. We introduce a new semantics describing the commit of sets of cooperating actions, reflecting the possibility of establishing abort sets and commit sets dynamically according to the actual information flow in the system. By extending the notions of abort and commit towards abort-correctness and commit-correctness, we formally describe the fundamentals of recovery for cooperative actions.

REFERENCES

[1] C. Beeri, P.A. Bernstein, and N. Goodman, "A Model for Concurrency in Nested Transaction Systems," *J. of the ACM*, vol. 36, no. 2, Apr. 1989, pp. 230-269.

[2] P. A. Bernstein, V. Hadzilacos, and N. Goodman, *Concurrency control and recovery in database systems*, Addison-Wesley, Reading, Mass., 1987, p. 370.

[3] P. K. Chrysanthis and K. Ramamritham, "A Formalism for Extended Transaction Models,", *Proc. 17th Int. Conf. Very Large Data Bases* (VLDB 91), Morgan Kaufman Publishers, Barcelona, Spain, 1991, pp. 103 - 112.

[4] A.K. Elmagarmid, ed., *Database Transaction Models for Advanced Applications*, Morgan Kaufmann Publishers, San Mateo, Calif., 1992, p. 611.

[5] H. Garcia-Molina and K. Salem, "Sagas," *Proc. ACM Conf. on Management of Data* (SIGMOD 87), ACM Press, San Francisco, Calif., 1987, pp. 249-259.

[6] J. Gray, "The transaction concept: Virtues and Limitations," *Proc. 7th Int. Conf. on Very Large Database Systems* (VLDB 81), IEEE CS Press, Cannes, France, 1981, pp. 144-154.

[7] J. Gray and A. Reuter, *Transaction Processing Systems: Concepts and Techniques,* Morgan Kaufmann Publishers, San Mateo, Calif., 1993, p. 1070.

[8] S. A. Greibach, *Theory of Program Structures: Schemes, Semantics, Verification,* Springer, LNCS 36, Berlin, 1975, 364 p.

[9] V. Hadzilacos, „A Theory of Reliability in Database Systems," *J. of the ACM,* vol. 35, no. 1, Jan. 1988, pp. 121-145.

[10] K. H. Kim, J. H. You, and A. Abouelnaga, "A Scheme for Coordinated Execution of independently Designed Recoverable Distributed Processes," *Proc. 16th Int. Symp. Fault Tolerant Computing* (FTCS-16), IEEE CS Press, Vienna, Austria, 1986, pp. 130-135.

[11] B. Liskov and R. Scheifler, "Guardians and Actions: Linguistic Support for Robust Distributed Programs," *ACM Trans. Programming Languages and Systems* (TOPLAS), vol. 5, no. 3, July 1983, pp. 381-404.

[12] N. Lynch et. al., *Atomic Transactions,* Morgan Kaufmann Publishers, San Mateo, Calif., 1994, p. 500.

[13] M. Mock, *Aktionsunterstützung für kooperative Anwendungen - Konzept und Realisierung[Action support for cooperative applications – concept and implementation],* doctoral dissertation, Dept. Computer Sciences, Univ. of Bonn, 1994 (in German).

[14] E. Moss, *Nested Transactions,* MIT Press, Cambridge, Mass., 1985, p. 160.

[15] E. Nett, *Supporting Fault Tolerant Computations in Distributed Systems,* habilitation thesis, Dept. Computer Sciences, Univ. of Bonn, 1991.

[16] E. Nett and B. Weiler, "Nested Dynamic Actions - How to Solve the Fault Containment Problem in a Cooperative Action Model," *Proc. 13th Symposium Reliable Distributed Computer Systems* (SRDS-13), IEEE CS Press, Irvine, Calif., 1994, pp. 106-115.

[17] E. Nett and M. Mock, "How to Commit Concurrent, Non-Isolated Computations," *Proc. 5th IEEE Workshop Future Trends in Distributed Systems* (FTDCS 95), IEEE CS Press, Cheju Island, Korea, 1995, pp. 343-352.

[18] E. Nett, M. Mock, and P. Theisohn, "Managing Dependencies - A Key Problem in Fault-Tolerant Distributed Algorithms," *Proc. 27th Int. Symp. Fault-Tolerant Computing* (FTCS-27), IEEE CS Press, Seattle, Wash., 1997, pp. 2-10.

[19] C. Papadimitriou, *The Theory of Database Concurrency Control,* Computer Science Press, Rockville, Md., 1986, p. 239.

[20] M. Patino-Martinez, R. Jimenez-Peris, S. Arevalo, "Exception Handling in Transactional Object Groups", *in Advances in Exception Handling Techniques,* Springer, LNCS-2022, Berlin, 2001, pp. 165-180.

[21] K. Ramamritham and P.K. Chrysanthis, "In Search of Acceptability Criteria: Database Consistency Requirements and Transaction Correctness Properties," *in Distributed Object Management,* Özsu, Dayal, Valduriez, eds., Morgan Kaufmann Publishers, San Mateo, Calif., 1993.

[22] S.K. Shrivastava, G.N. Dixon, and G.D. Parrington, "An Overview of the Arjuna Distributed Programming System," *IEEE Software,* vol. 8, no. 1, Jan. 1991, pp. 66-73.

[23] B. Randell, "System structure for fault tolerance," *IEEE Trans. Software Eng.,* vol. 1, no. 2, June 1975, pp. 220-232.

[24] J. Xu et. al., "Fault Tolerance in Concurrent Object-Oriented Software through Coordinated Error Recovery," *Proc. 25th Int. Symp. Fault-Tolerant Computing* (FTCS-25), IEEE CS Press, Pasadena, Calif., 1995, pp. 499-508.

[25] J. Xu, A. Romanovsky, B. Randell, "Concurrent Exception Handling and Resolution in Distributed Object Systems," *IEEE Trans. Parallel and Distributed Systems,* vol. 11, no. 10, Oct. 2000, pp. 1019-1032.

APPENDIX

PROOF OF THEOREM 28: CRITERION FOR COMMIT-CORRECTNESS

Let $S = (OP^S, \prec^S)$ be a schedule for the actions $A = \{A_1, A_2, \ldots, A_n\}, n \in IN$ and let c^S be the commit events in S. S is commit-correct, if and only if:

$$\forall c_I \in C^S : \forall A_i \in CM(c_I) : AB_{S_{\leq c_I}}(A_i) \setminus CA(S_{<c_I}) \subset CM(c_I) \tag{1}$$

Proof: "$\Rightarrow$": We show the contraposition. Assume (1) does not hold. Then we have to show that S is not commit-correct, i.e., that there is a commit event in S, which is not permissible. If (1) is not fulfilled, then there is a commit event c_I in S with an action $A_i \in CM(c_I)$ that depends on another action $A_j \in AB_{S_{\leq c_I}}(A_i)$ that is not contained in $CA(S_{<c_I}) \cup CM(c_I)$. Let c_I a minimal (with respect to the schedule-precedence relation) commit event with this property. From the definition of $A_j \in AB_{S \leq c_I}(A_i)$, there is a sequence of length n≥0 of actions with:

$$A_{k_0} \xrightarrow[LVS_{<c_I}]{} A_{k_1} \xrightarrow[LVS_{<c_I}]{} \cdots \xrightarrow[LVS_{<c_I}]{} A_{k_{n+1}} \text{ with } A_{k_0} = A_j \wedge A_{k_{n+1}} = A_i \tag{2}$$

Let l be the largest index in (2) for which $A_{k_l} \notin CA(S_{<c_I}) \cup CM(c_I)$ holds. Then $A_{k_{l+1}} \in CA(S_{<c_I}) \cup CM(c_I)$. In particular, it holds that $A_{k_{l+1}} \in CM(c_I)$, since otherwise there would be another commit event for $A_{k_{l+1}}$ in $S_{<c_I}$, that, in contradiction to the minimality of c_I, precedes c_I in the schedule-precedence relation, and for which condition (1) does not hold (with respect to the action A_{k_l}). It follows that:

$$A_{k_l} \xrightarrow[LVS_{<c_I}]{} A_{k_{l+1}} \text{ with } A_{k_l} \notin CA(S_{<c_I}) \cup CM(c_I) \wedge A_{k_{l+1}} \in CM(c_I) \tag{3}$$

According to the definition 20 of the reads-from relation, it follows from (3), that $A_{k_{l+1}}$ must have directly read on object from A_{k_l}, hence

$$\exists R_{k_{l+1}p}(x) \in OP^S : H_{S_{\leq R_{k_{l+1}p}(x)}}\left(R_{k_{l+1}p}(x)\right) = H_{S_{\leq R_{k_{l+1}p}(x)}}\left(W_{k_lp'}(x)\right)$$
$$\text{and } a_{k_l} \notin S_{\leq R_{k_{l+1}p}(x)} \tag{4}$$

We now construct an extension S' of $S_{<c_I}$, which is not abort-correct for $A_{k_{l+1}}$. Since A_{k_l} is not committed in $S_{<c_I}$ (according to (3): $A_{k_l} \notin CA(S_{<c_I}) \cup CM(c_I)$), we can simply abort it. Hence, if $a_{k_l} \in S_{<c_I}$ (i.e. A_{k_l} is already aborted), then let $S' = S_{<c_I}$, otherwise let $S' = S_{<c_I} \circ a_{k_l}$. This changes the semantics of $A_{k_{l+1}}$'s read operation of x, as $a_{k_l} \in S'$ now $H_{S'}\left(R_{k_{l+1}p}(x)\right) \neq H_{S'}\left(W_{k_lp'}(x)\right)$ and hence because of (4): $H_{S'}\left(R_{k_{l+1}p}(x)\right) \neq H_{S_{\leq R_{k_{l+1}p}(x)}}\left(R_{k_{l+1}p}(x)\right)$. As the semantics of a read operation of $A_{k_{l+1}}$ has changed, there should be $a_{k_{l+1}} \in S'$ for S' being abort-correct for $A_{k_{l+1}}$. However, this contradicts with the assumption that $A_{k_{l+1}}$ is committed, i.e., according to (3), c_I constitutes a commit event for $A_{k_{l+1}}$ in S'. Hence, S' is an extension

of $S_{<c_I}$, which is not abort-correct for $A_{k_{l+1}}$, hence c_I is not permissible, hence S is not commit-correct.

"⇐": Assume (1) holds. We have to show: S is commit-correct. Assume S was not commit-correct. Then there would be a commit event c_I in S that is not permissible. According to definition 26, there must be an action $A_i \in CM(c_I)$ and an extension S' von $S_{<c_I}$, which is not abort-correct for A_i. As A_i is committed in $S_{<c_I}$, it cannot be aborted in S', hence $a_i \notin S'$. Since S' is assumed to be not abort-correct for A_i, it follows from the criterion 22 for abort-correctness, that there is an action A_j in the dependency set of A_i, which is aborted in S', formally $\exists A_j \in ABS_{S'}(A_i) \wedge a_j \in OP^{S'}$. In the following, we show that A_j already as been in the dependency set of A_i at the time of the commit event c_I, i.e.

$$A_j \in ABS_{S_{\le c_I}}(A_i) \tag{5}$$

From (5) together with (1) follows, that there must be a commit event for A_j in $S_{<c_I}$, therefore A_j cannot be aborted in S', since S' is an extension of $S_{<c_I}$. This contradicts with $\exists A_j \in ABS_{S'}(A_i) \wedge a_j \in OP^{S'}$, hence the assumption must be wrong and S must be commit-correct.

We still have to show (5). For this, we first note that the following property holds for A_i:

$$\forall A_j \in ABS_{S_{\le c_I}}(A_i) \cup \{A_i\}: \{t_j\} \cap OP^{S_{\le c_I}} \neq \emptyset \tag{6}$$

This is because all $A_j \in ABS_{S_{\le c_I}}(A_i)$ are committed in $S_{<c_I}$ according to (1) and therefore also must be completed in $S_{<c_I}$ (see definition 24). Now, we can show the following property, in which S' can be an arbitrary extension of $S_{<c_I}$ (derive (5) as a special case):

$$ABS_{S_{\le c_I}}(A_i) \supset ABS_{S'}(A_i) \tag{7}$$

Intuitively, the dependency set cannot grow after the commit because all contained actions are completed. Formally, we show first that the following condition holds:

$$\forall A_k \in A \forall A_j \in ABS_S(A_i) \cup \{A_i\}: A_k \xrightarrow[LVS']{} A_j \Rightarrow A_k \xrightarrow[LVS_{\le c_I}]{} A_j \tag{8}$$

Assume (8) would be wrong. According to clause 1) of the definition 20 of the reads-from relation, there would be an operation of A_j with $o_{jm} \in OP^{S'}$. As by assumption $\neg\left(A_k \xrightarrow[LVS_{\le c_I}]{} A_j\right)$, o_{jm} cannot be part of $S_{\le c_I}$, hence $o_{jm} \notin OP^{S_{\le c_I}}$. On the other hand, A_j is completed in $S_{\le c_I}$ as stated by condition (3), i.e. $t_j \in OP^{S_{\le c_I}}$. As the schedule-precedence relation $\prec^{S_{\le c_I}}$ complies with the precedence relation $\prec^{(j)}$ of A_j, o_{jm} must precede t_j, i.e. $o_{jm} \prec^{S_{\leq C_l}} t_j$. Hence it holds $o_{jm} \in OP^{S_{\leq C_l}}$ in contradiction to $o_{jm} \notin OP^{S_{\leq C_l}}$ as stated above. Hence, the assumption was wrong and (8) must be true. As the reads-from relation is transitive, it follows directly from (8)

$$\forall A_k \in A \forall A_j \in AB_S(A_i) \cup \{A_i\} : A_k \xrightarrow[LV_{S'}]{} A_j \Rightarrow A_k \in AB_{S_{\leq C_l}}(A_i) \tag{9}$$

Now, we can prove (7). Consider an action $A_l \in AB_{S'}(A_i)$. We have to show: $A_l \in AB_{S_{\leq C_l}}(A_i)$. According to the definition 20 of the reads-from relation, we have $A_l \xrightarrow[LV_{S'}^*]{} A_i$, hence it holds that either

$$A_l \xrightarrow[LV_{S'}]{} A_i \tag{10}$$

or

$$\exists A_{k_1}, \ldots, A_{k_n} \in A : A_l \xrightarrow[LV_{S'}]{} A_{k_1} \xrightarrow[LV_{S'}]{} \cdots A_{k_n} \xrightarrow[LV_{S'}]{} A_i \tag{11}$$

In case of (10), $A_l \in AB_{S_{\leq C_l}}(A_i)$ follows directly from (9). In case of (11), it follows from (9) that $A_{k_n} \in AB_{S_{\leq C_l}}(A_i)$, and therefore, again by applying (9), also $A_{k_{n-1}} \in AB_{S_{\leq C_l}}(A_i)$, and by repeated application of sentence (9) finally $A_l \in AB_{S_{\leq C_l}}(A_i)$. This concludes the proof of theorem 28.

$$A \bar{u} = \bar{b}$$ (10)

(11)

Chapter 13

GROUP TRANSACTIONS[*]:

An Integrated Approach to Transactions and Group Communication

Marta Patiño-Martínez
Ricardo Jiménez-Peris
Facultad de Informática
Technical University of Madrid
Boadilla del Monte E-28660 Madrid Spain
{mpatino,rjimenez}@fi.upm.es

Sergio Arévalo
Escuela de Ciencias Experimentales
Universidad Rey Juan Carlos
Móstoles E-28933 Madrid Spain
s.arevalo@escet.urjc.es

Abstract   Transactions and group communication are two techniques to build fault-tolerant distributed applications. They have evolved separately over a long time. Only in recent years researchers have proposed an integration of both techniques. Transactions were developed in the context of database systems to provide data consistency in the presence of failures and concurrent accesses. On the other hand, group communication was proposed as a basic building block for reliable distributed systems. Group communication deals with consistency in the delivery of multicast messages. The difficulty of the integration stems from the fact that the two techniques provide very different kinds of consistency.

        This chapter addresses the integration of both models and how applications using group communication can benefit from transactions and

[*]This research has been partially funded by the Spanish National Research Council CICYT under grant TIC98-1032-C03-01.

P. Ezhilchelvan and A. Romanovsky (eds.), Concurrency in Dependable Computing, 253–271.
© 2002 *Kluwer Academic Publishers. Printed in the Netherlands.*

vice versa. On one hand, groups of processes can deal with persistent data in a consistent way with the help of transactions. On the other hand, transactional applications can take advantage of group communication to build distributed cooperative servers as well as replicated ones. An additional advantage of an integrated approach is that it can be used as a base for building transactional applications taking advantage of computer clusters.

Keywords: Transactions, Reliable Multicast, Cooperative and Competitive Concurrency.

1.   Introduction

Two well-known techniques to build fault-tolerant distributed systems are transactions and group communication. Transactions [1] were developed to provide data consistency in the presence of concurrent accesses and failures. Group communication (multicast) [2, 3] was proposed as a building block for reliable distributed systems. Group communication provides different levels of consistency in the delivery of multicast messages. These techniques have evolved quite independently, transactions in the context of databases and group communication in the context of reliable distributed systems. It has not been until the last years when researchers have tried to integrate both techniques.

During the mid-nineties a debate [4, 5, 6, 7] in the distributed systems community took place about whether group communication was enough to build any kind of distributed fault-tolerant application. One of the conclusions of this discussion was that group communication and transactions are two complementary fault-tolerance techniques. Since then, several research groups have become interested in the integration of both models.

For instance, in [8] a basic mechanism it is studied, *Dynamic Terminating Multicast*, that can be used to build both transactional and group systems. This work takes advantage of the fact that commit and multicast algorithms are consensus-like problems and therefore similar. They propose *Dynamic Terminating Multicast* as a basic mechanism to build both kinds of algorithms on top of it. Although their work deals with the integration of transactions and group communication, it just deals with the implementation of the commit protocol. Another approach integrating group communication with atomic commitment is taken in [9] where the lower bound of three rounds for non-blocking atomic commitment [10, 11] is overcome by using optimistic delivery of uniform multicast.

[12] proposes an integration of two models of consistency namely, virtual synchrony [2] and linearizability [13]. In that integration services

can be requested to groups of objects. Virtual synchrony guarantees that all group members perceive membership (view) changes at the same virtual time. Linearizability is a relaxation of serializability [14] (that guarantees serial execution of concurrent transactions). Linearizability ensures that the result of a set of concurrent invocations on a given object is equivalent to a serial execution of them. This approach does not deal with the bulk of transactional systems that imply a stronger isolation condition, serializability, as well as failure atomicity. However, the paper points out that the inclusion in the model of these properties, serializability and failure atomicity, must be addressed.

[15] present a more complete approach. In this paper, the authors explore the role of group communication in building transactional systems. The point of the paper is that group communication primitives are an application structuring mechanism that provides transactional semantics by itself. A transaction is sent in a single reliable total-ordered multicast message to all the servers the transaction needs to contact. Transaction atomicity is provided by multicast atomicity. That is, a message is delivered to all group members or to none of them. The isolation is achieved by using total-order and by processing requests sequentially. This approach has some penalties: groups must be dynamic, increasing transaction latency as a consequence. There are some other issues that are not addressed in the paper like recovery and transaction nesting.

In contrast the approach taken in [16] provides transactions as a basic mechanism while multicast is hidden from application programmers. Transactions can access replicated objects and therefore provide high available data, but no support is provided for cooperative transactional applications.

Another approach combining competitive and cooperative concurrency control are coordinated atomic actions [17]. In this model, processes can join on-going atomic actions to cooperate within them. This is useful in those applications where processes are autonomous entities, that need to cooperate with some atomicity guarantees. However, this model is not suitable for transactional systems where servers are passive entities that are only activated when clients request services.

Some programming languages [18, 19] have incorporated group communication primitives and features for replication, recovery and failure notification. Although, no facilities for transaction processing are available.

A different integrative approach has been the use of group communication as a building block to implement database replication. This approach has been taken in [20, 21, 22, 23, 24]. In these papers, reliable total ordered multicast is used to propagate updates from a replica where a transaction has been executed to the rest of the replicas. However, the emphasis is on improving the implementation of database replication rather than providing an integrated model.

Corba [25] did not provide fault-tolerance and many research projects [26, 27, 28, 29] have addressed this topic using replication and group communication. As a result, Corba has been recently enhanced with replication (FT-Corba [30]). However, in [31] it is stated that the composition of Object Transaction Service (OTS) and FT-Corba does not result in any meaningful combination of their strengths.

In [32] it is stated that none of the previous systems considers the problem of integrating group communication with the transactional frameworks they extend. The paper also describes how to integrate group communication with Jini transactions [33] to provide transparently transactions over replicated objects.

In all the previously mentioned approaches the integration of transactions and group communication has been identified as a key issue "to extend the power and generality of group communication as a broad distributed computing discipline for designing and implementing reliable applications" [15]. However, all the mentioned approaches just consider group communication to build replicated systems, but groups can be used for other purposes [34]. In this paper we address a complete integration of transactions and group communication. *Group Transactions* is a new transaction model in which transactional servers are groups of processes, either cooperative or replicated. Clients interact with these transactional group servers by multicasting their requests to them.

The paper is structured as follows, Section 2 introduces some definitions. Section 3 presents the proposed model, *Group Transactions*. Section 4 shows some applications of the model. Finally, we present our conclusions in Section 5.

2.   Model and Definitions

2.1   System

The system consists of a set of nodes $S = \{S_1, S_2, ..., S_N\}$ that communicate by exchanging messages through reliable channels. We assume an asynchronous system where nodes fail by crashing (no Byzantine failures).

In each node there is a set of processes. Each process belongs to a group. A group is seen as an individual logical entity, which does not allow its clients either to view its internal state, nor the interactions among its members. Processes belonging to the same group share a common interface and application semantics. A group interface is a description of remotely callable services, which must be implemented inside each group member.

Sites are provided with a group communication system supporting strong virtual synchrony [35]. Group communication systems provide communication primitives and the notion of view (current connected sites). Changes in the composition of a view are delivered to the application. We assume a primary component membership [3]. Strong virtual synchrony ensures that messages are delivered in the same view they were multicast.

Group communication primitives [2] are used to communicate with groups. A request to a group is multicast to all the processes of a group. Multicast messages are reliable. That is, a message is delivered to all sites in the view or to none of them. Regarding message ordering we consider multicast primitives providing *FIFO order* (messages from the same sender are delivered in the order they were multicast) or *total order* (all messages are delivered at all processes in the same order).

We distinguish two kinds of groups, *replicated* and *cooperative* groups, according to the state and behavior of its members.

Replicated groups implement the active replication model, that is, they behave as state machines [36]. According to this model all the group members are identical replicas, that is, they have the same state and should run on failure-independent nodes. Clients use total ordered multicast to submit their requests to replicated groups (Fig. 1.b). Therefore, all group members receive the same requests and produce the same answers.

A replicated group can act as a client of another group. Replication transparency is provided by the underlying communication system that filters the replicated requests so that a single message is issued. This is known as "n-to-1" communication [34] (Fig. 1.c). This type of communication allows building programs with active replication and minimal additional effort from the programmer. That is, the programmer programs the group as if the group were made out of a single process. To our knowledge *Group_IO* [37] is the only protocol that supports "n-to-1" communication.

On the other hand, members of a *cooperative group* (Fig. 1.a) do not need to have either the same state or the same code. They are intended to divide data among its members and/or to express parallelism taking advantage of multiprocessing or distribution capabilities in order to increase the throughput. For instance, a cooperative group can be used to perform matrix multiplication. Each member of a cooperative

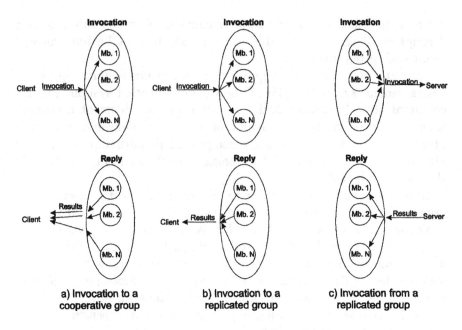

Figure 1. Group invocations and invocations from groups

group can compute a row. Each member of the group has a copy of the matrix and knows which elements it has to multiply.

Members of a cooperative group are aware of each other and they can communicate by multicasting messages to the group. This kind of communication is called *intragroup* communication. Invocations from a cooperative group are independent so they are not filtered by the communication system.

2.2   Transactions

A transaction is a sequence of operations that are executed atomically, that is, they are all executed (the transaction commits) or the result is as if none of them had been executed (it aborts). Two operations on the same data item conflict if they belong to different transactions and at least one of them modifies the data item. Transactions with conflicting operations must be isolated from each other to guarantee serializable executions [14].

A transaction that is executed in a single node is called a *local transaction*, while those that are executed in several nodes are *distributed transactions*.

Transactions can be nested [38]. Nested transactions or *subtransactions* can be executed concurrently, but isolated from each other. This kind of concurrency is competitive and only allows dividing a task into independent chunks (isolation forbids any cooperation). Transactions that are not nested inside another transaction are called *top-level transactions*. If a top level transaction aborts, all its subtransactions and their descendants will also abort, no matter whether they have committed or aborted. However, a subtransaction abortion does not compromise the result of its parent transaction (the enclosing one). Hence, subtransactions allow failure confinement.

3.   Group Transactions

Group Transactions is a transaction model that integrates nested transactions and process groups. In this model, transactional servers can be groups of processes. This kind of server is invoked from within transactions to enforce data consistency. Transactional group services are executed as distributed subtransactions or *multiprocess subtransactions*. The invocation of transactional groups within a transaction allows the isolation and atomicity of a sequence of group invocations, which it is not possible without transactional support.

Traditional transactions are single threaded. However, in order to use transactions in a more general setting, for instance to build fault-tolerant and high available concurrent and distributed applications, transactions might need to have multiple threads. The *intratransactional concurrency* provided by multithreading allows to transform easily concurrent applications into transactional ones. This intratransactional concurrency is cooperative, in contrast to the concurrency provided by subtransactions that is competitive. Transactions with local threads are called *multithreaded transactions*. Threads of the same transaction (siblings) can communicate among them.

Concurrency control mechanisms are used to guarantee the isolation of different transactions, however, those mechanisms do not apply to the local threads of a transaction. A local thread of a transaction could write a data item while a sibling is reading it. The underlying system must provide some kind of mutual exclusion to guarantee physical consistency, for instance *latches* [39].

Any transaction thread can start subtransactions. As a transaction can have several threads, a subtransaction and its parent transaction can run concurrently. Traditional nested transactions do not allow parent and child transactions to run concurrently. In our model, due to multithreading parent and child transactions can run in parallel. The semantics provided is that subtransactions are seen atomically by all the threads of its parent transaction. [40] study different forms of parent/child transaction concurrency, but they are based on explicit synchronization, whilst our approach provides an implicit synchronization closer to the transaction philosophy.

Members of a transactional group might have persistent state, which consistency is guaranteed by the transactional semantics. In case of failure, a recovery procedure takes place to recover the last consistent state.

3.1   Transactional Replicated Groups

An invocation to a replicated group is executed as a *replicated subtransaction*, the same in all the group members. If a member of a replicated group fails during the execution of a replicated subtransaction, the subtransaction will not abort as far as there is at least one available group member. Therefore, replicated groups can tolerate $k - 1$ failures, being k the number of group members. Transactional replicated groups provide high availability of both data and processing. If all the groups involved in a transaction (including the client) are replicated, the transaction will not abort in the presence of failures (either at the client or server side), hence, transactions will be highly available.

A transaction on a replicated group is executed by a thread at each group member. Those threads cannot create additional threads in order to maintain replica determinism. However, a replicated group can execute several transactions concurrently to provide an adequate level of concurrency. A transactional replicated group uses a deterministic scheduler [41], which ensures that all the replicas execute the same sequence of steps despite their multithreaded nature.

Since multicast messages are totally ordered and a deterministic scheduler is used, deadlocks on a single data item cannot happen. It is not possible an execution of two concurrent transactions where one of them locks an item in a subset of the replicas and the other locks the same item in another subset of the replicas. This problem happens in many replicated transactional systems.

Invocations from a transactional replicated group are filtered, so that only one invocation is made. These invocations are also executed as subtransactions of the calling transaction. The results of an invocation are sent back to all the members of the calling group. In Figure 2, there is a transactional replicated group (*gt1*) that invokes another transactional group (*gt2*). The *client group* invokes service *E1* in *gt1*. As a consequence a replicated subtransaction (*T1.1*) is created. If any of the two members of the replicated group fails, the subtransaction can still commit. When the replicas invoke service *E2* in *gt2*, a single request is made. The request result is returned to both members of the calling group.

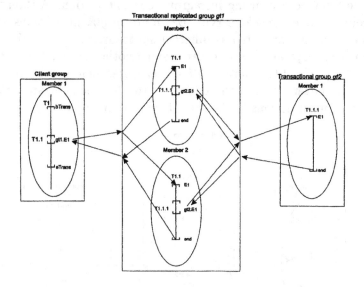

Figure 2. A transactional replicated group

When a failed member recovers, it performs a recovery process in order to undo the effects of uncommitted transactions on persistent data. Before joining the group, the state of the new member is updated with the state of a correct member. This state transfer is needed because the group could have been working while that member was down. The state transfer can be automatically performed, since all group members have the same state. State transfer is started once all the transactions, that were active when the join message was delivered, have finished their execution. The new member will execute the group invocations corresponding to transactions initiated after the delivery of the join message.

3.2 Transactional Cooperative Groups

Cooperative group invocations are executed as a *cooperative subtransaction*. Each of the group members executes a thread of the subtransaction in parallel. Since members of a cooperative group are aware of each other, they can use intragroup communication to cooperate. Members of a cooperative group can create new local threads to perform concurrently a service. The scope of these threads is restricted to the service where they are created.

Participants of a cooperative transaction can invoke other groups. These invocations are also executed as subtransactions. Figure 3 shows the interaction with a transactional cooperative group. Subtransaction *T1.1* is a cooperative subtransaction, where its participants can communicate (collaborate) using intragroup communication. Although the two group members invoke service *E2* in group *gt2*, invocations are independent and are executed as different subtransactions. Members of a cooperative group can also cooperate using another group. For instance, in the figure, if subtransaction *T1.1.1* executes before subtransaction *T1.1.2*, the latter will see the effects of the former subtransaction as both are subtransactions of the same transaction (*T1.1*).

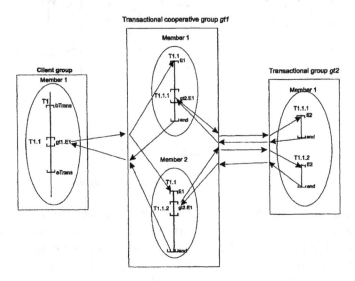

Figure 3.   A transactional cooperative group

Cooperative groups can have either of the following failure modes: all-commit-or-none and any-commits. In the former failure mode a transaction commits only if all the group members finish successfully. In the latter mode, if a node, where one of the group members resides, crashes while processing requests, the client will be notified and it will receive less answers from the group, but the transaction will not be aborted. The group could process further requests without all its members. This failure mode can be used when it is possible to perform services in a possibly degraded mode.

When a failed node restarts, group members in that node can join again their corresponding groups. Before joining the group a failed member will perform a recovery process. Since the rest of the group members could have been working in the meantime, the restarted member might need information from the group in order to update its state. The state transfer cannot be made transparently as it happens with replicated groups. The reason is that, in general, group members do not share the same state. Members of a cooperative group should define a recovery section to define the exchange of information needed before the new member joins the group.

Traditional transaction models have precluded cooperation within transactions due to their isolation property. Some advanced transaction models [42] have been proposed to deal with cooperative applications. However, their approach has been quite different. Cooperative transactions [43] relax serializability and offer different kinds of locks less restrictive than read/write ones, so transactions corresponding to different clients can cooperate. This is useful in cooperative applications like CAD environments.

4. Applications of the model

4.1 Cooperative Agenda

Let us see an example to illustrate the kind of cooperative applications for which cooperative groups are well-suited. The application under consideration will be in charge of the maintenance of the set of agendas of an organization or organization agenda. The application will register collective appointments (like department or section meetings) as well as private ones (go to the dentist). Each department of the organization keeps the agendas corresponding to its members or department agenda. A transactional cooperative group can be used to implement the organization agenda. The group provides services to access the distributed organization agenda. Each group member will keep a department agenda. Since the group is transactional, consistency of agendas is guaranteed in presence of concurrent accesses and node failures. This would have been impossible with a traditional non-transactional group.

A user can add, remove or modify entries in her agenda. An agenda resides in a single group member, and thus, this service does not require any cooperation. A more interesting service is the one of making a reservation for a set of people (i.e. a meeting). A reservation is made in two steps. First, the user asks for the free common slots in the set of agendas within a particular period of time. Then, the user chooses one of the slots and the reservation is made. Each step is implemented by a different group service. Clients want to make the reservation atomically, hence, both services should be called from within a transaction. The server group provides the `FindFreeSlots` service to search for all the common free slots in a set of agendas during a particular period of time. It also provides the `MakeCollectiveReservation` service to perform the reservation.

The `FindFreeSlots` service requires cooperation among the members of the server group due to common free slots cannot be found locally at one member. Common free slots can be obtained by intersecting the free slots in the requested period of time of all the involved agendas.

This intersection can be performed in two steps. A member of the group can coordinate this process. In the first step, the coordinator will multicast a request to the rest of the group members to perform the intersection of the involved local agendas. As a result of this request the coordinator will receive all the local intersections. In the second step, it will intersect all the local intersections to obtain the global intersection that will be returned to the client.

The global result can be computed in a more balanced way, if the coordinator sends its local intersection to the rest of the members. Thus, the rest of the members will intersect the coordinator local intersection with their local one, returning a (hopefully) smaller intersection and thus, the global intersection to be computed by the coordinator will be smaller.

As a result of `FindFreeSlots`, the client will receive the set of available free common slots. In the second step, the client will choose one of them to make the reservation through the `MakeCollectiveReservation` service. The reservation request will be multicast to all the group members and in response, they will make the reservations corresponding to involved local agendas.

A client might want to both make a reservation in a set of agendas as well as to book a meeting room. A server can be devoted to the reservations of meeting rooms in all the organization. In this case, the reliability requirements can be stronger and the organization can be interested in a highly available service, so even in the advent of node crashes the information about meeting rooms will be still available. Thus, a transactional replicated server can be devoted to held the information about meeting rooms providing the required availability. The client will make the reservation in the set of agendas and book a meeting room within the same transaction to guarantee that both reservations are done or none of them.

4.2   Fault-tolerant parallel computing

Most parallel programming languages have ignored the issue of fault tolerance because they focus on increasing the performance of a computation. Nowadays, there is an increasing trend to use large-scale distributed systems for parallel programs, as well as an increasing need for bigger computations. Parallel computations might run for days in hundreds or thousands of nodes, and in this context failures will be more likely. Therefore, fault tolerance of parallel computations should be addressed.

This topic has been addressed in [44] where the introduction of fault-tolerance in parallel applications using Argus [45] is studied. One of the examples proposed in [44] uses a master-slave scheme. The master distributes subcomputations to the slave processes. This master can be seen as a client of the slaves. The master splits a computation up into subcomputations that are executed on different slaves. Thus, subcomputations are executed as transactions what confines processor crashes to a single subcomputation, preventing the repetition of the whole computation. To prevent the loss of the whole computation due to a crash, checkpoints are written into stable memory. The master to achieve the checkpoints executes each checkpointed computation within a different top-level transaction. Thus, after a crash of the master it is only necessary the repetition of subcomputations not checkpointed before the master crashed.

However, it is not always feasible to split a computation into totally independent subcomputations. Some subcomputations might need to know intermediate results of other subcomputations. Traditional languages, like Argus, and models fail here, as transactions cannot cooperate. *Group Transactions* is an adequate model for fault-tolerant parallel computing, especially for those applications that need cooperation among subcomputations. Multiprocess and multithreaded transactions allow the work distribution in a cooperative way. Multiprocess transactions can be used to distribute a computation among a set of nodes, whilst multithreaded transactions can take advantage of multiprocessing (or multiprogramming) capabilities to run multiple threads of a transaction in parallel.

In [44] stable memory is used to save the results of subcomputations to prevent its lose in the advent of failures. The use of stable memory is quite expensive in terms of latency. In *Group Transactions* the creator of a transaction can be a replicated group. That group acts as a replicated master. Thus, subcomputations received by a replicated master can be stored in volatile memory and they will not be lost due to the availability provided by replication. Although group communication has a cost, it is much cheaper than stable memory that requires careful writes [46].

In the approach using Argus, each subcomputation checkpoint is achieved by running the subcomputation as a top-level transaction. Top-level transactions are expensive due to the atomic commitment protocol. Thus, another advantage of the proposed model is that the whole computation can be executed as a single top-level transaction in the replicated master. Subcomputations can be run as subtransactions, thus failure confinement is guaranteed with a cheaper solution.

Some parallel algorithms can perform more efficiently by using broadcast [47]. For instance, the parallel version of shortest path Floyd's algorithm [44]. As Argus only provides transactions, broadcasts can only be achieved by point-to-point messages with the corresponding loss of performance. Another advantage of *Group Transactions* is that members of a cooperative group can multicast messages to the other group members, this yields to an increase of performance with respect to a traditional transactional system without group communication like Argus.

4.3   Other applications

Database replication is another interesting application of the model. It has been recently studied how to take advantage of group communication in the implementation of replicated databases [20, 48, 23]. These approaches allow to manage replication of database systems. Replicated groups of *Group Transactions* can be used similarly to implement a replicated database.

Cluster computing has become a new paradigm for high performance computing. A cluster of computers is a collection of computers connected with a high speed reliable LAN that provides a set of services. A transactional group server can be run on top of a cluster to provide transactional services. The execution of these transactional services can be distributed among the cluster to reduce their latency. Traditional transactions preclude any cooperation within a transaction, and therefore cannot take advantage of cluster computing.

Transaction processing in multiprocessors is a different context where multithreaded transactions are interesting. Threads of a transaction can cooperate by means of shared memory and can be run on different processors to reduce the latency of the transaction.

5.   Current Work and Conclusions

Group Transactions have been incorporated into a programming language called *Transactional Drago* that is an Ada 95 extension. The language has already been defined [49] and a preprocessor is under implementation. The integration of exception handling with the model is addressed in [50]. The run-time support is provided by an object oriented library *TransLib* [51, 52] that implements *Group Transactions*.

In this paper we have presented an integration of transaction and group communication models into a new transaction model, *Group Transactions*. This new model provides multithreaded and multiprocess transactions, which are useful in many kinds of applications. The proposed model allows to build transactional distributed servers, either cooperative or replicated. Cooperative groups can be used to reduce the latency of transactional services by parallelizing transactions and thus, taking advantage of multiprocessors and/or clusters of computers. Replicated groups provide highly available transactional processing. The model has been formally described elsewhere [53] using the Acta framework [54].

Some applications of the model have been shown such as the agenda of an organization (a cooperative transactional application). This example has shown how some inherent distributed services can take advantage from an integrated approach for group communication and transactions. Fault-tolerant parallel computing is another field where group transactions can be extensively used. Our model allows the addition of fault-tolerance to parallel algorithms.

References

[1] J. Gray and A. Reuter. *Transaction Processing: Concepts and Techniques*. Morgan Kaufmann, 1993.

[2] K.P. Birman. *Building Secure and Reliable Network Applications*. Prentice Hall, NJ, 1996.

[3] G. V. Chockler, I. Keidar, and R. Vitenberg. Group Communication Specifications: A Comprehensive Study. *ACM Computer Surveys*, 2001.

[4] D. R. Cheriton and D. Skeen. Understanding the Limitations of Causally and Totally Ordered Communication. In *Proc. of ACM SOSP*, pages 44–57, 1993.

[5] K. P. Birman. A Response to Cheriton and Skeen's Criticism of Causal and Totally Ordered Communication. *Operating Systems Review*, 28(1):11–20, January 1994.

[6] R. Van Renesse. Why bother with CATOCS? *Operating Systems Review*, 28(4):22–27, October 1994.

[7] S. K. Shrivastava. To CATOCS or not to CATOCS, that is the ... *Operating Systems Review*, 28(4):11–14, October 1994.

[8] R. Guerraoui and A. Schiper. Transaction model vs Virtual Synchrony model: bridging the gap. In *Theory and Practice in Distributed Systems, LNCS 938*. Springer, 1994.

[9] R. Jiménez-Peris, M. Patiño-Martínez, G. Alonso, and S. Arévalo. A Low Latency Non-Blocking Atomic Commitment Protocol. In *Proc. of the Int. Conf. on Distributed Computing, DISC'01, LNCS-2180*, pages 93–107, 2001.

[10] C. Dwork and D. Skeen. The Inherent Cost of Nonblocking Commit. In *Proc. of ACM PODC*, pages 1–11, 1983.

[11] I. Keidar and S. Rajsbaum. On the Cost of Faul-Tolerant Consensus Where There No Faults - A Tutorial. Technical Report MIT-LCS-TR-821, 2001.

[12] K. P. Birman. Integrating Runtime Consistency Models for Distributed Computing. *Journal of Parallel and Distributed Computing*, 23:158–176, 1994.

[13] M.P. Herlihy and J. M. Wing. Linearizability: A Correctness Condition for Concurrent Objects. *ACM Transactions on Programming Languages and Systems*, 12(3):463–492, July 1990.

[14] P. A. Bernstein, V. Hadzilacos, and N. Goodman. *Concurrency Control and Recovery in Database Systems*. Addison Wesley, Reading, MA, 1987.

[15] A. Schiper and M. Raynal. From Group Communication to Transactions in Distributed Systems. *Comm. of the ACM*, 39(4):84–87, April 1996.

[16] M. C. Little and S. K. Shrivastava. Understanding the Role of Atomic Transactions and Group Communications in Implementing Persistent Replicated Objects. In *Proc. of 8th Workshop on Persistent Object Systems*, Sept. 1998.

[17] A. Romanovsky, S.E. Mitchell, and A.J. Wellings. On Programming Atomic Actions in Ada 95. In *Proc. of Int. Conf. on Reliable Software Technologies, LNCS 1251*, pages 254–265. Springer, June 1997.

[18] R. Schlichting and V. T. Thomas. Programming Language Support for Writing Fault-Tolerant Distributed Soft. *ACM Trans. on Comp. Syst.*, 44(2):203–212, 1995.

[19] J. Miranda, Á. Álvarez, S. Arévalo, and F. Guerra. Drago: An Ada Extension to Program Fault-tolerant Distributed Applications. In *Proc. of Int. Conf. on Reliable Software Technologies, LNCS 1088*, pages 235–246. Springer, June 1996.

[20] M. Patiño-Martínez, R. Jiménez-Peris, B. Kemme, and G. Alonso. Scalable Replication in Database Clusters. In *Proc. of the Int. Conf. on Distributed Computing DISC'00*, volume LNCS 1914, pages 315–329, Toledo (Spain), October 2000.

[21] F. Pedone, R. Guerraoui, and A. Schiper. Exploiting Atomic Broadcast in Replicated Databases. In *Proc. of Euro-Par Conference, LNCS 1470*, pages 513–520. Springer, 1998.

[22] B. Kemme and G. Alonso. A new approach to developing and implementing eager database replication protocols. *ACM TODS*, 25(3):333–379, September 2000.

[23] J. Holliday, D. Agrawal, and A. El Abbadi. The Performance of Database Replication with Group Communication. In *Proc. of FTCS'99*, 1999.

[24] U. Fritzke and Ph. Ingels. Transactions on Partially Replicated Data based on Reliable and Atomic Multicasts. In *Proc. of IEEE ICDCS'01*, pages 284–291, 2001.

[25] OMG. Corba services: Common object services specification, 1995.

[26] L. E. Moser, P. M. Melliar-Smith, and P. Narasimhan. A Fault Tolerance Framework for Corba. In *Proc. of the 29th IEEE Int. Symp. On Fault Tolerant Computing*, June 1999.

[27] S. Landis and S. Maffeis. Building Reliable Distributed Systems with Corba. *TAPOS*, April 1997.

[28] P. Felber, R. Guerraoui, and A. Schiper. The Implementation of a Corba Object Group Service. *Theory and Practice of Object Systems*, 4(2):93–105, 1998.

[29] G. Morgan, S. K. Shrivastava, P.D. Ezhilchelvan, and M.C. Little. Design and Implementation of a Corba Fault Tolerant Object Group Service. In *Proc. of the Int. Working Conf. on Distributed Applications and Interoperable Systems*, 1999.

[30] OMG. Fault tolerant corba specification, 1999.

[31] S. Frolund and R. Guerraoui. Corba Fault-Tolerance: Why it does not add up? In *Proc. of the IEEE Workshop on Future Trends in Distributed Computing*, December 1999.

[32] A. Montresor, R. Davoli, and O. Babaoglu. Enhancing JINI with Group Communication. Technical Report UBLCS-2000-16, Computer Science Dep., University of Bologna, 2001.

[33] K. Arnold, B. O'Sullivan, R. Sheifler, J. Waldo, and A. Wollrath. *The JINI Specification*. Addison Wesley, 1999.

[34] L. Liang, S. T. Chanson, and G. W. Neufeld. Process Groups and Group Communications. *IEEE Computer*, 23(2):56–66, February 1990.

[35] R. Friedman and R. van Renesse. Strong and Weak Virtual Synchrony in Horus. Technical report, CS Dep., Cornell Univ., 1995.

[36] F. B. Schneider. Implementing Fault-Tolerant Services Using the State Machine Approach: A Tutorial. *ACM Computing Surveys*, 22(4):299–319, 1990.

[37] F. Guerra, J. Miranda, Á. Álvarez, and S. Arévalo. An Ada Library to Program Fault-Tolerant Distributed Applications. In *Proc. of Int. Conf. on Reliable Software Technologies, LNCS 1251*, pages 230–243. Springer, June 1997.

[38] J. E. B. Moss. *Nested Transactions: An Approach to Reliable Distributed Computing*. MIT Press, Cambridge, MA, 1985.

[39] C. Mohan, D. Haderle, and B. Lindsay. ARIES: A Transaction Recovery Method Supporting Fine-Granularity Locking and Partial Rollbacks Using Write-Ahead Logging. In *Recovery Mechanisms in Database Systems*, pages 145–218. Prentice Hall, 1998.

[40] T. Haerder and K. Rothermel. Concurrency Control Issues in Nested Transactions. *Very Large Databases Journal*, 2(1):39–74, 1993.

[41] R. Jiménez-Peris, M. Patiño-Martínez, and S. Arévalo. Deterministic Scheduling for Transactional Multithreaded Replicas. In *Proc. of IEEE Int. Symp. On Reliable Distributed Systems (SRDS)*, pages 164–173, Nürenberg, Germany, October 2000.

[42] S. Jajodia and L. Kerschberg, editors. *Advanced Transaction Models and Architectures*. Kluwer, 1997.

[43] M. H. Nodine, S. Ramaswamy, and S. B. Zdonik. A Cooperative Transaction Model for Design Databases. In *Database Transaction Models*, pages 53–85. Morgan Kaufmann, 1992.

[44] H. E. Bal. Fault-tolerant parallel programming in Argus. *Concurrency: Practice and Experience*, 4(1):37–55, February 1992.

[45] B. Liskov. Distributed Programming in Argus. *Comm. of the ACM*, 31(3):300–312, March 1988.

[46] B. W. Lampson. Atomic Transactions. In *Distributed Systems*, pages 246–265. Springer, 1981.

[47] A. S. Tanenbaum, M. F. Kaashoek, and H. E. Bal. Parallel Programming Using Shared Objects and Broadcasting. *ACM Trans. on Computer Systems*, 25(8):10–19, August 1992.

[48] B. Kemme, F. Pedone, G. Alonso, and A. Schiper. Processing Transactions over Optimistic Atomic Broadcast Protocols. In *Proc. of ICDCS'99*, 1999.

[49] M. Patiño-Martínez, R. Jiménez-Peris, and S. Arévalo. Integrating Groups and Transactions: A Fault-Tolerant Extension of Ada. In *Proc. of Int. Conf. on Reliable Software Technologies, LNCS 1411*, pages 78–89. Springer, June 1998.

[50] M. Patiño-Martínez, R. Jiménez-Peris, and S. Arévalo. Exception Handling in Transactional Object Groups. In *Advances in Exception Handling, LNCS-2022*, pages 165–180. Springer, 2001.

[51] R. Jiménez-Peris, M. Patiño-Martínez, S. Arévalo, and F.J. Ballesteros. TransLib: An Ada 95 Object Oriented Framework for Building Dependable Applications. *Int. Journal of Computer Systems: Science & Engineering*, 15(1):113–125, January 2000.

[52] J. Kienzle, R. Jiménez Peris, Alexander Romanovsky, and Marta Patiño Martínez. Transaction Support for Ada. In *Proc. of Int. Conf. on Reliable Software Technologies*, volume LNCS-2043, pages 290–304. Springer, May 2001.

[53] M. Patiño-Martínez. *Language and Model for Cooperative and Replicated Distributed Transactional Systems*. PhD thesis, Technical University of Madrid (UPM), 1999.

[54] P. K. Chrysanthis and K. Ramamritham. Synthesis of Extended Transaction Models Using ACTA. *ACM Transactions on Database Systems*, 19(3):450–491, 1994.

Chapter 14

Checkpointing in Distributed Computing Systems

Lalit Kumar

Department of Computer Science & Engineering
Regional Engineering College, Hamirpur (HP) INDIA
lalitdec@rurkiu.ernet.in

Manoj Mishra

Department of Electronics and Computer Engineering
Indian Institute of Technology Roorkee, Roorkee INDIA
manojfec@rurkiu.ernet.in

Ramesh Chander Joshi

Department of Electronics and Computer Engineering
Indian Institute of Technology Roorkee, Roorkee INDIA
rcjfcc@rurkiu.ernet.in

Abstract   In this chapter, we present a message optimal non-intrusive checkpointing protocol for non-deterministic message passing distributed computing systems that does not require global time. Checkpoints in distributed systems can be coordinated, independent or quasi-synchronous. Coordinated checkpointing is attractive due to simple recovery, domino-freeness and optimal stable storage requirement. The quasi-synchronous checkpointing approach is also domino-free but may force processes to take multiple checkpoints. Independent checkpointing requires multiple local checkpoints of each node to be stored on stable storage and is affected by "domino effect". Coordinated checkpointing has been found better than independent checkpointing as it is domino-free and has minimum storage and performance overheads. So far, many coordinated checkpointing protocols have been proposed in literature for distributed computing systems. These protocols can be broadly classified as minimum process intrusive checkpointing protocols and non-intrusive checkpointing protocols. In this chapter, we present a non-intrusive coordinated checkpointing protocol for distributed systems with least failure-free overhead. The proposed checkpointing algorithm has optimal communication and storage overheads. It requires only $O(n)$ extra messages for taking a global consistent checkpoint. We introduce the concept of "odd" and "even" checkpoint intervals that replace the checkpoint sequence numbers that are generally piggybacked with each message to avoid orphan messages.

P. Ezhilchelvan and A. Romanovsky (eds.), Concurrency in Dependable Computing, 273–289.

1. INTRODUCTION

Checkpointing and rollback recovery is a technique, which has been used for transparently adding fault tolerance in distributed computing systems. During normal execution, each process saves its state on stable storage. This saved state is the checkpoint of the process. Now, if a fault occurs at a process, when it recovers, this process rolls-back to the last checkpoint and executes recovery protocol to bring the distributed system to a consistent global state. After rolling back to consistent global state, the computation restarts from that state and a greater effort of re-execution of computation at all processes from the start is saved.

A checkpointing protocol in distributed systems can be coordinated, independent or quasi-synchronous. Coordinated Checkpointing [3], [4], [7], [10], [16] is an attractive checkpointing strategy as it is *domino-free* [16] and requires a minimum number of checkpoints (maximum two checkpoints) to be stored per process on stable storage. In coordinated checkpointing all processes take checkpoints cooperatively and in a synchronized way. It is, therefore, also known as "Synchronous checkpointing". In this scheme the synchronization of processes is required for checkpointing and so, extra checkpointing messages are required to be exchanged between processes. Also, the underlying computation may have to be frozen. Once a synchronous checkpoint of the distributed computation has been recorded on stable storage, it can be used to recover from any future fault. If a fault occurs, all processes roll back and restart from the global consistent state given by this checkpoint. A global state of a distributed system contains one checkpoint of each process and is consistent if it does not contain any *orphan messages*. An orphan message is a message, whose receiving has been recorded by the destination process in its checkpoint but whose sending is not recorded by the sender in its checkpoint.

In 1985, Chandy and Lamport proposed the first coordinated checkpointing algorithm for the distributed systems. Their algorithm requires a special message called *marker* to be sent along each channel in the distributed computing system. Initially, a node takes a checkpoint and sends marker messages to all its neighbours. A node on receiving a marker i.e. inheriting a checkpoint request, takes a checkpoint and sends marker messages through all outgoing channels except to the process whose checkpointing request it has inherited. A process after receiving a marker from all the neighbours, sends a response to the process whose checkpoint request it has inherited. In this scheme the total message complexity required for synchronisation of n processes is $O(n^2)$.

Koo and Toueg [10] proposed a coordinated checkpointing protocol that requires a minimum number of processes to coordinate the checkpointing, but requires blocking. These protocols take the transitive closure of all processes that have communicated with the initiator process since the last checkpoint and force only those processes, which are in the direct or transitive set of the initiator, to take a checkpoint. In the worst case all processes may be in the transitive closure of the initiator and have to checkpoint with the blocking of all processes during checkpointing.

The quasi-synchronous approach or the communication-induced checkpointing approach [15], [20] piggybacks information on each message. This approach does not add any extra checkpointing messages and ensures domino-freeness by forcing processes to take additional checkpoints only when some conditions on the causal past of a receive event are met.

The other approach used for checkpointing is asynchronous or independent checkpointing [2]. Here, there are two different approaches which has been used. In the first approach, processes are non-deterministic in nature and this approach may be affected by domino effect. In the second approach, processes are assumed to be piece-wise deterministic (PWD). Here, independent checkpointing along with message logging [1], [5], [9], [19] is used to avoid domino effect, which is an uncontrolled cascaded rollback of processes to their initial state during recovery.. In independent checkpointing without message logging, all nodes take checkpoints independently and cooperate at the time of recovery to form a consistent global state. This scheme has minimum checkpointing overhead during normal execution, but may result in domino effect [16]. Domino effect can be avoided by increasing the frequency of checkpointing.

In this chapter, we propose a non-blocking coordinated checkpointing protocol for distributed systems with least failure-free overhead. Our algorithm not only tries to minimize the number of additional messages but also minimises the additional information carried by each message during normal execution. It requires only $O(n)$ messages to taking a global consistent checkpoint. The existing non-blocking coordinated checkpointing protocols either use a continuously increasing number for marking the consecutive checkpointing intervals [7], [17] or requires a high overhead of extra checkpointing messages [4], [13]. In the first scheme, each message carries this sequence number to identify the checkpointing interval to which the message belongs. This is needed to avoid orphan messages. The protocol proposed in this paper marks a checkpoint interval either as even or odd. This requires an overhead of only one extra bit per message.

2. SYSTEM MODEL

The model of distributed computing system used in this paper assumes that the processes communicate only by message passing. The system consists of n fail-stop connected through reliable channels with arbitrary but finite delays. Message arrival and reception are treated as two distinct events [7], [17]. A node can peek the contents of a message before receiving it. A message reception can be delayed as compared to its arrival at a node.

The communication channels are assumed to be FIFO [3], [4], [10], [16]. Processes do not share a common memory or clock. We use the terms node or process interchangeably in this paper.

2.1. Consistent Global State

A distributed computation is a finite set P of processes $\{P_1, P_2,...,P_n\}$ each running on a fixed node. These processes communicate by message passing only. A process may execute internal or communication statements. The communication statements are *send(m)* to P_j and *receive(m)* from P_j. The inter-process dependencies are created by these communication messages only. A pictorial representation of a distributed computation is shown in Figure 1. The pointed horizontal lines represent execution of processes in time and the slanting arrows between these horizontal lines represent the messages. The rectangular boxes are the local checkpoints of processes. The dotted lines are the global states of the distributed computation.

A *local checkpoint* [8] of a process P_i is its local state stored on stable storage and is denoted by $C_{i,k}$, where i denotes process P_i and k is the index of checkpoint. A *global state* of the system contains exactly one local checkpoint from each process and the state of different channels. The state of a channel between process P_i and process P_j contains messages sent by P_i before taking its local checkpoint $C_{i,k}$ and not received by the process P_j before taking its local checkpoint $C_{j,k}$ where both $C_{i,k}$ and $C_{j,k}$ belong to the same global checkpoint. Depending on the state of communication channels there may be three different global states. In the first case, there are no messages in the communication channels of the global state. We call this global state "*strongly consistent global state*" (Figure 1, cut R_2). In the second case, there may be messages in the channels, which have been recorded as sent in their sender processes but not yet received by the receiver processes in the global state. This global state is called "*consistent global state*" (Figure 1, cut R_3) and these messages (Figure 1, m_2, m_3) are called "*in-transit*" messages. In third case, there are messages in the channels, which have not been recorded sent by there

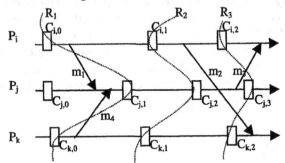

Figure1.Distributed Computation

sender processes but that have been recorded as received by the receiver processes in the global state. There may or may not be in-transit messages (Figure 1, cut R_1). This global state is called "*inconsistent global state* " and these messages (Figure 1, m_1, m_4) are called "*orphan messages*".

The strongly consistent global state is very difficult to achieve in real distributed systems due to the independence of processes and may require blocking of processes until all messages are flushed out of the channels. The inconsistent global state is useless as it has messages that have not been recorded as sent but that have been recorded as received. The only useful global state, therefore, is consistent global state, which has in-transit messages. This state can be achieved by recording a consistent global state and logging the state of the channels. If a fault occurs before receiving all in-transit messages, the state just before the fault will be reproduced using the consistent global checkpoint and the in-transit message logs.

Definition I: Let the total number of processes in the distributed system be n. A *global checkpoint* denoted by $GC \leftarrow (C_{1,x}, C_{2,y} ...., C_{n,z})$ consists of one *local checkpoint* from each process.

Definition II: Let m be any inter-process message. A *consistent global checkpoint* denoted by GCC is a global checkpoint $GCC \leftarrow (C_{1,x}, C_{2,y} ...., C_{n,z})$ such that:

$\forall m$ if *receive(m)* $\in C_{k,x}$ then *send(m)* $\in C_{l,y}$;

$$k, l \in (1..n); \quad k \neq l.$$

Definition III: We define that a virtual strongly consistent global checkpoint denoted by VSCGC is a global consistent checkpoint GCC and a log of messages such that:

if *receive(m)* $\notin C_{k,x} \wedge$ *send(m)* $\in C_{l,y} \wedge$ m has been received by P_k after $C_{k,x}$ then $m \in log(P_k)$ (1)

    where $k, l \in (1..n); k \neq l, C_{k,x}, C_{l,y} \in GCC$.

3.   CHECKPOINTING PROTOCOL

3.1. Basic Idea

A strongly consistent global state cannot be guaranteed in any distributed computing system as all processes are autonomous in executing *send* commands. Our protocol therefore tries to achieve a *virtual strongly consistent global state* defined in section 2.1 without blocking the underlying computation. Figure 2 explains the basic issue [6] that a non-blocking coordinated checkpointing algorithm needs to handle. Let P_0 be the initiator process for the consistent checkpoint algorithm. In Figure 2, process P_0 takes its checkpoint and sends messages (pointed dotted lines in Figure 2) to processes P_1 and P_2 to take tentative checkpoints.

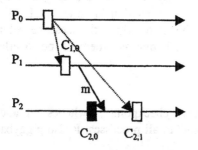

Figure 2

Process P_1 takes a checkpoint and sends a message m to process P_2. The message m reaches at P_2 before the message to checkpoint sent by P_0. P_2 should not receive this message before taking a checkpoint as this message belongs to a different checkpoint interval. Existing non-blocking coordinated checkpointing algorithms handle this situation either by sending a marker message before sending any message in a new checkpoint interval [4], [13] or by using a sequence number [7], [17]. The former approach requires $O(n^2)$ extra messages. In the latter approach the different checkpointing intervals have monotonically increasing sequence numbers. A message carries the sequence number of the checkpointing interval it belongs. The receiving process checks this sequence number and takes a checkpoint if the sequence number in the arriving message is greater than the sequence number of its current checkpointing interval.

Our protocol tries to minimize the number of extra messages and the size of each message. It uses the concept of *even* and *odd checkpoint- intervals* to replace the checkpoint sequence numbers of Elnozahy et al. [7] and the *marker* of   Chandy and Lamport [4]. Each process P_i maintains two vectors, *sent$_i$[ ]* *and receive$_i$[ ]*. These vectors are initialised to zero and used to identify in-transit messages. In-transit messages are those messages that are recorded as sent by the sender processes, but not recorded as received by the respective receiver processes. These in-transit messages are recorded in vector in_transit$_i$[]. Each message carries an extra bit to identify its checkpoint interval. P_i uses this bit along with the in-transit$_i$[] vector to record the checkpoints correctly. The in-transit messages need to be *logged* on stable storage as part of consistent state for possible replay. The next section explains the use of these vectors for recording the consistent global state and handling the in-transit messages.

Thus, our protocol achieves *virtual strongly consistent global state* (Equation 1) by piggybacking a single bit of information on each message regarding checkpoint interval and logging the in-transit messages on stable storage. The extra messages for checkpointing are also optimal.

3.2.   Algorithm

We consider a distributed computing system having a total of n processes. There is a centralised node called "initiator" that starts the algorithm. This condition is relaxed latter on. Each process execution is divided into "even" and "odd" checkpoint Intervals (CIs). Without loss of generality we can assume that all processes start the computation in an even CI. All messages have one control bit indicating the CI to which the message belongs. As a centralised node initiates the checkpointing, there is no overlapping of checkpointing protocols.

start
1.   Initiator takes a "tentative_checkpoint", switches CI and sends a message "take_checkpoint" to all processes. It also piggybacks its CI with the message.

2. A node takes a tentative checkpoint, if it has not taken a tentative checkpoint for the current initiation:
   - When it receives a message from the initiator to take a tentative checkpoint.
   - Or when it receives a message with a CI different than its own CI.
3. Whenever a node takes a tentative checkpoint, it switches its CI.
4. Whenever a process sends a message, it piggybacks its current CI with the message.
5. The processes continue to receive or send messages after taking tentative checkpoints.
6. A process after taking a tentative checkpoint for the current initiation may receive a message
   - To take a checkpoint from initiator. This message is discarded.
   - A message from other node who has not taken a tentative checkpoint for the current initiation. This message is logged for a possible replay in case of a fault followed by a rollback to the last consistent global checkpoint.
   - A message from a node that has taken a tentative checkpoint for the current initiation. The CI of this message and the current CI of the process will be same. This message is processed as a normal message.
7. All nodes after taking the tentative checkpoints send a "checkpoint_taken" message to the initiator.
8. After receiving "checkpoint_taken" message from all nodes, the initiator sends a "Commit" message to all nodes.
9. A process changes its tentative checkpoint into a permanent one on receiving a "Commit" and discards previous permanent checkpoint.
   End.

3.3. Data Structures

In this section we describe the data structures used by the process P_i for implementing the above algorithm.

i_flag: TRUE if for the current initiation of the checkpoint algorithm P_i has not taken a tentative checkpoint. Initially i_flag is TRUE for all processes.

CI: it is the checkpoint interval that can be "even" or "odd".

sent$_i$[]: The entry sent$_i$[j] is the number of messages sent by P_i to P_j in the current checkpoint interval; We assume no process sends messages to itself i.e., sent$_i$[i] =0.

recv$_i$[]: The entry recv$_i$[j] is the number of messages received by P_i from P_j in the current checkpoint interval. recv$_i$[i] =0;

in_transit$_i$[]: The entry in_transit$_i$[j] = sent$_j$[i] − recv$_i$[j] for all j; in_transit$_i$[i] =0.

m: m is any process to process application message.

m.CI: denotes the current CI of the sender of message m.

P$_i$.CI: denotes CI of process P_i.

m_type: indicates the type of message, which can be either an application message generated by the user process or control messages generated by the checkpointing or recovery procedures. Control messages are take_checkpoint, checkpoint_taken, abort, and commit.

s_buf[]: s_buf[] is used to temporarily store the value of sent$_i$[] at the time of recording tentative checkpoint (start of a new CI). In case of abort, this value is added to the new value of sent$_i$[].

r_buf[]: r_buf[] is used to temporarily store the value of recv$_i$[] at the time of recording tentative checkpoint (start of a new CI). In case of abort, this value is added to the new value of recv$_i$[].

All above vectors are of size n.

3.4. Issues

In this section we discuss the situations that require careful handling if we need to implement the scheme described above without creating any inconsistency. We first explain these situations and then show how they can be handled using the data structures described above.

Let us first consider the situation shown in Figure 3 where a process P_0 in its even "e" checkpointing interval receives two messages m and m$_1$ from process P_1. The CI carried by both m and m$_1$ is even but m belongs to a previous checkpointing interval and therefore needs to be logged for a possible replay during recovery. We call these messages in-transit messages. The message m$_1$ belongs to the same checkpointing interval and should be processed as a normal message. This situation may result in the loss of some messages like m if not handled properly.

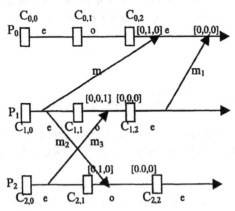

Figure 3. Lost message

In the second situation, shown in Figure 4, a message m sent by a process P_1 in an even CI is delayed and reaches the receiver P_0 in the next odd checkpoint interval. It will force a checkpoint at P_0 if not handled properly. P_0 after checkpointing its state may send further messages which can trigger other processes to checkpoint without having an initiation from the initiator. We call these checkpoints *false checkpoints* ($C_{0,2}$ in Figure 4). On the other hand message m_1 sent by P_1 should force a checkpoint. It will become an orphan message if P_0 records the checkpoint after receiving it. Message m is from a previous "even" checkpointing interval and should be treated as an in-transit message by P_0 and should not be allowed to initiate a checkpoint.

But message m_1 must initiate a checkpoint otherwise it will become an orphan message. We, therefore, need that P_0 should have enough information to differentiate between m and m_1.

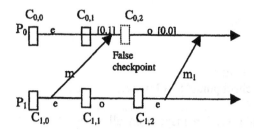

Figure 4. False checkpointing

To handle the situations described above each process P_i uses the i_flag and three vectors sent$_i$[], recv$_i$[] and in_transit$_i$[]. All nodes send their "sent" and "receive" vectors to the initiator with the "checkpoint_taken" message. The initiator computes the in-transit vectors for all nodes and sends them back to the respective nodes with the "commit" message.

In Figure 3 when m, a message from an even CI of P_1 reaches P_0 in even CI, the in_transit$_0$[1] = 1. Therefore P_0 treats m as a delayed message, decreases in_transit$_0$[1] = 0 and logs m. When P_0 receives message m_1 from P_1, in_transit$_0$[1] is 0. Therefore P_0 processes m_1 without logging.

Let us now explain how a node P_i uses the i_flag and the in_transit$_i$[] vector to handle the situation shown in Figure 4. Whenever a node takes a tentative checkpoint for the current initiation, it disables all further messages to initiate a checkpoint by setting the i_flag. After receiving the "commit" along with "in-transit" vector the process converts the tentative checkpoint into a permanent one and resets the i_flag again. If the i_flag is not set and P_i receives a message m from P_j with a different CI it takes a checkpoint only if in_transit$_i$[j] is zero as it indicates that this message belongs to a new checkpoint interval. If m is an in-transit message (i.e. in_transit$_i$[j] != 0) from P_j to P_i, then m is not allowed to force a checkpoint on P_i. P_i saves m for a possible replay in case of a recovery. If i_flag is set and in_transit$_i$[j] is zero, m is processed without logging as it belongs to the current checkpointing interval.

In Figure 4, when message 'm' from even CI of P_1 reaches P_0 in odd CI, in_transit$_0$[1] = 1. Therefore, P_0 treats this message as a delayed message. When message m_1 from even CI of P_1 reaches P_0 in odd CI, in_transit$_0$[1] = 0. Therefore, m_1 forces a tentative checkpoint at P_0.

Thus the use of in-transit vector at different processes takes care of the lost messages and the false checkpointing.

3.5.   Algorithm nbcmds()

//**timer, timer1** are counters at initiator;

//**timer_out** indicates that timer has hit minimum and interrupts the initiator to start checkpoint;

//**timer1_out** indicates that timer1 has hit the minimum and interrupts initiator to start abort;

//**in_transit_{commit,i}[j]** in_transit vector for i^{th} node sent by initiator piggybacked on to commit;

The algorithm executed by the initiator (coordinator) process P_c

```
main() {
  if(timer_out) {
      set(timer);
      set(timer1);
      take tentative_checkpoint;
      send message "take_checkpoint" to all nodes;
      repeat {
        receive "checkpoint_taken" message from all nodes;
          }until(timer1_out||checkpoint_taken received from all)
        if( checkpoint_taken received from all nodes) {
        get "sent" and "recv" vectors from all messages;
        calculate "in_transit" message vectors;
          send "commit" to all nodes and piggyback their "in_transit" vectors
          on it;
      }
    else {
          Abort tentative checkpoint;
          send "Abort" message to all processes;
          }
      } /* end of initiator part */
```

The algorithm executed by the process P_j, a checkpoint cohort of initiator P_c

```
main() {
  repeat {
    event_type ← next_event;
    switch (next_event) {
        case m_send:
            /*Pᵢ sends a message to Pⱼ*/
            m.CI ← pᵢ.CI;
            send(m, pⱼ);
            sent ᵢ[j ]++;
          break;
        case m_receive:
          /*Pᵢ receives a message*/
          switch(m_type) {
            case take_checkpoint:
                /*message to take tentative checkpoint*/
                if(i_flag == TRUE) {
                      i_flag ←FALSE;
```

```
                take tentative_checkpoint;
                append senti[] & recvi[] vectors to checkpoint_taken
                message;
                send(checkpoint_taken, Pc)
                change(CI);
                s_buf[]←sent[];
                r_buf []←recv[];
                sent[]← recv[]← 0;
                }
        else discard (take_checkpoint);
    break;
    case abort:
    /* message from initiator to abort*/
                abort tentative checkpoint;
                change CI;
                i_flag←TRUE;
                sent[]←sent[]+s_buf[];
                recv[]←recv[]+r_buf [];
    break;
    case commit:
                /*message to commit a checkpoint from initiator*/
                discard(permanent_checkpoint);
                make_permanent(tentative_checkpoint);
                for(j=1; j <= n; j++)
                in_transiti[j] = in_transiti[j]+ in_transitcommit.i[j];
                i_flag←TRUE;
                for(j =1; j<=n; j++) {
                 if((in_transiti[j] ! = 0) && (recvi[j] != 0)){
                    if(recvi[j] ≤ in_transiti[j] {
                        in_transiti[j] = in_transiti[j]–recvi[j];
                        recvi[j] =0;
                    }
                    else {
                recvi[j] =recvi[j]-in_transiti[j];
                in_transiti[j] =0;
                }
                }
            }
        }
    break;
    case application_message m:
      /* Pi receives a message from Pj*/
      if(i_flag == TRUE) {
        if(in_transit i[j] == 0) {
          if( m.CI != pi.CI) {
            i_flag ←FALSE;
            take tentative_checkpoint;
```

```
                append sent_i[] & recv_i[] vectors to checkpoint_taken
                        message;
                send(checkpoint_taken, P_c)
                s_buf ←sent[];
                r_buf []←recv[];
                sent_i[]← recv_i[]← 0;
                }
            receive(m);
            recv_i[j]++;
            }
        else { /* in_transit_i[j] !=0*/
        receive(m);
        log(m);
        in_transit_i[j]--;
        }
        else {/*i_flag !=TRUE */
         if (in_transit_i[j] == 0){
            recv_i[j]++;
            receive(m);
            }
         else {
            in_transit_i[j]--;
            receive(m);
            log(m);
            }
              }
              break;
              } /* end inner switch */
       break;
       /* end outer switch */
   until(computation_over)
 } /* end main */
```

3.6. Proof of Correctness

The proof of correctness for the proposed checkpointing protocol is presented here.

Theorem 1. Each node takes a checkpoint iff the initiator initiates a new checkpoint and takes exactly one checkpoint for each initiation of checkpointing algorithm.

Proof: Let us consider the situation when initiator initiates the ith checkpoint. We first show that a node cannot take a checkpoint unless and until the initiator has initiated one. A node P_i takes a checkpoint only if

(a) P_i receives a "take_checkpoint" message from initiator, or

(b) P_i receives a message "m" from a node P_k with a different CI.

P_i will not receive (a) if initiator has not initiated i^{th} checkpoint. As the channels are FIFO, P_i can't receive a take_checkpoint message of some previous initiation after receiving the commit for $(i-1)^{th}$ checkpoint. This also applies for all other previous checkpoints. If P_i receives m due to (b) and initiator has not initiated a new checkpoint then m should be from some previous checkpoint interval. Vector in-transit$_i$[k] will not be zero and P_i will not take a checkpoint.

We now show that all nodes take exactly one checkpoint for each initiation of the checkpointing algorithm. A node P_j takes a checkpoint $C_{j,i}$ either due to (a) or (b) which ever occurs earlier and disables the checkpointing (by setting i_flag) for the current checkpoint interval. This ensures that P_j cannot take more than one checkpoint for same initiation of checkpointing algorithm. Moreover if P_j is not faulty then it will either receive (a) or (b), which ensures that it takes a checkpoint.

Lemma1: All nodes take an equal number of checkpoints.

Proof : Theorem 1 shows that each node takes a checkpoint only when the initiator initiates a new checkpoint. Moreover each node takes exactly one checkpoint for every initiation of the checkpoint. This ensures that all nodes always take an equal number of checkpoints, one for each initiation.

Theorem 2: The global checkpoint $GC_i \rightarrow (C_{1,i}, C_{2,i} ...., C_{n,i})$ created by i^{th} initiation of the checkpointing algorithm is consistent.

Proof: A global checkpoint is inconsistent if it contains orphan messages, i.e. P_l sends a message m after taking $C_{l,i}$ and P_k receives it before taking $C_{k,i}$ (where $l,k \in 1..n$). If P_l has taken $C_{l,i}$ and P_k has not taken $C_{k,i}$ then P_k should be in the $(i-1)^{th}$ checkpoint interval as (a) initiator will initiate i^{th} checkpoint only when all processes will complete $(i-1)^{th}$ checkpoint and (b) P_k has not taken $C_{k,i}$. Moreover, P_l should send 'm' in i^{th} checkpoint interval as the $(i+1)^{th}$ checkpoint interval of P_l will start only after P_k will also take $C_{k,i}$ and i^{th} checkpoint will complete. The message 'm' received by P_k from P_l must have either

(i) m.CI = P_k. CI, or
(ii) m.CI != P_k. CI

As P_k is in the $(i-1)^{th}$ checkpoint interval (i) is possible only if P_l sends m after taking $C_{l,i+1}$, which is not possible.

(ii) is not possible as if P_k has not taken $C_{k,i}$ then 'm' will force a tentative checkpoint at P_k (different CI).

Theorem 3: Checkpointing algorithm terminates in finite time.

Proof: After the initiator initiates a new checkpoint following events should take place before the algorithm terminates.
(i)   All nodes take tentative checkpoints and inform initiator.
(ii)   After getting response from all nodes initiator sends a commit message to all nodes
(iii)   Nodes convert their tentative checkpoints into permanent after receiving commit from initiator.
We have already shown in theorem 1 that all nodes will complete (i) in finite time unless a node is faulty. As the channels are reliable and have finite

delays step (ii) will also complete in finite time. Step (iii) will complete in finite time for all nodes unless a node is faulty. If a node is faulty and does not respond to the initiator in finite time, the timer at initiator goes out and it sends an "Abort" message to all nodes terminating the algorithm.

Hence, it can be inferred that the algorithm terminates in finite time.

3.7.   Relaxing the condition of specific Initiator

It is possible to allow all nodes to initiate the checkpointing algorithm. To handle conflicts messages carry the "Identity of the Initiator". If a node receives multiple messages to checkpoint a simple rule that allows the "initiator with minimum address" or "initiator with maximum address" to continue may be used.

3.8.   Failure During Checkpointing

The failures during checkpointing can be:
- Initiator failure, or
- Any process failure

In case of initiator failure there can be two situations. Initiator fails after sending Commit or Abort then it does nothing for that checkpoint initiation. If it fails before sending a Commit or Abort then after restarting from the failure it aborts the checkpoint. In case of a non-initiator process if it has not taken tentative checkpoint then it sends abort to initiator otherwise if it has taken the tentative checkpoint and responded to initiator with checkpoint taken message then after restarting it finds out the initiators decision for tentative checkpoint. Then it requests to rollback.

4.   OPTIMIZATIONS

This section outlines some of the optimisations that can be done to reduce the checkpointing overhead. The main optimisations that can be made are:
- **Incremental checkpointing:** We propose to use *incremental checkpointing*. A process needs to transfer only those pages of its address space, which have been modified since last checkpoint. These pages are identified by "dirty bit" maintained by memory management hardware. Also, a process needs to checkpoint only if it has received or sent a message after last checkpoint, otherwise, its previous checkpoint can be used. Elnozahy, Johnson and Zwaenepol have studied the effect of incremental checkpointing in distributed systems. They observed that incremental checkpointing can reduce amount of data to be written for saving a checkpoint considerably depending on the application. In some cases incremental checkpointing reduces checkpoints to two percent of its actual size. Thus, this optimization can reduce the checkpoint data and checkpointing time exceedingly.

- **No purging Cost:** There is no purging cost involved as the permanent checkpoints of all nodes are discarded when a new permanent checkpoint is completed.
- **Minimum recovery cost:** As the global consistent checkpoint contains the last permanent checkpoint of each node, there is no extra cost involved for constructing a consistent checkpoint during recovery.
- **Minimum fault-free overhead:** During normal execution only one extra bit is transferred with each message, which is minimum. Also, each node stores not more than two checkpoints at any time. Piggybacking the CI value in the first message after a new checkpoint can further reduce this overhead as the channels are reliable and FIFO. This can be implemented by using the sent[] vector used in the checkpoint algorithm. If before sending a message to j^{th} process, entry $sent_i[j]$ is zero then CI is appended to that message, otherwise, message is sent without appending CI value. The overhead in sending the "sent" and "recv" vectors can be reduced by only sending the sent vector to the initiator. Initiator then sends back rearranged "sent" vectors to the processes in commit and nodes can compute in-transit messages.

5. COMPARISON

Chandy and Lamport [4] were first to present a checkpointing algorithm for static distributed systems. Their algorithm sends checkpointing messages on all channels in the system for collecting the checkpoint of the distributed system. Their approach has a message complexity of $O(n^2)$, whereas the approach proposed in this paper has a message complexity of $O(n)$ only.

Elnozahy, Johnson and Zwaenepoel [7] proposed a non-intrusive checkpointing algorithm that has a message complexity of $O(n)$. The algorithm uses a monotonically increasing integer to keep track of successive checkpointing intervals. This integer is piggybacked with every message and may be quite large in long computations. They also do not handle in-transit messages. In our approach, the piggybacked information is constant and is one bit only.

Silva and Silva [17] proposed a non-intrusive checkpointing algorithm and gave a recovery algorithm also. Their algorithm has a message complexity of $O(n)$ and requires two continuously increasing integers to be piggybacked with every message. Our approach requires only one extra bit to be appended with the messages.

Communication-induced checkpointing protocols [15], [20] have advantage of no extra checkpointing messages but may force number of checkpoints to ensure domino-freeness. These checkpointing protocols also have overhead of piggybacked information in each message that is utilized to take a decision to checkpoint before actually delivering the message. The piggybacked information varies with the protocol.

6.   SUMMARY

In this chapter, we have presented a non-intrusive coordinated checkpointing scheme for distributed computing systems. The proposed algorithm has a message complexity of $O(n)$. This ensures that the extra messages exchanged by the checkpointing algorithm are minimum. The information piggybacked on each message is only one extra bit as compared to two continuously increasing integers in [17] and one integer in [7]. Only in-transit messages received by a process need to be logged, which incurs minimum logging cost. We propose to use incremental checkpointing to reduce checkpointing overhead. In all, the proposed scheme is non-intrusive and optimal in terms of extra message communication overhead and information piggybacked on each message. The improvement in communication overhead is attributed to the use of even and odd checkpoint intervals that need only one bit overhead with each message. The number-warping problem will not be there in the proposed protocol as the numbers reach the upper limit that can be safely represented. This problem can be there with the protocols that use message sequence numbers [10] or with the protocols using checkpoint sequence numbers.

The further research direction in the proposed protocol is to minimize the number of processes to take checkpoint for any initiation of the protocol similar to protocol proposed by Koo and Toueg [10]. But, in case of our protocol if this modification is adopted as such, then it will take away the advantage of non-intrusiveness and will make the protocol intrusive. Also, the checkpoint intervals of different processes will be different and may not be able to avoid inconsistencies.

7.   REFERENCES

[1] Alviski L., Hoppe B. and Marzullo K. , "Nonblocking and Orphan-free message logging protocols," *Proceedings of 23rd Intentional Symposium on Fault-Tolerant Computing*, pages 145-154, 1993.

[2] Bhargava B. and Lian S. R., "Independent checkpointing and Concurrent Rollback for Recovery in Distributed Systems-An Optimistic Approach," *Proceedings Seventh IEEE Symposium on Reliable Distributed Systems*, pages 3-12, 1988.

[3] Cao G. and Singhal M., "Mutable Checkpoints: A New Checkpointing Approach for Mobile Computing systems," *IEEE Transactions On Parallel and Distributed Systems*, vol. 12, no. 2, pages 157-172, 2001.

[4] Chandy K. M. and Lamport L., "Distributed snapshots: Determining global state of distributed systems,". *ACM Transactions on Computer Systems*, vol. 3, no. 1, pages 63-75,1985.

[5] Elnozahy E.N. and Zwaenepoel W., "Mantho: Transparent Rollback-Recovery with Low Overhead, Limited Rollback, and Fast Output Commit," *IEEE Transactions on Computer*, vol. 41, no. 5, pages 526-531, 1992.

[6] Elnozahy E.N., Alvisi L., Wang Y. M., and Johnson D.B., "A Survey of Rollback-Recovery Protocols in Message-Passing Systems" *CMU Technical Report CMU-CS-99-148*, 1999.

[7] Elnozahy E.N., Johnson D.B., Zwaenepoel W., "The performance of Consistent Checkpointing" In *Proceedings of the International Symposium on Reliable Distributed Systems*, pages 39-47, 1992.

[8] Helary J.M., Netzer R., Raynal M., "Consistency Issues in Distributed Checkpoints" *IEEE Transactions Software Engineering*, vol. 25, no. 2, pages 274-281, 1999.

[9] Johnson D. B. and Zwaenepoel W., "Sender-based message logging" In *Proceedings of 17th Intentional Symposium on Fault-Tolerant Computing*, pages14-19, 1987.

[10] Koo R. and Toueg S., "Checkpointing and Roll-Back Recovery for Distributed Systems" *IEEE Transactions Software Engineering*, vol 13, no. 1, pages 23-31, 1987.

[11] Lai T.H. and Yang T.H., "On Distributed Snapshots" *Information Processing Letters*, vol. 25, pages 153-158, 1987.

[12] Lamport L., "Time, Clocks and the Ordering of Events in a Distributed System." *Communications of the ACM*, vol. 21 no. 7, pages 558-565, 1978.

[13] Li K., Naughton J.F., Plank J.S., "An Efficient Method for Checkpointing Multicomputers with Wormhole Routing," *International Journal Parallel Programming*, vol. 20, no. 3, pages 159-180, 1992.

[14] Manivannan D. and Singhal M., "Quasi-Synchronous Checkpointing: Models, Characterization, and Classification.," *IEEE Transactions on Parallel and Distributed Systems*, vol. 10, no. 7, pages 703-713, 1999.

[15] Mostefaui A.,Helary J.M., Netzer R., Raynal M., "Communication-based Prevention of Useless Checkpoints in Distributed Computation" *Distributed Computing*, vol. 13, no. 1, pages 29-43, 2000.

[16] Russel David R., "State restoration in Systems of communicating Processes," *IEEE Transactions on Software Engineering*, vol. 6, no. 2, pages 183-194, 1980.

[17] Silva L.M. and Silva J.G., "Global Checkpointing for Distributed Programs" *Proceedings of the International Symposium on Reliable Distributed Systems*, pages 155-162, 1992.

[18] Silva L.M. and Silva J.G., "The Performance of Coordinated and Independent Checkpointing" In *Proceedings 13th Intentional Symposium on Parallel Distributed Processing*, pages 280-284, 1999.

[19] Storm R. E. and Yemini S., "Optimistic Recovery in Distributed systems" *ACM Transactions. on Computer Systems*, vol. 3, no. 3, pages 204-226, 1985.

[20] Wang Y. M., "Consistent Global Checkpoints that Contain a Given Set of Local Checkpoints," *IEEE Transactions on Computers*, vol. 46, no. 4, pages 456-468, 1997.

V

CONCURRENCY IN REAL-TIME APPLICATIONS

Chapter 15

Concurrency in Dependable Real-Time Objects

Exploiting Concurrency in TMOs with Service Time Guarantees

K. H. (Kane) Kim
University of California, Irvine

Abstract: Producing complex real-time distributed computing systems with design-time
              guarantees of timely service capabilities is still considered by a predominant
              part of the research community to be a distant goal. Yet the recognition of the
              importance of facilitating such system engineering is steadily growing in the
              current century. This is because timeliness guaranteeing is a fundamental way
              of achieving a high degree of dependability. The TMO (Time-triggered
              Message-triggered Object) programming and specification scheme has been
              established in recent years to support such timeliness-guaranteed design. It is
              a high-level high-precision real-time distributed object programming scheme.
              The TMO scheme accompanies an execution scheme involving disciplined
              control of resources and services offered by typical commercial operating
              system platforms. Current versions of these schemes contain design and
              execution rules that prevent most important potential obstacles on the paths to
              timeliness-guaranteed design. However, there remain a number of challenging
              research issues which must be resolved satisfactorily before one can say
              whether the TMO scheme enables maximum exploitation of concurrency by
              programmers or not. Issues encountered in pursuing both goals together, i.e.,
              enabling timeliness-guaranteed design and enabling maximum exploitation of
              concurrency, as well as solution approaches identified are discussed here.

Key words: real-time, object, distributed computing, time-triggered, message-triggered,
              TMO, timeliness guarantee, execution engine, operating system

P. Ezhilchelvan and A. Romanovsky (eds.), Concurrency in Dependable Computing. 293–310.
© 2002 *Kluwer Academic Publishers. Printed in the Netherlands.*

1.   INTRODUCTION

Since early 1990's the author and his collaborating researchers have been pursuing the following real-time computing paradigms [5]:

1. *General-form design style*: Future real-time computing must be realized in the form of a generalization of the non-real-time computing, rather than in a form looking like an esoteric specialization.

2. *Design-time guarantee of timely service capabilities* of subsystems: To meet the demands of the general public on the assured reliability of future real-time (RT) computer systems in safety-critical applications, there does not appear to be any adequate way but to require the system engineer to produce design-time guarantees for timely service capabilities of various subsystems (which will take the form of objects in object-oriented system designs).

The motivating factors behind these paradigms which may be called the *GT (General-form Timeliness-guaranteed) design paradigms* are the newly improved hardware economy and component reliability which provide impetus in expanding the real-time computing application field. In non-RT distributed computing fields, object-oriented (OO) programming approaches gained a strong momentum in 1990's.   This is quite understandable, considering the natural modularity characteristics and the multi-level abstraction capabilities of the basic object structure.   Therefore, extending the prevalent OO design and programming approaches to support general-form design of RT distributed computer systems [1, 3, 7, 16, 17, 18] is also a natural step toward enabling GT design.

Concrete efforts made by the author and his collaborating researchers together were to establish an RT OO structuring approach called the *Time-triggered Message-triggered Object* (TMO) programming and specification scheme [4, 7, 9, 12]. It is a unified approach for design and implementation of both RT and non-RT distributed applications.   It offers the following important benefits to complex distributed application designers:

- (TB1) The TMO model is a natural and syntactically small extension of the conventional object model(s) such that typical OO programmers can adopt it with relatively small efforts.

- (TB2) The TMO scheme enables RT programming and distributed programming in a highly abstract and yet high-precision form, relieving the programmer of the burden of dealing with underlying OS services and network protocols and allowing the programmer to be highly productive and focused on essential design activities.

- (TB3) The scheme facilitates uniform structuring of
  (i) both RT and non-RT distributed application systems,
  (ii) both control computer systems and their application environment

simulators [7, 10, 13], and

(iii) requirement specifications and system designs arising at various phases of system engineering.

- (TB4) The scheme is devised to enable systematic design-time guaranteeing of timely service capabilities of objects.
- (TB5) TMOs can also be used as wrappers of legacy applications and physical devices.

We have conducted preliminary feasibility studies in recent years and the results obtained strongly indicate the potential of the TMO scheme in meeting its goals in the practicing field. The feasibility studies involved the development of practical execution engines centred around commercial operating system (OS) - hardware platforms, application programming interfaces (APIs) which wrap around the services of execution engines and approximate idealistic TMO programming languages.

In this chapter, we discuss some major issues to be addressed in realizing the second major component of the GT design paradigms with the TMO scheme, i.e., design-time guarantee of timely service capabilities of RT objects. First of all, the impacts of the OS services on the timely service capabilities of TMOs must be considered. Reasonable tight bounds on such impacts must be determined. Secondly, other program components that compete with the subject TMO for execution engine resources must be analyzed together. Finally, the available bandwidths of the communication networks that can be guaranteed during the execution of service methods in the subject TMO, must be determined.

The chapter starts in Section 2 with an overview of the essence of the TMO scheme. Major issues in facilitating design-time guaranteeing of timely service capabilities of server objects are then discussed in Section 3. One major issue is the acquisition of temporally reliable execution engines. This has been discussed in some depth before and thus is not dealt with here. The major issue discussed here is how to systematically analyze the loads which various objects and their components impose on shared execution engine facilities. Section 4 deals with this issue and Section 5 concludes the chapter.

2. AN OVERVIEW OF THE TMO PROGRAMMING AND SPECIFICATION SCHEME

The *Time-triggered Message-triggered Object* (TMO) scheme was established in early 1990's [4, 7, 9, 12] with a concrete syntactic structure and execution semantics for economical reliable design and implementation of RT systems. The TMO programming scheme is a general-style component programming scheme and supports design of all types of components including distributable hard-RT objects and distributable non-RT objects within one general structure.

TMOs are devised to contain only high-level intuitive and yet precise expressions of timing requirements. No specification of timing requirements in (indirect) terms other than *start-windows* and *completion deadlines* for program units (e.g., object methods) and *time-windows for output actions* is required. For example, priorities are attributes often attached by the OS to low-level program abstractions such as threads and they are not natural expressions of timing requirements. Therefore, no such indirect and inaccurate styles of expressing timing requirements are associated with objects and methods.

At the same time the TMO scheme is aimed for enabling a great reduction of the designer's efforts in guaranteeing timely service capabilities of distributed computing application systems. It has been formulated from the beginning with the objective of enabling *design-time guaranteeing of timely actions*. The TMO incorporates several rules for execution of its components that make the analysis of the worst-case time behavior of TMOs to be systematic and relatively easy while not reducing the programming power in any way.

2.1   TMO structure

TMO is a natural, syntactically minor, and semantically powerful extension of the conventional object(s). As depicted in Figure 1, the basic TMO structure consists of four parts:
- **ODS-sec** = object-data-store (ODS) section: list of object-data-store segments (ODSS's);
- **EAC-sec** = environment access-capability section: list of gates to remote object methods, logical communication channels, and I/O device interfaces;
- **SpM-sec** = spontaneous-method section: list of spontaneous methods;
- **SvM-sec** = service-method section.

Major features are summarized below. The second and third are the most conspicuous unique extensions of conventional object(s).

(A) DISTRIBUTED COMPUTING COMPONENT:
The TMO is a distributed computing component and thus TMOs distributed over multiple nodes may interact via remote method calls. To maximize the concurrency in execution of client methods in one node and server methods in the same node or different nodes, client methods are allowed to make non-blocking types of service requests to server methods.

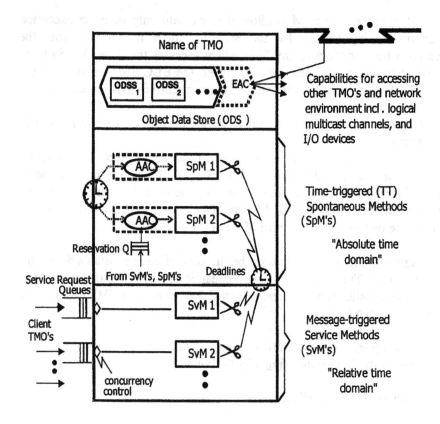

Figure 1. The basic structure of TMO (Adapted from [7])

(B) CLEAR SEPARATION BETWEEN TWO TYPES OF METHODS:

The TMO may contain two types of methods, *time-triggered (TT-) methods* (also called the *spontaneous methods* or *SpMs*), which are clearly separated from the conventional *service methods* (*SvMs*). The SpM executions are triggered upon reaching of the real-time clock at specific values determined at the design time whereas the SvM executions are triggered by service request messages from clients. Moreover, actions to be taken at real times *which can be determined at the design time* can appear only in SpMs.

(C) BASIC CONCURRENCY CONSTRAINT (BCC):

This rule prevents potential conflicts between SpMs and SvMs and reduces the designer's efforts in guaranteeing timely service capabilities of TMOs. Basically, *activation of an SvM triggered by a message from an external client is allowed only when potentially conflicting SpM executions are not in place.* An SvM is allowed to execute only when an execution time-window big enough for the SvM that does not overlap with the execution time-window of any SpM which accesses the same ODSSs to be accessed by the SvM, opens up. However, the BCC does not stand in the way of either concurrent SpM executions or concurrent SvM executions.

(D) GUARANTEED COMPLETION TIME FOR METHOD EXECUTION AND DEADLINE FOR RESULT RETURN:

The TMO incorporates deadlines in the most general form. Basically, for output actions and method completions of a TMO, the designer guarantees and advertises execution time-windows bounded by start times and completion times. In addition, deadlines can be specified in the client's calls for service methods for the return of the service results.

Triggering times for SpMs must be fully specified as constants during the design time. Those RT constants appear in the first clause of an SpM specification called the *autonomous activation condition* (AAC) section. An example of an AAC is

"for t = from 10am to 10:50am every 30min
start-during (t, t+5min) finish-by t+10min"

which has the same effect as

{"start-during (10am, 10:05am) finish-by 10:10am",

"start-during (10:30am, 10:35am) finish-by 10:40am" }

A provision is also made for making the AAC section of an SpM contain only *candidate* triggering times, not actual triggering times, so that a subset of the candidate triggering times indicated in the AAC section may be dynamically chosen for actual triggering. Such a dynamic selection occurs when an SvM within the same TMO object requests future executions of a specific SpM. Each AAC specifying candidate triggering times rather than actual triggering times has a name.

2.2 TMO structuring in environment modeling and multi-step multi-level design and implementation

The attractive basic design style facilitated by the TMO structuring is to produce a network of TMOs meeting the application requirements in a top-down multi-step fashion [7]. The engineering of an application system can start with a single TMO representation of the entire application environment (including the computer system to be designed) and proceeds through step-by-step expansion of the initial single TMO model toward a final implementation in the form of a network of TMOs executing on engines. This top-down process can also produce an RT simulator of the application environment, again in the form of a TMO network performing *distributed time-triggered simulation* (DTS) [13].

3. ISSUES IN FACILITATING DESIGN-TIME GUARANTEE OF TIMELY SERVICE CAPABILITIES

An underlying design philosophy of the TMO scheme is that an RT computer system will always take the form of a network of TMOs. TMO objects interact via calls by *client objects* for service methods (SvM's) in *server objects*. The caller may be an SpM or an SvM in the client object. In order to facilitate highly concurrent operations of client and server objects, *non-blocking* (sometimes called asynchronous) types of calls (i.e., service requests) can be made to SvMs.

Major issues in realizing server TMO objects with guaranteed timely service capabilities are discussed in this section.

3.1 Types of concurrency

In an RT distributed computing systems structured as a TMO network, concurrency may be exhibited among TMOs. SpMs belonging to different TMOs may be active concurrently. Also, SvMs belonging to different TMOs may be active concurrently. They have been called by remote SpMs. Or some of them have been activated by other SvMs via non-blocking calls.

Even within a TMO, the following major types of concurrency may be found:

1. Concurrency among SpM executions, i.e., the concurrency specified in an implicit but natural manner (e.g., two SpMs designed to be triggered at 10 am);
2. Concurrency among SvM executions;
3. Concurrency between SpM executions and SvM executions.

Concurrent SpM executions may be found to share ODSSs but they lock and release ODSSs in such a manner that yields relatively easy determination of the worst period in which any ODSS is locked or any method execution is blocked. This will be discussed in more detail later in

Section 4.2. The same is true for concurrent SvM executions. Concurrency between SpM executions and SvM executions is allowed subject to the BCC.

In order to maintain a high degree of timing behavior predictability in a TMO, concurrency within the object must be clearly understood and controlled.

3.2 Representation of timely service guarantees associated with server TMOs

The designer of each TMO provides a guarantee of timely service capabilities of the TMO. The designer does so by indicating the *guaranteed execution time-window for every output* produced by each SvM as well as by each SpM executed on requests from the SvM and the *guaranteed completion time* (GCT) for the SvM in the specification of the SvM (and some relevant SpM's). Such specification of each SvM is advertised to the designers of potential client objects. The specification of the maximum delay for an output from an SvM, which is the closing edge of the guaranteed time-window for the output, is a serious commitment on the part of the server object designer to the designers of potential client objects. Before determining the time-window specification, the server object designer must convince himself/herself that with the *object execution engine* (a composition of hardware, node OS, and middleware) available, the server object can be implemented to always execute the SvM such that the output action is performed within the time-window (in absence of intolerable component failures).

This means that the server object designer must consider:

1. The worst-case delay from the arrival of a service request from a client object to the initiation of the corresponding SvM by the server object, and

2. The worst-case execution time for the SvM from its initiation to each of its output actions.

The BCC contributes to major reduction of these burdens imposed on the designer. The designer of a TMO may also view SpMs as internal capabilities and SvMs as services advertised to all potential clients.

On the other hand, a client TMO object imposes a deadline on the server TMO object for creation of all the intended computational effects (i.e., all intended output actions). The deadline imposed by a client for the arrival of the result must not be earlier than the deadline guaranteed by the designer of the server object for completion of the corresponding SvM. This property is depicted in Figure 2.

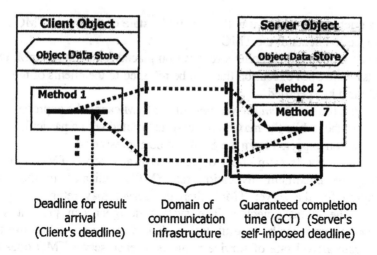

Figure 2. Client's deadline vs. Server's GCT (adapted from [11])

There are three sources from which a fault may arise to cause a client's deadline to be violated. They are
- (s1) the client object's resources which are basically node facility (hardware + OS),
- (s2) the communication infrastructure, and
- (s3) the server object's resources which include not only node facility but also the object code.

Thus while the server is responsible to finish a service within the guaranteed service time, the client is responsible for checking if the result comes back within the client's deadline or it does not due to a fault.

An output action of an SvM may be
- (o1) an updating of a portion of the ODS,
- (o2) sending a message to either another TMO (which may or may not be the client) or a device shared by multiple objects, or
- (o3) placing a reservation into the *reservation queue* for a certain SpM that will in turn take its own output actions.

The specification of each SvM which is provided to the designers of potential client TMOs must contain at least the following:
a) an *input specification* that consists of
  (a1) the types of input parameters that the server TMO can accept and
  (a2) the *maximum invocation rate* (MIR), i.e., the maximum rate at which the server TMO can receive service requests from client objects;
b) an *output specification* that indicates the *maximum delay* (not the exact output time) and the *nature of the output value* for every output produced by the SvM.

For an output value going into the ODS, its nature must be expressed in an abstract form consistent with the way the state of the server TMO is portrayed to clients of the TMO.

In the case of an output being a reservation placed for a certain SpM, the effects of the SpM execution that can be released to the clients of the TMO must be specified.

In general, the *maximum service time* of the SvM cannot be expressed as a single number while the maximum delay associated with a particular output action expected from the SvM can be expressed so.

If service requests from client objects arrive at a server TMO at a rate exceeding the maximum invocation rate (MIR) indicated in the input specification for the server TMO, then the server may return exception signals to the client objects. The system designer can prevent such "overflow" occurrences by careful design. The designer should ensure that the aggregate arrival rate of service requests at each server TMO does not exceed the MIR during any period of system operation. In order to satisfy greater service demands presented by the client objects, the system designer can increase the number of server TMOs or use more powerful execution engines in running server TMOs and revise the MIR accordingly. It is also conceivable that the system designer may deliberately interconnect TMOs such that non-negligible probability of overflow occurrences exists but also provide exception handlers in client objects with assurances that exception handlers will never fail to achieve the application goals satisfactorily (in absence of intolerable component failures).

As mentioned above, the specifications of the SpMs which may be executed on requests from the SvM must also be provided to the designers of the client objects which may call the SvM. The specification of such an SpM must contain at least the following:

1. an autonomous activation condition (AAC), and
2. an output specification.

There is no input specification in an SpM specification but the output specification for an SpM indicates, for every output expected from the execution of an SpM, the time-window during which the output action will take place and the nature of every value carried in the output action.

3.3 Inter-object dependency for guaranteeing timely services

Each TMO may play the role of a server object for a certain group of objects while at the same time playing the role of a client object for some other objects. The timely service guarantee associated with such a TMO is then dependent upon the timely service guarantees associated with the servers of the TMO. Therefore, during the early design phase in which different timeliness requirements are assigned to different TMOs, TMOs and their server TMOs must be considered together to ensure that the assignment of timeliness requirements is feasible.

On the other hand, suppose a TMO has been implemented to run on an execution engine and the server TMOs of the TMO have been defined to meet certain timely service requirements. The analysis of the implemented TMO can reveal the *service time bounds* of the TMO to be better than the assigned timely service requirements. In other words, the realized service time bounds may be better than the required service time bounds. This may result from the use of a very fast hardware platform for running the TMO. Or an efficient design and coding of every method of the TMO may produce such a result.

If the service time bounds of an implemented TMO can be determined by using the realized service time bounds of its server TMOs implemented rather than using the timely service requirements assigned to the server TMOs, then the service time bounds of the former implemented TMO may turn out to be even better. Conversely, during this analysis process, if a loose bound on the service time is attached to a TMO, then the service time bounds associated with the clients of the TMO will also become loose.

3.4 Timeliness-guaranteed execution engines

In order for TMOs to provide guaranteed timely services to external clients, the engine that supports the execution of TMOs must obviously provide guaranteed timely responses to service requests from the executing TMOs. In addition to containing a hardware platform, such an execution engine should be formed by a *timeliness-guaranteed OS*. Existing commercial OSs have improved in recent years and are still improving in their capabilities for providing guaranteed timely services needed by a great deal of RT application software [15].

The challenge is not just to realize a timeliness guarantee for an execution engine but rather it is to achieve a tight and low bound on the service time of an execution engine [8, 11]. In other words, claiming loose bounds (e.g., bounds in the order of tens of minutes in the 21st century) requires no efforts but it serves no useful purpose.

The communication network is often the most significant component of an execution engine in terms of impacting on the service time bound. In general, conventional system architectures yield poor worst-case delays in communicating service requests from clients to remote server objects [14, 15].

Since this subject has been discussed in some depth in literature, it is not dealt with any further here [8, 15].

3.5   Augmentation of service time bounds with statistical performance indicators

More often than not, hard-RT program components, implemented with currently available tools and execution engines, are associated with guaranteed service times of rather poor qualities, i.e., large service time bounds, but exhibit much better service times during most of their service executions. This is due to many factors, including fluctuations in the service times of an OS in supporting application program components, etc.

The communication infrastructure in many application environments has the same characteristics, i.e., service time bounds of poor quality and typical service times of much better quality.

Therefore, the designer of a client TMO can often run into a situation where available server TMOs do not provide guaranteed service times of acceptable qualities but their typical service times are far better than the client's requirements. A pragmatic compromise in such a situation is to augment each server TMO with a *statistical performance indicator* [11]. For example, an SvM of a server TMO can be put through a number, say 1000, of test-runs while the service time is measured in each test-run. Then the statistical distribution of the service time can be attached to the SvM of the server TMO as a statistical performance indicator.

The designer of a client TMO may use candidate server TMOs whose statistical performance indicators are good even if the guaranteed service times of the candidate TMOs are not acceptable. This means that the client TMO must be designed to impose on both the SvM of the server TMO and the client's execution engine a deadline for result arrival (DRA) which is smaller than maximum transmission times (imposed on the communication infrastructure) + guaranteed service time (of the server component). Moreover, the client TMO must be equipped with an alternate logic which will be invoked to accomplish the application objective of the TMO in time, in case a DRA violation results from the call for an SvM of the server TMO. This way the client TMO can satisfy its own guaranteed service time. Of course, the client TMO can also offer statistical performance indicators.

The need to provide an alternate logic is a price paid for relying on the statistical performance indicators of server TMOs, rather than relying on their guaranteed service times.

3.6   Competition among objects and among components of objects

In general, multiple TMOs can be co-resident in a processing node of a distributed and/or parallel processing execution engine. Such co-resident objects compete at a high frequency for execution engine node services. Therefore, such objects and the execution engine must be analyzed together to determine the service time guarantees to be associated with the objects. Even the methods in a TMO can compete among themselves for obtaining execution engine node services. The BCC simplifies the analysis of method-to-method competitions considerably but does not eliminate them completely.

The structuring of each individual method makes a significant impact on the difficulty of the analysis of method-to-method competitions. For example, a program loop of which the iteration bound is a function of an input-dependent variable (as opposed to a constant) contributes to the complexity of the competition analysis. The way ODS segments are locked and released is another major factor impacting on the difficulty of the analysis of method-to-method competitions.

More detailed discussions of these issues are given in the next section along with some simplifying approaches.

4.   ANALYSIS OF THE COMPETITIONS AMONG PROGRAM COMPONENTS

Determining service time bounds of server TMOs involves analyses of the competitions among various TMOs and parts of TMOs for using execution engine facilities. As mentioned earlier, multiple TMOs can be co-resident in a processing node of a distributed and/or parallel processing execution engine. Even when only one TMO is resident on a certain execution engine node, methods of the TMO compete among themselves for obtaining execution engine node services. Such situations are discussed in this section.

4.1   Execution time bounds and requirements of the SpMs and their impacts on the service time bounds

Due to the BCC adopted, the analysis of the execution time bounds and requirements of the SpMs does not need to involve the examination of possible interference from SvMs. It can become complicated somewhat by the presence of triggering time candidates and the dynamic selection of actual triggering times. Treating all triggering time candidates as actual triggering times during the analysis will often lead to an intolerably wasteful allocation of execution node facilities and an unnecessarily pessimistic determination of service time bounds of (the SvMs co-resident in) the TMO.

This means that different cases where different triggering time candidates become actual triggering times must be traced.

The other factor to consider here is the possibility of initiating or delaying SvM executions based not only on the ODS access requirements and execution engine time requirements of each SvM but also on the dynamic selection of triggering times which each SvM may make.

Therefore, if we were to avoid the simplistic approach of treating all triggering time candidates as actual triggering times during the analysis, the analysis of the execution time requirements of the methods must proceed in two steps as follows:

1. All SpMs associated only with actual triggering times are analyzed first.
2. The SpMs associated with triggering time candidates are analyzed together with all SvMs.

The step (2) in the above can be a great challenge if optimal decisions are aimed for. For example, if we know that certain reservations of an SpM, say, SpM1, and certain reservations of another SpM, SpM2, can never occur together, then we must take advantage of this in optimal determination of the service time bounds. Development of efficient suboptimal decision procedures is considered to be a meaningful topic for future research.

4.2   Ordered isolation (OI) rule

Another major factor impacting on the difficulty of the analysis of method-to-method competitions is the way ODS segments are locked and released. A simple approach which helps in easing the analysis of the service time bounds when incorporated into the TMO scheme, is to observe the rule called the *ordered isolation* (OI) rule [6]. The term *initiation timestamp* or *I-timestamp* used in the following discussion is defined as follows. In the case of an SvM execution, the *I-timestamp* is defined as the record of the time instant at which the execution engine initiated the SvM execution after receiving the client request and ensuring that the SvM execution can be initiated without violating the BCC and other execution rules. In the case of an SpM execution, the *I-timestamp* is defined as the record of the time instant at which the SpM execution was initiated according to the AAC specification of the SpM. Also, as mentioned earlier, the ODS segment (ODSS) is the basic unit of data storage which can be reserved for exclusive access by a method of a TMO. The OI rule has the following two parts:

– (OI-1) A method execution with an older I-timestamp must not be waiting for the release of an ODSS held by a method execution with a younger I-timestamp.

- (OI-2) A method execution must not be rolled back due to an ODSS conflict.

Practically, the OI rule dictates the locking of all ODSSs needed by a method in the order of their IDs. It also dictates that each used ODSS is locked and released exactly once during a method execution. ODSSs may be released in any order unlike the way they are locked. Suppose a method, say SxM5, has been registered with a TMO execution engine and the set of ODSSs that may be accessed by SxM5 have also been registered with the engine. $ODSS_5$ is the ODSS with the smallest ID in the set of ODSSs that may be needed by SxM5. Then when an SxM5 execution becomes necessary, a check is made as to whether for each on-going method execution with an older I-timestamp, say SxM3, every ODSS that may be needed by SxM3 and has the ID not greater than the ID of $ODSS_5$ has been locked and released. Only if the result is affirmative, then the SxM5 execution is initiated with the locking of $ODSS_5$. When the SxM5 execution tries to lock the next ODSS, say $ODSS_9$, the same check is made again. If the result of the check is affirmative, then the SxM5 execution proceeds with the locking of that $ODSS_9$. Otherwise, the SxM5 execution is blocked waiting until $ODSS_9$ is released by a method execution with an older I-timestamp and can be locked by the SxM5 execution.

Therefore, when a method is initiated under the OI rule, the number of methods with older I-timestamps is finite and does not grow thereafter. This makes it easy to find out the amount of time during which a method has to wait in order to access ODSSs due to the locks that other methods with older I-timestamps hold on those ODSSs. This contributes substantially to reducing the efforts required for determination of service time bounds.

The OI rule can be illustrated by considering two service methods, SvM1 and SvM2, that need to access the same ODSS, $ODSS_7$, mutually exclusively during their execution. Assume that a client request arrived first for SvM1 and another client request arrived later for SvM2. The execution engine will initiate SvM1 first with an older I-timestamp and SvM2 later with a younger I-timestamp. Both SvM1 and SvM2 executions may proceed concurrently. Then under the OI rule, the SvM1 execution should never have to wait for entering $ODSS_7$ due to the SvM2 execution accessing $ODSS_7$ at the same time. Moreover, meeting such a condition by forcing the SvM2 execution out of $ODSS_7$ and rolling it back to its beginning (i.e., by "wounding" the SvM2 execution) is not allowed. So, a practical implementation of the OI rule will involve locking $ODSS_7$ at the beginning of the SvM1 execution. Approaches that are less restrictive than the OI rule and yet ease the design-time guaranteeing of timely service capabilities of TMOs are certainly desirable but such approaches have not been established yet. Research in this area may benefit from the insights accumulated in the field of database transaction management [2].

4.3   Pipelined execution of the same SvM

Note also the possibility of *pipelined execution of SvMs*. When the service request rate for an SvM becomes high, multiple instances of the same SvM may be executed concurrently in a pipelined fashion to speed up the processing of client requests. This pipelined execution can be exploited subject to the BCC and the OI rule. In fact, under the OI rule, there is no real need to distinghish between pipeline execution of the same SvM and concurrent execution of different SvMs.

5.   CONCLUSION

Producing complex RT computer systems in safety-critical application environments with design-time guarantees of timely service capabilities is still a great challenge. The TMO programming and specification scheme has been devised to support such timeliness-guaranteed design. However, there are a number of challenging research issues which must be resolved satisfactorily before the timeliness-guaranteed design with the TMO scheme can become a common practice. Some of the most important issues were discussed in this chapter. Currently practicable approaches that enable both extensive exploitation of concurrency and systematic design and analysis for guaranteeing of service time bounds were discussed.

However, a number of challenging issues remain for, future research aimed for further optimization of the techniques. First, the inevitable gaps between the timely service requirements assigned to a server TMO and the service time bounds yielded by an implementation of the server TMO pose a challenge of keeping the sum of all such gaps contributed by the TMOs in a sizable client-server chain at an acceptable level. Similarly, analysis of the impacts of SpMs with candidate triggering times on the SvMs co-resident within the same TMO needs much further research. Thirdly, the search for approaches that are less restrictive than the OI rule and yet ease the design-time guaranteeing of timely service capabilities of TMOs is another highly meaningful research topic. In order to achieve significant progresses in research in these areas, large-scale experimental design and analysis as well as sizable investments in tool development are considered essential.

ACKNOWLEDGMENTS

The research on the timeliness guarantee was supported earlier by the US NSWC and the US DARPA under Contract N66001-97-C-8516. The current work is supported in part by the NSF under Grant Number 00-86147 (ITR), and in part by the US DARPA under Contract F33615-01-C-1902 monitored by AFRL. No part of this paper represents the views and opinions of any of the sponsors mentioned above.

REFERENCES

[1] Bollella, G., and Gosling, J., "The Real-Time Specification for Java", *IEEE Computer*, June, 2000, pp. 47-54.

[2] Gray, J., and Reuter, A., *'Transaction Processing: Concepts and Techniques'*, Morgan Kaufman Publishers, 1994.

[3] *ISORC (IEEE CS Int'l Symp. on Object-oriented Real-time distributed Computing)* Series; 1st held in April 1998, Kyoto, Japan; 2nd in May 1999, St. Malo, France; 3rd in March 2000, Newport Beach, CA; 4th in May 2001, Magdeburg, Germany. Proceedings are available from IEEE CS Press.

[4] Kim, K.H., Bacellar, L., and Kim, Y.S., , "Distinguishing Features and Potential Roles of the TMO Object Model", *Proc. 1994 IEEE CS Workshop on Object-oriented Real-time Dependable Systems (WORDS)*, Oct. 94, Dana Point, pp.36-45.

[5] Kim, K.H., "A Utopian View of Future Object-Oriented Real-Time Dependable Computer Systems", (Invited paper) *Proc. 1st Int'l Workshop on Real-Time Computing Systems and Applications (RTCSA)*, Seoul, Korea, Dec. 1994, pp. 59-69.

[6] Kim, K.H., "Towards Designing RTO.k Structured Server Objects with Service Time Guarantee", *Proc. SEKE '96 (8th Int'l Conf. on Software Engineering & Knowledge Engineering)*, Lake Tahoe, NV, June '96, pp.522-528.

[7] Kim, K.H., "Object Structures for Real-Time Systems and Simulators", *IEEE Computer*, August 1997, pp.62-70.

[8] Kim, K.H. and Subbaraman, C., "Principles of Constructing a Timeliness-Guaranteed Kernel and the Time-triggered Message-triggered Object Support Mechanism", *Proc. ISORC '98 (IEEE CS 1st Int'l Symp. on Object-oriented Real-time distributed Computing)*, Kyoto, Japan, April 1998, pp. 80-89.

[9] Kim, K.H., "Real-Time Object-Oriented Distributed Software Engineering and the TMO Scheme", *Int'l Jour. of Software Engineering & Knowledge Engineering*, Vol. 9, No.2, April 1999, pp.251-276.

[10] Kim, K.H., Liu, J., and Ishida, M., "Distributed Object-Oriented Real-Time Simulation of Ground Transportation Networks with the TMO Structuring Scheme", *Proc. COMPSAC '99 (IEEE CS Computer Software & Applications Conf.)*, Phoenix, AZ, Oct. 1999, pp.130-138.

[11] Kim, K.H., and Liu, J. "Deadline Handling in Real-Time Distributed Objects", *Proc. ISORC 2000*, Newport Beach, CA, March 2000, pp.7-15.

[12] Kim, K.H., "APIs for Real-Time Distributed Object Programming", *IEEE Computer*, June 2000, pp.72-80.

[13] Kim, K.H., and Paul, R., "The Distributed Time-Triggered Simulation Scheme Facilitated by TMO Programming", *Proc. ISORC 2001 (4th IEEE CS Int'l Symp. on OO Real-time distributed Computing)*, Magdeburg, Germany, May 2001, pp. 41-50.

[14] Kopetz, H. and Grunsteidl, G., "TTP-A: Time Triggered Protocol for Fault Tolerant Real-Time Systems", *Proc. IEEE CS FTCS-23*, Toulose, France, June 1993, pp.524-533.

[15] Kopetz, H., *'Real-Time Systems: Design Principles for Distributed Embedded Application'*, Kluwer Academic Pub., ISBN: 0-7923-9894-7, Boston, 1997

[16] Object Management Group, "The common Object Request Broker: Architecture and Specification", Revision 2.5, Sept, 2001, available from http://www.omg.org/.

[17] Schmidt, D.C. and Kuhns, F., "An Overview of the Real-Time CORBA Specification", *IEEE Computer,* June, 2000, pp. 56-63.

[18] *WORDS (IEEE CS's Workshop on Object-oriented Real-time Dependable Systems)* Series; 1st held in Oct. '94, Dana Point; 2nd in Feb. 1996, Laguna Beach; 3rd in Feb. 1997, Newport Beach; 4th in Jan. 1999, Santa Barbara; 5th in Nov. 1999, Monterey; 6th in Jan. 2001, Rome, Italy. Proceedings are available from IEEE CS Press.